STATELESSNESS
IN THE EUROPEAN UNION

Statelessness in the European Union draws together original research from over one hundred interviews in the United Kingdom, Slovenia, Estonia, and France, to provide one of the first comparative accounts of the *de facto* and *de jure* stateless populations in the European Union. It blends legal, political and empirical research to examine how non-citizens without secure status – in some cases, established undocumented migrants and their descendants – manage their lives in four EU member states. Normative and legal analyses of the practical meaning of basic human rights are combined with a ground-breaking investigation of the obstacles that prevent people from accessing essential services. Contrasting the situation of Europe's stateless now with that examined by Hannah Arendt over fifty years ago, it considers proposals for the future security of Europe's stateless people.

CAROLINE SAWYER is Senior Lecturer in Law in the Faculty of Law of the Victoria University of Wellington. A former practising solicitor, she has developed university teaching courses in migration and nationality issues for undergraduates and postgraduates and was also UK Country Expert for the European University Institute's comparative study of access to citizenship in Europe.

BRAD K. BLITZ is Director of Graduate Research Programmes at Kingston University, London, where he is also Professor of Human and Political Geography. He is also a Research Associate in the Department of International Development at the University of Oxford and Director of the International Observatory on Statelessness, a global web-based initiative which seeks to draw together academics, policy-makers, activists and others concerned about the human rights of stateless people.

STATELESSNESS IN THE EUROPEAN UNION

Displaced, undocumented, unwanted

Edited by

CAROLINE SAWYER

AND

BRAD K. BLITZ

CAMBRIDGE
UNIVERSITY PRESS

CAMBRIDGE UNIVERSITY PRESS
Cambridge, New York, Melbourne, Madrid, Cape Town, Singapore,
São Paulo, Delhi, Dubai, Tokyo, Mexico City

Cambridge University Press
The Edinburgh Building, Cambridge CB2 8RU, UK

Published in the United States of America by Cambridge University Press, New York

www.cambridge.org
Information on this title: www.cambridge.org/9780521191937

© Cambridge University Press 2011

First published 2011

Printed in the United Kingdom at the University Press, Cambridge

A catalogue record for this publication is available from the British Library

Library of Congress Cataloguing in Publication data
Statelessness in the European Union : Displaced, Undocumented, Unwanted /
[edited by] Caroline Sawyer, Brad K. Blitz.
p.   cm
Includes bibliographical references and index.
ISBN 978-0-521-19193-7 (hardback)
1. Stateless persons–Legal status, laws, etc.–European Union countries.
2. Immigration and emigration law–European Union countries.
I. Sawyer, Caroline, 1962–   II. Blitz, Brad K.
KJC6050.S73   2011
342.2408′3–dc22
2010045717

ISBN 978-0-521-19193-7 Hardback

CONTENTS

     CAROLINE SAWYER, BRAD K. BLITZ AND
     MIGUEL OTERO-IGLESIAS

8   Non-citizens in Slovenia: erasure from the register
     of permanent residents   195
     JELKA ZORN

9   The statelessness issue in Estonia   230
     RAIVO VETIK

10   The *sans papiers* in France   253
     ARNAUD LUCIEN, DAVID MARRANI AND THE EDITORS

11   Analysis: the practical and legal realities of
     statelessness in the European Union   281
     BRAD K. BLITZ AND CAROLINE SAWYER

12   Conclusions   306
     CAROLINE SAWYER AND BRAD K. BLITZ

     Bibliography   312
     Index   335

CONTRIBUTORS

Editors

CAROLINE SAWYER is currently Senior Lecturer in Law in the Faculty of Law of Victoria University Wellington. Having taken a first degree in languages and literature at the University of Oxford, she qualified and practised as a solicitor before taking an MA in Socio-Legal Studies at Brunel University and a PhD at the University of Bristol. She has previously written extensively on issues of property law and on the boundaries of legal personhood, especially in relation to the child/adult boundary and the rights of non-nationals. Caroline was involved in analysing the law that allowed British citizen children to be expelled from the United Kingdom and pressing for change. She has published in the *International Journal of Refugee Law, Public Law, Journal of Social Security Law*, the *International Journal of Children's Rights* and the *Journal of Social Welfare and Family Law*. She also co-ordinated the English team working on a *Dictionnaire plurilingue des droits de l'homme*, based at the Université de Poitiers and funded by the Centre National de la Recherche Scientifique, and was UK Country Expert for the comparative study on access to citizenship in Europe based at the European University Institute (EUI) in Florence.

BRAD K. BLITZ is Director of Graduate Research Programmes at Kingston University, London, where he is also Professor of Human and Political Geography. He is also a Research Associate in the Department of International Development at the University of Oxford and Director of the International Observatory on Statelessness, a global web-based initiative which seeks to draw together academics, policy-makers, activists and others concerned about the human rights of stateless people. He was previously Jean Monnet Chair of the Political Geography of Europe at Oxford Brookes University. He received his PhD in International Development from Stanford University and has published several studies on citizenship, statelessness, post-conflict development and minorities and human rights. He has served as a consultant to international agencies including UNICEF, the UN Office of the High Commissioner for Human Rights (OHCHR), the World Bank, the Council of Europe and the Organisation for Security and Co-operation in Europe (OSCE), as well as several governments. In 2006, he published *War and Change in the Balkans: Nationalism, Conflict and Co-operation* (Cambridge University Press) and in 2009 completed a multi-country study on the benefits of citizenship (with Maureen Lynch), a project funded by the Swiss and Norwegian Ministries of Foreign Affairs to support the sixtieth Anniversary of the Universal Declaration of Human Rights. He subsequently published books from this research, including *Statelessness and Citizenship: A Comparative Study on the Benefits of Nationality* (Edward Elgar, 2011, with Maureen Lynch). Recent articles have appeared in *Mobilities, Europe-Asia Studies, Politics, Contemporary European History*, the *Journal of Human Rights, Citizenship Studies*, the *International Journal on Multicultural Societies*, the *Journal of Refugee Studies, Political Studies*, the *Journal of South Eastern European and Black Sea Studies, International Studies Online*, the *Journal of European Social Policy*, the *Journal of Ethnic and Migration Studies* and *Human Rights Review*. He is currently completing a book on citizenship and mobility and is directing a comparative study of the livelihoods of stateless and formerly stateless people in Bangladesh, Kenya, Slovenia and Sri Lanka, funded by the US Department of State.

Contributors

MATTHEW J. GIBNEY is currently Reader in Politics and Forced Migration, University of Oxford and Fellow of Linacre College, Oxford. He received his PhD from Cambridge University, where he was a Commonwealth Scholar. He has also taught at Monash, Cambridge and Harvard Universities and since 1999 he has been Director of the International Summer School in Forced Migration at the University of Oxford. He has written widely on issues relating to refugees, migration control and citizenship from the perspectives of normative political theory and comparative politics. He is the author (with R. Hansen) of *Immigration and Asylum since 1900 to the Present*, a three-volume encyclopaedia; *The Ethics and Politics of Asylum: Liberal Democracy and the Response to Refugees* (Cambridge University Press, 2004); and *Globalizing Rights* (Oxford, 2003). Articles by him have been published in the *American Political Science Review*, the Georgetown *Immigration Law Journal*, the *Forced Migration Review, Government and Opposition* and other journals. He is currently writing a book provisionally entitled *Denationalization and the Liberal State*.

MONIKA KRAUSE is a Lecturer in Sociology at the University of Kent. She studied sociology at the universities of Munich and Cambridge and at the London School of Economics and holds a PhD from New York University. She is currently working on a book in the field of humanitarian relief NGOs. She is also a co-editor of *The University Against Itself: The NYU Strike and the Future of the Academic Workplace* (Temple University Press, 2008).

ARNAUD LUCIEN is a qualified French lawyer (*avocat*). He received his PhD in November 2007 from the Université du Sud – Toulon Var where he is Teaching and Research Fellow in the Faculty of Law. He is also a fellow of the Law Department at the University of Essex. He is involved in several research activities in the fields of Communications, Media and Semiotics and is also affiliated to 'Information, Milieux, Médias, Médiations – EA 3820', a respected French research institution. His published work covers intellectual property, judicial institutions as a symbolic system, justice and mediation and communications in the Euro-Mediterranean region.

DAVID MARRANI is Senior Lecturer at the School of Law of the University of Essex, where he is currently Co-Director of the double degree scheme, LLB in English law and Maitrise en Droit, and Director of LLM in EU Law and Comparative Legal Studies in the Department of Law. He holds degrees in Public Administration and Law from the Université de Nice Sophia Antipolis. He teaches French Public law and Comparative law. He is currently Visiting Professor at SciencesPo, Paris, the Universidad Autónoma de Barcelona, Spain and the University of Westminster, London.

MIGUEL OTERO-IGLESIAS is currently completing his doctorate on the role of the euro in the international political economy. His areas of research include the international monetary system, global economic governance and theories of money and power. He holds an MA degree in International Political Economy from the University of Manchester and a First Degree in Information and Communication Studies from the University of Santiago de Compostela. He has published in academic journals in the United Kingdom, Austria, Spain and China. A trained journalist, he is also a regular columnist on international affairs for various Spanish newspapers. He worked as a researcher for Brad K. Blitz throughout this research project.

RAIVO VETIK is Professor of Comparative Politics and former Director of the Institute of International and Social Studies at the University of Tallinn. He received his PhD in Political Science from the University of Tampere and has written extensively on inter-ethnic relations and identity, national integration policy, democratic processes and cultural semiotics in Estonia. In addition to numerous articles on nationality issues in Estonia and the Baltic states, he is the author of the *Estonian Sustainable Development Report* – the Estonian Official Report to the UN Johannesburg Summit on Sustainable Development, and *Perspectives on Democratic Consolidation in Central and Eastern Europe* (Columbia University Press, 2001).

JELKA ZORN is a senior lecturer at the University of Ljubljana, Faculty of Social Work. She is a trained sociologist and former Visiting Fellow at the University of Stirling. She is one of the authors of *The Erased: Organized Innocence and the Politics of Exclusion*, the first full account in English of the situation of persons who were rendered *de facto* stateless by Slovenia during the first stages of Slovenian independence. She has also published in several journals, most recently *Citizenship Studies*. A concerned activist, Jelka is also a central figure in the development of organisational support structures for asylum seekers, refugees and the Erased in Slovenia.

CASES

CONVENTIONS, COVENANTS AND TREATIES

xiv

ACKNOWLEDGEMENTS

Several people assisted in the production of this book. We are especially grateful to Sinead Moloney, Finola O'Sullivan and Richard Woodham at Cambridge University Press for their professional assistance throughout the publication process: it has been a pleasure to work with them all. We would also like to thank Tom de Freston for permission to use his superb artwork *Between Somewhere and Nowhere* on the cover.

This was a complicated research project which involved a team spread across the European Union. Dan Ozarow of Middlesex University conducted interviews in London and read drafts of the text. Colleagues at Oxford Brookes University also facilitated this project. We are especially grateful to Brian Rivers, Lucinda Frew, Jennie Cripps and Kevin Henderson. Tamsin Barber, formerly of Oxford Brookes University, also assisted with proof reading.

Sections of chapter 2 originally appeared as 'Undocumented Migrants: An Arendtian Perspective', *European Journal of Political Theory*, 7(3) (2008), 331–48. They are reproduced with the kind permission of Sage Publishing.

Sections of chapter 3 were previously published in 'Precarious Residents: Migration Control, Membership and the Rights of Non-Citizens', MPRA Paper, 19190, posted at www.mpra.ub.uni-muenchen. de/19190/, 11 December 2009.

Many colleagues provided comments and insights on both earlier versions of this study and public presentations of our research at our respective universities. Colleagues at the Refugee Studies Centre, University of Oxford, and at the University of Kingston also helped to guide the final product with probing questions during dedicated workshops and seminars. We are also grateful to our colleagues in the UNHCR's Statelessness Unit and at Refugees International, in particular Mark Manly and Maureen Lynch, respectively. They have both consistently supported our work and championed efforts to reduce statelessness.

Colleagues at the Victoria University of Wellington, also provided key research assistance. In particular we would like to acknowledge the support given by Professor Susy Frankel and our research assistant Sharma Taylor who provided useful editing services. Finally, a note of thanks to Hayley Blitz and Emily Sawyer for their comments, understanding and practical assistance throughout the course of this project and for their constant encouragement of our research.

ABBREVIATIONS AND ACRONYMS

ADALAH	Legal Centre for Arab Minority Rights in Israel
ADB	Asian Development Bank
AfriMAP	Africa Governance Monitoring and Advocacy Project
ANAEM	Agence Nationale de l'Accueil des Étrangers et des Migrations
APRODEPED	Action pour la promotion et défense des droits des personnes défavorisées
ARC	Asylum Registration Card
BVFG	Bundesvertriebenen- und Fluchtlingsgesetz
CADA	Centres d'Accueil pour Demandeurs d'Asile
CDCJ	Committee on Legal Co-operation (EU)
CEDAW	Committee on the Elimination of Discrimination Against Women
CEJIL	Center for Justice and International Law
CEMIRIDE	Centre for Minority Rights (Kenya)
CERD	Convention on the Elimination of Racial Discrimination
CESEDA	Code de l'entrée et du séjour des étrangers et du droit d'asile
CESP	Collectif des étudiants sans papiers
CIMADE	Comité Inter-Mouvements auprès des Evacués
CIS	Conference on Displacement
CPS	Crown Prosecution Service (UK)
EC	European Community
ECHR	European Convention on Human Rights
ECJ	European Court of Justice
ECOSOC	United Nations Economic and Social Council
ECRI	European Commission against Racism and Intolerance
ECSC	European Coal and Steel Community
ECtHR	European Court of Human Rights
EEA	European Economic Area
EEC	European Economic Community
EFTA	European Free Trade Association
EMHRN	Euro Mediterranean Human Rights Network
ERC	Estonian Refugee Committee
ERRC	European Roma Rights Centre (Hungary)

EU	European Union
EUMC	European Monitoring Centre on Racism and Xenophobia
EURODAC	European Dactyloscopy
DIP	Division of International Protection
FRA	Agency for Fundamental Rights (EU)
FRY	Former Republic of Yugoslavia
FSU	former Soviet Union
FYROM	Former Yugoslav Republic of Macedonia
GISTI	Groupe d'information et de soutien des Immigrés
HALDE	Haute autorité de lutte contre les discriminations
IABD	Inter-American Development Bank
ICC	International Criminal Court
ICCPR	International Covenant on Civil and Political Rights
ICESCR	International Covenant on Economic, Social and Cultural Rights
ICJ	International Court of Justice
ILC	International Law Commission
ILO	International Labour Organization
IOM	International Organization for Migration
IRO	International Refugee Organisation
JCWI	Joint Council for the Welfare of Immigrants (UK)
JNA	Yugoslav People's Army
JORF	*Journal Officiel de la République Française*
KSFHR	Kuwaiti Society for Fundamental Human Rights
KSHR	Kuwait Society for Human Rights
LDSG	London Detainee Support Group
MFN	most-favoured nation
MOU	Memorandum of Understanding
MUDHA	Centro de Mujeres Dominico-Haitianas
NATO	North Atlantic Treaty Organization
NGO	non-governmental organisation
NHS	National Health Service (UK)
NI	National Insurance (UK)
OAS	Organization of American States
OAW	Oxford Asylum Welcome (UK)
OFPRA	Office français de protection des réfugiés et apatrides (France)
OHCHR	Office of the High Commissioner for Human Rights (Council of Europe)
OISC	Office of the Immigration Services Commissioner
OPEC	Organisation of the Petroleum Exporting Countries
OSCE	Organization for Security and Co-operation in Europe
OSI	Open Society Institute
PA	Palestinian Authority

PAYE	Pay As You Earn (UK)
PCIJ	Permanent Court of International Justice (now ICJ)
PPG	Pastoralist Parliamentary Group (Kenya)
QMV	qualified majority voting
RAJFIRE	Réseau pour l'autonomie des femmes immigrées et réfugiées
RESF	Réseau éducation sans frontières
RSFSR	Russian Soviet Federal Socialist Republic
SFRY	Socialist Federal Republic of Yugoslavia
UAE	United Arab Emirates
UDHR	Universal Declaration of Human Rights
UKBA	United Kingdom Border Agency
UNDP	United Nations Development Programme
UNHCR	United Nations High Commission/Commissioner for Refugees
UNHRC	United Nations Human Rights Council
UNICEF	United Nations Children's Fund
UNRRA	United Nations Relief and Rehabilitation Administration
UNRWA	United Nations Relief and Works Agency
USCRI	US Committee for Refugees and Immigrants
VIS	Visa Information System (EU)
WARIPNet	West African Refugees and Internally Displaced Persons Network

PART I

The issue

Statelessness in the European Union

BRAD K. BLITZ AND CAROLINE SAWYER

In June 2008 the Council of Europe's High Commissioner for Human Rights, Thomas Hammarberg, made the bold statement that 'no one should be stateless in today's Europe'.[1] His comments called attention to a problem which, although noted by the Council of Europe, has persisted in several European states, including both 'old' and 'new' members of the European Union. The solution is still elusive. Yet the problem of statelessness is not new – indeed the rights to nationality and the prohibition against the arbitrary deprivation of nationality were included in the 1948 Universal Declaration of Human Rights (UDHR).[2] Over the past fifty years, both the Council of Europe and European Union have introduced enforceable human rights instruments, which are among the most far-reaching of the developed world, but they often offer little to Europe's stateless people. In practice, human rights do not cover everyone.

'Statelessness' in the legal sense describes people who are not nationals of any state. Although statelessness is decried in international law, and the UDHR proclaimed a right to a nationality,[3] the United Nations High Commissioner for Refugees (UNHCR) estimated that there were over half a million stateless people in the European region,[4] and perhaps 12 million stateless people worldwide.[5]

---

[1] T. Hammarberg, 'No One Should Have to be Stateless in Today's Europe', *Viewpoint* (9 June 2008), www.coe.int/t/commissioner/Viewpoints/080609_en.asp/, accessed 10 June 2008.

[2] United Nations General Assembly, *Universal Declaration of Human Rights*, (10 December 1948), 217A (III), www.unhcr.org/refworld/docid/3ae6b3712c.html.

[3] *Ibid.*, Article 15(1).

[4] United Nations High Commissioner for Refugees (UNHCR), *Statistical Online Population Database* (2009), http://apps.who.int/globalatlas/dataQuery/reportData.asp?rptType=1, accessed 27 November 2009.

[5] UNHCR, 'Addressing Situations of Statelessness', *UNHCR Global Appeal 2009 Update*, (1 December 2008), 45, www.unhcr.org/publ/PUBL/4922d4370.pdf.

Table 1.1 is based on data provided by UNHCR and provides an indication of the number of stateless people in the European region.

The figures in table 1.1 illustrate that the scale of statelessness is most pronounced in the Baltic states. That is not to say that non-citizens living in Estonia, Latvia and Lithuania enjoy few rights, on the contrary, unlike stateless populations in the developing world, they have considerably more rights; however, they are included in table 1.1 because they are not considered as nationals by any state under the operation of its law and in that sense are stateless.

The existence of stateless populations challenges some of the central tenets of international law and the human rights discourse that has developed over the past sixty years.

For the *de jure* stateless, the international statelessness conventions might offer either practical rights[6] or a route to a nationality.[7] Few states have, however, ratified the statelessness conventions, and while individual countries may nevertheless implement similar provisions in their domestic laws, nevertheless, the problem of disenfranchised minorities being left without nationality remains.[8] The denial and deprivation of nationality raises several important policy questions because it undermines human security since, in practice, people face difficulties accessing and exercising many basic rights, and their daily life itself may become precarious.[9] All too often, the births, marriages and deaths of stateless people are not certified and, as a result, many stateless persons lack even basic documentation, leaving them outside any social systems of protection or redress for wrongs.

The position of the *de facto* stateless is closely allied to that of the *de jure* stateless. Hannah Arendt herself formally linked the two concepts in 1951 in the ninth chapter of *The Origins of Totalitarianism* (1951), where she examined the practical position of those without any effective state

---

[6] United Nations, *United Nations Convention Relating to the Status of Stateless Persons*, 1954 Convention, UN Treaty Series, (1960), www.unhcr.org/protect/PROTECTION/3bbb25729.pdf.

[7] United Nations, *United Nations Convention on the Reduction of Statelessness*, 1961 Convention, UN Treaty Series, vol. 989, (1975), 175, www.unhcr.org/protect/PROTECTION/3bbb286d8.pdf.

[8] To date, sixty-five countries have become party to the 1954 Convention relating to the Status of Stateless Persons, and thirty-seven countries have acceded to the 1961 Convention on the Reduction of Statelessness.

[9] K. Southwick and M. Lynch, *Nationality Rights for All: A Progress Report and Global Survey on Statelessness* (Washington, DC: Refugees International, 2009), www.refintl.org/sites/default/files/RI%20Stateless%20Report_FINAL_031109.pdf.

Table 1.1 *Stateless persons in the European region, 2008*[a]

State	Numbers of stateless persons
Austria	464
Azerbaijan	2,078
Belarus	7,818
Belgium	548
Bosnia and Herzegovina	10,000
Croatia	180
Denmark	3,687
Estonia	110,315
Finland	1,397
France	1,006
Georgia	1,544
Germany	9,322
Greece	258
Hungary	241
Iceland	116
Italy	722
Latvia	365,417
Lithuania	5,900
Luxembourg	162
Montenegro	1,500
Netherlands	4,591
Norway	489
Poland	839
Portugal	273
Republic of Moldova	1,807
Romania	253
Russian Federation	50,000
Serbia	17,050
Slovakia	911
Slovenia	4,090
Spain	26
Sweden	6,239
Switzerland	75
Former Yugoslav Republic of Macedonia (FYROM)	1,051
Ukraine	56,350
United Kingdom of Great Britain and Northern Ireland	20

Source: [a] United Nations High Commissioner for Refugees (UNHCR), *Statistical Online Population Database* (2009), at http://apps.who.int/globalatlas/dataQuery/reportData.asp?rptType=1, accessed 27 November 2009.

to offer protection or support.[10] Where refugees and the *de jure* stateless may have access to travel documents equivalent to national passports issued by domestic governments voluntarily or under the terms of international treaties, and nationals themselves may have variable access to the enforcement of domestic rights, the distinction in terms of formal membership of a state is inevitably blurred. The issue of access to rights for those who are not citizens of the countries in which they have made their lives is, however, the same regardless of whether or not they hold another nationality, of a country – usually outside Europe – which they may feel no connection with and indeed may not know. All across Europe children may be non-nationals in the countries of their birth. Equally, there are thousands of 'unwanted' migrants, whether refused asylum seekers or irregular workers, whose nationality status offers little in the way of practical protection, and over time they may lose connections to their country of nationality. Effective statelessness thus remains an issue in the case of non-nationals who lack access to even basic rights.

The developing European human rights regime has not addressed the problem of effective statelessness as it has emerged since the founding of the current European institutions. The United Nations Declaration of Human Rights of 1948 lacked mechanisms for application and enforcement. The 1951 Convention on the Status of Refugees dealt with many of the *de facto* and *de jure* stateless after the Second World War, but had to be extended in the 1960s to cover subsequent refugee populations. With the advent of mass migration from the 1980s onwards, Europe started to close the borders. European states began to reinterpret their obligations under the 1951 Convention as unwanted immigration became a political issue and, by the 1980s, the application of the European Convention on Human Rights (ECHR) of 1950 had become contentious in cases of non-nationals.

Geo-political challenges as well as the development of new patterns of migration and settlement have since complicated attempts to prevent and reduce statelessness within Europe's borders. In addition to the ongoing nationality disputes that resulted from the break-up of the former Yugoslavia and former Soviet Union, thousands of former labour migrants who arrived in Europe, often during the height of Western European industrial expansion, never formally established their rights to reside and claim citizenship and, as a result, their status is a grey area. Equally, hundreds of thousands of new arrivals who applied for asylum

---

[10] H. Arendt, *The Origins of Totalitarianism* (New York: Schocken, 1951).

but were refused have remained on the territory, often leading settled lives without formal status. Unable or unwilling to return to their countries of origin, whether for fear of persecution or because their country of origin refuses to readmit them, or for economic reasons, they, too, have become effectively stateless.

This study examines the way in which those – both *de jure* and effectively – stateless people manage their lives inside the European Union. It is illustrated by case studies that record the realities of daily life for these non-citizens in four different European jurisdictions, namely the United Kingdom, Slovenia, Estonia and France. The study combines normative and legal analyses on the rights of others with an investigation of the practical obstacles that prevent people from accessing essential services and asks what provisions would make people more secure.

Review of relevant literature

The conceptual framework for this study is informed by a disparate but important collection of writings which has several intellectual sources. Some of the most widely cited publications on contemporary forms of statelessness include reports and articles by human rights advocates that have promoted the notion that statelessness should be viewed as a matter of human security and one that draws greater relevance from the anti-discrimination provisions regarding the rights of non-citizens.[11] Within the world of academia, one of the most influential writers on human security, Amartya Sen, has drawn attention to the problems associated with the lack of citizenship for personal and social development. Sen

---

[11] B. Aurescu, 'The 2006 Venice Commission Report on Non-Citizens and Minority Rights – Presentation and Assessment', *Helsinki Monitor*, 18(2) (2007), 150; J. Bhabha, 'Enforcing the Human Rights of Citizens and Non-Citizens in the Era of Maastricht: Some Reflections on the Importance of States' *Development & Change*, 29(4) (1998), 697; B. Frelick and M. Lynch, 'Statelessness: A Forgotten Human Rights Crisis', *Forced Migration Review*, 24, (2005), 65; J. A. Goldston, 'Holes in the Rights Framework: Racial Discrimination, Citizenship, and the Rights of Noncitizens', *Ethics & International Affairs*, 20 (2006), 321; Human Security Commission, *Human Security Now: Protecting and Empowering People* (New York: Commission on Human Security, 2003), www.humansecurity-chs. org/finalreport/English/FinalReport.pdf; M. Lynch, *Lives on Hold: The Human Cost of Statelessness* (Washington, DC: Refugees International (2005); D. Weissbrodt, *Final Report on the Rights of Non-Citizens*, UN Doc. E/CN.4/Sub.2/2003/23 (Geneva: UNHCR, 2003); C. Sokoloff and R. Lewis, 'Denial of Citizenship: A Challenge to Human Security', *European Policy Centre*, Paper 28, (1 April 2005), www.epc.eu/TEWN/pdf/724318296_ EPC%20Issue%20Paper%2028%20Denial%20of%20Citizenship.pdf; Southwick and Lynch, *Nationality Rights for All*.

argues that citizenship is integrally connected with the possible enhance-
ment of human capabilities; hence, the granting of citizenship removes
some of the 'unfreedoms' that place people at risk from want and fear.[12]
Others, however, challenge Sen's claims and note that human security
is often undermined by other domestic factors that operate at the subnational level. One important counter argument is that in both weak
and strong states where political divisions are defined by gender, ethno-
national, religious, tribal and party affiliations, there are many layers of
discrimination that dilute the potency of citizenship by reinforcing discriminatory structures.[13] Thus, rather than considering citizenship to be a
unifying force, one may speak of several classes of citizenship and a range
of entitlements.[14]

The vast majority of writing on statelessness and related issues, however, has not introduced theoretical considerations but has taken the
form of descriptive reports which have sought to set an agenda at critical times. In the late 1990s, a precursor to the discourse on statelessness – primarily a discourse on the rights of non-citizens who were not
necessarily stateless – centred on issues of equality and were justified
on the grounds that exclusion fosters inequality and hence, insecurity. Indeed, this was one of the central premises of the United Nations
Development Programme (UNDP) 1994 *Human Development Report*[15]
and the more influential Human Security Commission report entitled
Human Security Now: Protecting and Empowering People.[16] The reasons
why this discourse was important to the emergence of a new and explicit
discourse on statelessness lie in the fact that through these publications
the United Nations had identified a causal connection between developmental concerns such as poverty and deprivation, the protection of
human rights and problems of governance – all of which directly relate
to statelessness:

> In the final analysis, human security is a child who did not die, a dis-
> ease that did not spread, a job that was not cut, an ethnic tension that
> did not explode in violence, a dissident who was not silenced. Human

---

[12] A. Sen, *Development as Freedom* (Oxford: Oxford University Press, 2001).
[13] R. A. Elman, 'Testing the Limits of European Citizenship: Ethnic Hatred and Male
Violence', *NWSA Journal*, 13(3) (2001), 49.
[14] R. Cohen, 'Citizens, Denizens and Helots: The Politics of International Migration Flows
in the Post-War World', *Hitotsubashi Journal of Social Studies*, 21(1) (1989), 153.
[15] United Nations Development Programme (UNDP), *Human Development Report* (New
York: Oxford University Press, 1994).
[16] Human Security Commission, *Human Security Now.*

security is not a concern with weapons – it is a concern with human life and dignity.[17]

Over the past five years, the policy language has shifted from a development focus to a rights-based theme and, in addition to the UNHCR, a number of UN monitoring bodies and non-governmental organisations (NGOs) have drawn particular attention to the practice of denying and revoking rights to citizenship and the related problem of linking minority rights – namely, the rights to enjoy and practice one's culture, language, or religion – to citizenship status.[18] The topic of statelessness was elevated in diplomatic circles when, in 2008, the UN Independent Expert on Minorities devoted a section of her *Annual Report* to the arbitrary denial and deprivation of citizenship[19] and, shortly thereafter, the United Nations Human Rights Council (UNHRC) adopted a resolution on the human rights and arbitrary deprivation of nationality which named statelessness as a human rights issue and reaffirmed that the right to a nationality of every human person is a fundamental human right.[20]

To date, the most comprehensive studies on statelessness include the publication, *Nationality Matters: Statelessness Under International Law*, by Laura Van Waas (2008),[21] and the report by Katherine Southwick and Maureen Lynch on behalf of Refugees International, *Nationality Rights for All: A Progress Report and Global Survey on Statelessness* (2009).[22] Van Waas dissects the two statelessness conventions and related international

---

[17] United Nations Development Programme (UNDP), *Human Development Report* (New York: Oxford University Press, 1994), 22, http://hdr.undp.org/en/media/hdr_1994_en_chap2.pdf.

[18] Goldston, 'Holes in the Rights Framework, 321; Open Society Institute (OSI) Justice Initiative, *Human Rights and Legal Identity: Approaches to Combating Statelessness and Arbitrary Deprivation of Nationality, Thematic Conference Paper*, (May 2006), http://dev.justiceinitiative.org/db/resource2/fs/?file_id=17050; United Nations Human Rights Council (UNHRC), 'Arbitrary Deprivation of Nationality: Report of the Secretary-General', A/HRC/10/34 (26 January 2009), www.unhcr.org/refworld/docid/49958be22.html; UNHCR, 'The Excluded: The Strange Hidden World of the Stateless', *Refugees Magazine*, 147 (Geneva: United Nations High Commissioner for Refugees, September 2007), //www.unhcr.org/publ/PUBL/46d2e8dc2.pdf.

[19] Office of the High Commissioner for Human Rights (OHCHR), *Promotion and Protection of All Human Rights, Civil, Political, Economic, Social and Cultural Rights, Including The Right To Development: Report of the Independent Expert on Minority Issues, Gay McDougall*, A/HRC/7/23 (28 February 2008), www.unhcr.org/refworld/docid/47d685ea2.html.

[20] (UNHRC), 'Arbitrary Deprivation of Nationality'.

[21] L. Van Waas, *Nationality Matters: Statelessness Under International Law* (Antwerp: Intersentia, 2008).

[22] Southwick and Lynch, *Nationality Rights for All*.

instruments and examines the legal provisions for stateless people and the need for reform in key areas including conflict of laws, state succession and arbitrary deprivation of nationality, birth registration and migration. Her work also seeks to break down the distinction between *de jure* and *de facto* statelessness which she claims to be a false dichotomy since, in practice, those who cannot access their human rights cannot lay claim to protection. She is equally critical of the 1961 Convention which has remarkably few parties to it and is therefore of limited use under international law.

The report, *Nationality Rights for All: A Progress Report and Global Survey in Statelessness*, like the Refugees International study *Lives on Hold: The Human Cost of Statelessness* (2005),[23] provides a wide-ranging overview of the political and human rights challenges that stem from the lack of nationality and offers a useful global survey of the problem on a country-by-country basis. There is a considerable emphasis on the European region, and one of the most compelling aspects of these publications is their analysis of interview data gathered during field visits. The value added of the reports and field studies by Refugees International lies in the inclusion of historical details and micro-level descriptions of the way in which repression and the denial of human rights affects individuals on the ground.

Another influential publication is James Goldston's article in *Ethics and International Affairs* (2006).[24] Goldston acknowledges that while there is growing consensus that nationality laws and practice must be consistent with general principles of international law – above all, human rights law – there is a clear protection gap. He then illustrates how the denial of citizenship excludes people from the enjoyment of rights and pays particular attention to 'indirect discrimination' which occurs when 'a practice, rule, requirement, or condition is neutral on its face but impacts particular groups disproportionately, absent objective and reasonable justification.'[25] His conclusion that the growing divide between citizens and non-citizens in practice is 'primarily a problem of lapsed enforcement of existing norms' is especially relevant to the plight of *de facto* stateless people in Europe that need protection.[26]

In addition to the above experts, several academics have touched on the issue of statelessness in their philosophical and sociological studies; interpretations of international law; examinations of regional

---

[23] Lynch, *Lives on Hold.*   [24] Goldston, 'Holes in the Rights Framework', 321.
[25] *Ibid.*, 328.   [26] *Ibid.*, 341.

conventions and treaty systems; research on children, gender issues and birth registration; and, most recently, through their investigations of the effects of the war on terror, for individuals held in detention. The most prominent area of research on statelessness and the rights of non-citizens, outside legal studies, is to be found in the fields of social and political theory. In particular, there has been a growing interest in Hannah Arendt's work and a re-examination of her brief writings on statelessness included in the ninth chapter, 'The Decline of the Nation-State and the End of the Rights of Man', in her seminal work *The Origins of Totalitarianism* (1951).[27]

In Arendt's account, statelessness was symptomatic of the hollowness of human rights that could only be guaranteed by states and which, from the very start, lacked substantive support. Arendt provides an historical snapshot of the diplomatic wrangling that confined human rights discourse to a minority of concerned elites:

> Even worse was that all societies formed for the protection of the Rights of Man, all attempts to arrive at a new bill of human rights, were sponsored by marginal figures – by a few international jurists without political experience or professional philanthropists supported by the uncertain sentiments of professional idealists. The groups they formed, the declarations they issued, showed an uncanny similarity in language and composition to that of societies for the prevention of cruelty to animals. No statesman, no political figure of any importance could possibly take them seriously; and none of the liberal or radical parties in Europe thought it necessary to incorporate into their program a new declaration of human rights.[28]

While the nature of the human rights regime has expanded in both scope and substance to include a wider body of opinion, the essential problem of ensuring respect for rights bound to the state – especially in the case of nationality – has not been comprehensively addressed by social theorists. Few scholars have developed Arendt's theses on the tension between the nation (or, rather, national groups) and their attempt to dominate the state; and on the ineffectiveness of human rights instruments to provide protection to stateless populations today.[29] One notable exception is

---

[27] Hannah Arendt, *The Origins of Totalitarianism* (New York: Harcourt Brace, 1968).
[28] *Ibid.*, 292.
[29] M. Leibovici, 'Appartitre et visibilité: Le monde selon Hannah Arendt et Emmanuel Levinas', *Journal of Jewish Thought & Philosophy*, 14 (1–2) (2006), 55; S. Parekh, 'A Meaningful Place in the World: Hannah Arendt on the Nature of Human Rights', *Journal of Human Rights*, 31 (2004), 41; D. Tubb, 'Statelessness and Colombia: Hannah Arendt and the Failure of Human Rights', *Undercurrent*, 3(2) (2006), 39.

Richard Bernstein, a peer and colleague of Arendt who has retraced her arguments over evil, the nature of anti-semitism and the relevance of the author's own status as a formerly stateless person which influenced her thinking about effective protection.[30]

In general, however, the issue of statelessness has not been addressed squarely among contemporary theorists but indirectly in the context of alienage.[31] For example, Gillian Brock and Harry Brighouse make an important contribution to contemporary political theory and cosmopolitan claims to citizenship by bringing together scholars who examine the moral obligations to foreigner residents on the basis of national identity; but the authors do not single out those who are excluded from participating on account of their nationality status.[32] Yale political theorist Seyla Benhabib goes considerably further than Brock and Brighouse in her condemnation of the denial of access to aliens but it should be noted that the subject of her analysis is open to both foreign non-citizens who may have effective nationality but suffer from discrimination and *de facto* stateless persons who have no effective protection.[33]

Others who have approached the issue of nationality have often addressed the subject not from the perspective of rights *per se* but from a pragmatic problem of the politics of integration which has implicitly drawn attention to *de facto* stateless persons. For example, Rainer Bauböck records in his study on acquisition and loss of nationality (2006) that political pressure from pro- or anti-immigrant forces has been especially significant in helping to define the situation for non-citizens, some of whom have been regularised as a result of activist campaigns.[34] His study is more concerned with the content of citizenship and the adherence to human rights and the politics of inclusion that permits migrants to maintain ties abroad. Arguably, the primary contribution of scholars writing on citizenship has not been in defining the problem of statelessness but rather in pushing some of the boundaries of liberal political theory and articulating challenges to realist constants of sovereignty, fixed

[30] R. J. Bernstein, 'Hannah Arendt on the Stateless', *Parallax*, 111 (2005), 46; *idem.*, 'Are Arendt's Reflections on Evil Still Relevant?', *Review of Politics*, 70(1) (2008), 64.

[31] S. Benhabib, *The Rights of Others: Aliens, Residents, and Citizens* (Cambridge: Cambridge University Press, 2004); J. Carens, 'On Belonging: What We Owe People Who Stay', *The Boston Review* (summer 2005), www.bostonreview.net/BR30.3/carens.html.

[32] G. Brock and H. Brighouse, *The Political Philosophy of Cosmopolitanism* (Cambridge: Cambridge University Press, 2005).

[33] Benhabib, *The Rights of Others*.

[34] R. Bauböck (ed.), *Migration and Citizenship: Legal Status, Rights and Political Participation* (Amsterdam: Amsterdam University Press, 2006).

notions of membership and the conceptual division of state responsibility between domestic and external arenas as recorded in the literature on cosmopolitanism.

Within the field of international law, some older texts provide an interesting historical account of the development of UN legislation on statelessness and the impact of the conflict of nationality laws on the creation of stateless populations.[35] While these publications are set in the context of Cold War divisions, and have been supplemented by more recent writings that reflect contemporary geo-political realities in newly independent states,[36] one of the most comprehensive treatments of this subject from a rights-based perspective remains Paul Weis', *Nationality and Statelessness in International Law* (1979).[37] Weis addresses the conceptual challenge of placing nationality in the context of international law and examines conditions under which it may be withdrawn and multiple nationality granted. Among the most useful chapters is his study of nationality in composite states and dependencies, which pays particular attention to the operations of the British Commonwealth in the context of nationality rights; the chapter on conflict rules also offers an initial attempt to set out typologies of statelessness which is still helpful today.

Several well-known legal experts have further evaluated the right to nationality and the principle of non-discrimination within international human rights law.[38] Most influential of these is David Weissbrodt's *The*

---

[35] T.A. Aleinikoff, 'Theories of Loss of Citizenship', *Michigan Law Review*, 84(7), (1986), 1471–1503; I. Brownlie, 'The Relations of Nationality in Public International Law', *British Year Book of International Law*, 39 (1963), 284; G. Ginsburgs, 'Soviet Citizenship Legislation and Statelessness as a Consequence of the Conflict of Nationality Laws', *International & Comparative Law Quarterly*, 15(1) (1966), 1; E. Loewenfeld, 'Status of Stateless Persons', *Transactions of the Grotius Society*, 27 (1943), 59; W. Samore, 'Statelessness as a Consequence of the Conflict of Nationality Laws', *American Journal of International Law*, 45(3) (1951), 476.

[36] B. Bowring, 'European Minority Protection: The Past and Future of a "Major Historical Achievement"', *International Journal on Minority and Group Rights*, 152(3) (2008), 413; M. Craven, 'The International Law of State Succession', *International Law Forum du Droit International*, 23 (2000), 202.

[37] P. Weis, *Nationality and Statelessness in International Law* (Alphen aan den Rijn: Sijthoff & Noordhoff, 1979).

[38] Aurescu, 'The 2006 Venice Commission Report', 150; J.E. Doek, 'The CRC and the Right to Acquire and to Preserve a Nationality', *Refugee Survey Quarterly*, 25 (2006), 26; R. Donner, *The Regulation of Nationality in International Law* (Ardsley, NY: Transnational Publishers, 1994); Goldston, 'Holes in the Rights Framework', 321; D. Weissbrodt, *Prevention of Discrimination and Protection of Indigenous Peoples and Minorities – The Rights of Non-Citizens: Preliminary Report of the Special Rapporteur, Mr David Weissbrodt, Submitted in Accordance with Sub-Commission Decision*

Human Rights of Non-Citizens.[39] Weissbrodt reiterates his conclusion from his *Final Report* (2003) and argues that regardless of their citizenship status, non-citizens should enjoy all human rights just as formal citizens unless exceptional distinctions serve a legitimate state objective. Further relevant studies have appeared as a result of examinations of related international instruments including the Convention on the Rights of the Child.[40] Many of these studies are cited by Van Waas and Weissbrodt, who also includes a detailed review of the literature on the above-mentioned aspects of law.[41]

One central theme which links the studies on international instruments to the broader problem of human security and the practical aspects of protection is the issue of implementation and the identification of a gap between the rights that international human rights law guarantees to non-citizens and the realities they face.[42] Also relevant is the distinction between the treatment of refugees and stateless people under law and the human rights obligations of states to both populations.[43] In recognition of these obligations, some practitioners have sought to examine the possibility of transforming international legal principles into law.[44] For example, Van Waas presents an interpretation of the existing

2000/103, UN Doc. E/CN.4/Sub.2/2001/20/Add.1 (Geneva: UNHCR, 2001); *idem.*, *Final Report on the Rights of Non-Citizens*; *idem.*, *The Human Rights of Non-Citizens* (Oxford: Oxford University Press, 2008).

[39] Weissbrodt, *The Human Rights of Non-Citizens.*

[40] T. Buck, '*International Child Law* (London: Routledge/Cavendish, 2005); S. Detrick, *A Commentary on the United Nations Convention on the Rights of the Child* (The Hague: Martinus Nijhoff, 1999).

[41] Van Waas, *Nationality Matters;* Weissbrodt, *The Human Rights of Non-Citizens.*

[42] C.A. Batchelor, 'Stateless Persons: Some Gaps in International Protection', *International Journal of Refugee Law*, 7(2) (1995), 232; G. Gyulai, *Forgotten without Reason: Protection of Non-Refugee Stateless Persons in Central Europe* (Budapest: Hungarian Helsinki Committee, 2007); D. Hodgson, 'The International Legal Protection of the Child's Right to a Legal Identity and the Problem of Statelessness', *International Journal of Law, Policy and the Family*, 7(2) (1993), 255.

[43] A.B. Anderson, 'Missing Boundaries: Refugees, Migrants, Stateless and Internally Displaced Persons in South Asia', *Pacific Affairs*, 78(2), (2005), 320; Batchelor, 'Stateless Persons', 232; J. Boyden and J. Hart, 'The Statelessness of the World's Children', *Children & Society*, 21(4) (2007), 237; S. Grant, 'International Migration and Human Rights: A Paper Prepared for the Policy Analysis and Research Programme of the Global Commission on International Migration' (Geneva: Global Commission on Migration, 2007), www.gcim.org/attachements/TP7.pdf; D. Weissbrodt and C. Collins, 'The Human Rights of Stateless Persons', *Human Rights Quarterly*, 28(1) (2006), 245; Weissbrodt, *The Human Rights of Non-Citizens.*

[44] C.A. Batchelor, 'Transforming International Legal Principles into National Law: The Right to a Nationality and the Avoidance of Statelessness', *Refugee Survey Quarterly*, 25(3) (2006), 8; Gyulai, *Forgotten without Reason*; Van Waas, *Nationality Matters.*

international framework to explore the scope of the civil and political as well as the economic, social and cultural rights of stateless populations under international human rights laws. Others have suggested that at some point refugees should be considered stateless persons and that the rights of migrants, rather than the right to nationality, may provide a stronger mechanism for championing the plight of stateless people.[45]

Within the European region, there have been some notable studies of regional conventions and the commitments of regional treaty bodies with respect to stateless persons and non-citizens. Several have focused on the European Union[46] and the Council of Europe's Convention on Nationality; others have examined the problems of dual nationality and the challenges of state succession, most notably in the Baltic states and FSU.[47] Further, within the field of European studies more broadly, there has been renewed interest in the problems of nationality and the incorporation of non-nationals. One major tendency within a number of these studies has been their primary emphasis on legal residents often described as 'habitual residents' in legal instruments[48] and settled ethno-national minorities.[49] That said, the fate of undocumented migrants and the revision of nationality laws has featured in some excellent work. This includes reports on the resettlement of deported persons (principally Crimean Tatars), and evaluations of the Ukrainian government's efforts to reduce statelessness,[50] as well as critical studies on the barriers which Roma have

---

[45] OSI (2009).

[46] Batchelor, 'Stateless Persons', 232; F. Dell'Olio, *The Europeanization of Citizenship: Between the Ideology of Nationality, Immigration and European Identity* (Aldershot: Ashgate, 2005); J. Shaw, *The Transformation of Citizenship in the European Union: Electoral Rights and the Restructuring of Political Space* (Cambridge: Cambridge University Press, 2007).

[47] L. Barrington, 'The Domestic and International Consequences of Citizenship in the Soviet Successor States', *Europe-Asia Studies*, 49 (1995), 731; Bowring, 'European Minority Protection', 413; R. Brubaker, 'Citizenship Struggles in Soviet Successor States', *International Migration Review*, 26(2) (1992b), 269; N. M. Gelazis, 'The European Union and the Statelessness Problem in the Baltic States', *European Journal of Migration and Law*, 6(3) (2004), 225.

[48] L. Beckman, 'Citizenship and Voting Rights: Should Resident Aliens Vote?', *Citizenship Studies*, 10(2) (2006), 153; Dell'Olio, *The Europeanization of Citizenship*; C. Pattie, P. Seyd and P. Whiteley, *Citizenship in Britain: Values, Participation and Democracy* (Cambridge: Cambridge University Press, 2004); Shaw, *The Transformation of Citizenship in the European Union*; Y.N. Soysal, *Limits of Citizenship: Migrants and Postnational Membership in Europe* (Chicago, IL: University of Chicago Press, 1995).

[49] J. Minahan, *Encyclopaedia of the Stateless Nations: Ethnic and National Groups Around the World*, 4 vols. (Santa Barbara, CA: Greenwood Press, 2002).

[50] R. Ablyatifov, 'The Resettlement, Adaptation and Integration of Formerly Deported Crimean Tatars in Ukraine: Evaluation of Impact of Governmental Programmes of

faced as a result of discriminatory naturalisation requirements in the Czech and Slovak Republics.[51]

Some comparative studies and work on nationality issues in advanced states is also worthy of note.[52] In particular, there are some excellent accounts of the pressure to amend nationality laws in Germany[53] and Hungary.[54] A leading author in this area, as we have seen, is Rainer Bauböck whose research on ethnic Turks, the descendants of former guest workers in Germany and Austria, and recent pan-European investigations of membership rights in Europe, has influenced many research agendas.[55] In addition, recent writings on the problem of refused asylum seekers in the United Kingdom are also serving to fill an important gap.[56]

2002', Paper Presented at the 12th NISPAcee Annual Conference: 'Central and Eastern European Countries Inside and Outside the European Union: Avoiding a New Divide', Vilnius, (2004); G. Uehling, 'Evaluation of UNHCR's Programme to Prevent and Reduce Statelessness in Crimea, Ukraine', EPAU/2004/03, (Geneva: United Nations High Commissioner for Refugees Evaluation and Policy Analysis Unit, March 2004), www.unhcr.org/research/RESEARCH/405ab4c74.pdf; *idem.*, 'Livelihoods of Former Deportees in Ukraine', *Forced Migration Review*, 20 (2008), 19, www.fmreview.org/FMRpdfs/FMR20/FMR2008.pdf.

[51] R. Linde, 'Statelessness and Roma Communities in the Czech Republic: Competing Theories of State Compliance', *International Journal on Minority & Group Rights*, 13(4) (2006), 341; T. Perić, 'Personal Documents and Threats to the Exercise of Fundamental Rights of Roma in Europe', *Roma Rights*, 3 (2003), 7, www.errc.org/cikk.php?cikk=28; B. Struharova, 'Disparate Impact: Removing Roma from the Czech Republic', *Roma Rights*, 1 (1999), 47, www.errc.org/cikk.php?cikk=54.

[52] R. Hansen and P. Weil, '*Dual Nationality, Social Rights and Federal Citizenship in the US and Europe: The Reinvention of Citizenship* (New York: Berghahn, 2000).

[53] S. Green, 'Beyond Ethnoculturalism? German Citizenship in the New Millennium', *German Politics*, 9(3) (2000), 105; C.A. Groenendijk and B.D. Hart, *Multiple Nationality: The Practice of Germany and the Netherlands; Multiple Nationality: The Practice of Germany and the Netherlands* (The Hague: T.M.C. Asser, 2007).

[54] P.R. Magocsi, 'Mapping Stateless Peoples: The East Slavs of the Carpathians', *Canadian Slavonic Papers*, 39(3–4) (1997), 301.

[55] Bauböck (ed.), *Migration and Citizenship*; *idem.*, 'The Rights of Others and the Boundaries of Democracy', *European Journal of Political Theory*, 6(4) (2007), 398.

[56] B.K. Blitz and M. Otero-Iglesias, 'Stateless by Any Other Name: Unsuccessful Asylum Seekers and Undocumented Migrants in The United Kingdom' (*Journal for Ethnic and Migration Studies*, Forthcoming, 2011); Coventry Peace House, *Statelessness: The Quiet Torture of Belonging Nowhere* (Coventry: Coventry Peace House, 2008), www.stateless.org.uk/stateless_book.pdf, accessed 28 January 2009; London Detainee Support Group (LDSG), *Difficulties in Removal of Undocumented Iranian Nationals* (London: LDSG, 2007), www.ldsg.org.uk/files/uploads/dossierssummaries0708.pdf; *Difficulties in Removal of Undocumented Algerian Nationals* (London: LDSG, 2008), www.ldsg.org.uk/files/uploads/dossierssummaries0708.pdf; '*Detained Lives: The Real Costs of Indefinite Immigration Detention* (London: LDSG, January 2009), www.detainedlives.org/wp-content/uploads/detainedlives.pdf; C. Sawyer and P. Turpin, 'Neither Here Nor There: Temporary Admission to the UK', *International Journal of Refugee Law*, 17 (2005), 688.

For the purposes of this book, some of the most relevant studies that relate to the problem of statelessness tend to highlight the nationality problems associated with state restoration and the treatment of ethnic Russians in Estonia and Latvia[57] and other works on the case of the 'Erased' in Slovenia – the non-ethnic Slovenes who saw their residency rights cancelled shortly after Slovenia declared independence from the Socialist Federal Republic of Yugoslavia.[58]

Research design

The focus of this book is on non-nationals currently residing in the European Union without effective nationality. As noted above, this group may be considered *de facto* stateless in the sense that they have no effective nationality. The contribution which this study seeks to make is in its evaluation of the nature of effective statelessness in the European Union, which is measured by the degree to which such people can access rights such as the right to work or fulfil even basic needs such as food, housing and healthcare. We also examine the position of such people

---

[57] Barrington, 'The Domestic and International Consequences', 731; Bowring, 'European Minority Protection', 152(3), 413; A. Fehervary, 'Citizenship, Statelessness and Human Rights: Recent Developments in the Baltic States', *International Journal of Refugee Law*, 5(3) (2003), 392; G. Ginsburgs, 'The "Right to a Nationality" and the Regime of Loss of Russian Citizenship', *Review of Central and East European Law*, 26(1) (2000), 1; J. Hughes, 'Exit in Deeply Divided Societies: Regimes of Discrimination in Estonia and Latvia and the Potential for Russophone Migration', *Journal of Common Market Studies*, 43(4) (2005), 739; R. Kionka and R. Vetik, 'Estonia and the Estonians', in G. Smith (ed.), *The Nationalities Question in the Post-Soviet States* (London and New York: Longman, 1996), 129; R. Vetik, 'Ethnic Conflict and Accommodation in Post-Communist Estonia', *Journal of Peace Research*, 30(3) (1993), 271; *Democratic Multiculturalism: A New Model of National Integration* (Mariehamn, Finland: Åland Islands Peace Institute, 2001); 'The Cultural and Social Makeup of Estonia', in P. Kostø (ed.), *National Integration and Violent Conflict in Post-Soviet Societies: The Cases of Estonia and Moldova* (London: Rowman & Littlefield, 2002); M.H. Wiegandt, 'The Russian Minority in Estonia', *International Journal on Minority and Group Rights*, 3 (1995), 109.

[58] S. Andreev, 'Making Slovenian Citizens: The Problem of the Former Yugoslav Citizens and Asylum Seekers Living in Slovenia', *Southeast European Politics*, 4(1) (2003), 1; B.K. Blitz, 'Statelessness and the Social (De)Construction of Citizenship: Political Restructuring and Ethnic Discrimination in Slovenia', *Journal of Human Rights*, 5(4) (2006) 453; J. Dedić, V. Jalušič and J. Zorn, *The Erased – Organized Innocence and the Politics of Exclusion* (Ljubljana: Peace Institute, 2003); V. Jalušič and J. Dedić, 'The Erasure – Mass Human Rights Violation and Denial of Responsibility: The Case of Independent Slovenia', *Human Rights Review*, 9(1), (2008), 93; J. Zorn, 'Ethnic Citizenship in the Slovenian State', *Citizenship Studies*, 9(2) (2005), 135; 'The Right to Stay: Challenging the Policy of Detention and Deportation', *European Journal of Social Work*, 12(2) (2009b), 247–60.

regarding the wider rights to social participation including educating their children, accessing social services and the right to buy land and set up businesses.

The analytical framework presented offers an insight into three bundles of rights. The first bundle consists of basic rights; the second relates to social rights; and the third entails political rights more broadly:

(1) *Basic rights* include the means of everyday subsistence, such as the right to work and earn a living, the right to shelter and healthcare and the right to develop a personality and a personal life, including the right to family reunion. Such rights are often included in regional and international treaties which may purport to be universalist, but in practice even these basic rights may be difficult for non-nationals to access. If there are neither domestic rights nor any means of enforcing regional or international rights, then such rights are ineffective. Nevertheless, as this study shows, people do manage, and in reality there are often state or local systems and institutions which provide the means.

(2) *Social rights* are also vital to longer-term residents and their security and development. Rights to everyday participation in the life of society, such as access to education for one's children, are essential to the realisation of a future for both the individuals concerned and their families. If non-nationals cannot buy land, for example, or set up businesses, they will fall behind relative to nationals, and even if they are subsequently formally integrated and become citizens of the countries in which they live, their period of effective statelessness will have lasting deleterious effects, which will be particularly debilitating if they have included problems with obtaining education for children.

(3) Some elements of *political rights* are also important in this study. As Hannah Arendt notes, having a place in the world where one can voice concerns and make protests is central to the concept of citizenship and rights in modern European democratic states.[59] While the countries of the European Union often offer lawfully resident non-citizens certain political rights – such as the right to vote or to stand for local office – such opportunities to enhance one's sense of belonging by participation in political processes are not universal or consistent.

---

[59] H. Arendt, *The Origins of Totalitarianism* (New York: Schocken Books, 1951).

The issues of what to do with the unwanted are played out in the different European countries in the context of fundamental debates about who 'belongs'. Two of the selected case studies – France and the United Kingdom (chapters 10 and 7) – are 'old European' jurisdictions with contrasting histories. In France, citizenship, as the fundamental position of the citizen of the Republic, was traditionally of central importance to state structures. In Britain, by contrast, the position has long been much less clear, but the definition of 'belonging' is in the process of profound change. In both states, the situation of non-citizens and the prospect of their regularisation – or, conversely, removal – is subject to considerable concern and is a central plank in manifestos of the leading political parties. These two chapters examine the plight of refused asylum seekers, overstayers and the 'sans papiers' from a number of African, Asian and Middle Eastern countries as well as a selection of non-EU member states.

The other two jurisdictions, Slovenia and Estonia (chapters 8 and 9), belong to the 'new Europe'. Although they (re-)established their independence in 1991, in the context of nationality reform the 1990s brought an opportunity to start again. The two case studies differ in their selected populations and by the nature of political reform. A more conscious approach to citizenship is informed in the case of Estonia by the treatment afforded to ethnic Russians. In Slovenia, the national geographical boundaries within the former Yugoslavia became real and hard and were used to exclude those whose long-standing residence rights fell short of citizenship, namely the 'Erased'. In the case of Estonia, the non-nationals of concern are primarily Russian and other settled former Soviet nationalities from the neighbouring states; the 'Erased' in Slovenia cover nationals of former Yugoslav republics, including Roma.

Chapters 2–6 of this book examine the legal, normative and political frameworks that have developed in the European Union. The investigation begins with a review of the philosophical claims established by Hannah Arendt and subsequent scholars. Monika Krause in chapter 2 reconsiders Arendt's relevance to the plight of effectively stateless people – in this case, undocumented migrants – in the European Union. She argues that Arendt's writing on the rightlessness of migrants exposes the problem of 'total domination' by the state and recalls the essential contradiction between state-centred citizenship and the discourse of human rights. She concludes by identifying potential gaps within the dominating state that enable some stateless individuals to claim greater agency over their own lives, even if it is on the margins. Matthew J. Gibney in chapter 3 then surveys how additional bodies of political thought have responded to the question of the rights of non-citizens living in the polity who are excluded from most or all of the rights and benefits of citizenship. He argues that liberal political theorists have historically ignored distinctions between citizens and non-citizens, and as a result have overlooked the increasingly differentiated treatments afforded to non-nationals, above all those without secure status.

The philosophical discussion is followed by Caroline Sawyer's chapter 4 on the international and regional law relevant to statelessness. Sawyer examines the scope of the UN Conventions on *de jure* statelessness and related international Covenants and Conventions that may also apply to the *de facto* stateless before exploring the potential application of regional instruments, including the Council of Europe's convention on state succession, the evolution of European human rights law under the ECHR and the position of those migrants under the law of the European Union. She argues that given the origins of the Human Rights Convention in the aftermath of the Holocaust, it is surprising that EU law, originating in ideas of free trade as the means of preventing future wars between European states, now offers more personal rights and protection to third country national migrants.

Chapter 5, the final chapter in part I, surveys the development of an emerging regime on statelessness. Brad K. Blitz examines the strength of political claims for greater inclusion in both Europe and other regional contexts and describes the efforts by national and international actors to promote the rights of non-citizens and to prevent statelessness. Blitz assesses the actions of influential international NGOs and monitoring bodies – including the Council of Europe's Office of the High Commissioner for Human Rights (OHCHR), the UN High Commissioner for Human Rights and UN Independent Expert on Minorities, the UNHCR's Statelessness Unit, the Justice Initiative of Refugees International and the Open Society Institute (OSI) – and considers the degree to which they have successfully raised the profile of both *de jure* and *de facto* stateless populations. He also examines the development of mass protests organised in Europe and draws upon interview data to suggest that there is an emerging consensus among human rights bodies to provide greater protection to *de facto* stateless people in the European Union.

Within this framework, the five chapters in part II present the empirical findings based on interviews (*n* 100) and focus groups with stateless people in, the United Kingdom, Slovenia, Estonia and France. For analytical purposes, we suggest there are four key factors that influence state behaviour towards *de facto* stateless populations and affect their sense of stability and security. These include: (1) the importance of geography and sensitive political borders; (2) the size of the migrant population; (3) international relations between countries of origin and diaspora communities; and (4) political restructuring as a result of decolonisation, state succession, or state restoration. Throughout the case studies, the contributors evaluate how these factors have historically influenced the state's treatment of non-nationals, including effective stateless people, and how they may provide means to increase the agency of *de facto* stateless people and hence promote reform and greater inclusion.

Each case study begins with a review of the historical and legal treatment of *de facto* stateless people and an analysis of current citizenship policies. It then sets out the findings from interviews and focus groups. In the case of Estonia, Raivo Vetik in chapter 9 concentrates on the situation of the Russian-speaking community where, following independence, new tests for citizenship were introduced tending to disqualify this large and historically powerful group. He examines how both the Estonian state and Russian minority have adapted to the introduction of a 'grey passport' and intermediate form of citizenship that provides ethnic Russian non-citizens with most rights but does not address patterns of structural discrimination and social exclusion among this community. In the case of France, Arnaud Lucien and David Marrani in chapter 10 focus on the situation of the *sans-papiers*, the undocumented North African migrants now concentrated in Marseilles-Toulon and Paris; the treatment of other non-nationals from different regions is also assessed. Regarding Slovenia, Jelka Zorn in chapter 8 examines the 'Erased', some of the 25,000 former Yugoslav nationals who did not opt for Slovene citizenship in 1992 and as a result lost their residency rights and, with those, other essential rights. In the final case study, from the United Kingdom (chapter 7), Caroline Sawyer, Brad K. Blitz and Miguel Otero-Iglesias examine the impact of negative asylum application decisions on applicants' access to rights in the case of refused asylum seekers in Oxford and London.

The book provides, in chapter 11 by Brad K. Blitz and Caroline Sawyer, a comparative analysis of the state of law and protections afforded to stateless people in the European Union. The conclusion, by Caroline Sawyer and Brad K. Blitz, identifies common challenges facing stateless people in the European Union and suggests measures that would provide for greater security and fulfilment.

2

Stateless people and undocumented migrants: an Arendtian perspective

MONIKA KRAUSE[*]

Perhaps more than ever before, we live in a situation in which, as Hannah Arendt put it in her 1943 article, 'We Refugees', 'passports or birth certificates, and sometimes even income tax receipts, are no longer formal papers but matters of social distinction'.[1] In what constituted a drastic shift in policy, many Western governments curtailed legal means of entry and residence for foreigners from the mid-1970s onward.[2] States stopped admitting economic migrants. The signatory states of the Schengen Agreement (1985) and the TREVI group (1957) pushed asylum policies towards the lowest common denominator on a European level. Following the fall of the Berlin Wall, measures like the third-country rule, the introduction of visa requirements for refugee-producing countries and the extension of the policing of borders have made it almost impossible to claim or obtain political asylum in the European Union.

These measures have not been able to stop immigration. They have, however, illegalised work migration and driven many potential asylum seekers underground. Many foreigners already living on the territory found themselves, in different ways and to different degrees, illegalised. These people include rejected asylum seekers, visa overstayers and immigrants whose residence permit has not been renewed for a variety of reasons, such as losing employment, growing dependent on welfare benefits,

---

[*] A version of this chapter appeared originally as 'Undocumented Migrants: an Arendtian Perspective', in *European Journal of Political Theory*, 7 (2008), 331–48. I thank Sage Publishing for the permission to reproduce parts of that article in this volume.

[1] H. Arendt, *The Jew as Pariah* (New York: Grove Press, 1982), 65, 'We Refugees' was published in *Menorah Journal*, 31 (1943), 69.

[2] In the United Kingdom, successive governments limited the citizenship rights of former colonial subjects from 1962 onwards. Following the worldwide economic recession, Germany stopped recruiting guest workers in November 1973 and France officially closed its borders in 1974.

or having committed a crime, including having violated foreigner-specific restrictions.[3] As a result, we find on the territory of Western Europe a growing number of people who are not citizens and, lacking any formal right to residence and work, are not even 'denizens', according to Hammar's definition of the term.[4] Official estimates put the number of persons without valid documents at around 3 million for the European Union in the late 1990s, with increases each year of 500,000.[5] The Catholic Church estimated that there were 1 million undocumented foreigners in Germany alone.[6]

This group is the subject of an increasingly hostile discourse on 'illegal immigrants', 'bogus asylum seekers' and, since 11 September 2001, 'international terrorism'. This chapter explores what a re-reading of the work of Hannah Arendt can contribute to the analytical and political task of giving an alternative meaning to the presence of this group in our societies. An early post-national thinker, Arendt carves clearings into a thinking caught in a framework centred on the unity of nation, state, and territory, thus opening new ways of thinking and acting, and new questions for empirical research. She shows us the stateless as a victim, as an emblematic philosophical figure and as an important political actor.

Hannah Arendt today

The last ten to twenty years have seen a lot of detailed exegesis of Arendt's work, as well as imaginative applications of her concepts to

---

[3] For a useful overview of the variety of groups affected in France, see Nathalie Ferré, 'La production de l'irrégularité', in D. Fassin, A. Morice and C. Quimina (eds.), *Les lois de l'inhospitalité* (Paris: Éditions la Découverte, 1997), 47; for Germany, see R. Weitkamp, 'Spielball des deutschen Arbeitsmarktes: Zur rechtlichen Hierarchisierung von MigrantInnen', in BUKO (ed.), *Zwischen Flucht und Arbeit: Neue Migration und Legalisierungsdebatte* (Hamburg: Verlag Libertäre Assoziation, 1995), 93 and H. Lederer, 'Typologie und Statistik illegaler Zuwanderung nach Deutschland', in E. Eichendorfer, *Migration und Illegalität* (Osnabrück: Universitätsverlag Rasch, 1999), 53.

[4] T. Hammar, *Democracy and the Nation State* (Aldershot, Avebury, 1990).

[5] International Organization for Migration, *World Migration Report 2000* (Geneva: IOM, 2000); International Labour Organization (ILO), *Towards a Fair Deal for Migrant Workers in the Global Economy* (Geneva: ILO, 2004); see C. Pinkerton, G. McLaughlan and J. Salt, *Sizing the Illegally Resident Population in the UK*, Home Office Online Report 58/04 (2004) for a survey of efforts to measure the illegal population.

[6] See J. Alt, *Illegal in Deutschland* (Karlsruhe: Von Loeper Literaturverlag, 1999), 48, but also his updated 'Groessenschätzungen für Deutschland', www.joerg-alt.de/publikationen/materialanlagen/materialanlagen.mtml, accessed December 2006.

the contemporary moment.[7] To some extent independently of content or concepts, her *style* of thinking has inspired writers across disciplines.[8] This work has relied on a wide range of interpretations of Arendt; this diversity of uses is credit to the richness of her work and has been fruitful. But there are also some missed opportunities in these discussions: an opportunity to read different parts of her work together, an opportunity to capture the most original Arendt and an opportunity to make Arendt's work, as a whole, most relevant to the present day.

The most imaginative applications of her work have sometimes chosen not to explore its inner unity. Many of those who have, have done so from within established traditions of political theorising. Discussions about whether or not Arendt is a communitarian, a liberal, a modernist, an anti- or postmodernist, or a feminist have made her accessible as a resource for the theoretical tradition and such analysis has clarified parts of her work and the tensions within it.[9] Yet, if we try to make her fit any one of these pre-conceived labels, we are in danger of losing sight of the originality of her work.

There has been some debate regarding the basis of her own rethinking of politics. An isolated reading of *The Human Condition* led many to reproach her with a nostalgic longing for the Greek past. A focus on the experiences described in Part III of *The Origins of Totalitarianism* induced Margaret Canovan to emphasise Arendt's anti-modern, and

---

[7] Among key works of that period are M. Canovan, *Hannah Arendt: A Re-Interpretation of Her Political Thought* (Cambridge: Cambridge University Press, 1992); J. Isaac, *Arendt, Camus and Modern Rebellion* (New Haven, CT: Yale University Press, 1992); M. Passerin d'Éntreves, *The Political Philosophy of Hannah Arendt* (London: Routledge, 1994); S. Benhabib, *The Reluctant Modernism of Hannah Arendt* (London: Sage, 1996); R. Bernstein, *Hannah Arendt and the Jewish Question* (Cambridge, MA: MIT Press, 1996). For more recent contributions by many pioneering and influential Arendt scholars, see the special issue of *Social Research*, 69(2) (2002). Among the many contributions to the centennial of her birth E. Young-Bruehl, *Why Hannah Arendt Matters* (New Haven, CT: Yale University Press (2006) stands out.

[8] See, e.g., the work of J. Shklar (ed. with S. Hoffman), *Political Thought and Political Thinkers* (Chicago, IL: Chicago University Press, 1998) or G. Agamben, *Means Without End* (Minneapolis, MN: University of Minnesota Press, 2000).

[9] See Benhabib, *The Reluctant Modernism*; D.R. Villa, *Politics, Philosophy, Terror: Essays on the Thought of Hannah Arendt* (Princeton, NJ: Princeton University Press, 1999); G. Kateb, *Hannah Arendt: Politics, Conscience, Evil* (Totowa, NJ: Rowman &Allanheld, 1984); B. Honig (ed.), *Feminist Interpretations of Hannah Arendt* (University Park, PA: Pennsylvania State University Press, 1995).

especially her anti-Marxist, traits.[10] I argue for a reading that, instead, places statelessness at the centre of her work.[11]

Arendt, herself a refugee and for years a stateless person, was one of the few in her time to engage with what she analysed as the 'newest mass phenomenon in contemporary history': statelessness. Following the upheavals of the First World War, she witnessed the emergence of an increasing number of people for whom there was 'no appropriate niche in the framework of the general law'.[12] She was unique in her attention to statelessness:[13] and a reading that takes this experience seriously can gauge the originality of her work. A reading of her work that places statelessness at its centre provides a thread connecting *On Totalitarianism* and *The Human Condition*, and her reflections on power, states and revolutions. Arendt on statelessness is also Arendt on states. The reading presented here can be an important resource in our current attempts to interrogate the state and to think democratic politics beyond it.

The migrant as victim: total domination

Against a discourse that, not unlike now, tended to ignore the presence of these groups according to the principle that what must not be, cannot be, Arendt shows us the stateless as victims. In chapter 9 of *The Origins of Totalitarianism*, Arendt analysed very clearly what it means to be 'illegalised' in one's very existence. She begins from the fundamental observation of the 'illegal's' rightlessness. I discuss what this rightlessness entails for today's undocumented people. Then I present Arendt's interpretation of the political dimension of their situation. For her, the stateless suffer from a deprivation more fundamental than any material deprivation or denial of specific rights. It is a deprivation that cannot be thought of within the model of a political community: the stateless are deprived of the right to have rights and are subject to 'total domination'. We thus find one of the elements of totalitarianism within formally democratic societies.

[10] M. Canovan, 'The Contradictions of Hannah Arendt's Political Thought', *Political Theory*, 6 (1978), 5.

[11] Bernstein, *Hannah Arendt*; see also M.-C. Caloz-Tschopp (ed.), *Les sans-État dans la philosophie de Hannah Arendt* (Lausanne: Éditions Paliot, 2000b).

[12] H. Arendt, *The Origins of Totalitarianism* (New York: Harcourt Brace Jovanovich, 1968), 278.

[13] See M. J. Gibney, chapter 3 in this volume, for a more comprehensive account of the problem of statelessness in the history of political theory.

Rightlessness today

Arendt observed that to be stateless is to be 'an outlaw by definition'. The stateless person 'without right to residence and the right to work had of course constantly to transgress the law. He was liable to jail sentences without ever committing a crime.' Having been forced beyond the pale of law, the stateless person has 'no rights whatsoever and lives under the threat of deportation'.[14] She lacks any form of social, economic, or legal protection. Because she simply does not exist in terms of the law, she is exposed to the arbitrary rule of the executive – she is left 'completely at the mercy of the police'.[15] The stateless share with the subjects of totalitarian countries the destruction of their juridical personality, the life in a realm of lawlessness and an arbitrary form of domination that dominates each individual 'in every aspect of their life'.[16]

One might wonder whether migrants with rights in other countries are really rightless. In Arendt's time, as in ours, it has been difficult to distinguish between stateless persons, refugees and other kinds of migrants. Then, as now, refugees often claim statelessness in order to avoid being deported. States have also often de-nationalised refugees for political reasons. Arendt cited legal experts who then, as today, tended to resolve this ambiguity by arguing that all refugees could be considered stateless.[17] Ultimately, her analysis, which I follow, is based on the argument that undocumented migrants – subject to removal – are rightless to the extent that they want to stay on the territory. All undocumented migrants – as opposed to tourists – share this rightlessness as the limit function of their political existence on the territory, even though the degree to which they can claim rights elsewhere will affect the impact this rightlessness has on their quality of life. They share rightlessness despite immense differences in their material living conditions.

This reading suggests a set of questions for comparative research into the lifeworlds of undocumented migrants. How does the impact of rightlessness depend on peoples' education, the available social networks and on the degree of regulation in a given society? How does it affect the experience of the labour market? How does it impact the experience of

---

[14] Arendt, *The Origins of Totalitarianism*, 286.
[15] *Ibid.*, 283.   [16] *Ibid.*, 456.
[17] Simpson, quoted in Arendt, *The Origins of Totalitarianism*, 281; I. Brownlie, *Principles of Public International Law* (Oxford: Clarendon Press, 1998), 560.

public space? How does it shape the interaction with the state? How does it affect those who are not yet illegal but whose rights of residence or work depend on a partner or an employer? Such questions are explored in subsequent chapters of this volume.

The denial of the right to have rights

Whereas present research often focuses exclusively on the undocumented people's loss of legal status or material need, Arendt's interpretation emphasises the loss of political status. The stateless is denied the fundamental human capacity to act. The denial of agency is also implicit in the fact that nothing she does makes any difference to her illegal status.

For those who are outlawed by definition, the 'deprivation of legality, i.e., of all rights, no longer has any connection with specific crimes'.[18] It is in this context that we must understand Arendt's emphasis on the innocence of those subject to total domination. This innocence does not just add to our concern about how unjust their treatment is, it also underlines the implicit denial of agency. She writes that their 'innocence … was their greatest misfortune. Innocence in the sense of a complete lack of responsibility was the mark of their rightlessness as it was the seal of their loss of political status.'[19] Had they been persecuted for anything they did or said, this would at least have acknowledged the fundamental human capacities of action and speech. It would also have entailed, in retrospect at least, the attribution of a certain choice, however minimal it might be, to comply and be spared – a choice that the subject of the most intolerant regime retains. 'One had at least to be an enemy of tyranny in order to be persecuted by it.'[20] Here again, the stateless, to the extent that she cannot or does not want to leave the country, finds herself in a situation that bears similarity to the one of the 'objective enemy', as identified by the totalitarian regime. It is the situation of the Jew facing biological anti-semitism who, unlike the victim of traditional cultural anti-semitism, cannot even change her faith to influence her situation.[21]

In fact, as Arendt notes, the stateless can improve her legal – if not in all cases, her actual – position by committing a crime: 'The best criterion by which to decide whether someone has been forced outside the pale of law is to ask if he would benefit by committing a crime. If a small burglary is likely to improve his legal position, at least temporarily, one may be

---

[18] Arendt, *The Origins of Totalitarianism*, 295.
[19] *Ibid.*   [20] *Ibid.*, 433.   [21] *Ibid.*, 432.

sure he has been deprived of human rights ... Even if he is penniless he can now get a lawyer, complain about his jailers, and he will be listened to respectfully.'[22] When Arendt writes about the stateless' 'rightlessness', she does not primarily think of the deprivation of a number of discrete rights that one could list. She notes that formulas such as life, liberty, or equality before the law are terms designed to solve problems within a political community. The stateless' deprivation is more fundamental; they are deprived of the 'right to have rights' – the basic right to belong to an organised community.[23]

Total domination, according to Arendt, is thus fundamentally opposed to human freedom, but not to a negative freedom in the sense of an undisturbed privateness. In fact, the stateless 'might enjoy more freedom of movement than a lawfully imprisoned criminal or ... enjoy more freedom of opinion in the internment camps of democratic countries than they would in any ordinary despotism, not to mention in a totalitarian country.' The point is that neither physical safety nor 'freedom' of opinion affects what matters about their situation. 'Their freedom of movement ... gives them no right to residence ... and their freedom of opinion is a fools' freedom; nothing they think matters anyhow.'[24]

The stateless loses a freedom that can only be realised by acting together in the public realm. The stateless' 'fundamental deprivation is manifested first and above all in the deprivation of a place in the world which makes opinion significant and actions effective'.[25] With the loss of a realm of action, speech and human relationships, the stateless loses some of the essential characteristics of human life. The stateless is thrown back into a 'state of nature'.[26]

The migrant as figure: the *aporias* of state-centred thinking

Some of the passages just cited might leave us wondering whether Arendt, in depicting the stateless as living in 'conditions of savages',[27] is not colluding in the very dehumanisation she describes. However, a one-sided 'catastrophic' reading of Arendt's perspective on statelessness would be misleading.[28] To see how the stateless turn into privileged political actors in her work, it is important to analyse what the stateless shows us as an

---

[22] *Ibid.*, 286–7.   [23] *Ibid.*, 296–7.   [24] *Ibid.*
[25] *Ibid.*, 296.   [26] *Ibid.*, 297.   [27] *Ibid.*, 302.
[28] For an example of such a catastrophic reading, see H.-M. Enzensberger, *Die große Wanderung* (Frankfurt/Main: Suhrkamp, 1994).

'emblematic philosophical figure'.[29] What Arendt described as the 'sufferings of more and more groups of people to whom the rules of the world around them have ceased to apply'[30] casts doubt on the very rules in question. The stateless is the 'other' – the 'limit concept' of established political thinking that centres on the unity of the sovereignty of the state, nation and territory and exposes its contradictions.

The nation-state

The nation-state links the sovereignty of the state, territorial and ethno-cultural closure and the democratic claims of representative democracy. While formally democratic, the model of political membership as articulated in the French Revolution entailed 'the formal delimitation of the citizenry; ... the legal rationalization and ideological accentuation of the distinction between nationals and foreigners; the articulation of the doctrine of national sovereignty and of the link between citizenship and nationhood'.[31] The world is ideologically, and in institutional practice, constructed as neatly divided in territorially based, national, sovereign units.

From the perspective of the stateless person, this model is exposed as a power-produced construction and its exclusionary consequences unmasked. By definition, the stateless questions the distinction between national citizen and foreigner because she is neither. In doing so, she questions the equation of man with the citizen on which the system of nation-states bases its legitimacy.

Arendt explicitly addresses the ethno-cultural element of modern nationhood. We can take from her an analysis of how ethno-cultural closure followed the construction of the modern state. Writing on the French Revolution, Arendt emphasises that, in 1789, the 'nation had conquered the state'. The state, inherited from the absolutist regime, 'has been transformed from an instrument of law into an instrument of the nation'.[32] The privileges of the aristocracy were abolished, but popular sovereignty was, in the very historical moment of its birth, equated with national sovereignty. The democratic idea of government 'by the people, for the people'

---

[29] M.-C. Caloz-Tschopp, 'La figure-sujet des sans-Etat dans l'œuvre de Hannah Arendt', in Caloz-Tschopp, *Les sans-État*, 30–47.

[30] Arendt, *The Origins of Totalitarianism*, 267.

[31] R. Brubaker, *Citizenship and Nationhood in France and Germany* (Cambridge, MA: Harvard University Press, 1992a), 35.

[32] Arendt, *The Origins of Totalitarianism*, 230.

was from then on thought of as to be realised in ethnically defined, culturally homogenous collectives. The Minority Treaties confirmed this development after the First World War. Their real significance was 'the recognition that millions of people lived outside normal legal protection and needed an additional guarantee of their elementary rights from an outside body'. They made explicit 'that only nationals could be citizens, only people of the same national origin could enjoy full protection of legal institutions', and that 'the law of a country could not be responsible for people of a different nationality'.[33]

This ethno-cultural element might not be equally important for all modern nation-states. There is a long tradition of contrasting the French (civic) to the German (ethnic) tradition of nationhood.[34] According to the 'ideal type' of French citizenship, the nation is defined in a purely political manner in relation to the territorial and institutional framework of the state. However, the stateless' exclusion is not only due to the equation of political community with a pre-politically constituted nation. For the stateless person, who is neither a member of the nation nor a member of the state, it is not that decisive whether the nation creates the state or the state creates the nation. At the very least, the stateless person on French territory, by definition, shows the practical failure of the ideology of the French Revolution, according to which 'the only foreigner in France is the bad citizen'.[35]

The stateless person problematises also the other two elements of the trinity of nation, state and territory. In moving or having moved, she undermines and exposes the exclusionary consequences of the territorial closure of political community. By laying open the divergence between those present in the public space and the apparatus that claims to be representing them, she leads us to question the idea of a sovereign state that, in its power to decide 'in the last instance', places itself above the present inhabitants of the territory. The stateless person induces us to grow fully aware of the anti-democratic implications of the fact that in the modern nation-state, it is, in any case, the state that constitutes the citizenry, and not the other way round.[36]

---

[33] *Ibid.*, 275.
[34] H. Kohn, *The Idea of Nationalism* (New York: Macmillan, 1944); Brubaker, *Citizenship and Nationhood.*
[35] Tallien, quoted in R. Brubaker, *Citizenship and Nationhood.*
[36] For an explicit opposition of a *democratic* and a state-centred perspective on citizenship, see A. Stewart, 'Two Conceptions of Citizenship', *British Journal of Sociology*, 46 (1995), 63.

Arendt writes on the 'damage' the stateless inflict on the distinction between nationals and foreigners and on the legal structure of the state. Which side is she on in the clash between stateless and nation-state? Arendt values the nation-state as a solid man-made structure in which people could feel at home and for which inhabitants can take responsibility. In *The Origins of Totalitarianism*, she wrote on the decline of the nation-state against the background of the experience of what had followed: race imperialism. Whatever its historical merits, it seems clear that, for her, under the conditions created by an international economy, the nation-state is at least no longer a viable model. It is worth remembering that Arendt actively opposed the foundation of a Jewish nation-state in Palestine.[37] She agitated against a solution of the Jewish question 'that merely produced a new category of refugees, the Arabs, thereby increasing the number of stateless and rightless by another 700,000 to 800,000 people'.[38]

Human rights

In both Arendt's time and today, what is opposed to the particularity of membership in the nation-state is the idea of individual and universal human rights. Following the 'natural law' tradition of classical liberalism, the French Revolution had declared them to be innate, inalienable and independent of any government. The undocumented should therefore embody the concept of human rights more than anybody else: 'If a human being loses his political status, he should according to the implications of the inborn and inalienable rights of man come under exactly the situation for which the declarations of such general rights provided.'[39] Ironically, it is precisely the stateless that reveals the crisis of human rights.

The fate of the stateless, when they appear in great numbers, calls attention to the fact that for all practical matters, the rights of man are still identified with the rights of citizens. As Arendt noted: 'The Rights of Man proved to be unenforceable – even in countries whose constitution was based upon them – whenever people appeared who were no longer citizen of any sovereign state.'[40] The decades that have followed the writing of Arendt's original text have witnessed the erection and elaboration

---

[37] Arendt, *The Jew as Pariah*, 134–61.
[38] Arendt, *The Origins of Totalitarianism*, 290.
[39] *Ibid.*, 300.   [40] *Ibid.*, 293.

of a global human rights regime based on the Universal Declaration of Human Rights (UDHR) of 1948 complemented by regional protection mechanisms. But as the right of the state to grant or refuse residency remains unchallenged the situation, and the situation for the increasing number of undocumented people, has not changed: threatened by immediate removal, they simply lack the presuppositions for making an individual public appearance as a subject of human rights (see also Sawyer, chapter 4 in this volume).

For Arendt, the existence of stateless people exposes the abstract, formal, individualistic and, above all, apolitical character of the concept of human rights. Arendt observes that 'from the beginning the paradox involved in the declaration of inalienable human rights was that it reckoned with an "abstract" human being who seemed to exist nowhere, for even savages lived in some kind of social order'.[41] For Arendt, the concept of man underlying the Enlightenment notion of inalienable human rights is unrealistically worldless and atomistic:

> The conception of human rights, based upon the assumed existence of a human being as such, broke down at the very moment when those who professed to believe in it were for the first time confronted with people who had indeed lost all other qualities and specific relationships except that they were still human. The world found nothing sacred about being human. And in view of objective political conditions, it is hard to say how the concept of man upon which human rights are based – that he is created in the image of god (in the American formula), or that he is the representative of mankind, or that he harbors within himself the sacred demands of natural law (in the French formula) – could have helped to find a solution to the problem.[42]

The title of Arendt's chapter, 'The Decline of the Nation-State and the End of Rights of Man' in *The Origins of Totalitarianism*, suggests a strong link between a political thinking and reality centred on the nation-state and the concept of human rights. Natural human rights suddenly appear not as a solution to the problem of statelessness against the nation-state, but as part of the same discourse as the latter. The stateless questions the identification of man and citizen, thereby disrupting the discourse in which abstract human rights transferred to nature and the sovereignty of the state refer to each other and turn against the self-determination of the concrete plurality of human beings.

---

[41] *Ibid.*, 291.   [42] *Ibid.*, 299–300.

For Arendt, the French Revolution confronts us 'with the serious attempt to reduce the political to the natural'; a move that always arouses suspicions as to its ideological functions. The concept of individual, natural, innate rights is revealed as the means by which the sovereign state transfers the foundation of its power from god to nature. As Arendt writes, 'The French declaration of human rights was from the start aimed at establishing a source of political power and authority, it claimed to be the foundation of the state and not only the fundamental means to prevent the state from abusing its power. The state itself was meant to be based on the natural rights of man.'[43] An appeal to the notion of innate human rights might then affirm the sovereignty of the state based on the promise to enforce them.

The existence of stateless persons shows that rights are precisely not independent of this human plurality of history and society. Arendt reminds us of the need for a practical political solution to the problems of human organisation, as opposed to a philosophical, theoretical one. A political solution that seems all the more without alternative, as history has shown that, in the end, as Arendt wrote, 'no one seems to be able to define what these general human rights, as distinguished from the rights of citizen really are'.[44] Arendt insists that, 'Equality, in contrast to all that is involved in mere existence, is not given to us, but is the result of human organization insofar as it is guided by the principle of justice. We are not born equal; we become equal as members of a group on the strength of our decision to guarantee ourselves mutually equal rights.'[45]

Arendt is doubtful about the existence of any transcendental norms. This has disturbed many and brought against her the accusation of an irresponsible anti-foundationalism, a political existentialism and a Nietzschean aestheticism.[46] Yet, she affirms the 'existence of a right to have rights'. It is the right 'to live in a framework where one is judged by one's actions and opinions'.[47] Arendt's right to have rights is precisely not an abstract right, but a claim rooted in the concrete plurality of human beings – the fundamental human condition that we share the world with others who are both like and unlike ourselves. It is the right to participate in the discourse of plural human beings. The right to have 'rights' is

---

[43] *Ibid.*, 138.   [44] *Ibid.*, 393.   [45] *Ibid.*, 301.

[46] M. Jay, 'The Political Existentialism of Hannah Arendt', in M. Jay (ed.), *Permanent Exiles: Essays on the Intellectual Migration from Germany to America* (New York: Columbia University Press, 1996), 237.

[47] Arendt, *The Origins of Totalitarianism*, 296–7.

also the right to belong to a community that then only determines what the 'rights' and 'duties' of its members are. These secondary 'rights' and 'duties' are then not of a pre-political nature, but the outcome of a historically particular public debate.

The migrant as political actor: the power of concerted action

Arendt does not show us the undocumented only as victims, or as a disturbing signifier on the level of philosophical representation. By questioning state-centred thinking, the migrants appear also as political actors whose public appearance can be potentially explosive and liberating. I briefly discuss how Arendt's concept of the conscious pariah can help us understand the impact of the *sans papiers* movement in France, and how her concept of power is illustrated by their collective action.

The pariah as a privileged actor

It is important in this context to bear in mind the emphatic sense that action and politics carry for Arendt. The capacity to act is 'the capacity to begin', the capacity to create the new, and to do the unexpected. Action is boundless. It is tied to the human condition of *natality*. With action and speech, we insert ourselves into the human world, and this insertion is 'like a second birth'.[48] Human agency can assert itself even in the midst of seemingly automatic historical processes: 'If it is true that action and beginning are the same, it follows that a capacity to perform miracles must likewise be within the range of human faculties. It is in the very nature of every new beginning that it breaks into the world as an "infinite improbability."'[49] Action is inseparably linked to freedom. Arendt asserts that, 'Men are free – as distinguished from their capacity to freedom as long as they act, neither before nor after; for to be free and to act are the same'.[50] Politics derives its *raison d'être* from this freedom as experienced in action. Politics and freedom are two sides of the same coin.[51]

Arendt's emphasis in parts of *The Human Condition* on the Greek hero, who is concerned with the display of his excellence as one of few equals, earned her the accusation of an anti-democratic elitism.[52] Jennifer Ring has usefully emphasised another dimension of Arendt's

[48] H. Arendt, *The Human Condition* (Chicago, IL: Chicago University Press, 1958), 176.
[49] H. Arendt, *Between Past and Future* (London: Faber & Faber, 1961), 171.
[50] *Ibid.*, 153, emphasis in the original.   [51] *Ibid.*, 99.
[52] Canovan, 'The Contradictions', 26.

theory of action by demonstrating that besides the Greek aristocrat, the pariah, history's outsider, is an important actor in her work.[53]

The pariah has figured prominently in Arendt's books. Her fascination for the pariah is connected to her interest in the Jewish question. She presents Bernhard Lazare as the model of the 'conscious pariah'. Lazare believed that the Jew should come out openly as the representative of the pariah 'since it is the duty of every human being to resist oppression.' His case shows that 'as soon as the pariah enters the arena of politics, and translates his status into political terms, he becomes perforce a rebel.'[54] Because the stateless embodies the contradictions of the arrangements that exclude her, her public appearance is explosive and potentially liberating.

Arendt wrote that, 'those few refugees who insist on telling the truth, even to the point of indecency, get in exchange for their unpopularity one priceless advantage: history is no longer a closed book to them and politics is so longer a politics of gentiles. Refugees driven from country to country represent the vanguard of their peoples.'[55] There are strong indications that more and more *sans papiers* have opted to take history into their own hands throughout Europe in the past decade. France's immigrants have a long history as political actors, and as noted in subsequent chapters of this volume, the *sans papiers* began fighting for their right to stay and work as early as the 1970s.[56] Since the late 1980s we have witnessed an unprecedented degree of militancy; the now legendary founding event of the present movement was the occupation of the Parisian church of Saint-Bernard by 300 West African *sans papiers* in 1996. The eviction of the protesters and their consequent deportation did not prevent the spreading of the movement throughout France, and to other countries.[57]

A closer look at the French movement reveals what warrants us speaking of those activists as conscious pariahs who really do 'translate their status in political terms'. In their self-designation as 'sans papiers', they

[53] J. Ring, 'The Pariah as Hero: Hannah Arendt's Political Actor', *Political Theory*, 19 (1991), 433.

[54] Arendt, *The Jew as Pariah*, 71.   [55] Arendt, *The Jew as Pariah*, 66.

[56] C. Withol de Wenden, 'Immigrants as Political Actors in France', *West European Politics*, 17 (1994), 91; J. Simeant, *La cause des sans-papiers* (Paris: Presse de Sciences Po, 1998).

[57] Indeed, 1997 saw the foundation of the 'Caravan of Migrants' in Germany. *Sans papiers* in Switzerland had their first national demonstration in September 2001, and have continued to fight for collective regularisation after government initiatives to consider their fate on a case-by-case basis. In Northern Italy, migrants organised a month of protests in the Spring of 2001, a development that gained special significance considering that Italy had only recently turned from an emigration to an immigration country. See Nicole Montagna, 'La primavera dei migranti', *Posse* 2 (2001), 12.

define themselves not by having fled as 'refugees', not by having come in as 'immigrants', not even by moving as 'migrants', but by the mere fact that they are in France without the required documents for residence and work. As Madjiguène Cissé, a spokeswoman of the French movement, put it in a speech in 1997:

> We are here. That was our first rallying cry. We are here. We are men and women who chose to live in France. Each of us has tried his best on his own to get hold of documents and it did not work out. That is why we came together and occupied a church to show to people what is going on.[58]

The *sans papiers* have defended this political stance against the authorities, which would often close both eyes to their presence as long as there were no political demands, and sometimes even grant amnesty as long as it was an exception for an individual case. A spokesperson of the group of the *sans papiers* de Saint-Bernard quotes one of the policemen sent to evacuate the church: 'Return to your homes quietly, disappear into nature, and there will be no arrests.'[59]

Militants have also repeatedly resisted attempts to divide them into 'worthy' and 'unworthy'. In view of increasingly restrictive legislation, supportive organisations had in the preceding years often limited their activities to the defence of individual cases at the cost of collective struggles. In a practice of 'self-censorship', they had only presented to the authorities the cases that had the greatest prospect of benevolent consideration, thereby inevitably employing the criteria defined by the state itself. The *sans papiers* of Saint-Bernard have repeatedly been advised to dissolve the group and concentrate on the fight for the right to stay for the families among them, but they have opted to stay together.[60] The insistence on solidarity and collective action has been their great strength. Less than perhaps any other group, they can be incorporated via a model of identity politics. Their status is purely imposed by the state. They ask not for recognition of their status, but for the end of their identity.

The portable polis *and social power*

Arendt asserts the primacy of plurality and of concerted action to all formal political institutions. She insists on the primacy of plurality, the fact

---

[58] M. Cissé, 'Sans Papiers: Wir sind da! Die Bewegung der Illegalen in Frankreich', *Interim*, 433 (1997), 12.
[59] C. Rodier, 'Le mouvement de sans-papiers en France', in Caloz-Tschopp, *Les Sans-État*, 186.
[60] Cissé, 'Sans Papiers', 12–14.

that human beings share the world with others who are both the same and different. She insists that it is political action itself that creates public space: 'The public realm rises directly out of acting together, the sharing of words and deeds. Thus action not only has the most intimate relationship to the public part of the world common to us all, but it is the one activity that constitutes it.'[61] Arendt presents us with a model of the political realm that is, at times, 'astonishingly portable' (Ring 1991: 439). For Arendt, as for the Greeks,

> the polis properly speaking is not the city-state in its physical location; it is the organisation of the people as it arises out of acting and speaking together, and its true space lies between people living together for this purpose, no matter where they happen to be. 'Wherever you go, you will be a polis': These watchwords of Greek colonization express the conviction that action and speech create a space between the participants, which can find its proper location almost at any time and anywhere.[62]

Thus, Arendt helps us appreciate the political meaning of the *sans papiers*' protests. With their actions, they create spaces of public freedom. It is worth contrasting this perspective with the official view on these events. Rather than as a hostile seizure of public space from the outside, these actions appear as democratic re-conquests against the state. Etienne Balibar brings out this point:

> Paradoxically, the struggles of the Sans Papiers – perceived by the government as disturbances of the public order, as blackmailing out of despair or products of a conspiracy the wire-pullers of which have to be identified among the immigrants' 'criminal sons' – have been and are privileged moments in the development of an active citizenship (or of direct participation in public affairs) without which precisely there is no cité but just a statist form cut off from society and paralysed in its own abstraction.[63]

Protesters met fierce repression from the authorities and police. Occupied churches and buildings were cleared. Activists were deported despite resistance. The protests, however, continued and were not curbed in the climate hostile to migrants after 11 September 2001.

For Arendt, there is a strong link between the shared public realm and social power. She states that human beings, by acting together, by their joint presence, discover among themselves a potency quite disproportionate to their individual resources. In her famous re-definition of power in

---

[61] Arendt, *On Violence* (London: Allen Lane, 1970), 198.   [62] *Ibid.*

[63] E. Balibar, 'Le droit de cité ou l'apartheid', in E. Balibar *et al.* (eds.), *Sans-Papiers: l'archaïsme fatal* (Paris: Éditions La Découverte, 1999), 113.

contrast to individual strength and instrumental violence, Arendt wrote that, 'power corresponds to the human ability not just to act, but to act in concert. Power is never the property of an individual: it belongs to a group and remains in existence only so long as the group keeps together.'[64]

The experience of the power 'that springs up whenever people get together and act in concert'[65] is reflected in many activists' accounts. By leaving the clandestine situation forced upon them and by entering the public, they have, as individuals, re-gained a feeling of existence. 'Before, we were only shadows', one woman put it. With their struggle and the experience of solidarity they have reconquered a sense of dignity and power they had been denied.[66] Madjiguène Cissé, for example, describes a case of direct confrontation with the violence of the state apparatus: 'we have gained a status as sans papiers. To name but one example: it has now become possible for us to go to the police headquarters in Paris and say: "we are the sans papiers of Saint-Bernard and we have business in this building." And it does work. You could not have imagined this before the struggle of the sans papiers. That sans papiers come to a policeman who is told every morning: "go through Paris and look for sans papiers"; that sans papiers come to him and say: I am a sans papiers, I have a few things to do here. This has been very important.'[67]

Conclusion

Against a discourse that denounces 'illegal immigrants' and 'bogus asylum seekers' in the same breath as it targets 'international terrorism', Arendt offers an alternative analytical perspective on today's undocumented migrants. In this chapter, I conceptualised the specific situation of domination in which these migrants find themselves as 'total domination', a situation of radical rightlessness. The analysis of rightlessness invites comparison among excluded groups across history that brings out similarities and differences that require investigation, one of the central aims of this book. Such scholarship might offer analytical grounds for new solidarities in the face of similar forms of domination. These are especially pertinent in the face of the new powers many states assumed in the wake of 11 September 2001 and tighter controls on immigration and removal which extend rightlessness among non-citizens, and to some

---

[64] Arendt, *On Violence*, 44.   [65] *Ibid.*, 52.
[66] Fassin, Morice and Quimina, *Les lois de l'in hospitalité*, 107–23.
[67] Cissé, 'Sans Papiers', 12.

extent citizens as well. The contemporary situations facing undocumented migrants call into post-national membership question in a particularly urgent way. Here Arendt's work offers a distinct perspective on the current debate. It is a perspective that shows the political suffering created by the system of nation-states, but also cautions against hasty celebrations of post-national citizenship.

Arendt is an early theorist of the post-national. Race imperialism and the chaos of the interwar years for her were already symptoms of the practical exhaustion of the nation-state. Many commentators have picked up on further signs of this exhaustion of national citizenship in the period since the 1970s.[68] The difficulty lies in distinguishing the symptoms of the crisis of nation-state citizenship from the beginnings of a resolution of the problems caused by it. For Arendt, statelessness is not a symptom of specific policies. Instead, it reveals the inner contradictions of the nation-state. She offers a democratic critique not just of the nation-state, but of the sovereign state itself and, by implication, any top-down institution.

Practices on other scales, for example – such as the urban, the professional level, or the global level – do not by themselves overcome the democratic deficit of top-down citizenship. The appeal to supra-national formal legal guarantees or an abstract cosmopolitanism, as offered by the European Union, may also be a symptom of the hollowing out of the nation-state rather than a solution. Dual citizenship and arrangements to accommodate a select group of migrants may just contribute to hierarchisation of the population by legal status, as discussed by Morris.[69]

Arendt's critique of the state is based not on abstract legal principles, but on the primacy of the concrete plurality of the present population. Rather than recite the abstract cosmopolitanism of the Enlightenment, she discusses an institutional alternative to the sovereign state: the council system, which is based on direct representation and active participation of the citizen, organised on a local level, building up in a pyramidal structure to a federal system. She observed this form emerge spontaneously whenever action asserted itself against history. While not

[68] S. Sassen, *Territory, Authority, Rights* (Chicago, IL: Chicago University Press, 2006); Y. Soysal, *The Limits of Citizenship: Migrants and Postnational Membership in Europe* (Chicago, IL: University of Chicago Press, 1994); E. Isin (ed.), *Democracy, Citizenship and the Global City* (New York: Routledge, 2000).

[69] L. Morris, *Managing Migration: Civic Stratification and Migrants' Rights* (London: Routledge, 2002).

a realistic blueprint for policy, as a vision guiding reform, it calls for the democratic reconstruction of citizenship on all institutional levels.

Arendt's concept of power also helps us to make sense of the successes of migrants' mobilisation in the face of severe repression and an initial extreme lack of material and symbolic resources. While there is little systematic research on the outcomes of the movement, we do know that participants themselves have gained a sense of recognition and respect, a theme picked up in subsequent chapters of this volume. Moreover, since the late 1990s, the movement in France has been able to reframe the immigration debate and thus exert a degree of influence over the development of policy.[70]

Undocumented people, including the *sans papiers* in France, have succeeded in mobilising support from parts of the broader public. In gathering this support, they have not only strengthened the cause of undocumented immigrants. They have challenged others to make choices *vis-à-vis* them as illegal residents, and with that *vis-à-vis* their own state. They have been encouraged to rethink their own citizenship practices in a democratic way. These practices of solidarity across the line drawn by the state between citizen and non-citizen could be the beginning of an active citizenship that changes the state and affects everyone who is part of it.

[70] C. Lloyd, 'Anti-Racism, Racism and Asylum-Seekers in France', *Patterns of Prejudice*, 37(3) (2003), 323.

3

The rights of non-citizens to membership

MATTHEW J. GIBNEY*

Introduction

Citizenship in the modern European state is Janus-faced. On the one hand, it is a *unifier*. It offers a status – a common identity – for integrating residents from varied backgrounds and social situations and even nationalities. In its ideal form, as an egalitarian status, it cuts through barriers of class, status and local identity to offer residents of a territorially defined area a common set of rights, entitlements, privileges and obligations under law that link them to each other and to the state.[1] On the other hand, citizenship is a *divider*. The status for members it creates is purchased at the price of creating non-members, people excluded from its benefits for reasons of parentage, place of birth, or the possession of another citizenship.

In the contemporary world, the inequalities associated with this exclusive dimension of citizenship weigh heavily. This is partly because globalisation has made it more apparent than ever that the citizenship into which one is born is likely to have a dramatic impact upon the kind of life one will live. If one is lucky enough to be born a citizen of Sweden, the result is first prize in the lottery of life: one can expect to live to seventy-eight years of age and be provided with cradle-to-grave care in a stable and prosperous state. If, by contrast, one is born in Somalia, one is unlikely to live beyond forty-eight years of age, due to the dangers associated with a society and economy that has been wracked by intense civil conflict. Migration is one way that people attempt to respond to such inequalities. As life expectancies and economic opportunities have increased in recent

---

* A version of this chapter appeared originally in 'Precarious Residents: Migration, Control, Membership and the Rights of Non-Citizens', Human Development Research Paper, UNDP, 2009–10, posted at www.hdr.undp.org/en/reports/global/hdr2009/papers/HDRP_2009_10.pdf, 11 December 2009.
[1] B. Parekh, 'Three Theories of Immigration', in S. Spencer, *Strangers and Citizens* (London: River Orams Press, 1994).

decades, Europe has become, with deep ambivalence, a host to many millions of migrants from across the developing world.[2]

Migration, then, acts as an often uncomfortable reflection of the deep inequalities that exist between Europe and states in the developing world. But it also serves to create its own inequalities by changing the composition of people *within* European states. Every European state is currently populated by a mixture of citizens and non-citizens of various types living together and contributing to the same economy and, at least in principle, bound by the same laws. While citizens and non-citizens may face similar threats to their welfare from a range of social and political forces including crime, economic downturn and the actions of the state, they often possess vastly different rights to protect themselves from these forces.

In recent years scholars from sociology, law and political science have focused on the fact that increasingly permanent resident non-citizens in Western and Northern European countries have come to possess in law rights very similar to the citizens of these countries. Some have suggested that rights have now become disentangled from citizenship or membership in modern state. There has been a great deal of debate over the true nature and significance of this closing of the 'rights gap' between permanent residents and citizens. Some, like Yasemin Soysal, attribute it to the influence of post-national human rights norms, which have been an external force shaping national courts and civil society in ways conducive to the rights of non-members.[3] She suggests that personhood not membership is now the most important source of one's entitlements and protections in the modern European state. Christian Joppke and Randall Hansen are more sceptical.[4] They have attributed the closing of the 'rights gap' to factors internal to liberal states (such municipal courts) and have seen international law as effective only when incorporated into domestic law. Others such as Zolberg have pointed out that the harsh practical realities facing immigrants in Western European societies escape what can be gleaned by concentrating on formal laws and institutional discourses of legitimation.[5]

---

[2] S. Castles and M. Miller, *The Age of Migration*, 3rd edn. (Basingstoke: Palgrave, 2003).

[3] Y. Soysal, *The Limits of Citizenship* (Chicago, IL: University of Chicago Press, 1994).

[4] See C. Joppke, 'Asylum and State Sovereignty', in C. Joppke (ed.), *Challenge to the Nation State: Immigration in Western Europe and the United States* (Oxford: Oxford University Press, 1999) and R. Hansen, *Citizenship and Immigration in Post-War Britain* (Oxford: Oxford University Press, 2000).

[5] A. Zolberg, 'Review of Y. Soysal, Limits of Citizenship' in *Contemporary Sociology*, 24 (4) (1995), 326.

It is important not to exaggerate recent changes in the distribution of rights across the citizen/non-citizen divide. Even if many of the *privileges* once available solely to citizens are now legally available to permanent residents (access to public housing, welfare, education, etc.), two other major citizenship goods – what I will call *voice* and *security* – are usually enjoyed by them only on attenuated terms. *Voice* involves the right to air in public *fora* views about the use and abuse of government power and the direction of society, and to participate in (or to be elected to) political organisations that fashion society's direction and government policy.[6] The *sine qua non* of citizenship is often thus seen as embodied in key rights associated with voice, namely rights 'to vote, hold elected and appointed government offices, to sit on various sorts of juries, and generally to participate in debates as equal community members'.[7] The good of *security*, by contrast, is evident in the fact that the possession of citizenship offers a unique level of security of residence or presence in a state. Citizens, unlike non-citizens, typically cannot be deported or expelled, making their access to other goods enjoyed in the state uniquely robust.[8] Moreover, they may leave and re-enter the state at will, and claim consular protection abroad.

While it is clear that a gap still distinguishes the rights of permanent residents from those of citizens living in European states, a huge chasm separates other types of resident foreigners and citizens. Unlawful migrants, asylum seekers awaiting status determination or removal and foreign workers on temporary contracts are what we might describe as 'precarious residents'. Depending on their immigration status, the state may be able to hold them in detention for long periods, deny them access to welfare and other social provisions, refuse them permission to work and bar them from accessing citizenship. For many of these non-citizens, the possibility of removal or even deportation casts a long, dark shadow over their daily lives, threatening at any moment to take away from them the little they have gained by residence in the host country and their hopes for the future.

---

[6] A. Shachar, 'Birthright Citizenship as Inherited Property: A Critical Inquiry' in S. Benhabib and I. Shapiro (eds.), *Identities, Affiliations, and Allegiances* (Cambridge: Cambridge University Press, 2005).

[7] R. M. Smith, 'Modern Citizenship', in E. Isin and B. Turner (eds.), *Handbook of Citizenship Studies* (New York: Sage, 2002), 105.

[8] M. J. Gibney and R. Hansen, 'Deportation and the Liberal State', UNHCR New Issues in Refugee Research Working Paper, 77 (February 2003) and G. Goodwin-Gill, *International Law and the Movement of Persons Between States* (Oxford: Clarendon Press, 1978).

The very limited social, economic and political rights of precarious non-citizens are often a consequence of deliberate policy on the part of the state. The withholding of their rights is motivated by a desire to encourage their departure from state territory or, according to some, to keep them vulnerable to economic exploitation. The state cannot therefore be counted on to be an ally in the search for social and economic security by these vulnerable men, women and children. Even so, the experience of a (near) rightless life in Europe may for some precarious residents be preferable to returning home. Departure or removal may involve abandoning families, employment and social networks in the host country that have been established over many years. They may mean returning to the dim economic, social and political prospects that led to immigration in the first place.

In this chapter I will survey how political thought has responded to the question of the rights of non-citizens living in the polity who are excluded from most or all of the rights and benefits of citizenship. Much recent political thought has ignored the ethical issues raised by resident non-citizens.[9] Concerns about the way that constructions of race, gender, class and sexual preference interfere with the exercise of meaningful citizenship have been privileged over questions concerning the constitution of the *demos*. Distinctions between citizens and non-citizens have thus often been considered unproblematic. Nowhere has this been more evident than in the most influential work of political philosophy of the last fifty years, John Rawls' *Theory of Justice*.[10] Rawls' work, which attempts to describe and analyse the features of a just society, takes as its starting point the assumption of a 'bounded community' of members. Erased from consideration is the fact that each and every actual liberal democratic society is at any time composed by citizens and various categories of non-citizens, often possessing vastly different rights, obligations and levels of security.

In recent years, however, the issue of the non-citizen has emerged from the shadows of political theory. The reality of growing migration pressures, controversy over large numbers of refugees and asylum seekers and awareness of unlawful migration across Europe and North America have made it impossible to ignore the question of what justifies differences in the rights of citizens and the 'rights of others', especially when both live in

---

[9] L. Bosniak, *The Citizen and the Alien: Dilemmas of Contemporary Membership* (Princeton, NJ: Princeton University Press, 2006).

[10] J. Rawls, *A Theory of Justice* (Cambridge, MA: Harvard University Press, 1971).

the same territory. A range of theorists from different political perspectives, including communitarians, civic republicans, deliberative democrats, global liberals and statist liberals have begun to reckon with the fact that their conceptions of citizenship are racked by a tension between the universal and particular: between a commitment to universal equality on the one hand and the bounded nature of modern democracy on the other. This tension is incarnated in the figure of the resident foreigner who lives among citizens but is excluded from many of the rights they possess, including rights of political participation. As Jean Cohen has noted, while in its juridical mode citizenship may be 'universalising and inclusive but apolitical and individualistic', in its democratic mode, 'it is internally egalitarian and uniform but externally exclusive and particularising'.[11] A challenge for all these strands of political thought has been how to recognise the moral claims of each and every person in the polity without undermining the existence of a meaningful democratic community of members.

In the discussion that follows I will begin by outlining two contrasting historical perspectives on the rights of non-citizens: ancient republicanism and the early liberalism of Hobbes and Locke. After discussing the work of the late nineteenth–early twentieth-century liberal, Henry Sidgwick, I turn to examine the civic republican philosopher Hannah Arendt, whose work placed those excluded from citizenship at the centre of political thought for the first time through her analysis of the stateless people and refugees generated by the entrenchment of the modern nation-state in the early twentieth century. I then suggest that Arendt's concerns about rightlessness need now to be extended to those, like unlawful migrants and asylum seekers, who currently live within modern European states but do not or cannot claim the protection of membership in these states. I refer to such people as 'precarious residents'. The remaining sections draw from recent political theory to examine the case for including such residents in the community of rights-holders in European states. I consider their claims to human rights, then the case for considering them moral members of the societies in which they reside. I outline a range of different standards of membership that might be used to justify the inclusion of 'precarious residents' into some or all of the rights of members. I conclude the chapter by considering the unanswered questions raised by this membership-based approach.

---

[11] J. Cohen, 'Changing Paradigms of Citizenship and the Exclusiveness of the Demos', *International Sociology*, 14 (1999), 250.

Civic republicans and liberals: the ancient Greeks
and the early liberals

There is nothing historically new about citizens and non-citizens sharing same political society and living together under conditions of inequality. However, that the distinction between citizens and 'aliens' raises complex and significant moral issues is a more recent development. Certainly, in ancient Greece, birthplace of the republican conception of citizenship that would later inform the political theories of Jean-Jacques Rousseau in the eighteenth century and modern-day communitarians, the question of excluding foreigners was so integral to political life as to be virtually taken for granted. As William J. Booth has noted,[12] for Athenians to interrogate the boundaries between citizens and aliens would have involved questioning the idea of man as a *zoon politikon* at the centre of their social and political world. In this conceptualisation, citizenship involved participation in a 'closed community' of equals who were male, free and economically independent. Socrates, for example, spoke derisively of democracy as a place where the 'metic [resident alien] is on an equal level with the townsman and townsman with metic and similarly with the foreigner [*xenos*]', knowing that his audience would have understood this kind of equality as perverse. According to Booth, the

> perversity would have resided in a failure to distinguish a good from a debased regime, friends from enemies, Greeks from barbarians. It would have been seen as a most radical misunderstanding of the nature of political life. That townsmen would prefer townsmen, that their lives of political activity, language, religion and history, would set them apart from others, make their association a source of special obligations and devotion, and raise it above anything shared with foreigners: these no doubt would have seemed natural and unproblematic.[13]

This ancient republican view of political community rested on the face-to-face interaction of small communities of citizens with a strong commitment to the civic good. The outsider or the foreigner – '*xenos, metikos, barbaros*' – was someone by definition outside the circle of citizenship; someone whom one might fear, exploit, or show hospitality to, but not someone to whom one owed duties of justice or the rights and privileges of citizenship.[14] In a society where slaves existed and women were

---

[12] W. J. Booth, 'Foreigners: Insiders, Outsiders and the Ethics of Membership', *Review of Politics*, 59 (1997), 259.
[13] *Ibid.*, 261.   [14] *Ibid.*

barred from citizenship, the exclusion of the foreigner was simply one of a range of social and political exclusions upon which citizen equality was premised. Indeed, in most respects the (non-slave) foreigner was better off than these other excluded groups. In classical republicanism, it was at least conceivable for citizenship to be granted to the selected outsider, even if admission to citizenship was not seen as involving issues of justice. The idea that the grant of citizenship was discretionary was inherited by latter forms of republicanism. As Rainer Bauböck notes, in the classical republican tradition, citizens 'could admit or reject those who wanted to join and could modify the rules for the acquisition of citizenship at birth according to their own demographic needs.'[15]

If the ancient republican view of citizenship set in train one way of viewing the citizen/non-citizen relationship based on exclusive ideas of identity, the early theorists of the modern state of the seventeenth century offered a different perspective. When Thomas Hobbes[16] and John Locke provided their accounts of why one should obey the modern state as a concentrated form of political power, they stressed the goods that the state as a service provider could secure for those living under its authority. Individuals had good reason to obey the state – they had reason to accept the duties of citizenship – because the state could secure for them goods that they could not achieve on their own, notably civil peace and protection of their rights. Central to this idea of the modern state was the idea of consent – that the state's legitimacy derived from the fact that each and every individual adult male living under it could consent, in principle, to its authority in return for the goods it provided.

This contractual and instrumental view of citizenship was, as Melissa Lane has noted,[17] very congenial to placing native-born and resident foreigners on an equal footing. While Hobbes and Locke largely ignored discussion of the question of foreigners living in the polity, their accounts offered support for the idea that the state needed in principle to legitimate itself to each and every male adult, irrespective of birthplace, under the sovereign authority of the state. According to Lane, in this view, 'the real core of the doctrine of sovereignty is individual consent, not state control [over immigration], and this means that sovereignty is rightly understood

---

[15] R. Bauböck, *Transnational Citizenship: Membership and Rights in International Migration* (Aldershot: Edward Elgar, 1994), 2.

[16] T. Hobbes, *Leviathan*, ed. C.B. Macpherson (Harmondsworth: Penguin, 1968).

[17] M. Lane, 'A Philosophical View on States and Immigration', in K. Tamas and J. Palme (eds.), *Globalizing Migration Regimes: New Challenges to Transnational Cooperation* (Aldershot: Ashgate, 2006).

as a guide to naturalisation (which is in these theories eminently possible) rather than as a barrier to it'.[18] Hobbes and Locke seemed to assume that this justification would apply simply to established communities of members: their theories were intended to provide justifications for the obedience of current members rather than to re-write the boundaries of membership. The idea that coercive rule must be legitimated, however, provided grounds for the inclusion of resident foreigners that differentiated this approach from the early civic republican position.

The civic republican and the liberal mark out, then, two alternative visions of political life, the nature and significance of citizenship, and the status of non-citizens. But, as we have seen, in these early articulations the claims of non-citizens in the polity were rarely addressed explicitly. This deficiency was addressed only partly by international law writers in the seventeenth and eighteenth century, such as Hugo Grotius (1925)[19] and Immanuel Kant (1991).[20] These writers argued that states had certain duties to admit foreigners. Kant, for example, wrote of a duty of hospitality to foreigners;[21] Grotius acknowledged a right of refuge for those needing, in the face of necessity, to enter another state.[22] Neither, however, had much to say of foreigners actually living under the state's authority. It took till the late nineteenth century for a theorist of note to engage the alien question with any seriousness.

Liberals and civic republicans: Sidgwick and Arendt

In his *Elements of Politics* (1987 [1891]), the liberal-utilitarian political theorist Henry Sidgwick[23] tackled directly the issue of the responsibilities of states to foreigners living on their territory. Sidgwick placed the question of responsibilities to resident foreigners in the context of the broader question of the state's right to control immigration. Evincing an early version of the tension in liberal democratic ideas between universal community and statism, Sidgwick described two contrasted views of the state on the issue of immigration: a *nationalist* one in which the state is seen as the representative of a distinct and unique community, whose duty was to further the collective interests of its members; and a *cosmopolitan* one,

---

[18] *Ibid*, 134.
[19] H. Grotius, *De Jure Belli Ac Pacis Libri Tres, Book II*, trans F.W. Kelsey (Washington, DC: Carnegie Institute, 1925).
[20] I. Kant, *Political Writings*, ed. H. Reiss (Cambridge: Cambridge University Press, 1991).
[21] *Ibid*., 105–6.   [22] Grotius, *De Jure Belli*.
[23] H. Sidgwick, *The Elements of Politics*, 2nd edn. (London: Macmillan, 1987).

in which the state is tasked merely with maintaining order over a particular piece of the earth's territory and has no interest or right to control entry or residence.[24] Sidgwick dismissed the cosmopolitan view as at best an 'idea of the future' too inattentive to 'patriotic sentiments' and the need for social cohesion to be currently viable.[25] This dismissal led him to give short shrift the rights of foreigners resident inside the state. States, he argued, may impose '*any conditions* on entrance or any tolls on transit and subjecting them to any legal restrictions or disabilities that it may deem expedient'.[26]

However, in other parts of the *Elements*, Sidgwick shows signs of a more inclusive liberalism. He states, for example, that all aliens must be subjected to common laws *qua* aliens. It is thus impermissible to discriminate between different foreigner groups – that is, to treat the French in England one way and the Dutch in England in another. Moreover, if the state changes the conditions of residence under which foreigners must live, the residents must be given significant notice so that they may leave the state if they so desire. Finally, and most significantly, resident foreigners should generally be able to access citizenship 'provided they have, by sufficiently long, orderly, and unblemished residence within its territory, both shown a settled preference for the social order that it maintains, and acquired a sufficient acquaintance with its laws and political habits'.[27]

Despite these qualifications, convention wins out over reform and statism is dominant over liberalism in Sidgwick's approach to the rights of non-citizens. His defence of a wide-ranging right of states to determine the terms on which foreigners reside on their territory reflected (as well as legitimated) the practices of early twentieth-century states. It is no coincidence that he wrote at a time when European legislatures were introducing some of the first national laws to restrict the entrance and residence of foreigners, complete with extensive deportation powers.

Half a century after Sidgwick, the exiled German political theorist Hannah Arendt offered the most sustained attempt to analyse statelessness in *The Origins of Totalitarianism* (1949). What was new about Arendt's focus was that the non-citizen was no longer at the periphery of political thought, but at its centre. For Arendt, the stateless, specifically, are 'the most symptomatic group in contemporary politics'.[28]

The symptomatic role of the stateless was, for Arendt, their revelation of the emptiness of human rights in the context of a modern nation-state

---

[24] *Ibid.*   [25] *Ibid.*   [26] *Ibid.*, emphasis mine.   [27] *Ibid.*
[28] H. Arendt, *The Origins of Totalitarianism* (London: André Deutsch, 1986), 277.

system. The parlous situation the stateless (a term that for Arendt included many refugees) encountered throughout Europe clearly demonstrated that once states wielded denaturalisation as a weapon against unwanted subjects, and refused to accept stateless people or refugees into membership, the essential hollowness of the so-called inalienable Rights of Man, as rights held over and above state authorities, became evident.[29]

In Arendt's view statelessness involved three distinct losses, each with powerful implications for the individuals concerned. The first was the 'loss of a home'. This meant 'the loss of the entire social texture into which they were born and where they established for themselves a distinct place in the world'.[30] In a world now exhaustively divided among territorial nation-states, there was 'no place on earth where migrants could go without the severest restrictions, no country where they could be assimilated, no territory where they could found a new community of their own'.

The second loss was that of 'government protection'.[31] While citizens could leave their homes and still be protected by state membership as a result of a range of reciprocal treaties between states, those expelled or denationalised found themselves cast out of legality altogether, and they would receive assistance from state authorities or private organisations only as a 'matter of charity not of right'.[32] As noted by Monika Krause, they were placed so far beyond the pale of the law that their situation actually improved if they were charged with committing a crime, since they then obtained the procedural protections inherent in the criminal justice system (see also chapter 2 in this volume).[33]

The third and final loss associated with statelessness was the withdrawal from such individuals of 'a place in the world which makes opinions significant and actions effective'.[34] This loss involved 'something much more fundamental' than the simple fact that the stateless could no longer enjoy the benefits of 'freedom and justice' in a society.[35] They lost the mutual recognition necessary for a political life and thus their very 'right to have rights'.[36]

It is, then, according to Arendt, the stateless who expose the new and terrifying consequences of the spread of the state system across the globe. The plight of the stateless is not the result simply of 'civilization,

---

[29] *Ibid.*, 299.   [30] *Ibid.*, 293.   [31] *Ibid.*, 294.

[32] *Ibid.*, 294.   [33] *Ibid.*, 286.   [34] *Ibid.*, 296.

[35] R. J. Bernstein, *Hannah Arendt and the Jewish Question* (Cambridge, MA: MIT Press, 1996), 82.

[36] Arendt, *The Origins of Totalitarianism*, 296–7.

backwardness, or mere tyranny'. They have emerged because 'whether we like it or not we have really started to live in One World. Only with a completely organised humanity could the loss of home and political status become identical with expulsion from humanity altogether.'[37] The rise of statelessness is a product, then, of the conquering of the globe by the nation-state model. As the existence of the stateless demonstrate: 'belonging to the community into which one is born is no longer a matter of course and not belonging no longer a matter of choice.'[38] Membership in a modern state is now essential but not guaranteed.

If human rights proved hollow as soon as they were needed because they were contingent upon the willingness of a particular state to respect them, a world government might seem the obvious response. A single state could prevent people from being forced outside humanity. But Arendt was deeply sceptical of world government. As Seyla Benhabib has noted, she was concerned that 'world government would destroy the space for politics in that it would not allow individuals to define shared public spaces in common'.[39]

Instead, Arendt's work seems to vindicate a more modest view of the ideal political community as one that was civically rather than ethnically based; one which rests on 'the assumption that we can produce equality through organisation, because man can act and change and build a common world, together with his equals and only with his equals'.[40] Nevertheless, this does not seem to guarantee that individuals will not fall between the cracks of the membership policies of particular states; so it is not a complete resolution to the problem of expulsion from humanity. In this respect, Arendt ultimately offers a powerful diagnosis of a key aspect of the emerging problem of the non-citizen, but she fails to resolve it.

Forms and patterns of statelessness since Arendt: precarious residence

In Arendt's conceptualisation, the problem of rightlessness is something that confronted people, such as the stateless or refugees, without citizenship in *any state whatsoever*. Refugees and stateless people were

---

[37] *Ibid.*, 297.   [38] *Ibid.*, 296.
[39] S. Benhabib, *The Rights of Others: Aliens, Residents, and Citizens* (Cambridge: Cambridge University Press, 2004), 20.
[40] H. Arendt, quoted in S. Benhabib, *Transformations of Citizenship* (Amsterdam: Van Gorcum, 2001), 20.

vulnerable fundamentally because of their lack of citizenship precluded them from claiming even the most basic of rights. Such people were effectively 'orphans' of the nation-state system,[41] people who for whom no state claimed paternity and thus had no duty to protect and secure. Since the end of the Second World War, the international community has made a number of efforts to draft treaties, including the 1951 UN Convention Relating to the Status of Refugees, the 1954 Convention Relating to the Status of Stateless People and the 1961 Convention on the Reduction of Statelessness to prevent the creation of such 'orphans' and to provide them with a new state of citizenship when they do emerge. *De jure* statelessness is still a huge international problem, albeit not a problem in Europe of the same magnitude as in the first half of the twentieth century.

Yet as the issue of *de jure* statelessness has receded in significance, globalising forces and revolutions in transportation and communications have made European societies (often) unwilling hosts to large numbers of migrants from other continents. Such migrants include those considered 'trespassers' in European states, like the undocumented (e.g. illegal entrants, visa overstayers, failed asylum seekers), and those holding temporary forms of status preventing them from accessing permanent residence, or making them subject to deportation or immigration detention (e.g. asylum applicants, those enjoying complementary protection, those in immigration jails). These migrants are rarely formally stateless and are often not refugees. The problem they face is not the lack of a nationality; they cannot be said, unlike Arendt's stateless, to have been expelled from humanity altogether. Rather, they are people who lack security, basic civil, political and economic rights, and opportunities for membership *in the countries where they are making their lives*. Their daily experience is characterised by statelessness in the sense of an effective absence of state protection where they need it.

Such 'precarious residents' are some of the most vulnerable people in modern European states today. Practically, they may have little or no standing to claim even basic rights because in the eyes of state officials (and of large sections of the public) they have no right to be present in the state in the first place. The injustices and humiliations they face are thus often seen as self-inflicted because they result from their own decision to enter or remain living unlawfully in a state not their own. Yet the existence

---

[41] J. H. Carens, 'Migration and Morality: A Liberal Egalitarian Perspective', in B. Barry and R. Goodin (eds.), *Free Movement: Ethical Issues in the Transnational Migration of People and Money* (Hemel Hempstead: Harvester Wheatsheaf, 1992), 23.

of people effectively living outside the community of rights-holders seems an affront to standards of decency and justice. What arguments might be available in political theory for bringing them into the community of rights-holders?

In broad terms, there are two different pathways available in contemporary political thought which I will consider in the rest of this chapter. The first is by conceiving of 'precarious residents' simply as human beings; the second is by conceiving of them as members of the societies in which they live.

The human rights of 'precarious residents'

One obvious answer to the question of the rights of 'precarious residents' lies in the idea of human rights. In this view, precarious non-citizens should be seen as human beings possessing fundamental rights by virtue of their humanity and independent of their immigration or citizenship status. Everyone within a European state, regardless of their background or official status, should have the right not to be exploited, assaulted, tortured, or held in custody without reason. They should have the right to access emergency healthcare treatment, police and emergency services, and the courts. Such rights may be basic but they are in no way trivial to the day-to-day lives of precarious non-citizens who are often particularly vulnerable to private exploitation (from employers, traffickers and landlords). They represent a kind of moral minimum that is owed to anyone in the territory of the state, even the tourist passing through a country on holiday.

Many would push the argument for human rights further and argue that there is a moral right to sufficient resources (food, clothing, shelter) to ensure that destitution (or at least starvation) is avoided.[42] Some would suggest that there is a right of all children regardless of the immigration status of their parents to access primary and secondary schooling.[43] This right might be said to derive both from the enormous human cost of illiteracy and innumeracy and the principle that children should not suffer for the sins (the unlawful status) of their parents. Some may even claim that everyone *living* in the state (i.e. with no immediate prospect for return) should have the right to seek paid work and to access basic

---

[42] See StillHumanHere (2008), www.stillhuman.org.uk/.
[43] See, for example, the majority decision in the US Supreme Court in *Plyler* v. *Doe* 457 US 202 (1982).

welfare resources.[44] These more expansive claims are controversial (and less widely accepted by states) than the moral minimum outlined above. They illustrate that there is little consensus on where basic human rights claims end, even if there is an overlapping consensus on the importance of some basic rights.

Putting aside for the time being the question of the likelihood that all these rights would be accepted by states, a major problem, noted by a number of scholars, exists in accessing these rights. Ruth Rubio-Marin has, along with many others, pointed out that for unlawful migrants even the most basic rights may be hollow. She writes that the 'absolutely precarious and residential and working status' of unlawful migrants 'places them in a vulnerable and exploitable position from which even the enjoyment of these rights and guarantees theoretically granted to them is often practically impossible'.[45] This is the problem of what might be called the 'rights trap': in order to claim rights and state protections, unlawful migrants must bring themselves to the attention of state authorities (they must, for example, call upon the police or judicial authorities). By doing so, they risk advertising their unlawful presence and thus their eligibility for deportation. As appalling and dangerous as it may be to live rightless in a European state, it may be preferable, from the migrant's perspective, to the prospect of deportation.

One response to this problem has been suggested by Joseph Carens. He argues that if states and their citizens are serious about everyone's access to basic rights, states should build a 'firewall' between the authorities who act to guarantee these rights and those whose job is to enforce immigration laws.[46] The presence of such a firewall would mean that if an immigrant unlawfully in the country accessed the police or an emergency ward at a hospital, officials would be under an obligation not to pass on any information they may have garnered about the person's status to immigration authorities, directly or indirectly.

While Carens offers an ingenious way around some of the problems of rights protection, the human rights approach generally remains a very limited response to the plight of 'precarious residents'. The root of the problem recalls Arendt's diagnosis. The recognition of an individual's human

[44] J. H. Carens, 'Immigration and the Welfare State', in A. Guttman (ed.), *Democracy and the Welfare State* (Princeton, NJ: Princeton University Press, 1988).

[45] R. Rubio-Marin, *Immigration as a Democratic Challenge: Citizenship and Inclusion in Germany and the United States* (Cambridge: Cambridge University Press, 2000), 81.

[46] J. H. Carens, 'On Belonging: What We Owe People Who Stay', *The Boston Review* (Summer 2005), www.bostonreview.net/BR30.3/carens.html.

rights by a particular state can only be fragile when the state concerned has wide-ranging rights to expel the individual concerned. Without a right to reside in the state, any human right recognised by the state can simply be annulled through the act of deportation, enabling the authorities to wash their hands of the individual concerned. Just as Arendt saw human rights as hollow without citizenship, human rights in a modern Europe state may be empty without a right to reside.

Is it possible, then, to see a right to reside as a human right, one that is enjoyable independent of nationality? Joseph Carens, drawing upon a cosmopolitan liberal framework, has argued so. He claims that as a corollary of the fundamental right of people to move freely *within* societies, all people should be able to move freely *between* societies. 'Every reason why one might want to move within a state may also be a reason for moving between states. One might want a job; one might fall in love with someone from another country; one might belong to a religion that has few adherents in one's native state and many in another.'[47] Others, however, are more sceptical. Critics have countered that the right to move freely within national societies is far more circumscribed than free-movement proponents typically acknowledge. Liberals usually view as uncontroversial many restrictions on movement that protect private property, public goods, national security and environmentally endangered sites. If these internal restrictions are justified, even greater constraints on movement would seem appropriate globally where the volume of people who might move is far larger.[48] From another angle, David Miller has suggested that the range of choices open to individuals within most societies is extensive enough to make freedom of movement less compelling internationally than domestically.[49]

A more fundamental concern about the idea of a human right to reside where one wishes is that it conflicts with the fundamental value of membership in political communities.[50] From this point of view, liberal states must be able to exercise some controls on the residence of

[47] Carens, 'Migration and Morality', 27–8.

[48] M. J. Gibney, *The Ethics and Politics of Asylum: Liberal Democracy and the Response to Refugees* (Cambridge: Cambridge University Press, 2004) and B. Barry, 'The Quest for Consistency: A Skeptical View', in B. Barry and R. Goodin (eds.), *Free Movement: Ethical Issues in the Transnational Migration of People and Money* (Hemel Hempstead: Harvester Wheatsheaf, 1992).

[49] D. Miller, 'Immigration: The Case for Limits' in A. Cohen and C. Wellman (eds.), *Contemporary Debates in Applied Ethics* (Oxford: Blackwell, 2005).

[50] M. Walzer, *Spheres of Justice: A Defense of Pluralism and Equality* (Oxford: Martin Robertson, 1983).

foreigners because closure is required for democratic politics. Liberal democracy involves the meshing of two ideas: that rights matter and that the *demos* rules. But the second idea axiomatically requires the identification of a *demos* – a community of members – which makes collectively binding decisions that shape the direction of the state over time. This is the idea of a democratic sovereignty. An approach, like Carens', which proclaims a right to reside, *seems* (as I will suggest later, this is not necessarily the *actual* implication) to make membership insignificant because the state would deprive the members of any right to control the distribution of citizenship.

'Precarious residents' as members

Thus the human rights approach has some fundamental weaknesses. On the one hand, it appears inadequate unless accompanied by protection from deportation through a right to reside. Yet such a right appears to conflict with the value of membership. One potential way around this impasse is critically to examine the question of how we should define the boundaries of membership in the modern state.

A virtue of the human rights approach is that it offers exactly the same answer to the question of what is owed to each and every non-citizen in the state, from the tourist to the permanent resident. But this is also one of its major limitations. The human rights approach offers non-citizens *residing* in the state only those rights available to those simply passing through it in transit or on holidays. This lack of discrimination between different types of non-citizens does not do justice to the deep reliance of some non-citizens on state protection and assistance by virtue of their residence. It ignores the fact that a key problem raised by 'precarious residents' is that, morally, they often seem more like members than strangers. To do justice to 'precarious residents', then, we need to consider not just what is owed to them by virtue of their humanity but also what is owed to them by virtue of their status as moral members.

Different political theories give conflicting answers to the question of what distinguishes citizens from strangers and thus legitimates their different rights. In what follows, I will draw from contemporary political thought to consider the applicability of three different standards that might be used to reconceptualise precarious members as residents. Before doing so, however, it is important to consider how European states currently distribute citizenship. Despite much national variation, where one will receive citizenship is determined almost entirely by three principles: the principle of *jus soli*, whereby individuals born on the territory of the state are entitled to citizenship in the state; the principle of *jus sanguinis*, whereby individuals gain citizenship by being born to a citizen – i.e. through descent; and, through the process of *naturalisation*, whereby state officials define, through some political process, the requirements of foreigners being admitted to citizenship.

These bases for distributing citizenship are seen by political theorists of various stripes as problematic, for a number of reasons. First, as was evident in the work of Hannah Arendt, they do not prevent people being trapped in situations of *de jure* or *de facto* statelessness. As no state is legally obliged to naturalise any particular outsider except in terms of the criteria of its municipal law, adherence to these principles can leave substantial numbers of people without (effective) nationality or citizenship, as a result of state persecution or state dissolution and division. Second, these principles result in practice in a world where the bulk of the world's population find changing citizenship impossible. Only a tiny proportion of the world's population (2 per cent) have gained their current citizenship through naturalisation.[51] This is particularly dubious because, as I have suggested, citizenship is a key determinant of the quality of the economic, social and political goods that one will be able to access in the course of one's life, so people may have a powerful interest in acquiring a new citizenship.

A key problem with the way citizenship is currently distributed is that it makes one's life chances dependent upon caprice or the luck of birth. Citizenship has thus been described by liberals as 'arbitrary',[52] a quasi-'feudal status',[53] or as resting upon 'historical contingencies'.[54] If considerations of race, gender, or sexual preference are rightly seen as arbitrary bases for the distribution of rights and other social goods within society, it is no surprise that liberals find it equally troubling that where and to whom one is born determine membership.

Creating a morally defensible basis for the acquisition of membership is, however, a complex task. Political theorists are generally reluctant to abandon the system of birthright citizenship despite the fact that as 'an entitlement allocation scheme ... it is neither just nor fair in its distributive implications'.[55] The risks of generating stateless people and ignoring

---

[51] A. Shachar, 'Children of a Lesser State: Sustaining Global Inequality through Citizenship Laws', Jean Monnet Working Papers, 2 (2003), http://jeanmonnetprogram.org/papers/03/030201.html, 21.

[52] *Ibid.*, p. 8.   [53] J. Carens, 'Migration and Morality', 26.

[54] Benhabib, *The Rights of Others*.   [55] Shachar, 'Children of a Lesser State', 50.

people's genuine attachment to birthplace seem too great to entertain such an idea. Furthermore, open immigration policies and the global redistribution of resources seem to offer less severe ways of dealing with the inequalities resulting from birthright citizenship. But theorists have offered a range of different standards for the acquisition of membership in the modern state, designed to make the status less problematical from a moral perspective. These standards have direct implications for re-conceptualising precarious non-citizens as members with accompanying rights. I shall now spell out in some depth three different standards for membership – choice, subjection and societal membership – before considering the ways in which they clarify (and fail to clarify) the moral responsibilities of European states to non-citizens living in their territory.

Choice as a basis for membership

One potential standard for defining membership in the state is the principle of *choice*. In this account, membership should be available to *anyone* who chooses to live in a particular state. This approach is commonly identified with cosmopolitan liberalism. It is grounded in a view that recognises the moral right of people to reside where they wish and the inherent moral arbitrariness of state borders. As I mentioned above, Joseph Carens is perhaps the best-known adherent of the choice position. He derives a right of people to move freely between states and thus to change their membership communities by extending the basic liberties and difference principles of John Rawls from domestic society to the global realm.[56] The basic liberties principle suggests that the right to move freely is valuable internationally for exactly the same reason that it is fundamental domestically: it is necessary for individual autonomy. The difference principle demands fair equal opportunity and thus renders problematic restrictions on freedom of movement internationally because they perpetuate unfair economic inequalities.[57]

On its face, the principle of choice, as noted above, seems destructive of the very idea of membership. A situation of open borders globally would appear effectively to delegitimate citizenship (or membership) as a basis for differentiating between the rights of people. However, this conclusion is too hasty. The principle of choice may be consistent with forms

---

[56] Carens, 'Immigration', 44.   [57] *Ibid.*

of cosmopolitan federalism that attempt to retain different rights for members and strangers. For example, just as internal states (or provinces) within national federal states have internal freedom of movement in conjunction (in some cases) with residency requirements (a short period of continuous stay, owning or renting a house with the territory of the state, etc.) to determine who qualifies for certain local benefits (access to welfare, discounted university education, the right to vote in provincial elections, etc.), so one could envisage a right of free movement internationally with residency requirements in a particular state in order to claim the full rights of members.

Indeed, in a discussion of the need to preserve the welfare state in the context of open borders, Joseph Carens suggests that while closed borders are inconsistent with liberal cosmopolitan principles a 'commitment to free movement is compatible with short term residency requirements, so that one must live somewhere for a few months before being eligible for social programmes'.[58]

The deliberative democrat, Seyla Benhabib, has also sketched out a form of cosmopolitan federalism consistent with a differentiated approach to rights. In *The Rights of Others* (2004) Benhabib states that no one in the polity should be considered illegal (regardless of their nationality or mode of entrance). At the same time, she suggests that a right to 'first admittance' should not imply a commitment to 'automatic membership'. In her cosmopolitan federalism, 'Democratic peoples will still have to devise rules of membership at the national, subnational, regional and municipal levels'.[59] Benhabib's approach thus raises the question of how a general right to remain in the state derivative of her rejection of the idea of illegal migration is to be reconciled with excluding people from 'automatic membership'.[60] Benhabib indicates that the resolution of this question needs to be sought in forms of public argument and deliberation that contextualise universal principles. However, it is clear that the kind of residency requirements discussed by Carens above offers one way in which this circle might be squared.

What implications would adherence to the principle of choice have for 'precarious residents'? Clearly, it would dissolve the category of unlawful resident: deportation would no longer be a threat and, consequently, rights could be claimed and held in a context of security. Furthermore, access to membership in the state, and full rights to vote, to welfare, and

---

[58] Carens, 'Migration and Morality', 42.
[59] Benhabib, *The Rights of Others*, 177.   [60] *Ibid.*, 177.

to work in key public jobs, would open to all *residents* of the state, regardless of how they came to be there.

However some important questions are left unanswered in the choice approach, specifically in its cosmopolitan federal version. First, how would an individual's desire to *reside* in the state be evinced? There are many possible ways: a continued period of residence, paying tax and working there, enrolment of children in school. A key point of the cosmopolitan liberal attitude to membership seems to be that the standards should not be onerous, though it is open to different theorists to interpret the particular standards differently. A second question is: what rights should transients, or those waiting to prove that they are residents, have? A plausible response is that they should enjoy the kind of human rather than membership rights outlined above (though of course they would also have a right to reside).

Subjection as a basis for membership

An alternative way of conceptualising 'precarious residents' involves emphasising their situation as *subjects* of state power; as people who live under the laws of a particular state. According to Michael Walzer, 'men and women are either subject to the state's authority, or they are not, and if they are subject, they must be given a say, and ultimately an equal say, in what that authority does'.[61] The key idea in this approach is that any state that rules (i.e. exercises coercive force) over a people is legitimate only if the people in question consent to such rule.

This position is common to a range of different liberal and democratic theories of politics, even though they differ on what constitutes the giving of *consent*. A key distinction between liberal and democratic theories, for example, is that while liberal approaches engage 'in a strategy of hypothetical justification to establish the justness of institutions and laws through which political power is exercised', democratic approaches demand 'actual participation in institutionalised practices of discursive justification'.[62]

I showed above that classical liberal theorists, such as Locke, using hypothetical consent theories to justify coercive power by the state, were consistent with an inclusive account of membership. Some contemporary liberals

---

[61] Walzer, *Spheres of Justice*, p. 61.
[62] A. Abizadeh, 'Democratic Theory and Border Coercion: No Right to Unilaterally Control Your Own Borders', *Political Theory*, 36(1) (2008), 41.

have, by contrast, tried to use the coercion argument as a way of justifying *exclusive* practices towards foreigners, particularly in entrance controls. Michael Blake, for example, has argued that liberals 'value internal mobility and voting rights as part of the package of justifications for political *coercion*. We have no equivalent reason to extend these rights to individuals who are not part of the political community in question, but who merely seek to become so subject.'[63] Similarly, Stephen Macedo has suggested that 'the borders of political societies are morally significant ... because principles of social justice are designed to regulate and justify relations of participation in systems of collective self-governance. As members of a political community we are joined in a collective enterprise across generations through which we *coercively* impose a system of law on ourselves.'[64]

For each of these authors, subjection constitutes a powerful reason for citizens of a state possessing different rights and entitlements (such as a right to reside and other social and welfare related rights) than non-citizens. Yet, while these authors use the argument from subjection to justify preventing foreigners from entering the state, the principle has more inclusive implications for non-citizens who have already arrived. For *everyone* living in the state is subject to the state's coercive power, including 'precarious residents'. Indeed, it could be argued that 'precarious residents' are subject to state authority in uniquely powerful ways. As Walzer suggests, these non-citizens 'experience the state as a pervasive and frightening power that shapes their lives and regulates their every move – and never asks for their opinion'.[65] Since the state's power is territorial in nature, the argument from coercion grounds special rights not simply for members but for everyone *residing* (and perhaps even *present*) in the state.

Democratic theorists have offered a slightly different perspective on the moral issues arising from subjection by emphasising the issue of tyranny. The presence of large numbers of people, such as 'precarious residents', living in a democratic state but lacking rights of political participation jeopardises not just the rights of non-citizens, but also the overall health of democratic society. 'We ought not to subjugate immigrants', the legal theorist Owen Fiss has written, 'not because we owe them anything but to preserve our society as a community of equals'.[66]

---

[63] M. Blake, 'Discretionary Immigration', *Philosophical Topics*, 30(2) (2002), 273, emphasis mine.

[64] S. Macedo 'Immigration' (2008), ms on file with author, emphasis mine.

[65] Walzer, *Spheres of Justice*, 59.

[66] Quoted in Bosniak, *The Citizen and the Alien*, 128.

The democratic objection to individuals living in the state but outside the *demos* has been subtly explored by Michael Walzer. In *Spheres of Justice* (1983), Walzer argues that it was unjust for European states to take in immigrants on short-term contracts while forbidding them access to citizenship to encourage their eventual return home, like the Turks recruited for work in Germany during the 1950s and 1960s. The so-called 'guestworker system', according to Walzer, functioned because of the denial of political rights and civil liberties and the threat of deportation. Contrary to its name, it involved migrants living in the state not only as 'guests but also [as] subjects' and ruled by a 'band of citizen-tyrants'.[67] Moreover, even the fact that the immigrants concerned consented to the terms of their residence did not make the state's restriction of their rights and opportunities legitimate. Walzer argues that simple consent 'given at a single moment in time, while it is sufficient to legitimise market transactions, is not sufficient for democratic politics'.

> Political power is precisely the ability to make decisions over periods of time, to change the rules, to cope with emergencies; it can't be exercised democratically without the ongoing consent of its subjects. And its subjects include every man and woman who lives within the territory over which those decisions are enforced.[68]

Taking democratic principles seriously means that '[p]olitical justice is a bar to permanent alienage – either for particular individuals or for a class of changing individuals'.[69]

Similar conclusions to Walzer's can be found in the work of other political theorists who valorise democracy. Writing on immigrant integration, the philosopher David Miller has suggested that 'on democratic grounds it appears anomalous for someone whose interests are chiefly impacted by the policies of a particular state to have no say in determining those policies' (2008). '*Whatever the formal terms of admission*', Miller says, modern states must ultimately offer citizenship to all individuals who 'build their lives in the new country'.[70]

Both Walzer and Miller see the acquisition of citizenship as the only way of making subjection legitimate. But more radical democrats disentangle the right to vote from citizenship altogether. Some demand that the distribution of political rights, including voting, should be determined

---

[67] Walzer, *Spheres of Justice*, 58. [68] *Ibid.*, 58. [69] *Ibid.*, 61.

[70] D. Miller, 'Immigrants, Nations and Citizenship', Paper delivered at CRASSH Conference, Cambridge University (2004), emphasis mine, www.crassh.cam.ac.uk/oldwww/events/2003–4/MillerPaper.pdf, 6.

by *all who are affected by the laws* of a particular *demos*. Thus, rather than defining the *demos* in terms of legal citizenship (or even through length of residence), the right to participate politically would be determined by the 'contours of power relationships': those at the receiving end of a state's power should have a say in how that power is exercised.[71] Consequently, for Iris Young, 'a democratic decision is legitimate only if all those affected by it are included in the process of discussion and decision making'.[72] For example, because decisions on education typically touch upon the interests and well-being of citizens and non-citizens alike, as each are likely to have school-aged children, both groups should be entitled to participate in decision-making on this matter.

It is clear, then, that the idea of legitimate subjection grounds some or all precarious non-citizens possessing rights of political participation. The idea that all subject to state power should have a say in the exercise of that power can be derived from or is compatible with a number of different political theories, including liberal democracy, civic republicanism and deliberative democracy. That said, the extension of the democratic principle to non-citizens is controversial. It might be objected, for example, that the experience of 'precarious residents' of subjection is not similar to that of citizens and the claim of the former to be integrated into political life is thus less compelling. Non-citizens, unlike citizens, may escape the coercive power of the state by returning to their country of nationality. This objection, however, seems weak. Even putting aside the fact that most European states recognise dual citizens (who by definition enjoy political rights in more than one state), precarious non-citizens may have deep social, economic and emotional attachments to their country of residence which make departure from the state similar in its human costs to emigration for the citizen.[73]

This criticism does, however, raise important questions about subjection, the answers to which are not obvious in the work of the theorists who have developed the concept. First, at what point should a subject of state power qualify for political rights in the state? This is a question of the *scope* of the *demos*. 'Precarious residents' may include the illegal migrant who has lived in the state for ten years and asylum seeker who

---

[71] I. Shapiro, *The Moral Foundations of Politics* (New Haven, CT: Yale University Press, 2003), 220.

[72] I. Young, *Inclusion and Democracy* (Oxford: Oxford University Press, 2000), 23.

[73] See D. Kanstroom, *Deportation Nation: Outsiders in American History* (Cambridge, MA: Harvard University Press, 2007) and M. J. Gibney, 'Asylum and the Expansion of Deportation in the UK', *Government and Opposition*, 43 (2008), 146.

arrived yesterday. Should *anyone* subject to state power have political rights, or only those who have been (or intend to stay) in the polity for an extended period? Second, what *rights* should accompany the right to vote? Should those subject to state power be entitled to the same rights (to welfare, freedom for deportation, automatic naturalisation, to work) as citizens? Certainly, political rights would likely give politicians powerful reasons to take account of the interests of non-citizens and thus grant them economic and social rights. But there is another question here about whether genuine political participation positively requires a certain level of equality and security for all members of the *demos*. Notwithstanding these questions, it is clear that there is a wide consensus that it is dubious for any democracy to host people who live for many years subject to state power but with no say in how it is exercised.

The principle of societal membership

A third and final way of reconceptualising membership is through the principle of *societal membership*.[74] In this view, the membership of a state should be composed of everyone who has a significant stake in the development and direction of the society in question, a category that typically extends beyond citizens. While the principle of subjection concentrated on the injustice of not recognising individuals as *political* agents, the societal membership principle tends to attach weight to men and women as *social and economic* agents regardless of formal status.[75] For the societal membership principle, the test of membership is the depth of one's roots into a particular society, and the personal, social and economic costs of deprivation.

The societal membership principle is compatible with a range of different political theories. Communitarian theorists can see in the principle a way of defining what membership means – as social and economic belonging – that is not reducible simply to liberal rights. As one communitarian writes:

> Why should society take responsibility for people it tried to keep out of
> its territory [i.e. illegal migrants], for people who are not social members?
> Because in many respects they are social members. Although they are not
> citizens or legal residents, they may be diligent workers, good neighbours,

[74] R. Bauböck, 'Changing the Boundaries of Citizenship', in R. Bauböck (ed.), *From Aliens to Citizens* (Aldershot: Avebury, 1997).
[75] Lane, 'A Philosophical View', 132.

concerned parents, and active participants in community life. They are workers, involved in complex schemes of social co-operation.[76]

Joseph Carens, the liberal egalitarian, has also appealed to the principle in non-ideal mode. He argues that it is unjust for a state to deport any legal or illegal resident who has lived in the state for five years or more.[77] The time period he suggests simply acts as a proxy for the kinds of emotional and personal connections and social and economic roots that individuals can be expected to have established in a society over time.

Support for the principle of societal membership is implicitly part of the behaviour of most contemporary European states. When amnesty campaigns occur for illegal migrants, as they have done so in recent years in countries such as Britain, Belgium, France and Italy, the case for them typically rests on the belief that it is 'both impractical and apparently unjust' not to grant illegal immigrants who have 'integrated into the society in terms of work, education, residence, and social belonging' opportunities to gain formal citizenship or legal residence.[78] Accordingly it is common for such amnesties to require that unlawful residents show some evidence of integration into the society in question. One recent proposal in Britain for the regularisation of illegal migrants suggested that legal status should be made available to all who could speak English, had no criminal record, paid back taxes and had been present in the society for seven years.[79]

Perhaps the most developed account of societal membership is offered by Rainer Bauböck with his *stakeholder principle*. Bauböck's approach aims to fuse together an inclusive account of membership in the state consistent with liberal approaches with a view of the value of citizenship as a key human good distinctive of republican political thought.[80] The result of this fusion is an approach to membership that sees the subject-hood (or 'affected interest') principle as, on its own, problematic grounds for access to membership. One reason for this is that, if consistently applied, it would seem to require that at the same time as a non-citizen gains membership in their state of residence, they should lose citizenship

---

[76] J. Dwyer, 'Illegal Immigrants, Health Care and Social Responsibility', *The Hastings Center Report*, 34 (2004), 40.

[77] Carens, 'On Belonging'.   [78] Lane, 'A Philosophical View', 136.

[79] See *Strangers into Citizens* (2008), www.strangersintocitizens.org.uk.

[80] R. Bauböck, 'Changing Meanings and Practices of Citizenship', *PS: Political Science and Politics*, 28 (2005), 667.

in their country of origin because they are no longer subject to its laws or affected by its democratic decisions.[81] This result, however, is inattentive to the deep connections that individuals may still possess to their country of origin.

In the place of subjecthood, Bauböck proposes that non-citizens should be offered membership on the grounds that they have 'an interest in membership that makes the individual's fundamental rights dependent upon protection by a particular polity; and that ties an individual's well-being to the common good of that polity'.[82] According to this principle, citizenship, including voting rights, would be liberal and inclusive enough to accommodate the reality of societal membership as well as the right to hold multiple memberships simultaneously (in some cases). However, it would not be so inclusive as to rule out some requirements (e.g. a length period of residence to demonstrate a stake in society) for the gaining of citizenship.[83]

The principle of societal membership, expressed in various ways, provides a powerful account of why it is wrong to exclude long-term resident non-citizens from access to citizenship. This principle calls for an alignment between the reality of people's social existence – their level of effective integration into a society – and their legal status. Like the other principles outlined above, it seems to require an expansion in the boundaries of political community. However, also like the other principles, it leaves some important and difficult questions unresolved. For example, there is disagreement among adherents as to *how* societal integration is to be measured. For Carens, the passing of a certain period of time is enough. According to Miller, states can legitimately require that applicants for citizenship 'pass a language test and show basic knowledge of the history and institutions of the country' they live in.[84] In many actual regularisation campaigns, on the other hand, evidence of 'law abidingness' (not having a criminal record) is an important test of integration. Approaches, like the last two, that set (non-time-based) standards for regularisation or citizenship make it likely that some people living in the state whom are unlikely to be deported because of the length of their residence may never gain official status. It is thus important to consider at what point the reality of an individual's having made her life in a particular society should trump any subjective test of her integration.

---

[81] *Ibid.*, 686.   [82] *Ibid.*, 686.
[83] *Ibid.*, 686.   [84] Miller, 'Immigrants', 7.

Rethinking precarious residence

The three principles I have outlined offer ways of getting beyond the idea of 'precarious residents' simply as the bearers of human rights. They suggest that from a moral point of view these non-citizens are often members of the polity or society and should have rights (including protection from deportation) that reflect this fact. Each of the principles opens up the possibility of rethinking what membership in a modern European society should mean based on the commonly espoused values of autonomy, democracy and community.

Moreover, the principles I have outlined are not necessarily antagonistic to each other. It is possible to imagine arguments for the regularisation of unlawful residents based on both principles of subjection (deriving from democratic values) and societal integration (deriving from social reality and stake in the host country). Similarly, the choice-based (cosmopolitan–federal) approach might use principles of societal membership (degree of stake in society) to determine when a particular individual should be considered resident in a particular state, and thus be eligible to receive the full rights and entitlements of membership.

Non-citizens in the modern state are a diverse group. Whilst a transient non-citizen such as a visitor to an academic conference may have little obvious claim to a benefit such as state-subsidised healthcare, a longer-term resident, such as an asylum seeker (who may be in a state for over a year before her claim is decided) does have a legitimate claim. The challenge, then, is to provide an account of people living in the state who are entitled not only to human rights narrowly drawn, but also to benefits which currently may be restricted to those who have full formal membership, or citizenship, of the state, or some other immigration status. There is a further question as to how the rights of such people should evolve over time. This is a complicated issue. It may be useful to consider it a job requiring what Seyla Benhabib has called 'democratic iterations' or 'complex processes of public argument, deliberation, and exchange through which universalist rights claims and principles are contested and contextualised ... throughout legal and political institutions, as well as the associations of civil society' (2004: 179). Rather than attempting to resolve all questions of rights and responsibilities abstractly, this process aims to provide *fora* for deliberation among citizens and non-citizens, including those whose status is precarious, enabling membership to be revised to construct new ways of reconciling universal and particular principles.

Conclusion

The situation of the millions of people currently living in European states effectively outside the law, or enjoying its protection on only the most precarious of terms, is a profound challenge to the integrity of liberal democratic societies. As I have shown, it is a challenge that in many ways recalls the problems of statelessness diagnosed by Arendt in the immediate aftermath of the Second World War. A key aspect of this challenge, and one still invested with many of the Arendtian dilemmas, is to ensure that everyone within the territorial boundaries of European states has their basic human rights protected, including those who yesterday managed to sneak across the state's border or who are transiting through the country in search of asylum elsewhere. But another challenge is to rethink our conceptions of citizenship in the modern state, to consider whether these resident non-citizens should be considered members rather than strangers, or citizens in the making rather than unwanted guests.

I hope to have shown in this chapter that recent political thought across a wide range of approaches – global liberalism, statist liberalism, civic republicanism and communitarianism – offers ways of critically assessing the boundaries between members and non-members in the modern state. While each of these approaches has a different account of membership, ranging from choice, to subjection, to integration into the social and economic life of the society, each of them suggests that the long-term exclusion of resident non-citizens from membership is morally problematical.

4

Stateless in Europe: legal aspects of *de jure* and *de facto* statelessness in the European Union

CAROLINE SAWYER

Statelessness in international and regional law

While migration is a live topic of political discussion, less attention has been paid to the legal aspects of nationality and citizenship, and statelessness is still more neglected. These issues are sometimes perceived as purely policy issues or, even by lawyers, as small and rare technical legal questions, contentious for few people and essentially anomalous exceptions to the general rule that everyone has a fairly obvious nationality. There is perhaps also some moral difficulty, at least for lawyers, in allowing that the legal system might fundamentally fail some people, offering no jurisdiction within which they can frame their daily lives. But perhaps the greatest problem is that statelessness is essentially negative, and thus difficult to show or even to describe.

The International Court of Justice (ICJ) famously described nationality in 1955 as 'a legal bond having as its basis a social fact of attachment, a genuine connection of existence, interests and sentiments, together with the existence of reciprocal rights and duties'.[1] Statelessness is the obverse, describing a position of detachment, exclusion and abandonment. In the age of apparently universal basic human rights,[2] citizenship still provides the means through which those rights may be vindicated. The correlation of this is that those without a nationality may in practice be excluded from human rights. The premise of Hannah Arendt that citizenship is 'the right to have rights' still has a strong element of truth, and modern commentators such as Carmen Thiele are able to say even now: 'Citizenship ... remains an important consideration for full enjoyment of

---

[1] *Liechtenstein* v. *Guatemala (the Nottebohm case)* (1955) ICJ 4.
[2] United Nations Universal Declaration of Human Rights (UDHR), General Assembly GA Res. 217A, (1948) UN Doc A/810, Article 2(1).

all human rights.'[3] While Thiele's focus is that of enabling effective political participation, the more basic point relates to everyday rights, whether under international or regional law.

Citizens of EU countries have full entitlement not only to all political and social rights in their own country of nationality but also to the social advantages of EU citizenship elsewhere in the Union, such as the right to work. A lesser non-citizen status such as that of 'permanent resident' will generally mean that a person has access to day-to-day rights, even if not political ones, but such people usually also have a useful citizenship elsewhere. A lack of citizenship is not of basic import to permanent or temporary residents who may lawfully work or can otherwise be provided for. It is those who do not belong and are not wanted who have difficulty. Difficulties in a host country are solved by leaving, but for the stateless that is not always possible. Those who truly have no nationality – the *de jure* stateless – have no country of their own to go to; others have a nationality but do not want to go to their 'home' country, and remain *de facto* stateless in a country which regards them as an unwanted foreigner. Most countries, especially in Europe, make provision to grant citizenship to persons who are *de jure* stateless, but it may be impossible for them to show either that they are entitled to the nationality of a particular state or that they are stateless.[4] Those with an alternative nationality may not wish to go 'home' for a variety of reasons, including that they do not know the country at all, or that they fear for their lives there.

The difficulty for international law solutions to statelessness is that nationality and citizenship are both aspects of national sovereignty to be defined by the countries themselves. This is a long-standing and basic principle, affirmed particularly in the *Tunisia and Morocco* case in 1921.[5] Support for the proposition is also found in the *Research in International*

---

[3] C. Thiele, 'Citizenship as a Requirement for Minorities', *European Human Rights Law Review*, 6 (2005), 276.

[4] The difficulty of demonstrating statelessness is discussed by G. Ginsburgs, 'Soviet Citizenship Legislation and Statelessness as a Consequence of the Conflict of Nationality Laws', *International & Comparative Law Quarterly*, (15)1 (1966), 38.

[5] *Nationality Decrees Issued in Tunis and Morocco (French Zone) on 8 November 1921* [1922] PCIJ 3 (4 October 1922). The Court did, however, suggest that the scope of states' powers did not allow them to infringe obligations they had to other states (para. 12). *Stoeck* v. *Public Trustee* [1921] 2 Ch 67 and *Avis consultatifs, 1923*, C.P.J.I. série B no. 4, p. 24. Some jurisdictions distinguish between nationality (as membership of the country or state), and citizenship (as the political element of nationality). In some cases, these are two aspects of the same concept, but they may be very different – as where, for example, in the FSU one's citizenship was Soviet but one's nationality was, broadly, one's ethnicity.

Law carried out by the Harvard Law School,[6] as well as, later, in the work of Manley O. Hudson, the Special Rapporteur of the International Law Commission (ILC), who considered the issue in the early 1950s. Following a widespread general failing of the system in Europe, Hudson still said that 'in principle, questions of nationality fall within the domestic jurisdiction of each State'.[7] The court in the *Tunisia and Morocco* case did not, however, entirely rule out the idea that international law would be capable of affecting states' competence in determining their own nationals, particularly where this would also entail determining the nationality of other states' nationals. Articles 1 and 2 of the 1930 Hague Convention[8] asserted that it was for each State to determine under its own law who its nationals were in accordance with their own laws, but with the proviso that the law should be recognised by other states insofar as it was consistent with international conventions, international custom and the generally recognised principles of nationality law. The overall effect, in the early days of modern international law, was to entrench a rule that it was for states to define their own nationals, in accordance with their own systems of nationality law, with a small window of possibility for national laws to be influenced by international law.[9]

The problem is nevertheless an international one. People who belong nowhere, or only somewhere they cannot reasonably live, are not only personally vulnerable but of concern to the international community, practically as well as morally. If people have no system within which to live reasonably and lawfully, they must live unlawfully, if at all. They may not be easily expellable, and the next generation – children born neither stateless nor entitled to the nationality of the only country they know – compounds the issue. While they remain in their unwilling host country, outside the effective protection of the legal system, the *de facto* stateless are vulnerable to abuses of their rights, including their basic human rights. All the regulation of aspects of daily life, such as working, receiving welfare benefits or publicly funded healthcare, falls to a state whose concern may not be to protect that individual but to expel them. International law

---

[6] Part I, *Nationality* (Cambridge, MA: Harvard University Press, April 1929), 17 ff.
[7] Document A/CN.4/50(1952-II), *Yearbook of the International Law Commission*, 7.
[8] Convention on Certain Questions Relating to the Conflict of Nationality Laws 1930.
[9] See further, J.M.M. Chan, 'The Right to a Nationality as a Human Right', *Human Rights Law Journal*, 12 (1991), 1 and I. Brownlie, 'The Relations of Nationality in Public International Law', *British Yearbook of International Law* 139 (1963), 284. A. Grossman deals interestingly with the opposite situation, where persons seek to define their nationality without a state: 'Nationality and the Unrecognised State', *International & Comparative Law Quarterly*, 50 (2001), 847.

has no real solutions to either *de jure* or *de facto* statelessness, and as yet the problems such as war and poverty that make people move to countries that are unwilling to accept them, and which also do not make those people refugees within the meaning of international law, have not been resolved either. Regional law in Europe is only now dealing with the issue of how states treat long-term unwanted residents, and is beginning to bring them and their rights within states' obligations under the restrictive terms of the ECHR.

Nationality and citizenship in Europe

Questions of legal or *de jure* statelessness, where a person has no nationality or citizenship, are involved with issues about the definition of 'who belongs' within the modern nation-state. There are four essential bases for nationality or citizenship, and individual systems operate a mix of them. The *jus soli* (law of land) is the system under which a person born on the territory of a state has the citizenship of that state. The *jus sanguinis* (law of blood) grants citizenship to the children of citizens, whether or not they are born in the territory.[10] Citizenship may also be granted on the basis of a period of residence, or lastly may be granted to those who choose it, on the basis of the individual's wishes.[11] Most nationality systems operate a variation on one of the first two themes, but usually with elements of all the others. It is generally within the competence of any state to decide what system to operate, and various systems operate in practice and are generally internationally accepted.[12]

The schemes of nationality rules practised within Europe vary, both geographically and over time, and for reasons of history as well as philosophy. More Eastern states in particular have had more ethnically based concepts of citizenship of the political state. The end of the Soviet era,

---

[10] Hudson remarked of the *jus sanguinis* that 'it is more serious, as it tends to make statelessness hereditary' (Document A/CN.4/50(1952-II), 17).

[11] The ILC in 1936 favoured the operation of nationality law under a *jus connectionis*, so that people would belong to the state they led their lives in: *Report of the Thirty-Ninth Conference*, 13–51.

[12] See, however, the *Nottebohm* case (n. 1). There, Guatemala objected to Mr Nottebohm's acquisition of Liechtenstein citizenship, granted with unusual rapidity and when he was mostly resident in Guatemala, to avoid the personal consequences of being an enemy alien, and regarded him as still having his previous German nationality. The ICJ agreed broadly with Guatemala, but see the dissenting judgment of Guggenheim. See also J. M. Jones, 'The *Nottebohm* Case', *International & Comparative Law Quarterly*, 15 (1956), 230.

ending political union across states, led not only to notable outbreaks of ethnic warfare but also the quieter problems of defining the membership of the new nation-states which gave rise to much of the statelessness in Eastern Europe. Between the settling of its modern concept of nationality in 1913[13] until the turn of this millennium, Germany had a strong policy of *jus sanguinis*, recognising as citizens the descendants even of those who had emigrated in previous centuries[14] but denying citizenship to the German-born children of resident foreigners until, following pressure from the United Nations, they instituted a policy with far stronger elements of the *jus soli* in 2000.[15] The United Kingdom, in contrast, moved during the twentieth century from an inclusive concept where anyone born in the British Empire was equally a subject of the monarchy[16] to a complex and essentially *jus sanguinis* scheme of different forms of British nationality, under which British people based in the United Kingdom have the right to enter and live in UK territory but those from outside the United Kingdom do not.[17] France has long had a strongly *jus soli* policy, as befits a country that focuses on the rights of the citizen as first promulgated in the Revolution of 1789, but it is a 'double *jus soli*', so referring an individual back to the status of their parents, as does the essentially *jus sanguinis* system now obtaining in the United Kingdom. The loss of the domestic *jus soli* in the United Kingdom and the Republic of Ireland, in 1983 and 2004, respectively,[18] were apparently prompted at the domestic level by concerns about citizenship being obtained by the children of temporary migrants. The changes coincide, however, with the rise of the contested concept of 'Fortress Europe', where those within the polity have broad rights throughout it, but those formally outside it have trouble getting in at all. The issue of 'European citizenship' attracts much current debate but, while there are rights available to certain 'third-country' nationals, the allocation of European citizenship is on the basis of being a citizen of one of the EU member states. The loss of the *jus soli* in Western Europe, together with the hardening of the *jus sanguinis* already in place in Eastern

---

[13] Staatsangehörigkeitsgesetz vom 1. Januar 1871; Reichs- und Staatsangehörigkeitgesetz vom 22. Juli 1913.

[14] Bundesvertriebenen- und Fluchtlingsgesetz 1953 (BVFG).

[15] Gesetz zur Regelung von Fragen der Staatsangehörigkeit 1999.

[16] The *jus soli* was established in case law in *Calvin's Case* 77 ER 377 (KB 1608) and codified in section 1 of the British Nationality and Status of Aliens Act 1914.

[17] See currently British Nationality Act 1981, as amended.

[18] British Nationality Act 1981, section 1 and Irish Nationality and Citizenship Act 2004, amending Irish Nationality Act 1956.

Europe, means that it is also more difficult for European citizenship to be
obtained by the next generation even if they are European-born.[19]

International law and the issue of statelessness

The historical events that prompted the earliest concerns of modern international law with the issue of statelessness were the Russian Revolution of
1917 and the Armenian massacres of the period of the First World War
and into the 1920s. A decree of 15 December 1921 deprived an estimated
2 million people of Russian nationality, leading J. Fischer Williams to
suggest that, as granting nationality is an act of sovereignty, deprivation
of citizenship ('denationalisation') is like cession of territory. He found a
basis for arguing that states had a duty in international law not to leave
people effectively stateless:

> While positive international law does not forbid a state unilaterally to
> sever the relationship of nationality so far as the individual is concerned,
> even if the person affected possesses or acquires no other nationality, still
> a state cannot sever the tie of nationality in such a way as to release itself
> from the international duty, owed to other states, of receiving back a per-
> son denationalized who has acquired no other nationality, should he be
> expelled as an alien by the state where he happens to be.[20]

The emphasis of the international law relating to stateless persons and
refugees was, from the outset, to have them return to their countries of
origin if possible, and that, along with the general idea of protection of
their basic interests in the meantime, has remained the case.

The legal consolidation of the concept of universal human rights was
strengthened in reaction to the abuses in Europe of the mid-twentieth
century. Among these rights was the right to a nationality first stated in
the United Nations Declaration of Human Rights (UDHR) of 1948 and
repeated subsequently in other international instruments.[21] The right
not to be arbitrarily deprived of one's nationality likewise appears in

---

[19] D. Weissbrodt has said that '[i]n view of the nearly universal ratification of the Convention
of the Rights of the Child, the principle of *jus soli* (citizenship based on the place of birth)
has emerged as the overriding international norm governing the nationality of children born to non-citizen parents' (D. Weissbrodt, *The Human Rights of Non-Citizens*,
Oxford: Oxford University Press, 2008, 75), but this is not the case in modern Europe.

[20] J.F. Williams, 'Denationalization', *British Yearbook of International Law*, 8 (1927), 45, 61.

[21] Article 14, Universal Declaration of Human Rights 1948; Article 24(3) International
Covenant on Civil and Political Rights 1966 and Article 7 (1) United Nations Convention
on the Rights of the Child 1989.

the 1948 Declaration.[22] This Declaration was, however, of no practical validity,[23] having only at most 'moral value and authority' even if that was 'without precedent in the history of the world'.[24] Relatively few provisions of international law are directly enforceable, especially at the instigation of individuals. The only means of enforcement is usually some form of political embarrassment if a state does not comply with the terms it has agreed to. International law, even more than domestic laws, is a game that works only if, and only insofar as, everyone agrees to play.[25] The International Criminal Court (ICC) deals with war crimes, and the ICJ does decide contentious cases, but only states may be parties to those cases, and it gives advisory opinions only to a select few UN organisations.[26] There are no international human rights courts for individuals. As Lea Brilmayer says, 'treaties, like contracts, were intended as reciprocal exchanges, of mutual benefit to the signing parties but of little or no legal concern to the rest of the world. Most modern treaties still take this form. This exchange model of treaty relationships, however, is not well suited to human rights agreements.'[27]

International law after the Second World War: refugees and the *de jure* stateless

There is much factual overlap, as well as some general confusion, between the international regimes governing asylum and statelessness, but the lack of enforceability is a common theme. Even the Convention on the Status of Refugees of 1951, which is generally applied across Europe, has no international enforcement system, though a parallel European system is developing. Having provisions of international law to deal with refugees and stateless persons was not, however, a new idea arising from

---

[22] Article 15(2).

[23] H. Lauterpacht, 'The Universal Declaration of Human Rights', *British Yearbook of International Law*, 25 (1948), 354.

[24] Belgian Delegate A/PV 181, 47 (adoption of the Universal Declaration of Human Rights).

[25] The perception that law is unhelpful if it is not enforceable, and perhaps that it is the displaced who are in particular need of practically enforceable law, is not new: see (albeit particularly on the point of delay in international law) C.J.B. Hurst, 'Wanted! An International Court of Piepowder', *British Yearbook of International Law*, 4 (1925), 61.

[26] This is the successor to the Permanent Court of International Justice (PCIJ), which was set up in 1922 and dissolved in 1946. See n. 5 above.

[27] L. Brilmayer, 'From "Contract" to "Pledge": The Structure of International Human Rights Agreements', *British Yearbook of International Law*, 77 (2006), 163, 165.

the Second World War.[28] There had been earlier provisions dealing
with specific groups, beginning with provision made for the support of
Russian refugees by the League of Nations in the aftermath of the 1917
Revolution, extended to cover refugees from the Armenian massacres in
the 1920s. Later international arrangements and conventions were made,
covering especially refugees coming from Germany in the 1930s.[29] The
United Nations Relief and Rehabilitation Administration (UNRRA)
was created in 1942, and the First Session of the General Assembly of
the United Nations in 1946 decided that an international body should
determine the future of refugees, always focusing, however, on assisting
repatriation where possible. This led to the creation of the International
Refugee Organisation (IRO), which in 1947 began to develop basic international standards for dealing with large-scale migration – looking,
however, only at refugees and displaced persons. Across Europe, many
people displaced by changes in regime or by the war had been deprived
of their legal citizenship, and state boundaries had changed. Some refugees were not stateless, but others were – or preferred to be.[30] The international instruments drawn up to deal with the position still govern it
today, though the political scene has changed.[31]

The first major post-war act of the United Nations was the UDHR
in 1948, which related to all persons regardless of status. As well as the
(unenforceable) right to a nationality, the UDHR contains a right to seek
asylum which is similarly unenforceable for practical purposes as there
is no corresponding obligation on any state to grant it. Subsequently, and
more directly practically, the United Nations Convention on the Status of

[28] See, for example, L. W. Holborn, 'The Legal Status of Political Refugees', *American
Journal of International Law*, 32 (1938), 680.

[29] Provisional Arrangements Concerning the Status of Refugees Coming From Germany
(4 July 1936) and Convention Concerning the Status of Refugees Coming from Germany
(10 February 1938).

[30] The post-war repeal by the Allies' Military Government in Germany of the Reich citizenship laws of 1935, which had deprived many people of their German citizenship, thus
restored that citizenship to people who by then did not want it back but preferred to
re-settle elsewhere, even as stateless persons (Law No. 1 of the Military Government of
Germany (Supreme Commander's Area of Control) issued on 18 September 1944 and
re-issued on 20 September 1945 by the Control Council). Many such people were deeply
disadvantaged by being German rather than stateless, as they then became subject to the
'discriminatory, confiscatory, and repressive measures' then governing Germans abroad.
See H. Lauterpacht, 'The Nationality of Denationalized Persons', *Jewish Yearbook of
International Law* (1948–9), 164.

[31] See also J.C. Hathaway, 'The Evolution of Refugee Status in International Law 1920–1950',
International & Comparative Law Quarterly, 33 (1984), 348.

Refugees 1951 was drafted on the basis of defining states parties' agreed obligations to the foreign refugees resident in their territory in the aftermath of the war. That instrument is still the most relevant instrument in force and has been called an 'apology for the Holocaust',[32] but might also alternatively be seen as an administrative arrangement for allocating and accepting refugees and displaced persons who were still often in a limbo of status some years after peace was restored. Like the UDHR, the Refugee Convention contains no right for a person to claim asylum in any particular state, let alone a process of individual enforcement.[33] It requires some process for determination of refugee status, but does not impose any consequential duty beyond that of non-refoulement (see below).[34] Refugee status depends on having been persecuted by state authorities, or with their connivance. Fleeing civil strife, famine or war is not enough: the persecution must be for reason of race, religion, nationality, membership of a particular social group, or political opinion. Without requiring the acceptance of refugees' presence or residence in the state, the Convention sets out duties to refugees who are lawfully present in the relevant territory, and to those who are lawfully resident – the difference between these concepts is rooted in the law of some jurisdictions, but not all. These duties amount essentially to granting certain socio-economic rights usually on a similar basis to the provision made for nationals. Refugees are to be issued with travel documents[35] and provision is to be made for the naturalisation of refugees who are accepted as residents. The obligations on states under the Convention even towards those who fulfil its definition of 'refugee' are therefore relatively limited – if the refugee is given no lawful status, the only prohibition is on refoulement, or forced return to the country of persecution. There is no Convention obligation to allow the refugee to settle and make a life.

---

[32] F. Klug, personal communication.

[33] C. Harvey, 'The Right to Seek Asylum', *European Human Rights Law Review*, 4 (2004), 17. It also has no prescribed process for dealing with applications for asylum, beyond stating that some process must exist.

[34] United Nations Convention on the Status of Refugees, 1951 Article 33: the right of refugees not to be returned to the frontiers of the country from which they have fled. This is the only Convention right that states must, under the Convention, accord to all refugees.

[35] Travel documents for those who could not obtain them from a country's government were first instituted after the Russian Revolution of 1917 led to mass emigration. The League of Nations began issuing such documents in 1922. The 'refugee passports' were designed by a Norwegian explorer, Fridtjof Nansen, and are often known by his name. For more on his work, see also N. Bentwich, 'The League of Nations and Refugees', *British Yearbook of International Law*, 16 (1935), 114.

The 1951 Refugee Convention was designed specifically and solely for the aftermath of the Second World War. Subsequent refugees were only brought within it after a Protocol was made in 1967 extending its provisions to later refugees as well.[36] Many categories of people are specifically excluded from the scope of the Convention, such as war criminals, serious non-political criminals and those who fall within the scope of other UN assistance, especially the United Nations Relief and Works Agency (UNRWA). The Convention is currently enforced, if at all, by reports made by each state to the United Nations at intervals: no sanction for breach exists beyond the possibility of international disapproval. Commenting on the 'direct conflict between the needs of law and the demands of sovereignty', the commentator R.Y. Jennings said: 'It is not enough to have rules of law. If the law is to be effective there must also be courts to determine the application of the law to the circumstances of a particular dispute.'[37] Subsequent developments have not changed the position; there may be a right to seek asylum, and there may be international discussion as to asylum policies, but there is no corresponding right in any individual to be granted refugee status.[38]

What refugees, displaced people and the stateless face in host countries remains the need to make a life, which applies equally, regardless of the reason for the displacement. The first issue identified by a commentator in 1939, reporting the concerns of the League of Nations in 1936, was that a refugee who could not return to that person's country of origin should, in the delay before the hoped-for naturalisation in the new country, obtain 'such identity papers and passports ... as may secure a certain minimum of "personality", stability, freedom of movement and freedom to return, if desired, to the point whence he came'.[39] This commentator goes on to discuss the question of the definition of a refugee, since earlier definitions

---

[36] Protocol Relating to the Status of Refugees ESC Res. 1186 (XLI) 18 November 1966; GA Res. 2198 (XXI) 16 December 1966, in force 4 October 1967.

[37] R.Y. Jennings, 'The Progress of International Law', British Yearbook of International Law, 34 (1958), 334. At p. 355, Jennings notes: 'This picture will disappoint cynic and sciolist alike; both regard international law as a panacea, though the one thinks it an imagined one whereas the other believes it needs only to be "applied." International law can never be a panacea, for law is only one aspect of the immensely complex as well as immensely urgent problem that faces our civilization today. But international law is, if only one aspect, nevertheless an essential aspect.'

[38] G. S. Gilbert, 'Right of Asylum: A Change of Direction', International & Comparative Law Quarterly, 31 (1983), 633.

[39] R.Y. Jennings, 'Some International Law Aspects of the Refugee Question', British Yearbook of International Law, 20 (1939), 98.

were specific to countries of origin, and in the course of this he identifies the refugee as a *de facto* stateless person, since 'he does not *in fact* enjoy the protection of the government of his state of origin, whether he is legally entitled to such protection or not'.[40]

As the situation of stateless refugees was covered by the Refugee Convention, the situation of stateless persons who were not refugees had to be considered separately. In April 1954, the United Nations Economic and Social Council appointed a Council of Plenipotentiaries to deal with the issue, and a Convention on the Status of Stateless Persons was made the same year, drafted on the basis of the Refugee Convention and often adapting its provisions so little as to constitute effectively adopting them.[41] There are a few less favourable elements, however: refugees would have a 'most-favoured-nation' right of association, whereas the status of stateless persons was aligned with that of aliens generally, if as favourably as possible. Likewise, with the right to work, where refugees should be favourably treated and, after three years' residence, put on a par with nationals, stateless persons were to be treated as favourably as possible and merely not less favourably than aliens generally. Nor, importantly but logically, is there the prohibition on penalties for unlawful entry into the territory found at Article 31 of the Refugee Convention. Noticeable and also logical is the lack of any equivalent to Article 33, non-refoulement. There was and is no separate authority for the stateless equivalent to the Office of the United Nations High Commissioner for Refugees, who now, however, includes them in his remit.[42] The twenty-two original signatories included France and the United Kingdom, but neither the Soviet Union nor its successor states has ever signed the Convention, which came into force in 1960.

Paul Weis, in discussing the 1954 Convention, considered the differences between refugees and stateless persons, as well as the overlap. He noted: 'So far, international efforts to define the status of unprotected persons have been concentrated on refugees ... refugee movements are more likely to arouse international interest from the humanitarian and political angle. Stateless persons, on the other hand, are a rather amorphous

---

[40] *Ibid.*, 99, emphasis in the original.
[41] See also P. Weis, 'The Convention Relating to the Status of Stateless Persons', *International & Comparative Law Quarterly*, 10 (1961), 255.
[42] The travel document issued under the statelessness Convention to those who are stateless but not refugees is identical to the 'refugee passport', save that it does not have the two black diagonal lines across the corner.

group.'[43] Citing Article 5 of the Statelessness Convention ('nothing in the Convention shall impair rights and benefits granted to stateless persons elsewhere than the [Refugee] Convention, which should be applied in preference'), Weis suggested that there were four possible outcomes for stateless persons. First, if they were also refugees, they would be protected by a state's implementation of the 1951 Refugee Convention. Secondly, they might fall within the definition of a Convention refugee but not be under the protection of any state. Thirdly, stateless persons within the meaning of the Statelessness Convention might be in states ratifying the Convention and would have protection once it came into force. Fourthly, stateless persons in states which were not parties to the Statelessness Convention would therefore be unprotected. He felt that the Convention would 'probably not affect to any great extent the status of stateless persons' in their signatory host states, though it might benefit them abroad, and that the main significance of the Convention lay 'in its very existence'.[44]

The UN Convention on the Reduction of Statelessness followed in 1961. Its primary provision was the obligation of a state to grant its nationality to a person born (or a foundling found) in its territory who would otherwise be stateless, provided a timely application was made (Article 1). Provision was also made to deal with those who failed to apply in time. The loss of nationality on marriage or divorce, or some similar change of status such as adoption, was made conditional on possession or acquisition of another nationality (Article 5), and the deprivation of nationality leaving a person stateless was not permitted (Article 8), save in cases of fraud or disloyalty. Deprivation of nationality on racial, ethnic, religious, or political grounds was not permitted either (Article 9). Article 10 required provision to be made to prevent statelessness following the transfer of territory. Article 11 of the 1961 Convention envisaged the establishment of an international body to which individuals might apply to claim the benefit of the Convention's provisions. The Article thus envisages the institutional separation of statelessness and refugee issues. Nevertheless, it has not resulted in anything like a mechanism for individual petition in seeking assistance in obtaining a valid nationality. The prevention of statelessness was entrusted to the High Commissioner for Refugees, and the preoccupation remained with the refugee mandate.[45] The 1961

---

[43] See Weis, 'The Convention', 262.   [44] *Ibid.*, 263.

[45] UN General Assembly Resolution, GA Res. 3274 (XXIX) of 1974. See further, P. Weis, 'The United Nations Convention on the Reduction of Statelessness, 1961', *International & Comparative Law Quarterly*, 11 (1962), 1073. See also L. van Waas, *Nationality Matters: Statelessness Under International Law* (Antwerp: Intersentia, 2008).

Convention had only thirty five states parties as at 1 October 2008. Its influence has, however, often produced relatively solid practical results, with states making domestic provision for those born *de jure* stateless on their territory to claim citizenship. Such statelessness is rare, and also hard to prove. It tends to entail proving a negative not only about yourself but also about parents and grandparents whose status might entitle you to claim a citizenship by descent. Aside from the comparatively rare case of demonstrable *de jure* statelessness at birth in the territory, there are not merely unenforceable obligations but no international obligations to grant citizenship at all.

The rights of *de facto* stateless persons in international law

In an age where migration is a major political issue, for a state to be obliged to accept allegedly stateless persons easily as citizens would be to invite abuse and to offer a simple way of avoiding the domestic rules of naturalisation and asylum. Basic rights for all persons might appear to be the way to prevent blameless individual or group suffering, but recognition of *de facto* statelessness is, however, far from new. Well over fifty years ago, the Special Rapporteur Manley O. Hudson considered that 'fruitful' attempts to eliminate statelessness would only be those that improved people's status, giving them their 'effective nationality'.[46] There was discussion at the time of the making of the Statelessness Conventions as to the definition of statelessness, and whether or not it included those who were *de facto* stateless. Like Hudson, Weis also preferred the term 'unprotected'.[47] The drafters of the Convention included, at the proposal of the Belgian Delegation, alternative provisions which would include as 'stateless' persons who invoked valid reasons (in the view of the host state) for renouncing the protection of their country of nationality. The UK Delegation proposed to include those refused protection and assistance by their own states. In the end, no such provisions were made. Instead, a Recommendation

---

[46] 'Purely formal solutions which do not take account of this desideratum might reduce the number of stateless persons but not the number of unprotected persons. They might lead to a shifting from statelessness *de jure* to statelessness *de facto* which, in the view of the Rapporteur, would not be desirable', Document A/CN.4/50(1952-II), *Yearbook of the International Law Commission*, n. 7 above, 20.

[47] P. Weis, 'Legal Aspects of the Convention of July 28, 1951, Relating to the Status of Refugees', *British Yearbook of International Law*, 30 (1953), 480 and G. Scelle, 'Le problème de l'apatridie devant la Commission due Droit International de l'ONU', *Die Friedenswarte*, 52 (1954), 142.

was adopted inviting states to consider sympathetically giving the Convention rights to a person who had renounced the protection of the country of which they were a national, for reasons the host state regarded as valid, and for that position then to be recognised by other states. This, clearly, has no legal force.

Those who are *de facto* stateless, or who cannot prove their *de jure* state-lessness, must therefore look elsewhere for rules obliging states to offer them protection on another basis. Their greatest hope must be rooted in the modern international human rights system, which appears to give rights to all regardless of status. It includes practical rights of the sort that allow a person to conduct a daily life, such as the right to work or to obtain healthcare or education for one's children, rather than the more prin-cipled political rights such as the right to vote that citizenship brings, or even the more cultural rights such as that to burial in the territory. These may be perceived as imposing a potential or actual burden of expense on the state involved, or as offering it human assets. States generally, how-ever, give status to those in the latter category. Where a person is part of the social fabric in practice, they acquire ever stronger moral claims to political belonging as well, and to the admission of their families. But a state's control of its resident and practically entitled population is closely allied to its control of definition of its own nationals, and states are rarely inclined to allow any diminution of that.[48]

In 1966, two wide-ranging Covenants were made, to which most countries, including those in this study, are parties. The International Covenant on Economic, Social and Cultural Rights (ICESCR) focuses on the rights of peoples rather than of persons – to self-determination and the pursuit of their economic, social and cultural development – but goes on to state the rights as those of individuals. The provisions as to non-discrimination, and those which are framed to apply to all persons, do present difficulties for states which have resident persons or populations whose access to these rights would conflict with the state's exercise of its sovereignty. Part III sets out the rights that affect individ-uals which are recognised by states parties to the Covenant: the right to work and to appropriate conditions of work, to equal treatment for men and women, and the right to join a trade union; to social security, including social insurance; to the protection of the family; to adequate

---

[48] H. Fields, 'Closing Immigration throughout the World', *American Journal of Inter-national Law*, 26 (1932), 671 and R. Plender, 'Immigration Law Trends', *International & Comparative Law Quarterly*, 35 (1986), 531.

food, clothing and housing and to health and education, especially free primary education; and to participation in cultural life. Part IV gives, among other things, the means by which action shall be taken on implementing the provisions of the Covenant: reports from individual states on how they are complying with those provisions, with more direct action in the form of conventions, recommendations, technical assistance and the holding of meetings.[49] Thus while this Covenant appears useful to stateless persons, it is so only in the broadest and least applicable of terms. States may, in endeavouring to adhere to it, grant greater rights to non-nationals in general. But there is not always a route for complaint if they do not.[50]

The contemporaneous International Covenant on Civil and Political Rights (ICCPR) also begins with the rights of peoples to self-determination, acknowledging however that such self-determined peoples might decide nevertheless to adhere to internationally agreed rules. Article 2 requires states to make laws implementing the guaranteed rights, which then include many standard individual rights, and to make provision for effective remedies for individuals in the event of breach, with considerable exceptions where a public emergency threatening the life of the nation has been proclaimed. The rights to life and not to be tortured may not be derogated from; similarly with the right not to be held in slavery or servitude (though forced labour may be permissible in states of emergency). There are equally strict prohibitions on the arbitrary prevention of a person's entering his own country, the expulsion of aliens without giving reasons, and inequality and incomprehension before courts and tribunals.[51] The right to recognition as a person is furthered by Article 24, which requires that children should be registered at birth and given a name, and that every child has a right to acquire a nationality: that the right is to 'acquire' a nationality must entail that a person might be born stateless. The ICCPR has two optional Protocols, the first authorising the Monitoring Committee to receive individual complaints and the second affirming a commitment to the abolition of the death penalty. All EU member states are parties to the ICCPR, and all of those

---

[49] Article 23 of the International Covenant on Economic, Social and Cultural Rights 1966. France has entered a declaration that rules governing the right of aliens to work are not affected. See Articles 6, 9, 11 and 13.

[50] France, for example, has specifically declared that it does not affect the rights of aliens to work or establish residence requirements for the allocation of certain social benefits.

[51] Articles 3, 12, 13 and 14, respectively, of the International Covenant on Civil and Political Rights 1966

except the United Kingdom have ratified the first Protocol and all except France have ratified the second.[52]

The level of international concern about the rights of migrants also led the International Labour Organization (ILO) to make a series of instruments designed to protect their rights,[53] but neither these nor the subsequent UN instruments are effective in practice. The Declaration of the Rights of Persons Who Are Not Nationals of the Country in Which They Live was made in 1985.[54] It is remarkably limited in scope as well as (by virtue of being only a Declaration) ambition. After defining those to whom it refers in Article 1, it goes on to emphasise in Article 2 that nothing in the Declaration should be taken to legitimise the position of irregular migrants. Following articles dealing with basic human rights, such as that not to be subject to torture, Article 8, which refers to working rights as well as rights to healthcare, education and social services, is restricted to those 'lawfully residing in the territory'.

In December 1990 the UN also adopted the International Convention on the Protection of the Right of All Migrant Workers and Members of Their Families.[55] One of the aims was the harmonisation of states' policies towards non-citizen resident workers; another the expectation that if irregular migrants had greater employment rights, not only would they be less vulnerable themselves but also less desirable employees to rogue employers, thus discouraging the phenomenon of irregular migration itself. Refugees and stateless persons were, however, expressly excluded from the Convention.[56] It accords rights reminiscent of those in the

---

[52] France also entered various declarations and reservations, including one relating to Article 13, on the expulsion of aliens, declaring that Chapter IV of Order No. 45–2658 of 2 November 1945 on the sojourn of aliens, and other similar provisions, took precedence. O. A. Hathaway, 'Do Human Rights Treaties Make a Difference?', *Yale Law Journal*, 111 (2002), 1870.

[53] Convention concerning Migration for Employment (No. 97); Convention Concerning Migrations in Abusive Conditions and the Promotion of Equality of Opportunity and Treatment of Migrant Workers (No. 143); Recommendation Concerning Migration for Employment (No. 86); Recommendation Concerning Migrant Workers (No. 151); Convention Concerning Forced or Compulsory Labour (No. 29); Convention Concerning Abolition of Forced Labour (No. 105). In 1998 the ILO also produced a *Declaration on Fundamental Principles and Rights at Work* (1998) and a *Follow-Up*, referred to in the *Non-Binding Principles and Guidelines for a Rights-Based Approach to Labour Migration* (2006), which both require the human rights of all workers to be respected regardless of their status (Part V, para. 8) and confirm that governments should work towards the prevention of irregular migration (Part VI, para. 11).

[54] Adopted Res. 40/144 13 December 1985.   [55] Res. 45/158.

[56] Article 3 (d) of the International Convention on the Protection of the Right of All Migrant Workers and Members of Their Families 1990.

better-known ECHR to all migrant workers and their families, and to documented workers whose presence in the state is regular it gives rights which are close to those of citizenship. Again, however, it offers little to those whose status does not allow them to work or is more generally irregular, and so really gives no help to those of the *de facto* stateless who have no private financial resources on which to build a life.

The UN Convention Against Torture and other Cruel, Inhuman or Degrading Treatment or Punishments was made in 1975. It defines torture and prohibits it absolutely, without allowing for any excuses. In particular, no expulsion or return or extradition into danger of being tortured is permitted, such danger to be assessed among other things by looking at the record of the country in question.[57] The Convention Against Torture opened for signature in 1985 and, as with the International Covenants, most countries are party to it, with Rwanda becoming its 146th party in December 2008.[58] The Convention Against Torture is potentially a useful practical tool, since breach of it appears to cause considerable embarrassment. This usefulness would be unusual in international law, where the 'rights' granted are often more akin, for practical purposes, to political aspirations. They do not generally even purport to constitute binding and enforceable obligations on the signatory states. Moreover, even where obligations are created by international treaties, states may avoid fulfilling those obligations.[59]

Statelessness and the rights of persistently disadvantaged groups in international law

Some groups are more likely to suffer disenfranchisement. Women and children have attracted particular attempts at international protection, being both historically vulnerable to not being considered legal persons and being particularly liable not to acquire citizenship or to lose it, and also, at the social level, liable to oppression for sexual reasons. Those from routinely disadvantaged ethnic groups, especially the Gypsies, have also attracted attention. In the context of nationality and statelessness (and

---

[57] Article 3. This makes the provision broader than that in the United Nations Convention on the Status of Refugees 1951 (Refugee Convention), which arguably requires the asylum seeker to show that they, as an individual, reasonably fear persecution.

[58] See, for example, M. D. Evans and R. Morgan, *Preventing Torture* (Oxford: Oxford University Press, 1998).

[59] E. Bates, 'Avoiding Legal Obligations Created by Human Rights Treaties', *International & Comparative Law Quarterly*, 57 (2008), 751.

consequently the context of migration, since this may lead to naturalisation), ethnic discrimination is permissible, and any system based on the *jus sanguinis* principles that now permeate Europe will favour the existing ethnic mix over changes from immigration. Problems of ethnic and cultural identity and citizenship rights are not confined to the Eastern mind-set, though that is where they have recently been most obviously controversial.[60] Minority group rights are among the Copenhagen criteria for admission to the European Union, but the position reflects that of citizenship in international law: states parties will only alter their own policies and practices up to a certain point, and where there is no political will anywhere to go further. Going further would often be perceived as, for example, inviting Gypsies into individual states, something which states are often astute to avoid.[61]

The most widespread nationality issue for women stemmed from their historical lack of a legal personality capable of persisting through a marriage. Married women habitually lost their citizenship on marriage and took that of their husband. This could lead to effective statelessness if, say, their husbands then died, leaving them unable to return to their original home.[62] The Convention on the Nationality of Married Women 1957 and the Convention on the Elimination of All Forms of Discrimination against Women 1979 dealt with the particular problem of women losing their citizenship on marriage to a foreigner. Treating the phenomenon as one of sex discrimination, Article 9 (1) of the latter requires: 'States Parties shall grant women equal rights with men to acquire, change or retain their nationality', reflecting Article 1 of the Convention on the Nationality of Married Women 1957. This has been arguably the most

---

[60] For interesting discussion, see D. I. Kertzer and D. Arel (eds.), *Census and Identity: The Politics of Race, Ethnicity, and Language in National Censuses* (Cambridge: Cambridge University Press, 2001).

[61] See, for example, Z. Barany, 'The Socio-Economic Impact of Regime Change in Eastern Europe: Gypsy Marginality in the 1990s', *East European Politics and Societies*, 14(2) (1998), 64 and the UK case of *R. v. Immigration Officer at Prague Airport, ex parte European Roma Rights Centre* [2004] UKHL 55, in which the House of Lords found that procedures established by the UK Home Office to prevent persons of Gypsy ethnicity, considered likely to claim asylum on arrival in the United Kingdom, from boarding aeroplanes bound for the country at Prague Airport, contravened domestic race relations legislation.

[62] Examples of the effects of this are given by L. Kerber, 'The Stateless as the Citizen's Other: A View from the United States', in S. Benhabib and J. Resnik (eds.), *Migrations and Mobilities* (New York: New York University Press, 2009). For an earlier work on statelessness in the United States, see C. Seckler-Hudson, *Statelessness: With Special Reference to the United States* (Washington, DC: Digest Press, 1934).

effective of the international instruments in giving an entitlement to citizenship, since there is a considerable imperative to comply with it. It does not, however, deal with allocating citizenship where someone has none. Moreover, though all member states of the European Union have ratified the Convention, none of the countries considered in this study has ratified the Optional Protocol that allows the Monitoring Committee to receive individual complaints of breach, and the United Kingdom has also not signed it.

The United Nations Convention on the Rights of the Child was made in 1989. Children are particularly relevant to any system of allocation of nationality; all the more so where, as in Europe, the tendency is to a *jus sanguinis* system. Like the UDHR, it suffers from problems of enforceability, though it is phrased with more practical detail of persuasive force given the widespread approval of the Convention and the political embarrassment of contravening it.[63] It is also liable to reservations: the United Kingdom in particular entered a reservation in relation to 'the entry into, stay in and departure from the United Kingdom of those who do not have the right under the law of the United Kingdom to enter and remain in the United Kingdom, and to the acquisition and possession of citizenship, as it may deem necessary from time to time'. It also entered a reservation to the requirement under Article 37 (c) that children in detention be accommodated separately from adults, in relation to young offenders 'or where the mixing of adults and children is deemed to be mutually beneficial'. This enables the United Kingdom to make no provision to make it possible for British citizen children, entitled to citizenship under the existing *jus sanguinis* system (this having come into force in 1983, there are no longer minor children born under the *jus soli*), to be brought up in the United Kingdom if they are the children of a mixed British and non-British relationship and the British parent dies or deserts them. If the foreign carer parent does not find some independent right to remain in the United Kingdom, the children will be effectively expelled with them.[64]

---

[63] See D. A. Balton, 'The Convention on the Rights of the Child: Prospects for International Enforcement', *Human Rights Quarterly*, 12 (1990), 120: there is 'relatively little attention ... focused on the prospects for legal enforcement.'

[64] C. Sawyer, 'Not Every Child Matters: The UK's Expulsion of British Citizens', *International Journal of Children's Rights*, 14 (2006), 157. Note that section 73 of the Nationality, Immigration and Asylum Act 2002, adding section 10A to the Immigration Act 1971, appeared to allow not merely effective expulsion but also formal removal. The United Kingdom has not ratified the regional Protocol against expulsion of a country's own citizens.

The International Convention on the Elimination of all Forms of Racial Discrimination explicitly draws from the idea of universality in the UDHR of 1948. The Preamble is framed in very strong terms as to the repugnance of racial discrimination and there appears to be an element of surprise inherent in the alarm that racial hostility is still evident. But Article 1, as well as devoting one paragraph to defining 'racial discrimination' and another to asserting states' rights to positive measures (affirmative action), uses its other two paragraphs to state first that the Convention does not apply to distinctions between citizens and non-citizens and secondly that, provided that there is no discrimination against any particular nationality, it does not apply to a state's definition of a citizen.[65]

In our time: statelessness in international law since the end of the Cold War

By the 1980s, while it was becoming apparent that statelessness was not disappearing, it was however still often perceived as a refugee issue. The consequences of flight on the next generation of children, born to the displaced, were also becoming apparent. In 1980 the UNHCR began to acknowledge the problem and to exhort states to deal with it. The approach was not necessarily to exhort those states to naturalise foreign refugees resident in their territory, but emphasised the desirability of repatriation. The United Nations called upon governments to provide travel documents to repatriating refugees and to help with the practicalities of their return, including intervening to arrange for the restoration of any previous but lost nationality, and in 1987 expressed concern about the growing number of stateless refugee children.[66] The close connection between refugees and statelessness (rather than an assumption that they were different sides of the same coin) was noted and states were invited to accede to the 1954 Convention on the Status of Stateless Persons and 1961 Convention on the Reduction of Statelessness, making domestic provision for the rights of stateless persons in their territories.[67] By the time these concerns were

---

[65] Though this Convention, and the Committee monitoring its implementation, has nevertheless been very productive of persuasive observations, especially about the rules for the transmission of nationality from parents to children, which may have a particular impact on minority communities. Elsewhere, the post-Dayton Bosnia-Herzegovina Constitution has been condemned for elements of racism in its electoral system: *Sejdić and Finci v. Bosnia and Herzegovina (Applications No. 27996/06 and 34836/06), Judgment 22 December 2010.*

[66] Conclusion No. 18 (XXXI) 1980; Conclusion No. 47 (XXXVIII).

[67] Conclusion No. 50 (XXXIX).

confirmed in 1991, the Conclusion included the idea that the UN human rights bodies should focus on the issue of statelessness as such, and mentioned the problems of deprivation of nationality and the 'content of the right to a nationality', and the High Commissioner was called upon to continue working towards the appropriate international instruments to set up an international body to deal with statelessness.[68]

By this time the ILO had begun formulating migrant workers' rights in 1990,[69] and the consequences of the collapse of the Soviet bloc were about to become apparent. Statelessness had previously been treated as a minor issue partly because, during the Cold War, states were relatively stable and so the numbers of stateless people in Europe were relatively small. Ethnic definitions of nationality in the Eastern states had been subsumed under political citizenship, but the political re-organisation of Eastern Europe meant that practical efforts were called for to ensure that everyone had a political citizenship, in the context of the redrawing of membership rules in the newly independent states, often on ethnic lines, and the resulting exclusions of whole communities.[70] The ILC began to focus on nationality in relation to the succession of states, and the Executive Committee called on the UNHCR to strengthen its efforts on practical issues, such as the training of staff and government officials. A systematic gathering of information, with reporting back to the Executive Committee, was required, and by the mid-1990s there was broad concern about statelessness in an age of political turbulence.[71] Stateless refugees and immigrants cannot be repatriated, but host states were increasingly failing to grant them citizenship or its incidents.

This was the era of mass flight from the former Yugoslavia. The general provisions as to states' obligations to deal with *de jure* statelessness were effectively reconfirmed,[72] and specific steps were taken, albeit institutionally, within the remit of refugee issues. A legal expert in statelessness, Carol A. Batchelor, was recruited to develop a strategic approach. Programmes of disseminating information, training staff and heightening awareness about the Conventions were instigated, and reporting procedures introduced. The High Commissioner's

---

[68] Conclusion No. 65 (XXXIX); Conclusion No. 68 (XLIII).

[69] In force 2003.

[70] UNHCR, *The State of the World's Refugees – A Humanitarian Agenda* (Oxford: UNHCR and Oxford University Press, 1997), see esp. 227.

[71] 45th Session, 1993, No. 3274; 1994 Conclusion No. 74 (XLV), Conclusion No. 78 (XLVI) of 1995, General Assembly Res. 49/51.

[72] UN General Assembly Res.50/152 of 21 December 1995.

work on stateless persons was affirmed as 'part of her statutory function of providing international protection and of seeking preventive
action'.[73] The United Nations began to focus more on statelessness in its
co-operation with the Council of Europe, the Organization for Security
and Co-operation in Europe (OSCE) and various NGOs, with particular reference to the perceived major problem areas, many of which were
the former Eastern bloc states in Europe and on her borders; indeed,
these states have received most of the UNHCR's attention in relation to
statelessness, as well as most of its resources.[74] There were, however, no
apparent new ideas as to what to do in practice.[75] In October 1998 the
UNHCR began an earnest campaign to encourage states to accede to
the Refugee and Statelessness Conventions and related instruments; in
1999 the persistence of statelessness problems was noted with concern,
and with no particular hopes of improvement mentioned.[76] A closer

[73] The United Nations, EC and General Assembly asked the UNHCR to 'provide relevant
technical and advisory services', and about 200 states were given active help with draft-
ing reforming legislation designed to implement nationality rules that were adequate but
lacked implementation. For publications by C. A. Batchelor see, for example, 'Stateless
Persons: Some Gaps in International Protection', *International Journal of Refugee
Law*, 7(2) (1995), 232; 'Statelessness and the Problem of Resolving Nationality Status',
International Journal of Refugee Law, 10 (1–2) (1998), 172; 'Transforming International
Legal Principles into National Law: The Right to a Nationality and the Avoidance of
Statelessness', *Refugee Survey Quarterly*, 25(3) (2006), 8.

[74] M. Engstrom and N. Obi, *Evaluation of the UNHCR's Role and Activities in Relation to
Statelessness* (UNHCR Evaluation and Policy Analysis Unit EPAU/2001/09), 2001, 3,
www.unhcr.org/research/RESEARCH /3b67d0fa7.pdf.

[75] In 1996, Conclusion No 79. (XLVII) recalled the problem as well as the Conventions
designed to alleviate it, and noted the accession of certain non-European states, as well as
the United Nations' efforts on training, especially in relation to refugees. Conclusion No.
80 (XLVII) of the same year focused on displacement, identifying the right to a nationality in the wider context of human rights generally and including the right to leave one's
country and the right to return. A new requirement was made of the UNHCR's field offices
that they should report on statelessness in their annual protection reports. Conclusion
No. 81 (XLVIII) of 1997 reiterated similar points and, the following year, Conclusion No.
85 (XLIX) reaffirmed the importance of the right to a nationality and, for the first time,
mentioned specifically the issue of the stateless children of refugees and asylum seekers born in the countries of refuge. The UNHCR Division of International Protection
(DIP) issued *Guidelines: Field Office Activities Concerning Statelessness* (September 1998)
(Inter-Office Memorandum No. 66/98 and Field Office Memorandum No. 70/98). The
General Assembly passed Resolutions 51/160 on 16 December 1996, resolving to work on
the topic; 52/156 on 15 December 1997, alerting states to the issue and seeking comment;
and 54/112 on 9 December 1999, including drafts in its agenda for action. By Resolution
55/153 of 12 December 2000, the General Assembly took note of the finalised articles and
recommended their dissemination; by Resolution 59/34 of 2 December 2004 it invited
states to take note of the Articles.

[76] Conclusion No. 87 (L).

focus emphasising the elements of law and practice that lead to state-lessness, with a clearer appreciation of the differences between issues of statelessness and refugee issues, was however apparent, together with an appreciation of the disproportionate impact of nationality and birth registration rules on women and children, as well as the effects of the practice of international human trafficking.[77]

Engstrom and Obi published their commentary on the United Nations' practical activities in the field of statelessness in 2001.[78] Most notably, they identified the disparate and perhaps disorganised way in which the issue had been approached. Citing queries posed by UNHCR staff on the practical and pertinent issues of what officers should or could do about stateless persons,[79] the authors recommended that such guidelines as had been produced should be consolidated into a single document and given easier circulation, and that guidelines for use at the national and regional level should be produced on the model of the non-specialist 'advocacy papers' of the Regional Bureau for Europe in relation to asylum procedures. Statistics presented particular problems, among them being states' varying descriptions of stateless persons in their territories as 'foreigners' or 'non-citizens', or their not registering their residents at all. The UNHCR similarly had a range of categories – refugees, asylum seekers, internally displaced persons, 'others of con-cern' – into which stateless persons might fall, and its field officers made no distinction between refugees with and without a nationality (that is, *de facto* and *de jure* stateless refugees). Moreover, perhaps the Formerly Deported Peoples of the former Soviet Union (FSU) aside, stateless people are usually relatively invisible. These recording problems were identified as making the facts appear unreliable and so state support

---

[77] Conclusion No 90 (LII) of 2001. UNHCR programmes had by this time been instigated in the former Soviet bloc states, beginning with the Czech Republic on the break-up of Czechoslovakia and moving on notably to the Ukraine before dealing with almost all the former Soviet countries. UNHCR worked with the IOM, the OSCE and the CIS Conference on Displacement and adopted a Programme of Action which included the principles of the 1961 Convention on the Reduction of Statelessness. The United Nations was, however, less active in other geographical areas of concern, such as the Middle East, Africa and Myanmar (Engstrom and Obi, *Evaluation*, 21–3).

[78] See n. 76 above.

[79] Engstrom and Obi, *Evaluation*, 9, cite UNHCR officials' practical questions: 'What are we supposed to do if a person claiming that he has nowhere to return to, but clearly not fulfilling the refugee criteria, comes to our doorstep and asks for assistance? What if we receive a report that a person of unidentified nationality calls for assistance from the immigration detention centre, but there is only one protection officer, whose capacity is already overstretched?'.

and funding difficult to attract.[80] The UNHCR did, however, begin in some earnest, though perhaps with mixed effects, to carry out training, to assemble information about nationality laws and jurisprudence and to ensure the dissemination of information, and try actively to work with other regional organisations. By the early twenty-first century, as well as exhorting states to take back their own displaced nationals, as well as granting status to the *de jure* stateless, the United Nations was encouraging states and the UNHCR to co-operate in resettling the displaced in new countries.[81] By the time of its report of its global survey on statelessness in 1994, it was speaking of 'an important step towards establishing a common understanding of a problem affecting all regions of the world'.[82]

There were still, however, concerns about the protracted nature of the problem, and the unwillingness of some states to accept the return of those who had previously fled as refugees.[83] Focusing in particular on problems caused in Eastern Europe by state succession issues, and leaning on an earlier assertion that states' competence to define their own nationals was bounded by the limits allowed in international law,[84] by 2006 the European Commission was ready to produce a very substantial set of re-affirmations and exhortations in its Conclusion of 2006 on Identification, Prevention and Reduction of Statelessness and Protection of Stateless Persons.[85] This urged the identification of the stateless, citing their difficulties, by programmes of birth registration and population data updating and the sharing of data and statistics among states and the UNHCR. The Conclusion includes considerable detail about how a person may be stateless, including following 'arbitrary deprivation of nationality' and such deprivation resulting from discriminatory practices. Again, the United Nations exhorted states to accede to the statelessness Conventions. The General Assembly adopted another resolution dealing with both refugees and stateless persons, emphasising, however, that although individual states should deal with refugees, the UNHCR had a primary role in relation to the *de jure* stateless. There was only a brief mention of 'other persons of concern', with no clear or concrete ideas, let

---

[80] Engstrom and Obi, *Evaluation*, 15, paras. 64–5.
[81] Conclusion No. 95 (LIV) of 2003, Conclusion No. 96 (LIV) of 2003.
[82] Conclusion No. 99 (LV) of 2004.   [83] Conclusion No. 101 (LV) of 2004.
[84] 'Nationality in Relation to the Succession of States', *Yearbook of the International Law Commission 1999* A/CN.4/SER.A/1999/Aid.1(part 2), 19 (referring to, among other things, para. 1 of the Preamble to the Venice Declaration).
[85] Conclusion No. 106 (LVI).

alone a general proposal that states be exhorted to take on enforceable commitments to protect the unwanted non-citizen.[86]

The Council of Europe and European human rights law

The experience of war in Europe lay behind not only the modern international human rights system but also the creation of the Council of Europe in 1949, as well as the industrial trade organisation that became the modern European Union.[87] Perhaps the greatest creation of the Council of Europe is the European Court on Human Rights, made in 1950 and in force in ratifying states since 1953. States parties, of which there are now forty-seven, guarantee certain rights to 'everyone within their jurisdiction'.[88] Convention rights may be enforceable at the domestic level as well as at the European Court of Human Rights (ECtHR) in Strasbourg, which has power to order offending states parties to pay damages to individuals for breach of their Convention rights. It has an established jurisprudence which continues to develop, the Convention often being referred to as a 'living instrument'. The rights are nevertheless very specific and limited, and have been criticised as individualist and Eurocentric in their construction. This is perhaps historically inevitable. When it was suggested to him on behalf of the British Government that 'there were territories in the world, such as Iraq, for which the Convention was not designed and for which they might not be ready', the English judge Rix, LJ responded that this was because '[t]he Convention was not created because of the humanity of Europe, but because of its failures'.[89]

It is often thought that 'human rights' are now universally guaranteed in Europe. It is in that idea that the merit of the ECHR might lie for the stateless, since it is of little direct help in relation to the condition of statelessness itself. There is a useful political need for states to adhere to it – especially the requirement that member states of the European Union recognise the rights under it – and its enforcement mechanisms make it of great practical importance. There is a right of individual petition to the

---

[86] Res. 60/129 of 24 January 2006, para. 20.

[87] For a heartfelt discussion of this see P. Modinos, 'Effects and Repercussions of the European Convention on Human Rights', *International & Comparative Law Quarterly*, 11 (1962), 1097.

[88] Article 1 European Convention on Human Rights 1950 (ECHR).

[89] *R (On the Application of Al-Skeini and Others) v. Secretary of State for Defence* [2004] EWHC 2911 (Admin), para. 279.

ECtHR at Strasbourg for anyone who is a victim of a breach perpetrated by a public body,[90] and the court itself is very active, though often criticised for delays. Nevertheless, the ECHR often fails the stateless of Europe and, however ironically, aspects of the case law are developing so as to exclude them.

The ECHR is even more directly rooted in the events of the Nazi regime and the Second World War than is international law. The institution that created it, the Council of Europe, was set up in May 1949, Article 1 of its Statute asserting the Council's aim to be 'to achieve a greater unity between its members for the purpose of safeguarding and realising the ideals of principles which are their common heritage and to facilitate their economic and social progress'. Article 3 required every member to accept the principles of the rule of law and the enjoyment by 'all persons within its jurisdiction of human rights and fundamental freedoms'. Work on the ECHR proceeded apace, and despite considerable redrafting and revision,[91] the Convention was signed in November 1950, about a year and a half later. The question of what individuals' rights were guaranteed does not feature much in discussions of its drafting: it was apparently assumed to be universal. The question of enforcement mechanisms attracted much more debate. It was argued that the Convention was a form of international law, the only proper subjects of which are states but, as one commentator has pointed out:

> [t]he weakness of this argument in relation to human rights is to be found in practical considerations of common sense. The object of the Convention on Human Rights is to protect the rights of the individual citizen – of the man on the Clapham omnibus. If it should happen that his rights, as defined in the Convention, are violated, this violation will in all probability be committed by his own government.[92]

A right of individual petition was therefore included in the Consultative Assembly's original proposals of August 1949, which were largely approved and reproduced in the final Convention. The creation of the Court itself was the subject of profound disagreement, and its place as the fount of European jurisprudence took longer to establish. Nevertheless, as Robertson has said, the ECHR was:

---

[90] Article 17 ECHR 1950.
[91] The UK contribution to the drafting of the text is often mentioned; see, for example, G. Marston, 'The United Kingdom's Part in the Preparation of the European Convention on Human Rights, 1950', *International & Comparative Law Quarterly*, 42 (1993), 796.
[92] A.H. Robertson, 'The European Convention for the Protection of Human Rights', *British Yearbook of International Law*, 27 (1950), 145.

a great advance on the Universal Declaration of Human Rights of the United Nations, since the latter amounted in the last analysis to nothing more than an expression of intentions, whereas the European Convention contains specific legal commitments ... the most important [being] the granting to individuals whose rights are denied of direct access to an international organ capable of protecting them; and the institution of a judicial body on the international plane competent to sit in judgement on national governments.[93]

The Convention entered into force in 1953, only four years after its conception.

The ECHR has a hold on the imagination of not only human rights activists but also the general public all over Europe and beyond. Its limitations in relation to statelessness are however profound, notwithstanding the apparent requirement to protect the rights of individuals 'within their jurisdiction'.[94] Perhaps surprisingly given its roots in reaction to the Holocaust, to which deprivation of the normal rights of citizenship was fundamental,[95] its provisions about the equal treatment by a country of its own nationals are often fragile or optional, and the protection against racial discrimination is limited to the context of the other rights under the Convention.[96] This may be because most European countries operate on a civil code model built on a written constitution giving fundamental rights to all citizens, so that differential treatment of nationals is unlawful in domestic law. Provisions explicitly requiring equal treatment of non-nationals are notably absent, and as there is no requirement on states to recognise anyone in particular as a citizen or a lawful resident, and little restriction on the expulsion of non-nationals,[97] so the unwanted may be defined as foreigners liable to exclusion, and thus beyond the practical protection of the ECHR.

---

[93] *Ibid.*, 162.

[94] Article 1 ECHR. This has become particularly obviously controversial in relation to extra-territoriality (see, for example, *Banković* 52207/99, 19 December 2001); the rights of stateless persons are the obverse of that issue.

[95] The Weimar Constitution was not abandoned under the Hitler regime in Germany, but some citizens were retained as nationals while being deprived of their civil rights, usually for reasons of race, and could subsequently be relatively easily deprived of their nationality altogether: *Reichsbürgergesetz, Gesetz zum Schutz des deutschen Blutes und der deutschen Ehre (Nürnberger Gesetz*, or 'Nuremberg Laws').

[96] See, for example, *Sejdić and Finci* (n. 65 above): race discrimination contrary to Article 14 ECHR was found in the Bosnia-Herzegovinian Constitution, related to Article 3 of Protocol No. 1 (free elections) and Article 1 of Protocol No. 12 (against discrimination), as it limited high offices to certain ethnic groups.

[97] Even the restriction on the expulsion of citizens is optional: see Protocol No. 4.

Moreover, the rights guaranteed by the ECHR are very limited. They are often characterised as 'negative' – the right not to suffer state interference with how one conducts one's life, rather than to have state provision of such positive rights as food or shelter. Though those rights do not immediately appear to address the primary concerns of those in this study, the Convention as a 'living instrument' has been subject to interpretation that does affect them. Some of the rights are absolute, and apply without qualification, apparently to all persons. Thus the right to life[98] and the right not to be subjected to torture or inhuman and degrading treatment[99] are to be respected by all states and for everyone, and where these rights conflict with the right to control population and borders, they should take precedence. A person may not only not be tortured within the states parties to the ECHR, but may also not be expelled by them to a place where they would suffer the same fate.[100] The right not to be discriminated against on the basis of nationality or national origin, however,[101] is very narrow in its application and more fragile. It applies only in relation to other Convention rights, and it does not apply in cases of admission or expulsion.[102] Indeed, if it did, it would be hard to see how any system of immigration control could work at all, since it is of the essence that foreigners are treated differently from citizens. It is at this point, where apparent universalism meets democratic accountability to a citizen electorate, that the limits of the European human rights regime – thought of as involved with or even inseparable from democracy – begin to bite.[103]

The usefulness of the ECHR to the stateless focuses on those Articles which may protect a person from being removed or deported, and to a lesser extent these may help that person establish or maintain a life in the host country. Removal or deportation may be prevented by appeal either to Articles 2 or 3, in relation to the risks that might await the person on arrival in the receiving country, or to Article 8, on the grounds that removal would split up a family or damage an established personal life in the host country. Articles 3 and 8 may also be used to challenge

---

[98] Article 2 ECHR.   [99] Article 3 ECHR.
[100] But for the application of this principle see p. 97.   [101] Article 14 ECHR.
[102] *Abdulaziz, Balkandali and Cabales* (1985) 7 EHRR 471.
[103] '[O]ne of our hard-rooted political and legal beliefs is the idea that the nation state is the one and only frame of reference in which the democratic ideal is to be implemented. The idea that there is no democracy without a nation state … remains, as to date, the central tenet of our democratic thinking': A. Verhoeven, 'Europe Beyond Westphalia', *Maastricht Journal of European and Comparative Law*, 5 (1998), 369.

the treatment of a stateless person by the host state as a resident of that state.

The Strasbourg jurisprudence on Article 3 as a means for non-nationals to resist removal, deportation or extradition[104] has largely been fuelled by the United Kingdom. *Soering* v. *UK* established that a person may not be extradited to face a trial the result of which might be the death penalty.[105] The case was developed through the judgment in *Cruz-Varas* v. *Sweden*,[106] extending it from extradition to other forms of expulsion. A medical patient in *D* v. *UK* successfully resisted deportation at the end of a sentence for drug-dealing by establishing that he was dying of AIDS and had been treated on a long-term basis by the National Health Service. He was undergoing death counselling and would die rapidly and horribly if deported; his deportation was declared contrary to Article 3.[107] However, in *N* v. *UK*, following greater publicity about unwanted foreigners using public health care in the United Kingdom and the inception of serious Europe-wide attempts at harmonising asylum and immigration processes with a general view to more efficient exclusion, the Grand Chamber confirmed that removal or deportation could be resisted for reason of illness and treatment only in the most exceptional cases, where the process of removal itself would contravene Article 3.[108] This accords with the idea that the ECHR does not affect immigration policy, but begins to raise the question as to whether the refusal of positive rights, such as the means to obtain basic necessities such as shelter and food, can amount to a breach of the Convention's negative rights.

The right in Article 8 of the ECHR to respect for one's family and private life[109] is subject to the 'margin of appreciation' which allows its application to be tempered by considerations of 'public order', including the state's interest in immigration control.[110] Moreover, the ECHR

---

[104] Removal (the French call this 'conduite à la frontière') is the least of the processes and occurs when someone with no right to be in the country is required to leave. Deportation is a more formal and personal idea: the individual has done something making the continuation of their stay undesirable, usually the commission of a criminal offence. Extradition is the removal of a person to stand trial in another country. Some countries extradite their own citizens as well as other countries' and some, as a matter of their domestic constitution, do not.

[105] (1989) 11 EHRR 439.

[106] ECtHR 20 March 2001, Case 15576/89, Series A, No. 201.

[107] (1997) 24 EHRR 423. No recounting of this case is complete without mention that D's treatment continued to be successful over many years.

[108] *N* v. *UK* (App. No. 26565/05) 27 May 2008.   [109] Article 8.

[110] This is clearer in the French 'ordre public', on which the English phrase is based, rather than in the English itself, which tends to suggest the prevention of riot. For more

does not require any bias towards the right to family integrity being respected in the country in which it is sought, or within Europe at all. A state may lawfully find that its own citizen could reasonably carry on family life in the country of a foreign spouse, rather than that spouse should be admitted to the country in question. While this could not apply in the case of a *de jure* stateless person, the situation might be less clear for the *de facto* stateless persons if the reasonableness of life in their home country were in dispute. The vindication of rights can be hedged about with procedural requirements, overt or merely factual, which make them unreachable. How far this is permissible can be the subject of debate. For example, the right in Article 12 to marry and found a family may be limited to attempt to prevent 'marriages of convenience' made for immigration purposes, but this will then have effects on the resident citizen population as well, both as to complying with the procedural rules and as to restricting whom they may marry.

Article 8 has been the subject of considerable case law, both at the domestic level and in Strasbourg. It is most associated with its protection of the right to respect for 'family life', but also encompasses 'private life', which has gradually become more important. Hugo Storey identified the Article 8 jurisprudence in immigration cases as beginning to develop in the Commission in the 1980s, though showing a narrower approach to family life in that context than elsewhere.[111] He commented, however, that the Commission was 'too wedded to the view that Article 8 cannot be breached if family members ... are able to resume family life "elsewhere"'.[112] Later commentators took varying views. Writing in 1994, Cholewinski approached the issue on the one hand more as one of community relations in the host country, focusing on the results of post-war labour policies on the recruitment of overseas workers,[113] and on the other as a means by which the ECtHR was developing an effective policy towards the protection of second-generation

generally, see N. Lavender, 'The Problem of the Margin of Appreciation', *European Human Rights Law Review*, 4 (1997), 380. See also N. Rogers, 'Immigration and the European Convention on Human Rights', *European Human Rights Law Review*, 4 (2003), 53.

[111] H. Storey, 'The Right to Family Life and Immigration Case Law at Strasbourg', *International & Comparative Law Quarterly*, 39 (1990), 28. The same trajectory was apparent in the European Community: see Case 249/86 *Commission of the EC v. Germany* [1989] ECR 1263.

[112] Storey, 'The Right to Family Life', 343.

[113] R. Cholewinski, 'The Protection of the Right of Economic Migrants to Family Reunion in Europe', *International & Comparative Law Quarterly*, 43 (1994a), 568.

migrants;[114] whereas van Dijk saw the developing jurisprudence as one of protection for those who in this study would be called *de facto* stateless – long-term non-citizen residents.[115] The ECtHR dealt with an expulsion as a breach of the Article 8 right to family life in 1991,[116] and gradually developed an approach to long-term residents that combined the protection of family and private life.[117] Later commentators turned to the use of Article 8 as a means of regularising irregular migration, with Marie Dembour discussing its potential use for 'quasi-nationals'.[118] Several cases have been dealt with by the Grand Chamber, where appeals from the ECtHR are heard. In 2001 the Court found that the deportation of an Algerian national from Switzerland was in violation of Article 8, notwithstanding his conviction for violent offences, because his wife could not reasonably accompany him to Algeria.[119] A later notable case was *Üner* v. *Netherlands*, in which it was held proportionate to expel a long-term-resident Turkish national who had been convicted of violent offences, notwithstanding that his partner and children were Dutch nationals who did not speak Turkish.[120] In a more recent case, however, the deportation of a Pakistani national who had lived in the United Kingdom since the age of three, for an isolated conviction relating to the importation of heroin when he was twenty-eight, was declared disproportionate given his family circumstances.[121]

Of particular relevance to this study is the line of cases dealing with the disenfranchised Russophone minorities in the Baltic states: *Slivenko et al.* v. *Latvia* and *Sisojeva et al.* v. *Latvia*.[122] These have been identified as having implications for the wider Europe by Daniel Thym, who also

---

[114] R. Cholewinski, 'Strasbourg's "Hidden Agenda": The Protection of Second-Generation Migrants from Expulsion', *Netherlands Quarterly of Human Rights*, 12 (1994b), 287.

[115] P. van Dijk, 'Protection of "Integrated" Aliens Against Expulsion under the European Convention on Human Rights', *European Journal of Migration and Law*, 1 (1999), 293.

[116] *Moustaquim* v. *Belgium* (App. No. 1231/86) [1991] ECHR 3, 8 February 1991.

[117] Largely through a line of cases against France: *Boujlifa* v. *France* (App. No. 25404/95), ECtHR, 21 October 1997; *Ezzouhdi* v. *France* (App. No.47160/99 13 February 2001); *Dalia* v. *France* (App. No. 26102/95 33) EHRR 625.

[118] M.-B. Dembour, 'Human Rights Law and National Sovereignty in Collusion: The Plight of Quasi-Nationals at Strasbourg', *Netherlands Quarterly of Human Rights*, 21 (2003), 63.

[119] *Boultif* v. *Switzerland* (App. No. 54273/00) 2 August 2001.

[120] App. No. 46410/99. Judgment of the Grand Chamber 18 October 2006.

[121] *A. W. Khan* v. *UK* (App. No. 47486/06).

[122] Apps. Nos. 48321/99 and 6654/00. See also N. Gelazis, 'The European Union and the Statelessness Problem in the Baltic States', *European Journal of Migration and Law*, 6(3) (2004), 225.

suggests that Article 8 might be a means to regularise an illegal stay.[123] He refers in particular to the judgments in *Mendizabal* v. *France*[124] and *Sisojeva et al.* v. *Latvia* as showing that the ECtHR now uses the provision as capable of regulating immigration practices in their broadest sense independent of family circumstances. The cases of *Shevanova* and *Kaftailova* v. *Latvia*, in which the ECtHR had found a violation of Article 8 in relation to long-term stateless ethnic Russian residents of Latvia, were resolved by the granting of long-term residence permits.[125] Thym comments that the case law appears to extend the scope of the Convention but does not, however, 'appear as a generous extension of the human rights status of illegal immigrants'. It merely makes immigration policy a factor to be considered, rather than one of overwhelming priority, in the granting of residence permits to foreign nationals.

There are additional Protocols to the ECHR, which are not always signed and ratified by all states parties to the Convention. Protocol No. 4 prohibits any expulsion by a country of its own nationals, and the collective expulsion of aliens. Most, but not all, EU states are parties to this Protocol, including the states in this study, save for the United Kingdom, which has signed but not ratified it. Optional Protocol No. 7 deals with, amongst other things, the expulsion of aliens. It addresses the codification of procedural safeguards, rights of review and of compensation. Turkey, Belgium, Germany, Spain, Ireland, the Netherlands and Portugal have signed it but not ratified it. Only the United Kingdom has not even signed it. Accession to Protocol No. 12, which prohibits all forms of discrimination (rather than just discrimination in relation to Convention rights) is very patchy. The United Kingdom and France have not signed it; Estonia and Slovenia have signed but not ratified. The first judgment that Protocol No. 12 had been breached was given in 2009.[126]

The Council of Europe has dealt elsewhere with issues affecting migrants, such as the European Convention on Establishment, made in 1955 and in force in 1965. Of the countries in this study, only the United

---

[123] D. Thym, 'Respect for Private and Family Life Under Article 8 ECHR in Immigration Cases: A Human Right to Regularize Illegal Stay?', *International & Comparative Law Quarterly*, 57 (2008), 87. Thym points out, however, that the judgment in *Slivenko* is very restrictive of the definition of 'family' (91).

[124] App. No. 51431/99 17 January 2006. Here, Article 8 was used to castigate the French government for its persistent failure to grant an appropriate long-term residence permit to a long-term-resident Spanish national who claimed no potential breach of any family connection were she to be expelled and was, in any event, under no such direct threat.

[125] Apps. Nos. 58822/00 and 59643/00, respectively. Grand Chamber decision 7 December 2007.

[126] See n. 65 above.

Kingdom has ratified it; France has signed it. Parties cannot expel nationals of other states parties after ten years' lawful residence unless there are compelling grounds such as national security.[127] This treaty has attracted relatively little support, being ratified broadly by the older member states, though Turkey has also ratified it. In the countries where it has effect, its usefulness is considerable, but only for those whose residence has been demonstrably lawful. The European Convention on the Status of Migrant Workers of 1977, which entered into force in 1983, makes provisions for recruitment, testing and granting permits to migrant workers, and also in relation to family reunion. As with the ILO instruments on the same issues, those referred to are, however, regular or lawful migrants. Moreover, very few states have signed this Convention, though of the countries in this study France has both signed and ratified it.

Of the countries in this study, none is a party to the European Convention on Nationality, though France has signed it. It was made in 1997 and entered into force in 2000, and has been described as a 'remarkable convention'.[128] It provides, among other things, for rights of naturalisation for long-term residents and requires states to grant citizenship to children born in the territory to lawful residents. The Convention does have some exhortatory strength, and indeed the changes to German nationality law at the turn of the millennium, for example, have been in accordance with it, notwithstanding that Germany did not sign or ratify the Convention until much later.[129] Of the countries in this study, only France has signed it and none has ratified it. Similarly perhaps, the 2006 Council of Europe Convention on the Avoidance of Statelessness in Relation to State Succession has few signatories or ratifications, and none from this study.

EU law

The European Union was a broader reaction to the disastrous conflict of the Second World War than the Council of Europe. The involvement

---

[127] G. Goodwin-Gill, 'The Limits of the Power of Expulsion in Public International Law', *British Yearbook of International Law*, 55 (1974–5), 55.

[128] See G.-R. de Groot, 'The European Convention on Nationality: A Step Towards a *ius commune* in the Field of Nationality Law', *Maastricht Journal of European and Comparative Law*, 7(2) (2000), 117.

[129] *Micheletti* 7 July 1992 Case C-369/90 [1992] ECR I-4239. See also G.-R. de Groot, 'The Relationship between the Nationality Legislation of the Member States of the European Union and European Citizenship', in M. La Torre (ed.), *European Citizenship: An Institutional Challenge* (The Hague, London and Boston: Kluwer Law International, 1998), 115.

of the legislative provisions on human rights and related issues made by
the European Union in the ECHR can cause confusion between the two,
particularly perhaps because the European Union is not seen as a human
rights institution, or even because the European Parliament, an EU institution, is located in Strasbourg, the home of the ECtHR, leading to frequent confusion – at least in the media – of the ECtHR with the Court
of Justice of the European Union (ECJ), which is nevertheless located in
Luxembourg. Moreover, persistent contravention of the ECHR has been
asserted as a reason why Turkey might not join the European Union and
the European Union has considered acceding to the ECHR.

What is now the European Union has expanded from its original six
central members to its current twenty-seven members,[130] with Turkey and
Croatia currently hoping for admission within the next few years. When
states first accede, it is permitted for them to be integrated slowly, so there
may be some delay in according full rights of movement and free labour.
European privileges generally apply to nationals of the wider European
Economic Area (EEA) and Switzerland rather than merely the Union
itself, but because the concept of European citizenship, established in the
Treaty of Maastricht, applies to citizens of the member states only, it is
thus founded in the national laws of the individual member countries
and applies to them only. The idea of the residence rights of permanent
residents of member countries who are non-European citizens being fully
recognised among other countries of the Union is gaining ground, but
has not yet been achieved.[131]

The origins of the Union may have been essentially the same as those of
the ECHR, but where the ECHR attempts to prevent oppression of individuals by protecting a bottom line of basic rights against breach by signatory states, the precursor of the current European Union attempted to
make a further war unthinkable or unworkable by committing a core of
Central Western Europe to co-operation in the production of coal and
steel through the European Coal and Steel Community. Through the rise
of market ideas in the later twentieth century, trade and the European
free market were developed (with growing central regulation – towards
state deregulation, or the withdrawal of state protectionism) of the free
movement of goods, capital and labour. Rules made by the European

---

[130] Germany, France, Belgium, Netherlands, Luxembourg, Italy, Ireland, Spain, Portugal,
Greece, Malta, Czech Republic, Slovakia, Slovenia, Lithuania, Latvia, Estonia, Hungary,
Poland, Finland, Austria, Cyprus, UK, Denmark, Sweden, Bulgaria and Romania.

[131] Council Directive 2003/109/EC concerning the status of third-country nationals who
are long-term residents.

Commission on behalf of the European Economic Community (EEC) and then the European Union are generally directly applicable within the member states, to the extent of arguably infringing state sovereignty in the areas in which those states have accepted the effective competence of Europe.[132] This means that whatever effective rules are made by the Union apply throughout the now considerable EU area.

The EU rules most relevant to this study are those that prohibit discrimination on the grounds of nationality,[133] and the copious rules related to freedom of movement. However, the scope of the impact of EU law is very different from that of the ECHR, because whereas the ECHR appears to be universalist but arguably applies somewhat less to non-nationals of the state against whom it is enforced, EU law appears to apply only to European citizens (citizens of a member state of the EU) but often gives rights to others, through agreements that cover other countries, such as the Accession and Mediterranean Agreements – or, more commonly, through the rights given to non-European members of the families of Union citizens. The EU requires that migrant workers from other member states must enjoy equal treatment in work and employment with the host country's own nationals.[134] To make the free movement of labour a realistic proposition, states are also required to permit the entry and residence of the family members of those citizens and to provide education for their children on the same basis as that of their own nationals' children. This area has given rise to a considerable body of case law and commentary, as has the developing law on residence rights for third-country family members.[135] The Union may give considerable rights to non-European citizens, especially where they are the members of EU nationals' families, but there is also a growing focus on the harmonisation and effective implementation of rules to identify unwanted immigrants, to prevent their entry into Europe and to make arrangements for their return, forcibly if necessary, to their countries of

---

[132] *Van Gend en Loos* [1963] CMLR 105.   [133] Article 12 (ex Article 6).

[134] This point, which is now well understood, seems to have been appreciated only slowly: see A. C. Evans, 'Development of European Community Law Regarding the Trade Union and Related Rights of Migrant Workers', *International & Comparative Law Quarterly*, 28 (1979), 354.

[135] See, for example, *Zhu and Chen* v. *UK* C-200/02 [2004] ECR I-9925. For commentary generally, see E. Guild, K. Groenendijk and H. Dogan, *Security of Residence for Aliens in Europe* (Strasbourg: Council of Europe, 1996), E. Spaventa, *Free Movement of Persons in the European Union: Barriers to Movement in Their Constitutional Context* (The Hague: Kluwer Law International, 2007).

origin. The focus is therefore on the importance of European citizenship, rather than on citizenship as a universal right.

The interrelationship between member state and European citizenship rules was notably tested in the case of *Janko Rottmann* v. *Freistaat Bayern*.[136] Here, Mr Rottmann became *de jure* stateless after he renounced Austrian citizenship in order to take up German citizenship, and his German citizenship was then withdrawn because of deception in the naturalisation process. Pointing out that the case 'raises for the first time the question of the extent of the discretion available to the member States to determine who their nationals are', in his Opinion, the Advocate General Poiares Maduro posited some possibility of a European-level governance of how member states might operate.[137] He suggested that 'although it is true that nationality of a Member State is a precondition for access to Union citizenship, it is equally true that the body of rights and obligations associated with the latter cannot be limited in an unjustified manner', but went on to say that, nevertheless, 'it cannot reasonably be inferred from this that it is absolutely impossible to deprive a person of nationality, where such deprivation would entail the loss of Union citizenship'.[138] The reason given is the 'fundamental nature of the Member States' autonomy' in deciding who their nationals are, and the impossibility of the maintenance of Union citizenship becoming a basis for demanding maintenance of citizenship of a member state. In the judgment itself, the ECJ avoids confronting the issue of statelessness directly, asserting that it was not contrary to EU law, in particular Article 17 EC, for Germany to withdraw a citizenship obtained by deception, provided the withdrawal is proportionate, and avoiding the issue of whether Austria could be obliged to take Mr Rottmann back by finding that it had not yet finally decided not to.[139]

Co-operation on the harmonisation of approaches to immigration was originally made in 1975, being put on a firm footing under the Treaty of Maastricht in 1993 and then given a legislative foundation under the Treaty of Amsterdam in 1999. A meeting in Tampere in October 1999 was devoted to creating a common European asylum system and a common asylum process. There had been a previous attempt to regulate and prevent 'asylum shopping' within Europe with the creation of the 'Dublin Convention' in 1990. This attempted to implement a system for returning asylum seekers from outside Europe to the first European country

[136] Case C-135/08.   [137] 30 September 2009.
[138] See n. 137 above, paras. 23–24.   [139] 2 March 2010, paras. 59 and 63.

in which they landed in order to have their asylum claim dealt with, so that effectively only one application could be made in Europe. As became apparent when it began operation in 1997, the 'Dublin Convention' was not easily implemented. 'Dublin II' is the later, more successful attempt at establishing criteria for deciding which member state would examine an asylum application.[140] The operation of this system relies at the practical level on the EURODAC fingerprint recording system, which began operating in 2003 and was originally designed to identify and track asylum seekers.[141]

The Treaty of Nice also came into effect in 2003, setting out how asylum decisions would be made in Europe, namely by qualified majority voting, and in November 2005 the Hague Programme set out plans for a comprehensive asylum and migration policy across Europe. Topics to be covered include plans for the integration of wanted migrants, uniform visa formats with harmonisation of visa systems and a central record of visas granted or refused,[142] and the return of the unwanted to their countries of origin. The last policy also included the negotiation of re-admission agreements with non-EU countries to which returns were historically difficult for practical or legal reasons, especially because there was a risk of contravention of Article 3 of the ECHR. Directives on a number of practical asylum issues were made.[143] These are of great importance because of their wide applicability. Further issues to be decided at a European level include measures to counter human trafficking, family reunion policy and the status of non-citizen permanent residents of EU countries, especially the extent to which they are permitted to take advantage of the freedom to cross internal borders within

---

[140] Council Regulation (EC) No. 343/2003 ('Dublin II') of 18 February 2003 and Commission Regulation (EC) No. 1560/2003 of 2 September 2003. See also chapter 10 in this volume.

[141] OJ 2000 C337 E/37; OJ 2001 C 29 E/1.

[142] The EU Visa Information System (VIS).

[143] Directive on Reception Conditions for Asylum Seekers 2003/9/EC; Directive regarding the Giving of Temporary Protection by Member States in the event of a mass influx of displaced persons (the Temporary Protection Directive) CD 2001/55/EC of 20 July 2001; Direction 2004/83/EC on minimum standards for the qualification and status of the third country nationals or stateless persons as refugees or as persons who otherwise need international protection and the content of the protection granted of 29 April 2004; Directive on minimum standards on procedures in Member States for the granting and withdrawal of refugee status 2005/85/EC of 1 December 2005. See also R. Plender, 'Competence, European Community Law and Nationals of Non-Member States', *International & Comparative Law Quarterly*, 39 (1990), 599 and H. Lambert, 'The EU Asylum Qualification Directive, its Impact on the Jurisprudence of the United Kingdom and International Law', *International & Comparative Law Quarterly*, 55 (2006), 161.

the Union. This applies particularly within the Schengen system, to which Estonia, France and Slovenia in this study belong, but the United Kingdom does not.[144]

The Union is now arguably of even broader relevance to the legal position of stateless persons in Europe than is the ECHR, though perhaps more at the policy level. The two systems are in any case becoming more closely entwined. Given their very different policies on the importance of citizenship, with the Union finding it fundamental in theory but granting wide rights to non-nationals in practice and the ECHR being apparently committed to universalism while in reality often being unavailable or unhelpful to non-nationals, this could be the most interesting element of the combination.

Conclusion

Domestic laws rarely give state support to non-citizens, and international and regional law rarely require it. The dictum of Hannah Arendt that citizenship is the 'right to have rights' and that the stateless are liable to be deprived of human rights remains largely true. International and regional law that appears to be universalist may be unenforceable because there is no means for individuals to vindicate the rights it appears to give or because states may avoid their obligations by a variety of means, including expulsion of the individual concerned. Some rights are more vindicable than others, such as the right not to be tortured, but the day-to-day positive rights that make general life workable, such as the right to shelter or to make a living, are not so widely or easily available.

European countries have more homogeneous state citizenship policies than they used to, but the current position still allows for statelessness. The reasons for this include the loss of the *jus soli* within Europe, so that many countries implement a *jus sanguinis* policy that effectively excludes large numbers of their long-term residents. These may include native-born residents who fall outside the definition of 'citizen' employed by that political state, either because they are the children of irregular migrants or, more broadly, because they are not of the approved ethnicity. In effect, current citizenship policies recognise not the results of established and continuing migration but only migration as desired and managed at state policy level. The physical exclusion of irregular migrants and their

---

[144] M. Colvin, 'The Schengen Information System: A Human Rights Audit', *European Human Rights Law Review*, 3 (2001), 271.

families is increasingly encouraged and enforced by the withdrawal of everyday rights. Where this does not result in those migrants leaving the country – and in many cases it does not – then the result is a disenfranchisement and dispossession at the state level which international and regional law rarely offers any practical means of countering. The apparently universal system of human rights offers little to someone who needs the practical wherewithal of everyday life, and, though there are policies for integration of regular settled migrants, the efforts of the European Union are focused on the exclusion of the unwanted. While some people leave, many do not, often because of conditions in the alternative country. The result over time is dispossessed communities living within but excluded from the citizenry.

5

Policy responses and global discourses on the rights of non-citizens and stateless people

BRAD K. BLITZ

Introduction

This chapter surveys the discourse on non-citizens and stateless people and assesses the degree to which it is affecting policy development and reform. It notes that this discourse is produced by a number of actors including the United Nations High Commissioner for Refugees (UNHCR), human rights monitoring bodies, domestic legislators, policy-makers and academics as well as a collection of grass-roots activists primarily based in Europe, North America, Asia and Africa. Recognising that, in contrast to the situation with the Refugee Convention, few states are parties to the Statelessness Conventions, the focus here is the development of a human rights discourse regarding the rights of non-nationals and the corresponding efforts by national, non-governmental and international actors to promote these rights. To this end, this chapter investigates the institutionalisation and diffusion of norms, principles and knowledge of the rights of *de facto* stateless people as set out in earlier chapters. I first examine the international relations literature on norms and international co-operation before considering the development of international advocacy on statelessness-related issues, and in particular the actions of the UNHCR and associated agencies. This is followed by a review of global and regional initiatives by international and local NGOs and civil society organisations. The chapter concludes with an evaluation of the discourse on statelessness on policy and considers ways in which policy co-ordination and co-operation in support of an inclusive agenda that respects the rights of *de facto* stateless people in Europe may be strengthened.

Research context

The situation of non-citizens in the European Union has attracted considerable interest among human rights activists, policy-makers and the wider public, though for different reasons. Europe is home to an estimated 69.8 million non-EU migrants (9.5 per cent of the total population) and the change in demography now poses an important test to its promises of liberalism, including the way in which non-citizens are treated.[1] Non-EU nationals have been the subject of intense political arguments over the degree to which individual member states have a responsibility to accept certain categories of migrants, including asylum seekers, and provide social assistance and services to them.[2] Further states, such as Italy,[3] have re-examined their commitments to non-EU nationals during a period of increasing xenophobia as migrants have been blamed for 'taking jobs' from nationals and have been identified with crime and other social ills. As scapegoats for failed social policies, above all failures in job creation and poverty reduction, migrants have also been the victims of violent attacks across Europe. On the French island of Corsica in 2006, there were 236 attacks on immigrants[4]; in May 2008, Roma camps in Ponticelli just outside Naples were destroyed by approximately 400 armed locals who proceeded to attack the residents with metal bars; in Belfast in June 2009 more than 100 Roma from Romania were attacked by locals[5] in what was described by the Simon Wiesenthal Centre as a 'pogrom'.[6]

---

[1] International Organization for Migration (IOM), *World Migration 2008: Managing Labour Mobility in the Evolving Global Economy* (Geneva: IOM, 2008).

[2] 'Social Security: Proposal to Extend Future Regulations to Foreigners', *European Report* (30 July 2007) and K. B. Richburg, 'Security Curtain Raised Along EU's New Eastern Front: Tightened Borders Draw Concerns About Impact on Neighboring Nations', *Washington Post* (July 31, 2003).

[3] See L. Clarke, *Editorial: Immigrants or Foreign Residents?* (17 February 2010), www.wantedinrome.com/articles/complete_articles.php?id_art=1000.

[4] United States Department of State, *2008 Human Rights Report: France, Bureau of Democracy, Human Rights, and Labor – 2008 Country Reports on Human Rights Practices* (February 25, 2009), www.state.gov/g/drl/rls/hrrpt/2008/eur/119079.htm, accessed 4 December 2009.

[5] 'On May 13, 300 to 400 local residents assaulted one of the largest Roma camps in the area, home to 48 families. Hooded men armed with metal bars pulled down a fence, shouted insults and threats, threw stones, and overturned some cars. Authorities evacuated encampments and relocated former residents to a larger camp protected by police. On May 14, two abandoned groups of shacks were set afire, presumably by the same group of vandals, and with the approval of some local residents, who heckled fire-fighters when they arrived. By May 15, all Roma in the area had been forced to leave the Ponticelli camps to go to camps and a school in other districts.' See United States Department of State, *2008 Human Rights Report*.

[6] See Simon Wiesenthal Centre, 'SWC to New European Parliament Head: Quarantine New MEPs Elected on Platform of Hate', (10 August) (Paris: Simon Wiesenthal Centre,

Public responses to the arrival and settlement of non-EU nationals have had a profound influence on the design of restrictive national policies regarding migration, asylum and law enforcement. Political leaders from Silvio Berlusconi to Gordon Brown have courted populist anti-immigrant sentiment in the run-up to national elections,[7] while other states have actively prevented migrants reaching places of safety by intercepting and returning them.[8] For example, in the Mediterranean, Greece has been accused of 'push-backs' – forcing ships carrying migrants including asylum seekers back into international waters – while Italy has similarly refused to allow ships to dock and has introduced a policy of finger-printing migrants.[9] Yet, the increasingly restrictive policies and questionable human rights practices have also generated protest and criticism over the treatment of non-nationals in the European Union. As Rainer Bauböck found in his study on acquisition and loss of nationality (2006), political pressure from *both* pro- and anti-immigrant forces has helped to define the situation for non-citizens and increase their profile since European governments tended to respond by refining legal provisions which have been open to challenge.[10]

State policies and actions against non-nationals have created a new, normative battleground over the rights of non-nationals inside the European Union. As noted in chapter 1, several contemporary social theorists have sought to clarify the standing of non-nationals in the liberal state. Such intellectual trends are significant because they also point to a rupture between Hobbesian claims of national sovereignty, with clearly demarcated lines of authority, and the development of a discourse on human rights which, though anchored to the national state system, is fundamentally universal and de-territorialised. Such tension is also at odds

---

2009), www.wiesenthal.com/site/apps/nlnet/content2.aspx?c=lsKWLbPJLnF&b= 5711841&ct=7298057.

[7] See D. Summers' two pieces, 'Gordon Brown's "British Jobs" Pledge has Caused Controversy Before', *The Guardian* (30 January 2009a), www.guardian.co.uk/ politics/2009/jan/30/brown-british-jobs-workers and 'Brown stands by British Jobs for British Workers Remark', *The Guardian* (30 January 2009b), www.guardian.co.uk/ politics/2009/jan/30/brown-british-jobs-workers.

[8] B. Frelick, 'Greece's Refugee Problem', *New York Times* (July 30, 2009); and Human Rights Watch, *Stuck in a Revolving Door: Iraqis and Other Asylum Seekers and Migrants at the Greece/Turkey Entrance to the European Union*, Human Rights Watch (Document 1–56432–411–7) (November 2008), www.hrw.org/en/node/76211/section/10.

[9] *Ibid.*

[10] R. Bauböck (ed.), *Migration and Citizenship: Legal Status, Rights and Political Participation* (Amsterdam: Amsterdam University Press, 2006).

with the longer-term history of foreigners who, as John Torpey records in *The Invention of the Passport: Surveillance, Citizenship, and the State* (2000), were until the eighteenth century able to travel quite freely both within and between European jurisdictions. While their fates were circumscribed by restrictions over involvement in military matters, with the exception of Jews and some other religious minorities there was considerably less societal discrimination against migrants than in the modern period. Indeed, during the Middle Ages, Charlemagne welcomed foreigners and there was extensive evidence of cross-border movements, many of which were voluntary.[11]

The rise in border controls and the creation of social hierarchies that divided individuals on the basis of formal membership accelerated periods of state development which were above all characterised by national integration projects and secessionist attempts from larger political units in the nineteenth and twentieth centuries. Arguably, in many parts of Europe today, similar tensions influence the way in which non-citizens are treated, especially in states which are still coming to terms with new national identities, following independence and the collapse of larger systems of political organisation (colonialism, imperialism and communism) and as a result of increased multicultural and multiethnic interaction. Such pressures challenge the idea of the Westphalian state where identities were seen as shallow and historically contingent and where rights were bestowed upon subjects rather than universally held.

One distinct consequence of the transformation of the modern state has been a substantive normative shift in the discourse on membership, which is of particular relevance to this book. While the European Union has extended considerable rights to non-citizens living within its borders, including the rights to vote in local elections, the principle of non-discrimination has been simultaneously developed as a tenet of international law. The spirit of non-discrimination, primarily on the grounds of race and religion, has now been extended to include a host of other social categories. As Rawls has noted elsewhere, if liberal states have

---

[11] Einhard writes, '[Charlemagne] liked foreigners, and was at great pains to take them under his protection. There were often so many of them, both in the palace and the kingdom, that they might reasonably have been considered a nuisance; but he, with his broad humanity, was very little disturbed by such annoyances, because he felt himself compensated for these great inconveniences by the praises of his generosity and the reward of high renown', see Einhard, *The Life of Charlemagne* (written *c.* 830) (Ann Arbor: University of Michigan Press, Ann Arbor Paperbacks, 1960), 49. J. Torpey, *The Invention of the Passport: Surveillance, Citizenship and the State* (Cambridge: Cambridge University Press, 2000).

not formally outlawed discrimination on ethnic and racial lines, as in the European Union, they have certainly made it distinctly unpopular and the subject of far-reaching moral condemnation.[12] For this reason, Seyla Benhabib (2004) argues there is now an accepted belief that, on the basis of human rights, minorities, foreigners, and others have legitimate claims on states where they reside, irrespective of their citizenship status.[13]

The 'shift' in states' attitudes towards non-citizens is particularly relevant to this study on *de facto* statelessness and exclusion in the European Union. Many non-citizens inside Europe would not be considered to be stateless in a legal sense, since the degree to which they have 'effective' nationality is open to debate and depends on individual case histories; their plight has nonetheless been associated with an emerging global discourse on the rights of foreigners and 'others' without regular immigration status, including unsuccessful asylum seekers, overstayers and other irregular migrants.

Normative development and international co-operation

Liberal approaches to international relations have given much consideration to mechanisms that foster shared expectations and encourage co-operation between states. One particular school of thought, 'regime theory', analyses co-operation with a view to understanding how institutions may bring together individual state actors. In this context, a regime is defined as a 'set of explicit or implicit principles, norms, rules and decision making procedures around which actor expectations converge in a given issue-area'.[14] Much of the literature considers regimes as deliberate constructions around particular issues and interests; how they develop, however, is varied.[15] Krasner identifies five basic causal variables that identify regime development and include (1) egotistic self-interest (on the part of states), (2) political power (expressed by particular states), (3) the diffusion of norms and principles, (4) custom and usage and (5) knowledge.[16]

---

[12] J. Rawls, *Political Liberalism* (New York: Columbia University Press, 1993).
[13] S. Benhabib, *The Rights of Others: Aliens, Residents, and Citizens* (Cambridge: Cambridge University Press, 2004).
[14] S. D. Krasner (1982), 'Structural Causes and Regime Consequences: Regimes as Intervening Variables', *International Organization*, 36 (1982), 185.
[15] A. Hasenclever, P. Mayer and V. Rittberger, 'Integrating Theories of International Regimes', *Review of International Studies*, 26 (2000), 3.
[16] Krasner, 'Structural Causes'.

The central importance of regimes is that in addition to facilitating co-operation, they affect the behaviour of states and may encourage joint or convergent policy responses – for example, around the reduction of carbon emissions or the practice of banning all but the 'dolphin-friendly' fishing for tuna. Although regime theory has historically prioritised the state as the key interlocutor in international relations, the role of non-governmental bodies and non-state norm-creating institutions has also received considerable attention over the past fifteen years and has given rise to the discussions about the intersection between ideas, interests and joint policy actions,[17] and the role of normative factors in the development of international co-operation.[18] Further attention to the role of trans-national, non-state and advocacy-based actors has also helped to shape a specific discourse on an emergent 'human rights' regime which embraces many of the benefits of increased global communication.[19] Such regimes are notably different from international regimes where specific institutions are forged out of state interests, for example, the Organisation of the Petroleum Exporting Countries (OPEC). Human rights regimes are not intended to address the challenge of collective action, and measuring their effectiveness is notably problematic.[20] One way to do so, however, is at the level of discourse.

Goldstein and Keohane, in their study of regimes and foreign policy, argue that while many ideas are expressed as rational interests, others develop differently; to this end, they identify 'world views', as illustrated by religious traditions; 'principled beliefs', which specify right from wrong; and causal beliefs which 'derive their authority from shared consensus', for example, those of scientists.[21] Of the above categories of ideas, principled beliefs are the most relevant to this study. As discussed by Monika Krause and Matthew Gibney in chapters 2 and 3 of this book, a central premise of this study is that there is convergence in social and

---

[17] J. Goldstein and R. Keohane, 'Ideas and Foreign Policy: An Analytical Framework', in J. Goldstein and R. Keohane (eds.), *Ideas and Foreign Policy* (Ithaca, NY: Cornell University Press, 1993); K. A. Sikkink, S. Khagram and J. Riker (eds.), *Restructuring World Politics: Transnational Social Movements, Networks, and Norm* (Minneapolis, MN: University of Minnesota Press, 2002); and K. A. Sikkink and M. E. Keck, *Activists Beyond Borders* (Ithaca, NY: Cornell University Press, 1999).

[18] See R. Goodman and D. Jinks, 'How to Influence States: Socialization and International Human Rights Law', *Duke Law Journal*, 54 (2004), 621.

[19] Sikkink and Keck, *Activists Beyond Borders*; Kikkink, Khagram and Riker, *Restructuring World Politics*.

[20] Goodman and Jinks, 'How to Influence States'.

[21] Goldstein and Keohane, 'Ideas and Foreign Policy', 8–9.

political thinking on the rights of non-citizens, a claim which is increasingly upheld by human rights lawyers.[22] In addition, it is helpful to review the approach taken by Goodman and Jinks in their study of human rights regimes which advances an argument for *acculturation* and suggests that such social processes may inform our understanding of the ways in which 'norms operate in international society with a view to improving the capacity of legal institutions to promote respect for human rights'.[23] In this setting, acculturation explains how changes in the social environment can affect behaviour, often by tacitly encouraging conformity.

The central challenge, then, is to identify which norms have been expressed, establish how they are being disseminated and locate ways in which they have been institutionalised. Below we consider the human rights discourse around the principle of non-discrimination, as advanced in international law, through advocacy organisations and through social action and public campaigns initiated by *de facto* stateless people themselves. The principle of non-discrimination is centrally important because, as noted above, permanent residents are so close to citizens in all but formal status that to discriminate against them is contrary to the idea of universal human rights, especially in Europe where in the orbit of the European Convention on Human Rights (ECHR) human rights explicitly must be accorded to all those within the jurisdiction (Article 1).

Human rights discourses and international advocacy

In the context of *de facto* statelessness, international jurisprudence on the prohibition of nationality-based discrimination has recently been encouraged by the advocacy efforts of international organisations, non-governmental actors and particular states to respect the rights of non-citizens. High-profile organisations and individuals, including the UN Secretary General, have drawn an explicit link between the importance of nationality and the promotion and protection of all human rights, civil, political, economic, social and cultural rights, including the right to

---

[22] J. A. Goldston, 'Holes in the Rights Framework: Racial Discrimination, Citizenship, and the Rights of Noncitizens', *Ethics & International Affairs*, 20, (2006) 321; L. Van Waas, *Nationality Matters: Statelessness Under International Law* (Antwerp: Intersentia, 2008); D. Weissbrodt, *Final Report on the Rights of Non-Citizens*, UN Doc. E/CN.4/Sub.2/2003/23 (Geneva: UNHCR, 2003); D. Weissbrodt and C. Collins, 'The Human Rights of Stateless Persons', *Human Rights Quarterly*, 28(1) (2006), 245; D. Weissbrodt, *The Human Rights of Non-Citizens* (Oxford: Oxford University Press, 2008).

[23] Goodman and Jinks, 'How to Influence States', 621.

development.[24] Further publications by high-level working groups within the UN system, in addition to UN agencies and specialised NGOs, have put the issue of statelessness firmly on the global agenda.

Advocacy at the United Nations

Within the UN system, several working groups have sought to address the problems related to exclusion and denial of citizenship, above all the Committee on the Elimination of Racial Discrimination (CERD) which has consistently sought to raise awareness of this issue. In March 1997, at its fiftieth session, CERD proposed that the Sub-Commission on Prevention of Discrimination and Protection of Minorities prepare a study on the rights of non-citizens. Two years later, the Commission on Human Rights' Sub-Commission on the Prevention of Minorities Working Group on Minorities published a report entitled *Citizenship and the Minority Rights of Non-Citizens* (Eide 1999b). This report examined four questions in the context of citizenship controversies, namely, the status of those who: (a) already have the citizenship of the state concerned but are at risk of losing it, (b) live in a territory which has come under new sovereignty and thus need a new citizenship, (c) are stateless, or (d) have moved from their country of citizenship to another country to settle there. The report recorded that states may not make distinctions between different sets of applicants for naturalisation and that doing so might be a violation of the International Covenant on the Elimination of All Forms of Racial Discrimination. The report also noted that many states ignore this rule.[25]

In 2001, David Weissbrodt, UN Special Rapporteur on Non-Citizens, issued his preliminary report entitled, *Prevention of Discrimination and Protection of Indigenous Peoples and Minorities –The Rights of Non-Citizens*, which was followed by a final report two years later.[26] In these reports, Weissbrodt highlighted the use of measures by states to exclude

---

[24] See United Nations General Assembly, *The Right to Development: Report of the Secretary-General on the Right to Development*, Document A/63/340, Sixty Third Session (2 September 2008) http://daccess-dds-ny.un.org/doc/UNDOC/GEN/N08/493/97/PDF/N0849397.pdf?OpenElement.

[25] A. Eide, 'The Non-Inclusion of Minority Rights: Resolution 217C(III)', in G. Alfredsson and A. Eide (eds.), *The Universal Declaration of Human Rights – A Common Standard of Achievement* (The Hague: Martinus Nijhoff, 1999), 701.

[26] D. Weissbrodt, *Final Report on the Rights of Non-Citizens*, UN Doc. E/CN.4/Sub.2/2003/23 (Geneva: UNHCR, 2003).

persons and deprive them of their most fundamental rights, including the right to citizenship. The 2003 report considered the problem of denial of citizenship with particular reference to state succession and provided a working definition of discrimination as an action which 'lacked objective and reasonable justification'.[27] It also established the parameters under which states may differentiate in their treatment of citizens and non-citizens and criticised the design of restrictive citizenship laws that have either the purpose or effect of discriminating on the basis of race, ethnicity, national origin or other prohibited criteria.

Also in 2003, the UN Commission on Human Security produced a report, *Human Security Now*, that underlined the importance of citizenship for respect of other rights and the advancement of human security. It defined 'human security' as complementing state security, furthering human development and enhancing human rights; it also noted that the denial of citizenship undermined the promise of human security:

> Citizenship … determines whether a person has the right to take part in decisions, voice opinions and benefit from the protection and rights granted by a state. But the outright exclusion and discriminatory practices against people and communities – often on racial, religious, gender or political grounds – makes citizenship ineffective. Without it, people cannot attain human security.[28]

The argument that citizenship is essential for human security became a central focus of inquiry for CERD, which in 2004 issued its *General Recommendation No. 30* drawing attention to the practice of discrimination against non-citizens and connecting the issues of discrimination, denial of citizenship and the social and economic effects of exclusion. In this document, CERD made specific recommendations and noted the problems of denial of citizenship that resulted from barriers to naturalisation and the relationship between denial of citizenship and the Convention's anti-discrimination principles.[29]

In 2008, the Independent Expert on Minorities Gay McDougall, issued her own report on the discriminatory denial or deprivation of citizenship as a tool for exclusion of national, ethnic, religious and linguistic

---

[27] *Ibid.*

[28] Human Security Commission, *Human Security Now: Protecting and Empowering People* (New York: Commission on Human Security, 2003), 133, www.humansecurity-chs.org/finalreport/English/FinalReport.pdf.

[29] United Nations Committee on the Elimination of Racial Discrimination, *United Nations Committee on the Elimination of Racial Discrimination 2004. General Recommendation No. 30: Discrimination against Non-Citizens* (Geneva: Office of the High Commissioner for Human Rights, 2004), CERD/C/64/Misc.11/Rev.3.

minorities. McDougall claimed that discrimination was both 'a cause and a consequence of State actions that seek to marginalize minorities' and reiterated the finding of the Human Rights Committee, in its general comment No. 15 which argued against a firm distinction between aliens (non-citizens) and formal citizens. She also illustrated the extent of the problem by recording abuse against minorities who had been denied or deprived of citizenship in Africa, Asia, Europe, Latin America and the Caribbean. Her report concluded with further recommendations to correct and prevent situations that might give rise to the denial and deprivation of nationality – for example, by registering all children and issuing birth certificates immediately, allowing for the possibility of multiple nationality and providing full access to identity documentation in a non-discriminatory manner.[30]

In addition, it is important to highlight the work of the Human Rights Council which has passed several resolutions on issues relating to statelessness, most importantly, Resolution 7/10 of 27 March 2008 on Human Rights and the Arbitrary Deprivation of Nationality, which called upon the Secretary-General of the United Nations to gather information from states on this matter. In January 2009 the Secretary-General published reports received from twenty-nine states[31] and also included responses from the UNHCR, international organisations and non-governmental bodies, including Refugees International.[32] The Secretary-General's report enabled the UNHCR to make general recommendations and publicised the ongoing challenge of statelessness at the highest level within the UN system. It was followed up by another report in December 2009, which recalled states' obligations to implement fully the principle of non-discrimination and to prevent statelessness. It also addressed the question of the right to a nationality and arbitrary deprivation of nationality, in the context of state succession.[33]

---

[30] Office of the High Commissioner for Refugees (OHCHR), *Promotion and Protection of All Human Rights, Civil, Political, Economic, Social and Cultural Rights, Including the Right to Development: Report of the Independent Expert on Minority Issues, Gay McDougall*, A/HRC/7/23 (28 February 2008), www.unhcr.org/refworld/docid/47d685ea2.html.

[31] Responses were received from: Algeria, Angola, Azerbaijan, Belarus, Bosnia-Herzegovina, Bulgaria, Burkina Faso, Colombia, Congo, Costa Rica, Ecuador, Finland, Georgia, Greece, Guatemala, Iraq, the Islamic Republic of Iran, Jamaica, Kuwait, Mauritius, Monaco, Montenegro, Qatar, the Russian Federation, Spain, the Syrian Arab Republic, Ukraine and Venezuela.

[32] United Nations Human Rights Council (UNHRC), 'Arbitrary Deprivation of Nationality: Report of the Secretary-General', A/HRC/10/34 (26 January) (Geneva: UN Human Rights Council, 2009), www.unhcr.org/refworld/docid/49958be22.html.

[33] United Nations General Assembly, *Human Rights and Arbitrary Deprivation of Nationality, Report of the Secretary-General*, Document A/HRC/13/34, Thirteenth Session

The UNHCR and other UN bodies

Since 1974, when the Convention on the Reduction of Statelessness came into effect, the UNHCR has sought to examine and assist individual claims for protection under the category of stateless person. Although relatively few states are signatories to the statelessness conventions, since the mid-1970s the UNHCR's mandate has expanded and the agency now has a global mandate on statelessness which is not limited to states that are a party to either the 1961 or 1954 Conventions. The UNHCR now operates a dedicated unit devoted to the issue of statelessness which has become increasingly active, thanks in part to the ground-breaking work and publications by Carol Batchelor,[34] which have sought to examine ways in which international law could be clarified and used to protect stateless people. Subsequent efforts by Philippe Leclerc and Mark Manly have sought to draw more signatories to the UN Conventions while calling attention to the many ways in which protection can be afforded to stateless people and the fact that stateless people enjoy human rights.[35]

The UNHCR's 2006 Executive Committee Conclusion on statelessness has served as a blueprint for action on the issue and has led to a number of successes in the identification, prevention and reduction of statelessness and the protection of stateless persons. Over the past five years, the UNHCR has supported more training activities and has performed a vital public information role with the publication of several high-profile documents including the Inter-Parliamentary Union *Nationality and Statelessness: A Handbook for Parliamentarians* (2005), which aims to provide elected representatives with a broad description of the international principles regulating nationality and statelessness[36] and a general overview of the problem of statelessness in *Refugees Magazine* (2007).[37]

(December 14, 2009), www2.ohchr.org/english/bodies/hrcouncil/docs/13session/ A-HRC-13–34.pdf.

[34] C. Batchelor, 'Stateless Persons: Some Gaps in International Protection', *International Journal of Refugee Law*, 7(2) (1995), 232; *idem*, 'Transforming International Legal Principles Into National Law: The Right to a Nationality and the Avoidance of Statelessness', *Refugee Survey Quarterly*, 25(3) (2006), 8.

[35] See, in particular, UNHCR, *Action to Address Statelessness: A Strategy Note* (Geneva: UNHCR, 2010), www.unhcr.org/4b960ae99.html.

[36] Inter-Parliamentary Union, *Nationality and Statelessness: A Handbook for Parliamentarians* (Geneva: Inter-Parliamentary Union, 2005).

[37] UNHCR, 'The Excluded: The Strange Hidden World of the Stateless', *Refugees Magazine*, 147 (Geneva: UNHCR, September 2007), www.unhcr.org/pub//PUBL/46d2e8dc2.pdf.

Most important, the UNHCR has accelerated its campaign to prevent and reduce statelessness by providing guidelines to states and by setting ambitious goals of its own. The UNHCR recently set a target of increasing accession to the statelessness Conventions with the aim of reaching forty-one States Parties to the 1961 Convention and sixty-eight to the 1954 Convention by the end of 2011 and has prioritised the need to improve access to procedures to identify stateless persons by supporting population censuses and conducting surveys, most recently in Montenegro (2009) and Kyrgyzstan (2007–8). On a related note, in February 2009, the UNHCR published 'Statelessness: An Analytical Framework for Prevention, Reduction and Protection' which is a particularly useful tool that aims to facilitate statelessness determination procedures and provide a mechanism for analysing situations where persons are stateless or are at risk of becoming stateless.[38] According to the UNHCR, the Framework is designed to 'identify causes of statelessness, obstacles to acquisition of nationality and the risks faced by stateless persons as well as to highlight the capacities of all concerned stakeholders to minimise those risks'.[39]

The UNHCR is also becoming increasingly proactive in its efforts to prevent statelessness, and in its March 2010 *Strategy Note*[40] set out some of the conditions which could 'trigger' its involvement in *anticipation* that an individual or population might become stateless and identifies indicators, including: (1) the passage of national legislation; (2) information on the implementation of national legislation, including with regard to issuance of documents which constitute proof of nationality; (3) government statements on nationality of the persons in question. In addition, the UNHCR may become involved when there are gaps in nationality legislation which may require technical assistance to remedy or when there are administrative barriers to the acquisition or confirmation of nationality, or State succession.[41] In addition the UNHCR has developed a greater public presence by means of a new website and by promoting visual documentation on the lives of stateless people, through its collaboration with photojournalists, including Greg Constantine. Finally, as a result of the reorganisation of funding streams, the UNHCR is now also to devote more funding to its work on statelessness, allocating US$38.5 million for its statelessness operations in 2010 – approximately three times the expenditure on statelessness-related activities in 2009.[42]

---

[38] www.unhcr.org/refworld/docid/49a28afb2.html.   [39] *Ibid.*, iv.
[40] UNHCR, *Action to Address Statelessness*.   [41] *Ibid.*, vii.
[42] See UNHCR, *Addressing Statelessness* (Geneva: UNHCR, 2009c), www.unhcr.org/4b02c5e39.pdf.

In a different capacity, UNICEF and Plan International have worked simultaneously to call attention to the problems associated with the lack of birth registration which, though not coterminous with statelessness, is often an exacerbating factor.[43] Together these organisations spearheaded a ten-year-long campaign on universal birth registration which aimed to curtail some of the consequences of vulnerability which affect both *de jure* and *de facto* stateless persons and which include the challenge of proving one's nationality, accessing basic services, travelling, marrying, founding a family, having a child and protecting one's children from the dangers of legal anonymity. The case for universal birth registration was also made as a means of preventing trafficking. To this end, Plan launched a targeted global campaign in 2005–6 through its regional offices and, with the assistance of the United Nations Children's Fund (UNICEF), lobbied to ensure that birth registration, as a means of preventing statelessness was included as a recommendation in the 2006 *UN Secretary General's Study on Violence Against Children*.[44] The efforts of these two organisations in particular have drawn attention to the need to ensure that policies are in place to prevent statelessness at birth and also ensure that governments develop public information campaigns to reach out to those who are entitled to nationality but may not have been able to enjoy this right, for lack of proof of their nationality often as a result of insufficient funds or for other practical reasons.

The UNICEF and Plan campaigns have been most actively supported by the Organization for American States (OAS), together with the Inter-American Development Bank (IADB) which signed a tri-partite

---

[43] B. Crossette, 'Third of Births Aren't Registered, UNICEF Says', *New York Times* (July 8, 1998).

[44] Under Recommendation 11, 'Develop and implement systematic national data collection and research', para. 107, the UN Secretary General wrote: 'I recommend that States improve data collection and information systems in order to identify vulnerable subgroups, inform policy and programming at all levels, and track progress towards the goal of preventing violence against children. States should use national indicators based on internationally agreed standards, and ensure that data are compiled, analysed and disseminated to monitor progress over time. Where not currently in place, birth, death and marriage data registries with full national coverage should be created and maintained. States should also create and maintain data on children without parental care and children in the criminal justice system. Data should be disaggregated by sex, age, urban/rural, household and family characteristics, education and ethnicity. States should also develop a national research agenda on violence against children across settings where violence occurs, including through interview studies with children and parents, with particular attention to vulnerable groups of girls and boys.' See United Nations, *UN Secretary General's Study on Violence Against Children* (New York: United Nations, 2006), 27, www.unviolencestudy.org.

Memorandum of Understanding on 8 August 2006. This document formally links birth registration to human development, noting that the OAS General Secretariat is committed to

> strengthening governance through state modernization and by recognizing and strengthening the right to identity through programs and projects that broaden access to civil registry and build the capacity of institutions responsible for registry in the Latin American and Caribbean region as a cornerstone of its development activities. [45]

This Memorandum of Understanding (MOU) led directly to the establishment of the Inter-American Program *For A Universal Civil Registry And 'The Right To Identity'* which has paved the way for numerous operational and technical assistance projects to improve birth registration across the OAS region by means of awareness-raising, legal assistance, training of civil servants and identification of best practice.[46]

In parallel to the Plan/UNICEF campaign and the OAS activities, the Asian Development Bank (ADB) has examined the impact of birth registration campaigns in Asia. While the ADB recognises that birth registration may provide a route to security, field research in Bangladesh, Cambodia and Nepal revealed that other means of documentation are also increasingly important and may substitute for birth certificates. The increase in other methods of identification may conversely devalue real documents by encouraging bribery and corruption and the creation of black markets which negatively affect poor and vulnerable populations and may exacerbate their exclusion.[47] The ADB's findings raise important policy implications for advocates and national governments, not least the need for greater flexibility when determining nationality.

The Council of Europe and EU agencies

The Council of Europe has sought to raise awareness about statelessness in Europe by issuing public statements and through its Convention-related

---

[45] See AG/RES. 2286 (XXXVII O/07) Inter-American Program for a Universal Civil Registry and 'The Right To Identity' (Adopted at the Fourth Plenary Session, held on June 5, 2007), www.iin.oea.org/2007/Res_37_AG/Res_2286–37_en.pdf.

[46] For an overview of OAS activities, see www.oas.org/sap/english/cpo_modernizacion_puica_projects.asp.

[47] C. Vandenabeele, 'Establishing Legal Identity for Inclusive Development: Bangladesh, Cambodia, Nepal', Presentation at 'Children without a State: A Human Rights Challenge Birth Registration and Irregular Migration' (Kennedy School of Government, Carr Center for Human Rights Policy and Committee on Human Rights Studies, Cambridge, MA, Harvard University, 2007); and C. Vandenabeele, and C. V. Lao (eds.), *Legal Identity for Inclusive Development* (Manila: Asian Development Bank, 2007).

activities. One of the most vocal champions inside the Council of Europe is the current Commissioner for Human Rights, Thomas Hammarberg, who has issued several opinion pieces known as 'viewpoints' in which he has called attention to the plight of stateless people, including Roma minorities[48] and denationalised minorities in Greece.[49] In addition, legal experts initiated activities in 2009 to build on the two Council of Europe Conventions on statelessness with the aim of clarifying the rights of children and others affected by nationality problems. Also in 2009, the European Committee on Legal Co-operation (CDCJ) commissioned Jeremy McBride to prepare a report on access to justice for migrants and asylum seekers in Europe.[50] In addition, the Council of Europe has convened a specialist group of experts on nationality and has organised workshops in the preparation for the 4th Council of Europe Conference on Nationality in 2010. Most important, on 9 December 2009, the Council of Europe Committee of Ministers adopted Recommendation CM/Rec (2009)13 on the nationality of children prepared in the framework of the work of the Group of Specialists on Nationality. The recommendation includes chapters on reducing statelessness, nationality as a consequence of a child–parent family relationship, children born on the territory of a state to a foreign parent, position of children treated as nationals, rights of children in proceedings affecting their nationality and registration at birth.

The European Union Agency for Fundamental Rights (FRA), a relatively young organisation that grew out of the former European Monitoring Centre on Racism and Xenophobia (EUMC) in Vienna, has emerged as an important player in the struggle to promote equality and freedoms on several issues, including nationality. To this end, it works to provide comparative data, evidence-based research, expertise and advice to EU institutions and member states. An important illustration of its research and advocacy work is the study on the situation of irregular migrants in

---

[48] See 'Many Roma in Europe are Stateless and Live Outside Social Protection', Viewpoint 06/07/09, www.coe.int/t/commissioner/Viewpoints/090706_en.asp.

[49] See Report by T. Hammarberg, Commissioner for Human Rights of the Council of Europe, following his visit to Greece on 8–10 December 2008, Document Comm DH(2009)9, Strasbourg (19 February 2009), https://wcd.coe.int/ViewDoc.jsp?id= 1409353&Site=CommDH&BackColorInternet=FEC65B&BackColorIntranet=FEC65B& BackColorLogged=FFC679.

[50] J. McBride, *Access to Justice for Migrants and Asylum Seekers in Europe* (Strasbourg: Council of Europe, 2009), http://fra.europa.eu/fraWebsite/research/research_projects/ proj_irregularimmigrants_en.htm.

Europe which aims to describe the situation of irregular immigrants in all EU member states and the main problems they face primarily in the areas of health, education, housing, social care, employment status and fair working conditions, as well as access to remedies against abuse.[51]

National policy actions and state reporting on statelessness

While more states have been urged to accede to the statelessness Conventions, non-parties have been able to address some of the symptoms of statelessness through national legislation. The most high-profile example is the United States where a bill introduced by Rep. Sheila Jackson-Lee (Texas) in January 2009 was referred to the Committee on Foreign Affairs. The proposed legislation seeks to prevent statelessness by decreasing trafficking and discrimination. The authors note that the lack of nationality (citizenship) and the lack of national documentation often results in

> severe hardships and discrimination, particularly the inability to pursue lawful employment and a sustainable livelihood, own property, or enjoy legally protected family bonds and increases the likelihood that such persons may fall victim to traffickers and organized criminal groups who prey on the vulnerability of unprotected de jure or de facto stateless persons.[52]

Specifically, the bill seeks to increase political and financial support for the UNHCR's work on the prevention and elimination of both *de jure* and *de facto* statelessness, including US$5 million of appropriations to the UNHCR and US$3 million to UNICEF. It also calls for the creation of an Inter-Agency Task Force on Statelessness composed of representatives from the UNHCR, UNICEF and related UN agencies.

For the past four years there has been increased activity on the part of the US State Department. In 2006, the former Bush administration supported the adoption of the UNHCR's 'Executive Committee Conclusion on Identification, Prevention and Reduction of Statelessness and Protection of Stateless Persons', and called for the integration of stateless persons into US-funded development programmes. Most important, since 2008, the

---

[51] See *The Situation of Irregular Immigrants in the European Union*, http://fra.europa.eu/fraWebsite/research/research_projects/proj_irregularimmigrants_en.htm.

[52] United States Congress, HR 72 – To Increase Global Stability and Security for The United States and the International Community by Reducing the Number of Individuals who are de jure or de facto Stateless and at Risk of Being Trafficked (January 6, 2009), www.opencongress.org/bill/111-h72/text.

US State Department has monitored the situation of stateless people and detailed their conditions in its annual Human Rights reports. It has also dedicated staff in the Office of Policy and Resource Planning (based in the Bureau of Population, Refugees, and Migration) who are both monitoring the plight of stateless people and acting as a point of co-ordination regarding US governmental policy.[53]

In addition to the United States, a handful of advanced democracies have sought to address the problems of statelessness by introducing determination procedures and mechanisms for handling stateless populations within their borders, most notably Spain and Hungary, which have emerged as pace-setters by amending their nationality legislation to this end. In the case of Hungary, the government amended the Aliens Legislation to establish a formal statelessness determination procedure which 'ensures access to a legal identity and the right to a protection status on the sole ground of being stateless'.[54] High-level decisions and in some cases legislation introduced in Bangladesh, Sri Lanka, Nepal and Mauritania have helped to redress historic problems of statelessness.[55] The achievement of these countries in addressing the problem of statelessness, and specifically the creative approach taken by Hungary and Spain, sets an important precedent for other states.

NGOs in the West: information and advocacy

Several non-governmental actors have sought to advance an agenda to reduce statelessness. Among the most active are Refugees International

---

[53] For further information on commitments by the US government to address the challenge of statelessness, see E. P. Schwartz, Assistant Secretary, Bureau of Population, Refugees, and Migration, 'Protecting Stateless Persons: The Role of the US Government', Conference on Statelessness: Sponsored by Refugee Council USA, Washington, DC (October 30, 2009), www.state.gov/g/prm/rls/rmks/remarks/131183.htm.

[54] G. Gyulai, *Forgotten Without Reason: Protection of Non-Refugee Stateless Persons in Central Europe* (Budapest: Hungarian Helsinki Committee, 2007).

[55] For example, in May 2008, the Bangladesh High Court held that any Urdu speaker born in Bangladesh, or whose father or grandfather was born in Bangladesh, and who was a permanent resident in 1971 or who had permanently resided in Bangladesh since 1971 was a citizen 'by operation of law'. This essentially confirmed the citizenship of most members of this community. In Sri Lanka, the 2003 Grant of Citizenship to Persons of Indian Origin Act gave citizenship to persons of Indian origin residing in Sri Lanka since October 1964 and their descendants. This legislation essentially ended the problem of statelessness in Sri Lanka. For a good evaluation of these and other efforts, see B. K. Blitz and M. Lynch (eds.), *Statelessness and Citizenship: A Comparative Study on the Benefits of Nationality* (Cheltenham: Edward Elgar, 2011).

and the Justice Initiative of the Open Society Institute (OSI), which have paved the way for international advocacy efforts. Refugees International mapped out the problem of denial of citizenship in a study entitled 'Lives on Hold: The Human Cost of Statelessness' (2005).[56] This report was the first global survey of its kind and included case studies based on fact-finding visits to Bangladesh, Estonia and the United Arab Emirates (UAE) and brief reports on the situation in some seventy countries around the world. Refugees International published a follow-up, 'Nationality Rights for All: A Progress Report and Global Survey on Statelessness' (March 2009), which presented a more comprehensive view of the plight of stateless people and is the most authoritative survey on the subject.[57]

For its part, the OSI Justice Initiative has hosted several thematic sessions on nationality problems primarily, though not exclusively, in the African context. Through the OSI network, the Justice Initiative has carved out a particularly influential role by drawing together experts from the region, and based in the West, to design both legislation and support international litigation, most famously against the Dominican Republic in the case of *Dilcia Yean and Violeta Bosico* v. *Dominican Republic*[58] and currently, in the case of the Erased, *Makuc* v. *Slovenia*.[59] It has also filed multiple cases before the ECtHR, for example in the active cases of *Bagdonavichus* v. *Russia* (where Roma in Dorozhnoe, Kaliningrad, had seen their homes torn down when Russian authorities razed the village) and the ethnic segregation of

[56] M. Lynch, *Lives on Hold: The Human Cost of Statelessness* (Washington, DC: Refugees International, 2005).

[57] K. Southwick and M. Lynch, *Nationality Rights for All: A Progress Report and Global Survey on Statelessness* (Washington, DC: Refugees International, 2009), www.refintl. org/sites/default/files/RI%20Stateless%20Report_FINAL_031109.pdf.

[58] See, for example, www.unhcr.org/refworld/docid/44e497d94.html. The OSI has taken up other cases including: *Good* v. *Botswana* (see www.soros.org/initiatives/justice/ litigation/botswana/botswana_20080501.pdf), *People* v. *Côte d'Ivoire* (www.soros.org/ initiatives/justice/litigation/people), *Institute for Human Rights and Development in Africa* v. *Republic of Guinea Conakry* (www.ihrda.org/images/292-04%20IHRDA%20 v%20Angola.pdf) and *Makuc and Others* v. *Slovenia*, concerning the 'Erased' (Application No. 26828/06).

[59] Application No. 26828/06), ECtHR 31 May 2007, www.unhcr.org/refworld/docid/ 47fdfafdd.html, and *Written Comments on the Case of Makuc and Others* v. *Slovenia, Application No. 26828/06 – A Submission from the Open Society Justice Initiative to the European Court of Human Rights*, www.soros.org/initiatives/justice/litigation/ makuc/written-comments-20071015.pdf. See also *Bagdonavichus and Others* v. *Russia* (Application No. 19841/06), www.soros.org/initiatives/justice/litigation/bagdonavichus/ bagdonavichus_20060211.pdf.

Roma school children in the Czech Republic in *D.H. and Others* v. *Czech Republic*.[60]

In addition, through the Africa Governance Monitoring and Advocacy Project (AfriMAP), one of OSI's four African foundations, the OSI has also promoted advocacy work around gaps in citizenship protections at African Union level and is currently developing a protocol to strengthen protection for stateless people and unprotected minorities within the African Union. It has also suggested how one might be able to promote the human rights of stateless people, even in countries where states are not a party to the statelessness conventions – for example, by campaigning for stateless people to have status in the United States, similar to trafficked persons. In addition, the OSI has developed a new website to raise awareness of both the sources of statelessness and its achievements.

Two London-based organisations, the Equal Rights Trust, which works to combat discrimination and promote equality, and the London Detainee Support Group (LDSG), have highlighted the vulnerability of people who have been detained while their immigration status is under review; many of these people are *de facto* stateless.[61] LDSG, in particular, has considered the implications of indefinite detention and the human rights implications this poses for states parties to the above-mentioned international Conventions and European instruments. Finally, it should be noted that at particular times human rights organisations such as Amnesty International, Minority Rights Group International and Human Rights Watch have played a prominent role in advancing an agenda on behalf of stateless populations by publishing occasional reports, participating in parliamentary and congressional hearings and at the 2001 UN World Conference Against Racism in Durban, South Africa.

Local NGOs and grass-roots campaigns

Some of the above-mentioned organisations have worked in partnership with NGOs and stateless people in the field to advance agendas aimed at local policy-makers and to provide services. Jesuit Relief Services, for

---

[60] For a full account of OSI's submissions to the ECtHR, see www.soros.org/initiatives/justice/litigation/czechrepublic.

[61] See, in particular, *ERT Legal Working Paper: The Protection of Stateless Persons in Detention Under International Law* (4 February 2009a), www.equalrightstrust.org/view-subdocument/index.htm?id=398 and *ERT Research Working Paper: The Protection of Stateless Persons in Detention* (4 February 2009b), www.equalrightstrust.org/view-subdocument/index.htm?id=399.

example, has worked with several stateless and undocumented populations including the Rohingya, to deliver aid and assistance. The OSI network has collaborated with several African NGOs to support awareness-raising and project-monitoring, for example on the repatriation of Mauritanians from Senegal. Partners include Anti-Slavery International and the West African Refugees and Internally Displaced Persons Network (WARIPNet).

Local organisations, many composed of stateless and undocumented people, have also developed a particular capacity to address citizenship and nationality issues under the umbrella of human rights and equality. For example, from Kathmandu, JAGRIT Nepal has used the internet to send regular briefings to raise awareness in the West about mobilisation campaigns in support of the landless Madhesi communities in the Terai plains; the Association of Human Rights Activists has campaigned on behalf of the tens of thousands of refugees expelled from Bhutan on account of their contested nationality status. In South Asia, following a 2003 High Court ruling which allowed ten Biharis to obtain citizenship and voting rights in Bangladesh, organised Bihari groups became increasingly vocal and pressured the Bangladeshi government to bring a resolution to their protracted status as unwanted refugees and stateless persons born in Bangladesh.[62]

The Arakan Project, based in Bangkok but with field assistance in Bangladesh, has also worked to monitor the plight of the hundreds of thousands of Rohingya who have endured long-standing persecution by the Burmese Junta. Having become the most authoritative independent NGO working on this issue, the Arakan Project has also made several submissions before UN bodies, most recently, the Committee on the Elimination of Discrimination Against Women (CEDAW),[63] and has collaborated with Western-based organisations including the Equal Rights Trust. Through its work, the Arakan Project has raised media awareness and alerted human rights groups to the emergency situation of the large numbers of Rohingya boatpeople who have been captured by Thai and Indonesian authorities, and others who have drowned at sea.[64]

---

[62] See K. Southwick, in Blitz and Lynch, *Statelessness and Citizenship*.

[63] Arakan Project, *Issues to Be Raised Concerning the Situation of Stateless Rohingya Women in Myanmar (Burma). Submission to the Committee on the Elimination of Discrimination Against Women (CEDAW) for the Examination of the Combined 2nd and 3rd Periodic State Party Reports (Cedaw/C/Mmr/3) – Myanmar* (2008), www.burmalibrary.org/docs6/CEDAW_Myanmar_AP_Submission-Final-Web.pdf.

[64] S. Mydans, 'Thailand Is Accused of Rejecting Migrants', *New York Times* (January 17, 2009).

In Africa, the Nairobi-based Centre for Minority Rights (CEMIRIDE) has published extensive research on the situation of the statelessness Nubians in Kenya. Through media training, research and facilitated talks with the government of Kenya, CEMIRIDE has helped to provide a forum for stateless Nubians and has been credited with reactivating the Pastoralist Parliamentary Group (PPG) in parliament. Similarly, from the Great Lakes area, Action pour la promotion et défense des droits des personnes défavorisées (APRODEPED) has worked to advance the human rights of stateless Banyumulenge and others by providing legal aid and representation before the courts. In addition, the tireless work of Judge Unity Dow in Botswana should be recorded; most notably her efforts to challenge the citizenship laws. In *Attorney General* v. *Unity Dow* (CA No. 4/91, 3 July 1992) Dow, a distinguished human rights activist, successfully challenged the legitimacy of the Citizenship Act which denied Botswana citizenship to her children on the basis that her husband was a foreigner. The gender discrimination inherent within the Botswana Citizenship Act was found first by the High Court, and later by the Court of Appeal, to be in violation of the Constitution.[65]

In the Middle East, human rights organisations working on issues of nationality have had to contend with repressive governments and multiple forms of abuse including the withdrawal of citizenship, discrimination on the grounds of religious belief, and gender-based policies which have excluded women from enjoyment of their civil and political rights. The Kuwait Society for Human Rights (KSHR), has worked with independent film-maker Norah Hadeed who produced a short documentary on the plight of the Bidun. A new Islamic-based NGO, the Kuwaiti Society for Fundamental Human Rights (KSFHR), has also spoken out on the situation of the Bidun in Kuwait.[66]

Another long-standing Middle East issue is the situation of Palestinians within Israel, and those under the jurisdiction of the Palestinian Authority (PA) and the United Nations Relief and Works Agency for Palestine Refugees in the Near East (UNRWA) which operates in Gaza and the West Bank as well as Lebanon. Within Israel and the PA, the Legal Centre for Arab Minority Rights in Israel (ADALAH) has

---

[65] U. Dow (ed.), *The Citizenship Case – The Attorney General of The Republic of Botswana vs. Unity Dow: Court Documents, Judgements' Cases and Materials* (ENTSWE LA LESEDI (PTY) LTD, 1995), www.law-lib.utoronto.ca/Diana/fulltext/dow1.htm.

[66] United States State Department, *Kuwait – Country Reports on Human Rights Practices*, Bureau of Democracy, Human Rights, and Labor 2006. (March 6, 2007), www.state.gov/g/drl/rls/hrrpt/2006/78856.htm.

provided legal aid and supported both local and international advocacy campaigns. Most recently it has challenged the constitutionality of the Israeli Citizenship Law regarding the ban on family unification and the right to family life for Palestinians within the PA and East Jerusalem. In Lebanon, the Frontiers Ruwad Association, an NGO based in Beirut, has made a mark by defending and advocating on behalf of refugees, asylum-seekers and stateless persons. It is one of the few dedicated organisations which provides legal aid and legal training and monitors detention centres. Its work is publicised through research reports and briefs.

With offices in Washington, DC, San José (Costa Rica), Rio de Janeiro and Buenos Aires, the Center for Justice and International Law (CEJIL) has emerged over the past fifteen years as one of the most effective human rights advocacy organisations to champion the cause of nationality issues in the Americas. In collaboration with Roxana Altholz of the International Human Rights Law Clinic at the University of California at Berkeley, CEJIL worked to provide legal assistance to the Centro de Mujeres Dominico-Haitianas (MUDHA), as they took the case of *Yean and Bosico* to the Inter-American Court of Human Rights.[67] Both MUDHA and CEJIL have steadfastly kept the pressure on the government of Dominican Republic to implement the decision of the Inter-American Court.

In Europe, Roma organisations monitored the discriminatory treatment of minority groups and have provided legal aid, community support, education and training. Most notable is the Budapest-based European Roma Rights Centre (ERRC), a public interest law organisation which has led concerted advocacy campaigns at the international level, often in conjunction with the OSI to promote the rights of Roma, Sinti, Gypsy and other groups. The ERRC has also led domestic efforts to monitor and promote the implementation of anti-discrimination legislation. In particular, the ERRC has called attention to the problem of undocumented people who are unable to access public services and are, in many cases, *de facto* stateless.[68] While the ERRC works in over thirty European countries, there are a substantial number of organisations working on Roma issues such as the Roma Education Fund based in Budapest and the National Roma Centrum in Kumaovo, Macedonia, which provides legal aid.

---

[67] *Case of Yean and Bosico Children v. The Dominican Republic*, IACrtHR 8 September 2005, www.unhcr.org/retworld/docid/44e497d94.html.

[68] T. Perić, 'Personal Documents and Threats to the Exercise of Fundamental Rights of Roma in Europe', *Roma Rights*, 3 (2003), 7, www.errc.org/cikk.php?cikk=28, and B. Struharova, 'Disparate Impact: Removing Roma from the Czech Republic', *Roma Rights*, 1 (1999), 47–51, www.errc.org/cikk.php?cikk=54.

Grass-roots campaigns in the West have also played a key political role, raising awareness alongside international litigation. The focus of grass-roots efforts has been on both the need to regularise the status of irregular workers, unsuccessful asylum seekers and overstayers, and the inclusion of discriminated minorities. Some protests have been organised through local NGOs, such as the Joint Council for the Welfare of Immigrants (JCWI) in the United Kingdom, but other mass protests have been co-ordinated by non-professional associations, above all migrant community organisations and collectives. Notable events have taken place across Europe. In May 2007, there was a public rally entitled 'From Strangers into Citizens' which was motivated by the desire to create a one-off regularisation – or 'pathway into citizenship'. Specifically, the event aimed to ensure that migrants who had been in the United Kingdom for four years or more should be granted a two-year work permit and at the end of that period, subject to employer and character references, they should be granted leave to remain. The organisers claimed that such an approach would bring great benefits to the UK economy and society and that it has already been achieved elsewhere in the European Union and United States.

Other targeted campaigns have occurred in major European cities. In France, the debate over the *'sans papiers'*, the undocumented former migrants from North Africa, was revived following occupations of public buildings. In February 2005, the 9th collective, an organisation of undocumented migrants, occupied the headquarters of the Social Party in Paris,[69] and in April 2007, more than ninety people occupied the Church of Saint Paul de Massy in l'Essonne, just south of Paris, demanding that their contribution to the French economy be recognised and insisting on regularisation of their rights to work, social security and education. In other regions, the *'sans papiers'* have organised themselves into 'collectives' and have carried out co-ordinated activities. For example, the Collectif de soutien des exilés du 10e arrondissement de Paris publicises actions by organisations based in other European states including Greece, Italy, Norway and the United Kingdom. One organisation, the Collectif des sans papiers de Marseille, has a weekly radio broadcast, 'La Voix des sans papiers' which it uses to publicise its actions.[70] Other pan-European

---

[69] See '9ème collectif de sans papiers, Occupation de la Fédération 93 du PS' (14 February 2005), http://pajol.eu.org/article719.html.
[70] The broadcast is on Radio Galère: 88.4 FM (Marseilles) every Monday from 11.00 to 12.15.

actions included the 'caravan of the erased', where a convoy of activists travelled from Ljubljana to Brussels in November 2006 via several European cities to protest about the cancellation of residency rights and mistreatment of more than 18,000 people who were 'Erased' from the national register of permanent residents shortly after Slovenia achieved independence in 1991. They thus lost their social, economic and political rights, and after travelling some found themselves unable to re-enter the country. Local Slovene organisations including the Peace Institute/Mirovni Institut also sponsored the pending litigation before the ECtHR, *Makuc and Others* v. *Slovenia*, with the assistance of an Italian legal team and the OSI Justice Initiative.[71]

Discourse and policy development: an evaluation

There is a growing discourse around the rights of non-citizens which has been initiated by both local groups of stateless and undocumented people and NGOs such as Refugees International, Plan International and the OSI. This discourse has been used by UN agencies and specialist bodies and is influencing agendas on all continents, most notably in the OAS region where policy actions have been introduced to improve birth registration as a means of protecting the rights of children. The discourse on the rights of non-citizens has also drawn attention to particular regions and situations and has also cast a light on the work of the UNHCR and encouraged further funding of its work on statelessness.

NGOs and local groups have therefore performed a vital role by reminding states of their obligations and by setting out principles and recommendations which guide states to respect these rights. That governmental agencies such as the US State Department now include statelessness in their human rights monitoring reports and that non-discrimination in matters of nationality is among the Copenhagen Criteria which influence whether or not states may accede to the European Union, suggest that in some selected instances these norms and principles are in fact being taken seriously. Though far from universal, the decisions of some international courts, especially the ECtHR and the Inter-American Court, have further reinforced the prohibition on the denial or deprivation of nationality and have called on states to introduce reform.

The ways in which the discourse on the rights of non-citizens may influence states, however, needs further explanation. In contrast to most

---

[71] See *Makuc and Others* v. *Slovenia*, n. 58 above.

typical international regimes, including those that apply to the area of human rights, there is little evidence of 'egoistic self-interest' prompting national actors to take up the cause of statelessness at the international level. Few states are signatories of the Conventions and there is a recognised norm that nationality is determined by states and thus a sovereign right of states. Unlike other situations where it may be in a state's interest to use international *fora* to advance a particular agenda, the issue of statelessness does not attract any such attention. However, that is not to say that norms regarding the rights of citizens are not being widely disseminated, or that they have not been institutionalised. As discussed above, there is considerable evidence of a discourse on the rights of non-citizens which has principles of non-discrimination at its very heart and which has permeated the work of the CERD and other UN bodies. The advocacy efforts spearheaded by NGOs, such as the OSI, have further helped to inform where international law applies and where action by states is required. In this context, one effect of protest and social action by groups such as the '*sans papiers*' and the 'Erased' is the further institutionalisation of the rights of non-citizens in international and regional laws.

There is also some evidence of 'political power', the second of Krasner's causal variables, effecting change. As noted above, some countries have actively criticised other states on account of poor human rights practices, including nationality-based discrimination.

This is most apparent with respect to foreign policy negotiations in the case of norm-violating states such as the Dominican Republic, Myanmar and Democratic Republic of Congo – all of which have engaged in discrimination on the basis of nationality and in some instances race, too.[72] In a similar context, the European Council has consistently linked respect for nationality rights in accession talks with certain states, more recently Croatia.[73]

In some parts of the European Union, the situation is not especially optimistic – for example, in both the United Kingdom and France, amnesties issued for overstayers and irregular migrants already on the

---

[72] In the case of the Dominican Republic, criticism has been raised against its policies which deny Haitian-born children and those of Haitian descent the right to acquire a nationality; in the case of Myanmar, it is the continued discrimination against the Rohingya whose citizenship has been withdrawn; in Democratic Republic of Congo, it is the ethnic-Rwandese minorities, the Banyumulenge, who have been denied citizenship.

[73] See B. K. Blitz, 'Democratic Development, Judicial Reform and the Serbian Question in Croatia', *Human Rights Review*, 9(1) (2007), 123.

territory have been followed by increasingly coercive policies on removal and evidence of refoulement.[74] Further, it is important to note that the application of conditionality in the context of accession is not a panacea for reform. In contrast to Croatia, Estonia and Slovenia slipped into the European Union with the fate of the 'Erased' unresolved.

Finally, it is important to mention the degree to which the actions of these NGOs and local organisations have advanced knowledge of statelessness. As noted in chapter 1 there is an emerging body of commentary on nationality and citizenship, as well as on the rights of non-citizens and the undocumented, which has multiple sources. The primary sources of connection between these works remain analyses of international law (upon which there is already considerable agreement) and a more recent rights-based discourse over the relationship between nationality and human security. There is little empirical data on the plight of stateless people, though the survey reports produced by Refugees International has called attention to the global problem of statelessness and are increasingly cited as authoritative sources. In general, however, the level of knowledge about statelessness, and its causes and effects, remains rather limited.

Overall, it is fair to suggest that there is an evolving discourse on the rights of non-citizens, though the degree to which this discourse is able to influence the behaviour of many states is still open to question. It should, of course, be noted that the coalition of groups and organisations is currently operating in a context of high anti-immigrant sentiment and one which is not conducive to reform. There are nonetheless some trends one can identify – whether they are the result of normative shifts, political demands, protest, etc. remains to be determined. It is difficult to establish a causal connection, though there appears to be convergence in some instances. Positive results include the draft legislation in the United States and the introduction of regularisation programmes and statelessness determination procedures in Spain and Hungary, respectively.

---

[74] According to the US Committee for Refugees and Immigrants (USCRI), 'In March [2007], France forcibly returned a Chadian asylum seeker whose claim its Ministry of Interior rejected as "manifestly unfounded." Upon his return, Chadian authorities arrested, forcibly interrogated, and imprisoned him. See US Committee for Refugees and Immigrants, 'In November, the UK's House of Lords approved the forced return of non-Arab Sudanese from Darfur, reasoning that, even if they could not return to that province, the internally displaced persons squatter camps around Khartoum were "not ... unduly harsh," as the Court of Appeals had found.' World Refugee Survey, 2008, www.refugees.org/countryreports.aspx?id=2138.

Challenges to the discourse within Europe

In spite of the actions of the UNHCR, NGOs and local groups, states have often failed to embrace the message of non-discrimination and address the protection needs of non-citizens. In the case of the European Union – the focus of this book – the rights-based discourse identified above now sits uneasily in a highly differentiated context: on the one hand, skilled migrants are often welcome and the introduction of harmonising instruments, including the Reception[75] and Temporary Protection Directives[76] set out minimum standards of treatment for asylum seekers and those who, though not falling within the terms of the 1951 Refugee Convention, are accepted as being in need of protection because of the circumstances in their home state. On the other hand, those who do not qualify for protection under these policies are left with only the protection of last resort, namely a claim that to return them would breach their absolute rights to life or protection from torture or inhuman and degrading treatment under Articles 2 and 3 of the ECHR, such a claim being extremely hard to make out. For those who do not fall within the accepted categories and are consequently not given status, Europe is a hostile environment. In contrast to the prized highly skilled migrants, 'irregular' migrants who remain on the territory without status are generally unable to work legally but are denied benefits or social assistance and must often live clandestine lives, facing the constant threat of removal.

Moreover, it is almost impossible for poor and unskilled migrants from the developing world to seek asylum in, or migrate to, Europe through legal channels. The introduction of visa requirements and fees and the more coercive use of profiling and interception practices are all aimed at keeping such migrants out hence the coining of the term 'Fortress Europe'. For those who cannot afford the fees or obtain the relevant visas, the only way to Europe is by enlisting the support of a smuggler. Such 'help' comes at enormous cost, besides immediately putting the migrant

---

[75] See *Council Directive 2003/9/EC of 27 January 2003 laying down minimum standards for the reception of asylum seekers*, http://eur-lex.europa.eu/LexUriServ/LexUriServ.do? uri=OJ:L:2003:031:0018:0025:EN:PDF.

[76] The Temporary Protection Directive aims to harmonise temporary protection for displaced persons in cases of mass influx on the basis of solidarity between member states. See *Council Directive 2001/55/EC of 20 July 2001 on minimum standards for giving temporary protection in the event of a mass influx of displaced persons and on measures promoting a balance of efforts between Member States in receiving such persons and bearing the consequences thereof*, http://eur-lex.europa.eu/LexUriServ/LexUriServ.do? uri=OJ:L:2001:212:0012:0023:EN:PDF.

outside the law. Most migrants will exhaust their families' savings in their journey to 'freedom'. Once they reach the European neighbourhood, they must dodge patrols by Frontex and national coastguards whose job it is to prevent irregular migrants from reaching Europe's shores. One way in which they do so is by travelling in smaller vessels or packed in crates, in the hope they will pass unnoticed: every year hundreds if not thousands of migrants will die in transit. Others may be intercepted and returned, and even where a country was historically perceived to be too danger-ous for return, re-admission agreements may now be in place. In many cases, rather than reducing the risk of human rights abuses the signing of re-admission agreements may have the opposite effect.[77] Throughout the Mediterranean, migrants have been returned to countries such as Libya, where they face considerable risk of abuse and danger. While some of the most egregious returns have been conducted by Italy,[78] even northern states such as the United Kingdom have returned people to Libya,[79] to an uncertain fate.[80]

Most recently, Malta, another front-line state which has become an important destination for asylum seekers and irregular migrants, has rejected the expansion of Frontex since it objects to its rules of engage-ment which prevent it from returning migrants to countries of origin or, if that is not possible, the country hosting the Frontex mission.[81] Rather, Malta has suggested that if migrants cannot be sent back to their point of origin, they should be sent to the nearest harbour.[82] The Maltese objections recall a wider fear that migrant management is not evenly

---

[77] R. Andrijasevic reports that, according to NGOs, the signing of an agreement between Libya and Italy in August 2004 'led to widespread arrests in Libya of individuals from sub-Saharan Africa, and that 106 migrants lost their lives during subsequent repatriations from Libya to Niger', see: R. Andrijasevic, 'How to Balance Rights and Responsibilities on Asylum at the EU's Southern Border of Italy and Libya', COMPAS Working Paper, WP-06–27 (Oxford: COMPAS, 2006).

[78] Euro Mediterranean Human Rights Network (EMHRN) and Migreurop, 'Illegal Refoulement of 500 Migrants to Libya: The EU must Condemn Italian Authorities', Press release (11 May 2009), www.migreurop.org/IMG/pdf/CP-Libye-english.pdf.

[79] B. K. Blitz, 'Libyan Nationals in the United Kingdom: Geo-Political Considerations and Trends in Asylum and Return', *International Journal on Multicultural Societies*, 10(2) (2009), 106.

[80] Between 2003 and 2005, Libya repatriated 145,000 people, including some refugees to Egypt, famine-stricken Niger and war-torn Eritrea and was formally condemned by international monitoring organisations. See Blitz, 'Libyan Nationals'.

[81] 'EU Makes Proposals to Strengthen Frontex, but Avoids Rules of Engagement', *Times of Malta* (24 February 2010).

[82] *Ibid.*

distributed across Europe and that some states shoulder too much of the 'burden'.[83]

The challenges facing migrants who reach Europe are especially daunting, as vividly described in Omar Ba's recent testimony *Je suis venu, j'ai vu, je n'y crois plus* (*I came, I saw, I no longer believe*).[84] The 'jungle' camp episode of the Autumn of 2009 further illustrates the precarious situation in which migrants may have to – and be prepared to – live. Migrants camped on the beach just outside Calais, on the north coast of France, and lived for weeks without any form of housing, sanitation, or services until bulldozers were called in by the French government to raze the illegal dwellings. By the end of 2009, the Sarkozy presidency could boast that it had removed 30,000 people from France, to much celebration.[85] Notwithstanding considerable adverse press coverage of these events, and an increasingly noticeable discourse of rights, the Sarkozy presidency had set the tone of current policy.

Conclusion

The main findings of this chapter suggest that there is an international discourse on statelessness, consisting of selected activists, high-profile UN organisations and NGOs, as well as local groups, but there is limited co-ordination between them. The most potent ways in which these organisations have tried to influence state action has been by means of moral persuasion, by clarifying legal commitments and by reiterating states' obligations to protect non-citizens under international law. Unlike most international regimes, the call to protect the rights of non-citizens has not yet found a champion among national actors which has been prepared to take on the case of statelessness at the international and global levels. This finding suggests the need for more instrumental hooks to connect the rights-based discourse, as found in the above-mentioned research, writing and advocacy efforts, with interest-based agendas – indeed, an altogether stronger realist discourse that can broker global reform. Greater co-ordination between the key actors mentioned above and further support of the UNHCR would no doubt advance this goal.

[83] See I. Camilleri, 'Malta's Migration Burden Biggest in EU – Study', *Times of Malta* (4 March 2010), www.timesofmalta.com/articles/view/20100304/local/maltas-migration-burden-biggest-in-eu-study.

[84] O. Ba, *Je suis venu, j'ai vu, je n'y crois plus* (Paris: Max Milo Éditions, 2009).

[85] See C. Coroller, 'SOS Racisme milite contre les expulsions de la "honte"', *Liberation.fr* (21 January 2009), www.liberation.fr/societe/0101313547-sos-racisme-milite-contre-les-30–000-expulsions-de-la-honte.

In the context of the European Union, the call to develop more inclusive policies to protect the rights of non-citizens has been hampered by states' re-interpretation of their obligations under the ECHR and international law. The degree to which the post-Lisbon process may further embed stronger commitments to the protection of all within the EU's borders, remains a major challenge of the twenty-first century. Further positive decisions from the ECtHR will no doubt circumscribe states' actions and give greater weight to the discourse on the rights of non-citizens. In the meantime, advancing a principled argument for the rights of non-citizens through protest and social action by local groups and NGOs, and where possible the use of smart litigation, remain the critical mechanisms for reform, however slow and uncertain that may be.

PART II

The research project

6

Research design and methodology of the country studies

CAROLINE SAWYER AND BRAD K. BLITZ

Introduction

Conducting research on refugees, asylum seekers and stateless individuals is notoriously difficult. Not only are such populations often out of reach – understandably, individuals faced with the threat of removal often live clandestinely – but, with the exception of Estonia, there is little official information recorded on the populations of interest to this project. Estimates of *de facto* stateless individuals in the European Union vary widely and, with the introduction of increasingly restrictive laws on asylum and the cancellation of support and assistance to those without status, there are few direct ways of accessing vulnerable individuals who may be *de facto* stateless. The twin challenges of exploration and experimentation therefore shaped this project which sought to develop understanding of this uncharted area, the lives of *de facto* stateless people in Europe.

Given the lack of empirical investigations of stateless people in general, the research team reviewed some of the conclusions generated from social scientific research on the experiences of asylum seekers in order to evaluate the potential application of exploratory styles of research for this project. A central premise of this research is that, while the legal situations of stateless people and asylum seekers are legally distinct, commentary on the increasing restrictions on asylum seekers highlights some relevant problems regarding the ways in which vulnerable populations may access rights to educate their children, secure decent housing and receive healthcare.[1] Hence, it was hoped that the research team could learn from

---

[1] A. Bloch, 'Refugee Settlement in Britain: The Impact of Policy on Participation', *Journal of Ethnic and Migration Studies*, 26 (2000), 75; J. Dennis, *A Case for Change: How Refugee Children in England are Missing Out* (London: The Children's Society, Refugee Council and Save the Children, 2002); R. Sales, 'The Deserving and Undeserving? Refugees, Asylum Seekers and Welfare in Britain', *Critical Social Policy*, 22 (2002), 456.

the ways in which other researchers have considered the conditions of life of such populations.

A key concept was the notion of differentiation, namely that the increasing polarisation between people on the basis of entitlements has created new social categories (e.g. refugees, asylum seekers, unsuccessful asylum seekers, irregular migrants) which now dominates the political discourse. For example, the ramifications of the asylum-seeking process had produced highly differentiated outcomes in terms of how migrants, including children, have found security and a sense of home,[2] which informed the research team's approach to finding participants and assessing their experiences. Equally important was an appreciation of the contradictory nature of governmental policy which supports structuralist explanations for this trend in differentiation. For example, Yuval-Davis and her colleagues argue that contradictory policies on asylum and reception in the United Kingdom have undermined integration initiatives which aim to improve social cohesion. The net effect of governmental initiatives towards asylum seekers has been to foster deprivation and feed racism and anti-immigrant sentiment at home.[3] Within the field of social policy there is a related body of writing which reinforces the structuralist line and claims that governmental policies on asylum have been effectively designed with built-in biases that produce particularly negative gendered outcomes and foster social exclusion.[4] One further consequence of recent policy measures on asylum in Europe has been the stigmatisation of asylum seekers into categories of those 'deserving' and 'undeserving' of protection,[5] a fact equally relevant to stateless populations. One stigmatising central factor in the differentiation of asylum seekers is precisely the granting of particular categories of status, which bring with them different sets of entitlements, even basic ones, which reinforces the impression that some categories of people are less deserving of protection than others.[6]

In addition to the literature on differentiation, the research team considered the role of support organisations – usually seen as gatekeepers

---

[2] I. Gedalof, 'Unhomely Homes: Women, Family and Belonging in UK Discourses of Migration and Asylum', *Journal of Ethnic and Migration Studies*, 33 (2007), 77; N. Spicer, 'Places of Exclusion and Inclusion: Asylum Seekers and Refugees' Experiences of Neighbourhoods in the UK', *Journal of Ethnic and Migration Studies*, 34 (2008), 491.

[3] N. Yuval-Davis, F. Anthias and E. Kofman, 'Secure Borders and Safe Haven and the Gendered Politics of Belonging: Beyond Social Cohesion', *Ethnic & Racial Studies*, 28 (2005), 13.

[4] Gedalof, 'Unhomely Homes'; Sales, 'The Deserving and Undeserving?'; Yuval-Davis, Anthias and Kofman, 'Secure Borders'.

[5] Sales, 'The Deserving and Undeserving?'.   [6] *Ibid.*

and a central means of accessing vulnerable populations. One important element of analysis from the recent literature on support organisations which was taken into account in the conduct of this research was the place, role and politics of support organisations in the face of governmental cutbacks. Some commentators have questioned the degree to which support organisations work to mitigate the effects of social exclusion and deprivation and form 'social bridges',[7] in the face of restrictive policy developments. They claim that the role played by support organisations in the development of migrants' social capital has been increasingly abandoned as such organisations attempt to survive in a hostile policy environment which has introduced mechanisms and procedures such as dispersal, resettlement and removal that precisely deny migrants opportunities to form 'social bonds'.[8] The research team therefore recognised that while such organisations may still offer an effective way of accessing vulnerable populations, their own agendas needed to be taken into consideration during the interview and information-gathering process. Many organisations have been put in the difficult position of gathering data on migrants for research purposes and this may give the impression they they support government initiatives, such as profiling studies. As a result, their actions may be treated with suspicion by the people they seek to help.

From the very start, the research team recognised that it would be challenging to locate and interview *de facto* stateless people. Nonetheless, the researchers felt that it would be possible to gain an insight into the nature of stateless in Europe from a selective sample of twenty-five research participants/interviewees in each of the four countries. The researchers noted that, while interview-based research cannot demonstrate causal connections and is less suitable to the development of grounded theory – which was never the ambition of this project – even with a small number of participants such an approach could elicit a rich portrait of participants' lived experiences of selected situations. To this end, the researchers sought to design a qualitative research project suitable for exploring participants'

---

[7] A. Agar and A. Strang, *Indicators of Integration: The Experience of Integration – Final Report* (London: Home Office, 2004); H. Beirens, R. Hek, N. Hughes and N. Spicer, 'Preventing Social Exclusion of Immigrant and Asylum Seeking Children: Building New Networks', *Social Policy and Society*, 6(2) (2007), 219; R. Zetter, D. Griffiths, S. Ferretti and M. Pearl, *An Evaluation of the Impact of Asylum Policies in Europe* (London: Home Office, 2003).

[8] Beirens, Hek, Hughes and Spicer, 'Preventing Social Exclusion'; Zetter, Griffiths, Ferretti and Pearl, *An Evaluation*.

perceptions and recording accounts of exclusion and marginalisation that could only come from a personal, face-to-face, approach. Given the lack of precise data on such populations there was no claim that the study could be considered in any way representative; rather, the objective of this project was to use the personal data to develop further insight into the nature of *de facto* statelessness.

The approach taken by the research team also recognised certain limitations. The researchers acknowledged that valid quantitative sampling among this population would probably be unattainable: as noted above, one of the greatest difficulties of researching the *de facto* stateless is that they are by definition an inaccessible population: it is likely there will be no records of their presence at all. Although some may be lawfully present with their living arrangements recorded in whatever way is administratively appropriate in their area, collecting survey data raises important ethical considerations. Participants may fear being seen to say something that damages them or puts them at further risk. Others may fear exposure merely of their presence, as many are in hiding. Given the fact that many exist clandestinely, it would be difficult to assess the population from which one would take a representative sample, let alone how to design such a study. One has trouble finding the necessary subjects, let alone convincing them that they will not be exposed. The usual considerations about anonymity have a much greater resonance than usual with these subjects.

A quantitative method would also have entailed an amount of empirical work well beyond the financial scope of the project and the demands of the funding agency. Given the two-year duration of the project, to be carried out comparatively in four countries, it was felt that the most effective contribution the researchers could make to our understanding of statelessness in the European Union was to develop a case study approach. This would set out the legal and administrative frameworks within which the research participants live, illustrating how those translate into everyday life, through qualitative methods, and enable the team to then compare and contrast the results across the different European jurisdictions.

The research participants were sought among a population that was already identified as fulfilling a certain criterion – namely, a status of *de jure* or *de facto* statelessness. The aim was to ensure that the research team capture as full as possible a range of responses in relation to each issue investigated. Using the 'snowball' method of sampling, this research approach assumes that selection of subjects stops once it has reached its saturation point – when the same points are brought up repeatedly – and thus further investigation will not bring anything new to answering the research questions. This is the classic method for finding hidden populations.[9]

The name of the method indicates the way that the sample population is built up, by identifying and interviewing appropriate subjects and then asking them for referrals to others they know in the same situation. The method has both strengths and potential weaknesses. Its potential weaknesses are diffusion in the encounters with the subjects, which can be guarded against by determining the structure and detail of the participation process in advance to ensure that the material is validly comparable, or a failure to engage with the relevant networks to begin with, which is prevented by care in the selection of initial contacts. The strengths of the method are that it determines relevant subjects and that it can build on local and community networks to find subjects who would otherwise be difficult or impossible to discover. There is, moreover, probably no other feasible method of carrying out this sort of investigation.

In this type of study, finding the right subjects is the first and perhaps most difficult hurdle. A personal referral may overcome both the difficulty of finding the subject and that of persuading them that taking part will not put them at risk. (It is worth mentioning that not only may stateless individuals fear exposure but those who work with them openly may fear for them, or operate more broadly in fear, too: when two of the authors of this volume first approached a respected local charity working with asylum seekers in the United Kingdom, it was explained to them that – excellent as the project sounded – the proposal would have to go to the charity's trustees, who would inevitably refuse it because past 'researchers' had turned out in fact to be infiltrators from a far-right organisation opposed to the charity's endeavours. The authors were lucky that one had published a research paper with the only solicitor still practising asylum law locally, whom the charity trusted, and an academic colleague of both was one of the charity's trustees and could vouch for us personally.) Researchers working in the other European jurisdictions equally drew upon their personal contacts and knowledge of social work professionals, lawyers and journalists to gain access to participants. Both

---

[9] See, for example, M. Patton, *Qualitative Evaluation and Research Methods* (Newbury Park, CA: Sage, 1990); R. D. Petersen and A. Valdez, 'Community Sample of Gang-Affiliated Adolescents', *Youth Violence and Juvenile Justice*, 3 (2005), 151; C. M. Flanyak, 'Accessing Data: Procedures, Practices and Problems of Academic Researchers', in M. K. Dantzker, *Readings for Research Methodologies in Criminal Justice* (Oxford: Butterworth-Heinemann, 1992).

academic and professional contact networks were brought into play, as links to the sources and subjects as well as tools for conducting the research. This is a field in which one does make one's own luck by engagement, and while this would not necessarily suffice for quantitative representative work, establishing primary data, it does enable qualitative work to be done that would otherwise be impossible.

The case studies were selected from a pool of countries of particular concern to the Rothschild Foundation (Europe) (hereafter, the 'foundation'). The foundation had been contracted by the Ford Foundation to disburse monies through the Grant Programme to Study and Prevent Anti-Semitism, Racism and Xenophobia in Europe. The programme supports activities taking place within the EU member states, in particular France, Hungary, the United Kingdom, Poland, Belgium, Italy and Germany. Although the programme did not specify the involvement of countries including those in the former Socialist bloc, the research team suggested that the nationality problems in the former Yugoslavia and Baltic states were equally relevant.

Four countries were then selected as a means of examining the conditions of *de facto* stateless people in Europe. In light of the foundation's priorities, the research team selected the United Kingdom and France among the large, West European, countries of concern. In both France and the United Kingdom, it should be noted that while there has been considerable public reaction to the plight of *de facto* stateless people, this has rarely resulted in the publication of formal studies. As noted in the literature review above, while some researchers have highlighted new problems of destitution and commented on the racist and anti-immigrant sentiment which has been related to governmental policies regarding the large numbers of refused asylum seekers still remaining on the territory, this has not yet been informed by studies which focus on nationality – though in France, the '*sans papiers*' have themselves raised protests about their situation which invited further investigation, a challenge the team was keen to undertake.

The research team then decided that two smaller states from the 'new Europe', would provide an alternative focus which would be particularly valuable to the research study. Slovenia was selected in large part because of the protracted problem surrounding the issue of the 'Erased', the former residents who lost their residency rights shortly after Slovenia seceded from the former Socialist Federal Republic of Yugoslavia (FSRY). Slovenia was a particularly attractive case study because of the heightened protest and activism over the Erased and the fact that in 2007 an application was made to the European Court of Human Rights (ECtHR).[10] A local member of the research team had previously worked on this topic and liaised with other members, was familiar with the local conditions and had excellent supporting infrastructure which it was felt would facilitate the study.

Estonia was selected as an additional case study from the former Socialist bloc because, in contrast to Slovenia, the numbers of people affected relative to the overall population were very high – approximately 30 per cent of the overall population at the time of Estonia's restoration. Another important point of contrast was the state's history of nationality reform, and the involvement of that with the history of the country as a constituent state of the Soviet Union, together with the effects of its independence after the post-Soviet transition period. Estonia had been cited as a more positive example of reform by international agencies, including the UNHCR, which noted that from Estonia's declaration of statehood, the state had actively tried to address the problem of the disenfranchisement of the ethnic Russian population. It did so by declaring that these non-citizens should enjoy the same level of social protection as Estonian nationals. It thus presented a very different example from Slovenia, which had resisted the inclusion of existing permanent residents as citizens of the newly independent state and, on the contrary, had sought to exclude and 'erase' them.

The unifying context of the comparison among the chosen jurisdictions was the uniting feature of international and regional law, discussed in chapter 4. These elements are very different, but can interact. International law in this area encompasses the Convention on Refugees and the statelessness conventions. All the countries studied are members of the European Union and so bound not only by their own history and politics but by EU legal policies. The relevant EU law for third-country (non-EU) nationals is surprisingly well developed and often does give rights to non-EU citizens, usually but not always because of family connections with EU citizens. International law is unenforceable – there is no court in which the stateless, or refugees, may enforce rights under Conventions even if their host countries have ratified them – but of considerable political importance if the countries concerned value their

---

[10] Council of Europe, *Makuc and Others* v. *Slovenia*, Application No. 26828/06, European Court of Human Rights, 31 May 2007, www.unhcr.org/refworld/docid/47fdfafdd.html. See also *Written Comments on the Case of Makuc and Others* v. *Slovenia, Application No. 26828/06 – A Submission from the Open Society Justice Initiative to the European Court of Human Rights*, www.soros.org/initiatives/justice/litigation/makuc/written-comments-20071015.pdf.

place in the international community. Of course, if that community as a whole decides to flout the rules, that importance is lost. However, even formal and enforceable law is a game that requires the participants effectively to agree to continue playing, even if it is clearer when they have decided to abdicate that responsibility. EU law, on the other hand, has strong enforcement mechanisms. These may work for or against the stateless. Thus, for example, procedures under the so-called Dublin Conventions, whereby European states return asylum seekers to the first European country they land in, often appear to be a breach of Article 32 of the 1951 Refugee Convention, but are well established as a method of controlling 'asylum shopping' among the EU states, so that asylum seekers get only one chance.

Each of the country chapters begins with a description of the particular legal system obtaining in that jurisdiction in relation to attribution of citizenship and the rights afforded to non-citizens, in theory and in practice. The legal variations in the systems in each country depend largely on the history of each state; law generally, and perhaps especially the definition as well as the treatment of non-nationals, is a highly political subject. It states who 'belongs' in terms of rules of definition and it prescribes, permits and forbids behaviour towards those who do not as well as those who do. This study demonstrates not only the wide range of rules possible within the unity of international and especially EU law, but also the practical effects of such variations.

The countries chosen most obviously differ in that two are from the former Eastern bloc and two from the West. Estonia and Slovenia have, however, different histories that are reflected directly in their legal provisions relating to statelessness. The most subtle of legal exclusions surely relates to ethnicity. This element is found, differently, in all four of the chosen jurisdictions. Estonia was part of the Soviet Union, and so before the fall of the Wall and the Warsaw Pact, her citizens were Soviet citizens, defined only as to their nationality (as opposed to citizenship) as Estonian. In the East, ethnicity and nationality are closely tied, but while in Russia desovietisation weakened the link between ethnicity and nationality by the categorisation of willing permanent residents as citizens of the new Russia, in Estonia resentment of the Soviet occupation through the Russian army led to exclusion of those whose residence in Estonia arose through military connections and so, in effect, the exclusion and statelessness of many ethnic Russians.

Slovenia had been among the most fortunate of the former Yugoslav republics in that its citizens were formally defined as belonging to a constituent nation (*narod*) which guaranteed their status as nationals, rather than members of ethnic groups (*narodnosti*) who could not lay claim to a territorial unit within the former SFRY (e.g. Muslims, Roma, Albanians and Jews). During the 1980s this specificity was reinforced by intellectuals who promoted a cultural and linguistic nationalism that excluded other Yugoslav groups, including Roma.[11] It is interesting in considering the uses of law to note that the relevant Slovene citizenship laws do not state that this is their purpose; that would invite international condemnation, perhaps especially from EU sources. A study such as this can, however, not only show how those laws can be read that way but also illustrate how clear and accurate such a reading is through the narrated experiences of the use of those laws in practice.

The two Western countries also differ between themselves. The United Kingdom, which is still in theory (and to some extent in practice) a monarchy, has a long history of the pure *jus soli* based on a nationality system emphasising allegiance to the monarch. The loss of the domestic *jus soli* in 1983 was a major legal cultural change whose ramifications are only now being fully translated into legislation, but that translation has been accomplished by the use of a philosophy of 'connection' that emphasises ethnicity.[12] France, by contrast, has a long history of law based on citizenship of the post-revolutionary strong state,[13] within which there is no apparent room for ethnicity. Nevertheless, the philosophy of *laïcité* superimposed on a culture which to the outsider at least is fundamentally Catholic[14] is a good example of incidental exclusion with strong ethnic overtones. Again, too, the French 'double *jus soli*' allows citizenship on a basis that necessarily includes elements of heritage rather than merely individual choice and behaviour.[15]

As this study deals with those excluded from the definition of national or citizen, it also exposes how the rules for the lawful presence or residence

---

[11] B. K. Blitz, 'Statelessness and the Social (De)Construction of Citizenship: Political Restructuring and Ethnic Discrimination in Slovenia', *Journal of Human Rights*, 5(4) (2006), 453.

[12] See, for example, the judgement of the European Commission in *East African Asians* v. *UK* (1973) [1981] 3 EHRR 76.

[13] R. Brubaker, *Citizenship and Nationhood in France and Germany* (Cambridge, MA: Harvard University Press, 1992a).

[14] As, for example, the public holidays not only for Christmas but also for Toussaint (1 November).

[15] As to attempts to go further: 'to prove that one was French by virtue of descent from French parents, however, involved an infinite regress', Brubaker, *Citizenship and Nationhood*, 151–2.

of non-nationals differ among the jurisdictions. Perhaps the most striking element in this respect is the clarity of the rules in question, and the
extent to which whatever rules are formulated are applied in practice.
Estonia has rules that amount to official toleration, if not recognition, of
its Russian minority; Slovenia has relatively unclear rules but has undertaken a process of using them in order to exclude its Roma in particular.
In France, those who live outside the rules and *'sans papiers'* have managed to develop rules for living that way and some official acceptance of
that; in the United Kingdom, pervasive ambiguity about status also char-
acterises the way that those without status are treated, sometimes with
great forbearance and humanity, and sometimes with none.

It is of the essence of international law that states may define their
own nationals, and EU citizenship law is likewise based on the citizenship laws of the EU member states, as well as their relevant definitions
of permanent residents. The laws of the separate jurisdictions may then
be analysed against the wish-lists of international law texts to see how
they measure up. Indeed, this is essentially the closest process that international law has to enforcement; countries generally present periodical
reports on their conformity with, or discrepancy from, the statements
of the international treaty; serious discrepancy risks disapproval. EU
membership and, increasingly, EU law are bound up with the ECHR,
which is enforceable but does not deal in the sort of positive and practical
rights that are to be found in international law. In practice, EU member
states adhere to parallel systems of human rights law since the European
Union frequently invokes the growing body of international and
regional human rights jurisprudence as a condition for participation in
EU activities; for example, the various UN and especially the European
Conventions are now crucial anchors for transitional states seeking EU
support.[16] It should be noted that the parallel systems of international
law are also important, not least because they contain specific monitoring and reporting requirements by international bodies, including the
Council of Europe.

The approach of the EU court (ECJ) at Luxembourg and the ECHR
court (ECtHR) at Strasbourg as regards the importance of citizenship are
different in emphasis, with the ECJ finding it important to embody citizenship in realistic rights, and the ECtHR giving less weight to realising

---

[16] Especially, the Convention Against Torture, the European Convention on Human Rights
and the Convention for the Prevention of Torture and Inhuman or Degrading Treatment
or Punishment.

the positive incidents of citizenship.[17] It is the concept of the minimal rights guaranteed under the ECHR that is purportedly universalist, and yet because its system takes no concern of the necessity of state protection for the implementation of its apparently universal rights, even they are relatively easily avoided in the case of non-nationals, who may be denied basic rights because they are not in the Convention, deprived of the means of enforcement of the rights that are in Convention, or expelled from the jurisdiction of the Convention itself. It is of the essence of the legal element of this study that both domestic jurisdictions and these supra-national jurisdictions are compared and contrasted for their practical effects. Among non-lawyers, in particular, the existence of international treaties may give the impression that countries will implement those rights and that there is some means for individuals to obtain redress if those rights are infringed. As this study will show, this is not the position in either theory or practice. The relevant texts of international and regional law are explained in chapter 4, and where the domestic law of each country is set out in the relevant country chapter, that can be set against those international ideals. It is possible that the international ideal or the domestic embodiment, or both, may be found wanting, and the questions asked of the participants in the study covered the implementation of the legal rights set out in international and regional law, giving the views of those who have experienced the domestic practice of the rights that they apparently should have.

Investigating rights

The rights in question were those of the basic protections from want and oppression that many consider to be the fundamental achievement of the human rights endeavour in Europe. By examining how non-nationals living in those states experienced those protections, the study addressed the importance of status in accessing these apparently universal rights. The researchers asked how the participants perceived that their lack of immigration or nationality status affected their social and economic entitlements and personal life, using a series of specific examples of aspects of daily life. The right to work was of great importance, as was the ability to

---

[17] Compare, for example *Zhu and Chen* v. *UK* Case 2000/02 [2004] ECR I-09925 17 with *Jaramillo* v. *UK* (Application No. 24865/94) and *Sorabjee* v. *UK* (Application No. 23938/94). The outcome of the *Chagos Islanders* case (Application No. 35622/04) should also make for interesting reading in this respect.

obtain decent housing and sufficient income to cover not only food but a reasonably social life. The demographics of the participants varied across the study, reflecting the varying patterns of statelessness. In the United Kingdom, the stateless are most likely to be young, single and male; they tend to be former asylum seekers who have joined previous waves of co-nationals to British cities following the traditional pattern of chain migration,[18] whereas in Estonia they are just as likely to be middle-aged, the rules of nationality having changed around them. The questions put to the participants were thus of varying relevance to the different populations: the very young, or parents, are more concerned about the right to education than are men in their twenties or thirties, and older people may be more concerned about access to healthcare. Nevertheless the same range of questions was addressed in each country study, the issues covered being:

- The right to work and access to the labour market
- Access to health care
- Social security rights, such as welfare benefits or social housing
- Access to education
- The right to establish a business, practice a profession, or work in the public service
- The right to purchase land or other housing arrangements
- The right to marry and found a family
- The right to burial in the country of residence
- Feelings of safety and security of the person
- Being safe from removal from the country of residence
- Access to the courts and the justice system
- The right to vote.

While all issues varied in importance across the jurisdictions, some were of less importance to the participants. This was often foreseeable, though still worth asking about given the centrality of the issues to the *corpus* of human rights. Rights to purchase land and housing were likely often to be irrelevant to a population that was frequently disadvantaged economically as well as otherwise, and in no position to use any such right. The right to burial was contentious only in Slovenia; the right to vote was often so much the least of participants' troubles that it had very short shrift even in the context of addressing the legal background.

[18] S. Mayhew, *A Dictionary of Geography* (Oxford: Oxford University Press, 2004).

The context of the empirical work was the comparative legal regime in each jurisdiction and the practice of implementing the rights, or lack of rights, it embodied for non-nationals in each country. As explained in chapter 1, the rights were regarded as falling into three categories – namely, the most basic rights (the right to work and make a living; rights to healthcare and shelter), social rights (to education for children, and the establishment of rights to land and to establishment in business) and political rights (voting and standing for public office). In each case, the participants were asked about their experience of the availability of these rights, and the effects of having – or, especially, not having – those rights. The results were illustrative, not probative, of the regime in each country, but offer particular illumination of the practical meaning of the rules in each individual jurisdiction. The study enables a comparison of approaches among the different countries. The empirical evidence particularly aids a view of the breadth and variety in interpretation of international and regional rules, or perhaps in the apparent expectation of their enforcement. The questions to participants covered the variety of practical rights without distinguishing their origins in law; many rights, such as the right to marry, are found in several treaties. Participants were not asked about the rights to nationality or citizenship as such, as this is a fundamentally legal question rather than one about their experience. The empirical element of this study considers the personal and individual effects of the lack of nationality or citizenship, or of a practically comparable status, in the country of residence. Those effects are most graphically experienced as the lack of basic everyday rights, such as the right to work or to access some other means of subsistence.

The ability to obtain reasonably remunerative work, legally if possible, was a central theme especially for those participants who did not have the right to work under the local law and could only subsist either miserably, or illegally, or both. The importance of the right is shown by its centrality to a number of instruments, but despite its inclusion at Article 23 of the UDHR and elsewhere, the right to work may still be heavily restricted in practice, no doubt just because of its effectiveness in preventing unwanted people from establishing a life; experiences across the study show non-nationals being prevented from working, as well as others who have full rights to work and thus usually access to a life often broadly similar to that of their citizen neighbours. The ILO Employment Policy Convention 1964 (No. 122) says at Article 1 (2) that member states should ensure that 'there is work for all who are available for and seeking work', and the right is further recited in the International Covenant on Economic, Social and

Cultural Rights 1966, where it is promised at Article 6 and favourable conditions of work are promised in Article 7. In Article 1 of the European Social Charter, its contracting parties undertake to maintain full or high employment levels and protect workers' rights to earn their living in occupations freely entered upon. These rights do not, however, come as absolutes, and do not override the interests and rights of states in preventing access to this fundamental right for those for whom they would prefer not to have responsibility. Moreover, many of these treaties have no enforcement mechanism, so that even where countries have ratified them it is envisaged that implementation will not so much be enforceable as come about gradually. The expectation is that, by a process of reporting to each other on their practices and suffering (albeit largely moral) condemnation if they are not in compliance, the countries will gradually pull closer to the ideal. Moreover, rights may be less than absolute even within the terms of treaties. For example, at Article 4 the ICESCR admits of the limitation of rights. While it states that rights under it may be 'subject … only to such limitations as are determined by law only in so far as this may be compatible with the nature of these rights and solely for the purpose of promoting the general welfare in a democratic society', the rub lies especially in the last formulation: it may easily be suggested that the general welfare of a democratic society lies in excluding and expelling those who are not entitled to its benefits by virtue of membership, and often contribution, leaving more for those who are. Thus, while all the countries in this study have ratified the ICESCR, and its terms may suggest that it offers full basic rights to the *de jure* and *de facto* stateless, in reality it may provide little practical comfort.

It is important to remember that the participants in this study are those without status. The International Convention on the Protection of the Right of All Migrant Workers and Members of Their Families thus does not apply to them, since it relates principally to those that have status as workers and has little to offer those without status. Similarly, the Declaration of the Rights of Persons Who Are Not Nationals Of the Country in Which They Live 1985 declares the right to work, to healthcare, education and social services only for those 'lawfully' resident in the territory. The *de jure* stateless may find that they benefit from laws and policies designed to give them a practical status and rights and so are better off than the *de facto* stateless for whom their country of residence feels no moral responsibility.

The Conventions relating to the Status of Refugees 1951 and the Status of Stateless Persons 1954 contain rights to social security. This study did not concern refugees as such, in respect of whom there are various specific provisions in the separate jurisdictions, and of whose position there are many studies. This study rather deals with migrants who do not qualify for refugee status. The United Kingdom, France and Slovenia are states party to the Convention Relating to the Status of Stateless Persons 1954, but Estonia is not. However, that Convention deals with the *de jure*, rather than the *de facto* stateless. Its provisions require states variously to treat the *de jure* stateless either no less favourably than other aliens or no less favourably than nationals. The latter, useful, provisions are in Articles 20–24 and relate to rationing, housing, public education and public relief, labour legislation and social security. What mostly limits the relevance of this Convention in this study is, however, that the populations of concern were *de facto* rather than *de jure* stateless, except in Estonia – the non-signatory country.

Other basic issues are that participants' rights may be mentioned in treaties so that they appear attainable, but in practice may be much less so. The right of access to healthcare is recited at Article 25 of the UDHR as part of a general right to an adequate standard of living, and specifically at Article 12 of the ICESCR, which also contains at Article 11 the right to adequate food, clothing and housing (mirroring Article 25 of the UDHR). Such positive rights form no part of the ECHR, though in extreme situations Article 3 may be invoked. Article 3 prohibits not only torture but also 'inhuman and degrading treatment'; there is then, however, a problem in that this requires some 'treatment' of the complainant by the state, within which definition it is difficult to place neglect or abandonment.[19] These 'rights' are therefore to be found where they may carry no right of individual petition, or where they are not enforceable. The same applies to rights to social security and social insurance, which are found at Article 25 of the UDHR and Article 9 of the ICESCR.

For the many participants who were unable to earn a living, the right to social security and welfare benefits were particularly important, both in sustaining daily life and in making it reasonably enjoyable (as, for example, the right to 'participation in cultural life' mentioned at Article 15 of the ICESCR). The right to adequate resources in Article 9 of the ICESCR is the most specific apparent guarantee of reasonable subsistence, but there is a general statement of rights to social security at Article 25 of the UDHR and elsewhere in the ICESCR. States are, however, unlikely to

---

[19] For exploration of this point, see the UK case of *R. (on the application of Adam)* v. *SSHD* [2005] UKHL 66.

provide financial support for people without status as a matter of policy or politics, especially if there is any hope that making life difficult or unsustainable will persuade those people to leave.

The right to education was usually relevant to participants in one of two ways: either because they were themselves still studying because they were young, or because as parents they wanted to educate their children; the relevance therefore varied with the demographics of the cohort in each country, which itself varied with the local pattern of statelessness. Article 26 of the UDHR and Article 13 of the ICESCR both speak of the right of education, but again neither is generally useful to the individual. The right to establish a business, practise a profession, or work in the public service was personally relevant to relatively few of the participants, but for those to whom it was useful it ranked with the right to seek and obtain employment.

More personal rights, such as the right to marry and found a family, or the right to burial in the country of residence, and the central political right to the franchise, are of considerable potential interest. Rights to marry have a considerable impact on rights to family reunion, which in turn affect the rights of those without status to remain in their country of residence. What makes this particularly important is that a right to family reunion is contained at Article 8 of the ECHR, which is an individually enforceable instrument binding on all countries in this study and indeed in the European Union. What may make the right to marry less important in this context is that the right to family reunion under the ECHR, and increasingly in domestic jurisdictions, is not dependent on the marital family so much as the biological family, making provisions as to marriage much less relevant to those already in the country. Access to the right to vote may well be of longer-term or more strategic interest to the stateless as a whole, since their concerns are more likely to be addressed if they are perceived as a cohort with political power; individuals may, however, often find it of less immediate concern.

Perhaps the greatest gap between the formal legal structure of rights and the needs of the stateless is likely to be found in the area of rights to feelings of security and protection from removal. The importance to states of being able to define their own members and decline responsibility for others is fundamental to international law and also to domestic political policy. It entails the opposite of security for those without status, whether in the satisfaction of their everyday needs or in the more fundamental right to remain in the country. Countries may, however, practice more or less harsh or efficient policies of identification, detention, or removal of such persons. The persuasive effect of such policies often depends as much on the desperation of those liable to removal and the perceived efficiency of the agencies charged with carrying it out as it does on the rules themselves. Participants' own subjective feelings of security are therefore of particular relevance.

Interview process

The selected participants were informed of the scope and nature of the project in advance of interviews. Some were informed in writing, with notices being left for them with NGOs and support agencies that agreed to facilitate the research by putting the teams in contact with potential participants. Others were informed by NGO workers and contacts established by the research team. All participants were assured of anonymity insofar as this is possible in any research project. The characteristics of the participants could be ascertained in such a way as to prevent their identification without impacting on the value of their participation. For example, the researchers could be referred by a local organisation offering practical assistance to poor or destitute persons without status to a prospective participant whose details, as opposed to the method of referral, would not then need to be recorded. The participants were informed of the universities' procedures with regards to ethics approvals for studies with human subjects.

An interview schedule outlining the above questions was given to each researcher, as well as a consent form. Participants were asked if the researchers were allowed to record the interviews, which lasted on average forty-five minutes, with focus groups lasting approximately ninety minutes. Interviews were recorded using digital recorders and the findings then uploaded to computer. Verbatim transcripts were produced, where possible. This interview data were then analysed, with the research team checking for consistency across the transcribed reports and organising material thematically by the categories of rights specified above and in the interview schedules. It should be noted that while most participants felt the interviews were useful or interesting and co-operated fully, a small number found the process difficult, even painful. One female participant removed herself from an interview.

Finalising of country data

Each country team then analysed and presented the results of their country study, emphasising those elements considered most interesting or appropriate. The research team as a whole met on four occasions to compare the project and findings as they progressed in each country. This enabled discussion of the differences and similarities in each country, often illuminating for researchers aspects of their own country's approach which had previously not been apparent to them. The team met in the United Kingdom twice, in Oxford in 2006, at the start of the project, and in London in 2007; in Toulon in France and Ljubljana in Slovenia during 2007; and in Tallinn in Estonia in 2008. The progress of the interviewing process was regularly discussed and monitored to ensure consistency so far as possible across the jurisdictions.

Each team wrote up its detailed findings and analysis at the end of the research period and the teams subsequently liaised by e-mail in the preparation of the finalised country studies. These were put in the context of summaries of each country's legal structures, which were prepared in tandem with the data report and analysis.

Evaluation

While qualitative research of this kind, based on illustrative interviews, cannot demonstrate causal connections, it allows researchers to present a rich portrait of selected situations and is particularly suitable for exploring individual accounts of exclusion and marginalisation that would not necessarily be captured with a less personal approach. The aim of the interviews was thus to illustrate the types and impact of loss of status and state protection as reported. Given the lack of precise data on such populations there was no claim that the study could be considered representative; rather, the objective was to use the personal data to develop further insight into the nature of *de facto* statelessness.

The empirical element of the project was very much set in an Arendtian framework: it sought to demonstrate how a lack of protection by *and from* the state negatively impacts on one's personal identity and creates feelings and situations of arbitrariness, extreme vulnerability and rightlessness. The researchers sought to understand how *de facto* stateless people operate in a world where they may be exposed to the coercive power of the state to remove them, as well as deprived of its power to protect – for example, through law enforcement and the judiciary and by providing people with benefits and access to services.

Interview data generated five preliminary lines of inquiry: (i) the primacy of work for integration and advancement; (ii) practical challenges to integration; (iii) personal development; (iv) the arbitrariness of the asylum and related systems; and (v) the prospect of return and removal. These themes were then further investigated to consider the impact that change in status had on participants' lives and how their situation was suggestive of statelessness in terms of: (a) loss of a sense of home; (b) the loss of government protection; (c) loss of 'a place in the world'. While the small sample makes it difficult to generalise from this research study, certain conclusions can be reached regarding the methods applied and their relevance to the Arendtian framework. First, in terms of the methods, the difficulties encountered by the researchers in accessing *de facto* stateless people, especially in France, the United Kingdom and Slovenia, reflect their isolation within society but also draw attention to the importance of engagement with the support sector for social science research. Indeed, the research would not have progressed without direct and energetic personal engagement, as noted in the example of the British charity above.

The researchers benefited from contacts supplied by support organisations, social workers and activists on the ground. In several cases, the placement of research assistants in the offices of support organisations successfully built trust and facilitated access to sample populations. However, the organisations' capacity to guarantee access to participants was complicated by their own institutional priorities and limited resources, especially in the context of the negative impact of governmental policies on them – all of which affected the process of attracting research participants. Without question, future research of this sort would benefit from wider application, a longer timeline and continued engagement with support organisations over the course of the study.

7

De facto statelessness in the United Kingdom

CAROLINE SAWYER, BRAD K. BLITZ AND
MIGUEL OTERO-IGLESIAS

The United Kingdom: changing statuses in a country of historical immigration

The legal context for those without immigration status has changed fundamentally in the United Kingdom in recent decades; in British legal terms, this is a very short time scale. The issue is perhaps a bigger one, though – until the later twentieth century, the British law of belonging was structured as befitted a country of immigration that had acquired an Empire. Its inclusive approach to belonging encompassed anyone who chose to make a life in the United Kingdom, and the formal nationality structure was also inclusive, encompassing anyone born in the territory. The principle that anyone 'born within the dominion or allegiance' of the monarch was British was affirmed in *Calvin's Case* in 1608[1] and confirmed by codification in the British Nationality and Status of Aliens Act 1914. Nationality by descent and naturalisation processes were gradually established. Anyone born within the British Empire, which at one point covered about 20 per cent of the world, was British and could come to and live in the United Kingdom. By the end of the Second World War in 1945, the number of British people who could come and live in the United Kingdom and exercise all civic rights there was about 600,000,000.[2] After the Second World War, Britain began shed most of her colonies, and with them their people. Under the British Nationality Act 1948, it was intended that individuals should in effect transfer to their countries of residence as those countries became independent. Decolonisation was, however, so uncomfortable for minority

---

[1] 7 Coke Report 1a; 77 ER 377.
[2] R. Hansen, 'From Subjects to Citizens: Immigration and Nationality in the United Kingdom' in R. Hansen and P. Weill (eds.), *Towards a European Nationality* (Basingstoke: Palgrave Macmillan, 2001).

communities within some colonies that many people preferred to come to the United Kingdom.

The United Kingdom, however, became increasingly unwelcoming. In the 1960s, Britain restricted the right of abode (residence) in the United Kingdom to those with ancestral ties, using 'immigration' legislation.[3] Then in 1983, the rules of nationality and citizenship were redrawn under the British Nationality Act 1981. This instituted six kinds of British nationality, of which only one was called 'citizenship'. British citizenship – a phrase with no legal meaning before 1983 – was also the only status that gave the automatic right of abode in the United Kingdom. At the same time, the pure *jus soli* was attenuated, so that British citizenship was granted to those born in the United Kingdom only if one of their parents was British or 'settled' in the United Kingdom. Where few appreciated the effects of the second change, that was largely because the definition of British-born British citizen was still very inclusive. 'Settlement', like the idea of the *jus soli* throughout the Empire, was an old-fashioned concept, but one which is still important in legislation, where it is defined as presence in the country without restrictions on one's stay.[4] Leave to remain (residence granted to those without the right of abode) and citizenship were relatively generously given. Indefinite Leave to Remain was, for example, granted to anyone recognised as a refugee until August 2005. There were, and are, broad provisions for registration as a British citizen for those born in the United Kingdom without British citizenship at birth.

Even after these changes, in a country where record-keeping about individuals was somewhat haphazard and there was no practice of identity papers, at the level of day-to-day life there were still few or no practical differences between foreigners and British people. After the exclusion of the overseas-British in the 1960s and the withdrawing of the domestic boundaries of formal citizenship in the 1980s, the 1990s saw greater exclusions from everyday belonging. The effective system of belonging by presence and choice that had been encouraged by a longstanding laissez-faire attitude to immigrants was changed, both in the public imagination and by legislation. In the 1980s, the highly publicised advent of uninvited Tamils from Sri Lanka coincided with the end of the Cold War, and the

---

[3] The so-called 'patriality' rule, introduced under the Commonwealth Immigrants Acts of the 1960s. Informal discrimination on the basis of race was widespread: see, for example, P. Shah, *Refugees, Race and the Legal Concept of Asylum in Britain* (London: Cavendish, 2000).

[4] Section 33 (2) Immigration Act 1971.

perception of refugees as the occasional hero fleeing from East Germany gave way to one of streams of Eastern Europeans, only increased further by the wars in the Balkans in the 1990s. This in turn was easily, if inappropriately, confused in the mind of some with the influx of Eastern European workers after EU enlargement. Against a background of a perceived vast growth in the numbers of people seeking refuge in the United Kingdom, the concept of the heroic, deserving 'refugee' was replaced with that of the demanding, maybe 'bogus' 'asylum seeker'.[5] Legislation and its interpretation in case law over the following period reflected media concerns with a gradual but inexorable change of culture. Parliament led the way, the judiciary at first fighting but then effectively acceding to the fundamental shift from inclusion in the social fabric to exclusion and expulsion.

That the public debate was for many years conducted entirely with reference to 'asylum seekers' for a period of years is a symptom of the lack of clarity throughout the British system of immigration and nationality status. Among the variety of technical legal statuses, many were and are very unclear. The term 'asylum seeker' is itself a recent coining, and had no legal meaning until 2003.[6] Many asylum seekers were on 'temporary admission',[7] but it was unclear that the term denoted lawful presence in the United Kingdom until 2005, and even then the clarification was controversial.[8] Entitlement to social rights such as the right to work or claim welfare benefits was still based on residence rather than immigration status. The move from entitlement by residence to entitlement by status was and is very difficult to achieve, since it involves a change of administrative culture that re-defines an existing population. The early procedure of giving identity cards to asylum seekers clearly did not work; a person could simply say they did not have one, and so look British.[9] Eventually it was decided that the United Kingdom would adopt a system of formal identity cards for everyone, which government ministers have variously claimed is to help prevent identity fraud in money transactions, to assist in the detection of crime, or to establish who is entitled to be present or to work in the United Kingdom. Primary legislation was passed in 2006 for the

[5] S. Chakrabarti, 'Rights and Rhetoric: The Politics of Asylum and Human Rights Culture in the UK', *Journal of Law and Society*, 32 (2005), 131.

[6] SI 2003/1, bringing into force section 18 Nationality, Immigration and Asylum Act 2002. The term now officially encompasses many people who have never sought asylum at all, but no-one under eighteen, even if they have.

[7] Para 21, Sch. 1 Immigration Act 1971   [8] See n. 12 below.

[9] Asylum Registration Cards (ARC) were introduced in January 2002, replacing a Standard Acknowledgement Letter with a credit-card-style item identifying the holder by photograph and fingerprint.

setting up of an identity database which did not, however, clearly explain how it would be decided who would go on the database and with what status – nor indeed how individuals' status would be clarified in cases of doubt.[10] These plans became mired in moral and financial controversy as well as computer problems.

Legislation to disqualify first of all 'asylum seekers' and then others without immigration status from enjoying social rights in the United Kingdom was passed persistently, beginning with the Asylum and Immigration Appeals Act 1993. This Act included the first mention of the Refugee Convention in primary legislation; it fell well short of incorporating it into domestic law, merely saying that nothing in the Immigration Rules should contravene it.[11] The meaning of the term 'refugee' was re-defined by the House of Lords in 2005 to something so contrary to international and indeed European law that the United Kingdom could effectively refrain from taking any more refugees at all without any domestically apparent breach of her obligations.[12] The real targets were not asylum seekers, but uninvited immigrants. For a considerable period, given the lax practices of the Home Office, even an unjustified claim for asylum could give an immigrant a legitimate status sufficient to make a life, sometimes indefinitely. The practice was of long standing, and established by the Home Office's failure to keep records or follow up asylum applications, inviting the misuse of the process that was subsequently complained of.[13] The campaign against asylum seekers was in reality a campaign against those without status.

A series of parliamentary Acts, beginning in 1993, was intended to make life difficult for those without status.[14] Appended to the Immigration Act 1971, these have become officially known as the 'Immigration Acts'.[15] Step by step, sometimes after fights with the judiciary, the legislature withdrew the means of subsistence from those without formal status. They were prevented from working, from claiming benefits, often from obtaining medical help or legal advice, and generally from making a life. This was

---

[10] Identity Cards Act 2006.   [11] Section 2 Asylum and Immigration Act 1993.

[12] See *Szoma* v. *DWP* [2005] UKHL 64 and C. Sawyer, 'Elephants in the Room, or: A Can of Worms', *Journal of Social Security Law*, 17 (2007), 86.

[13] An incoming Home Secretary, John Reid, famously described the Home Office in 2006 as 'not fit for purpose' (a misquotation from the Sale of Goods Act 1979), http://news.bbc.co.uk/2/hi/uk_news/politics/5007148.stm.

[14] C. Sawyer and P. Turpin, 'Neither Here Nor There: Temporary Admission to the UK', *International Journal of Refugee Law*, 17 (2005), 688.

[15] Section 64 Immigration, Asylum and Nationality Act 2006.

intentional, but even then beset by ambiguity, given the lack of clarity of the statuses people might hold and the conflicting constructions of rights those statuses might bring.

Further changes to nationality law followed. The Nationality, Immigration and Asylum Act 2002 had also provided for easier deprivation of British citizenship and nationality, including from those born in the United Kingdom.[16] The Immigration, Asylum and Nationality Act 2006 produced the most draconian current law in Europe, allowing deprivation of citizenship if the Secretary of State considered that to be 'conducive to the public good'.[17] The Identity Cards Act of 2006 excited much debate, some of it over the cost and efficacy of the necessary computer system. The legislative reform of immigration and nationality was continued with the UK Borders Act 2007 and the Borders, Immigration and Citizenship Act 2009, and still continues.

Alongside the primary legislation restructuring the institutional framework, secondary legislation provided for the detail. These rules are made by ministers, usually without the scrutiny of Parliament. Most court cases about individual rights even now turn on these small provisions in secondary legislation, but so did one of the earliest, and most famous, judicial revolts. Commenting on an early provision withdrawing the means of subsistence from asylum seekers, Simon Brown, LJ in *JCWI* v. *SSSS* in 1996,[18] asserted that such a drastic step could not be made by secondary legislation. But eventually, when the highest court in the United Kingdom officially supported the abandonment of the international definition of 'refugee' and removed the basis for many asylum seekers' rights, it was Lord Brown of Eaton-under-Heywood, the former Simon Brown, LJ, who gave the judgement.[19]

Health system

The UK National Health Service (NHS), instituted following the Second World War and largely credited to Aneurin ('Nye') Bevan and Jennie Lee, was a system based on need and free at the point of delivery. In a country where identity cards were, until recently, deprecated, there was no real

---

[16] Section 4, adding the grounds for deprivation of doing something seriously prejudicial to the United Kingdom's interests.

[17] Section 56, with similar provisions in section 57 relating to the right of abode.

[18] *R (on the application of Joint Council for the Welfare of Immigrants)* v. *Secretary of State for Social Security* [1996] I WLR 275.

[19] See n. 12 above.

system of restricting access to free medical treatment, and such restrictions were generally regarded as contrary to the ethos of the health service itself. Those who were ordinarily resident could and still can obtain NHS treatment.[20]

The issue of 'ordinary residence' came to be disputed early, and the House of Lords case of *Shah*[21] remains good law. It was established there that it entails a regular habitual way of life in the place of residence, with a settled purpose and with some continuity, but not necessarily with permanence. A person may be ordinarily resident in more than one country at a time. Subsequent evidence may be adduced to give the benefit of hindsight.[22] However, in *Shah* Lord Scarman also said that unlawful presence could not constitute ordinary residence. At that time, the distinction between lawful and unlawful presence had yet to become a hotly debated topic, but was nevertheless known to be often unclear.

A strong media attack on the use by foreign nationals of NHS resources came in the summer of 2003, with particular reference to those who were obtaining HIV/AIDS treatment. The position of such people has been a particular source of legal tension in the United Kingdom, with two leading cases turning on it. The change in approach between the two cases shows a strong hardening of attitudes to their removal between cases in the mid-1990s and a decade later. In *D* v. *UK* (1996), the ECtHR had upheld Mr D's claim that to deport him at the end of his prison sentence to certain and immediate death would amount to a breach of Article 3 of the ECHR.[23] In *N* v. *SSHD* (2005), however, the House of Lords put an end to the previous understanding that longer-term residents without immigration status who were having AIDS treatment that would not be continued were they to be removed would be able to resist removal for that reason. Distinguishing *D* v. *UK* (1996), they said that removal would breach Article 3 only in the most exceptional circumstances. The tenor of the judgement suggests, indeed, that they might have liked to be able to reopen the issues in *D* v. *UK*, were it not for the precedent set by the Strasbourg court, though human sympathy was extended to the unfortunate Ms N and the hope expressed that the Home Office would extend it, too. The decision against Ms N was upheld in the Grand Chamber at Strasbourg.[24]

---

[20] H. Carty, 'Overseas Visitors and the NHS', *Journal of Social Welfare and Family Law*, 45 (1983), 258–264.

[21] *R* v. *Barnet LBC ex parte Shah* [1983] 2 AC 309.

[22] *R.* v. *IAT ex parte Siggins* [1985] IAR 14.

[23] *D* v. *UK* (1997) 24 EHRR 423; *N* v. *SSHD* [2005] UKHL 31.

[24] *N* v. *UK* [2008] ECHR 453; *N* v. *SSHD* [2005] UKHL 31.

Between the cases of *D* and *N*, the Department of Health made changes to the regulations and practice with the National Health Service (Charges to Overseas Visitors) (Amendment) Regulations 2004[25] which have had widely reported and serious effects on those who are without status and without financial resources. Figures of '£50 – £200 million' were given in Parliament as the costs of the treatment given to the unentitled, though enquiries as to the source for these figures elicited no response and the true figure was also put at considerably less.[26] Concerns over the public health effects of not treating certain communicable diseases have combined with some doctors' resistance to refusing to treat the sick or to checking immigration status have meant that attempts to remove NHS medical treatment from the unentitled have been only patchily successful and the position remains confused.[27] While medical treatment for some conditions whose lack of treatment would have serious social consequences – such as treatment for tuberculosis, antenatal care and midwifery, and emergency treatment – has therefore remained free, other treatments, including for HIV/AIDS (where the treatment is represented in the media as inviting foreigners who are sick with a stigmatised disease to come to the United Kingdom) is restricted.

The legal framework has been similarly awkward to change. In 2009, the discussion of the Court of Appeal in *R on the application of YA* v. *Secretary of State for Health* (2009),[28] the tenor of the discussion was clearly not whether asylum seekers should have to pay for their healthcare so much as the definition of 'the people of England', whom the NHS should treat free. Government Guidance[29] still refers to persons who are 'ordinarily resident' in England, and includes in that definition those who have been lawfully resident in England for the preceding twelve months. The Guidance refers to those who are 'settled', though clearly not using the term as the immigration legislation does.[30] The Court of Appeal's conclusion was

---

[25] SI 2004/614.   [26] Lords Hansard 9 December 2003 Col. 923.

[27] See n. 26 above and, for example, British Medical Association General Practitioners' Committee, 'Guidance for GPs' (2006), www.bedshertslmcs.org.uk/Guidance/guidance Documents/Overseas%20visitors%20March%202006.doc and I. Anya, 'The Right to Healthcare for Vulnerable Migrants', *The Lancet*, 370 (8 September 2007), 827.

[28] [2009] EWCA Civ 225.

[29] Guidance issued from government departments is not part of statute, but has the force of law.

[30] Department of Health, *National Health Service: Implementing the Overseas Visitors Hospital Charging Regulations: Guidance for NHS Trust Hospitals in England* (2009), www.dh.gov.uk/prod_consum_dh/groups/dh_digitalassets/@dh/@en/documents/ digitalassets/dh_081516.pdf, for example, says there is no minimum period of residence

largely that the rules on the giving and withholding of NHS treatment to those without the requisite status was unclear, save where treatment is 'immediately necessary', when it is given free, though if the patient will not be able to pay it may be limited to what will enable them to return to their home country. The NHS is very dear to the British public heart, and restricting its use is politically as well as practically sensitive.

Currently NHS treatment is thus available to anyone, without restriction as to status, for emergency treatment, antenatal and maternity care, and certain diseases such as tuberculosis, but not HIV/AIDS. Otherwise, it is available only to those who are ordinarily resident, which excludes all those whose presence in the United Kingdom is unlawful. Most adults have to pay a flat charge for prescriptions for medicines that are not given in hospital; the charges are high enough to cause difficulty for the poor, and there are schemes to exempt some, including children under sixteen. The provisions are overall a balance among considerations of humanity, the practical effects of untreated communicable diseases and the financial costs of treatment. Those of concern in this study would mostly be ineligible for free treatment; however, most were young and fit and this might not be high among their priorities.

Educational system

Although it is compulsory for those with the care of children to see that they are educated up to the age of sixteen, it is not compulsory to send the child to a school for that purpose, though it is usual. Local education authorities (councils) are obliged to make education provision for all school age children in their area, regardless of the children's immigration status or rights of residence, save in relation to children in accommodation centres.[31] Central funding to the local authorities is the same for all children, but there is additional funding support for schools with children whose first language is not English, and children who have arrived recently from overseas need not be counted in reports of central tests of school achievements – otherwise schools would be unwilling to take them, as good test results are valuable. Children in receipt

related to being 'settled', and suggests it is about intentions for the future (rather like domicile, a different legal concept), whereas the immigration legislation describes it as being in the United Kingdom without limitations on one's stay (section 33 (2A) Immigration Act 1971/section 50 (2)–(4) British Nationality Act 1981).

[31] Sections 13, 14 and 19 Education Act 1996; School Standards and Framework Act 1998, sections 86 and 118.

of state support, including welfare benefits or vouchers, are entitled to free lunches at school. Some local authorities may assist with the cost of school uniforms.

Admission to a school depends on acceptance by the school itself. State schools are controlled in the admissions systems they may operate. The system of geographical catchment areas within a local authority area usually means that a child is entitled to a place at the local state school, but over-subscribed schools may refuse a child if they are full; a place may then be available further away. School admissions policies generally are the subject of intense public debate and often legal challenge.

Full participation in school and related activities may involve travel abroad, which for those without a passport may be impossible. School visas exist, which cover a whole group, but obtaining such a visa involves the school investigating the position of each child. Where this presents difficulties schools will often decide not to seek the visa but to leave it to all the children to make their own separate passport arrangements.

It seems likely that most difficulties experienced in the education system by children of families without immigration status will however be financial rather than formal. Even 'free' state education now entails many expenses. University tuition is no longer free, and if a person without immigration status manages to obtain and take up a university place they will be charged the much higher fees payable by overseas students.

Employment

The persons of concern to this project generally have no right to work in the United Kingdom, though some people with a temporary and fragile immigration status do have it. 'Settled' persons have the right to work. 'Work permits' are granted specifically for the employee to take up a specific job. Those with other forms of leave, such as student visas, have more or less extensive rights to work as a secondary element of their leave to enter the United Kingdom. Some statuses are less clear. Asylum seekers or others on 'temporary admission'[32] have variously been granted that status with or without a restriction as to working. It is generally difficult to obtain the right to work after arriving in the United Kingdom without it; currently, asylum seekers usually do not have the right to work. There is continuing public debate on whether asylum seekers ought to work rather than have to be supported by the taxpayer, and whether immigrants

---

[32] See n. 14 above.

are an impediment to local workers seeking jobs or are necessary to the economy.

Working without permission attracts criminal penalties and renders a person liable to removal from the country if caught. A record of working without permission will mean that it is very difficult to obtain a lawful immigration status in future. The legal framework surrounding the employment of 'illegal' workers has gradually strengthened since section 8 of the Asylum and Immigration Appeals Act 1996, which was passed in an attempt to make real the prohibition on asylum seekers working. It provided for a penalty on those employing 'illegal' workers, with the proviso that it was a defence to show they had seen a relevant work document and taken a copy of it. As a result, everyone now generally has to take such papers to job interviews in the United Kingdom – this broke down somewhat the cultural resistance to carrying 'papers'. Formal restrictions on asylum seekers working ensued.

There is however a large underground economy employing 'illegal' workers. Periodically, substantial cohorts of such workers are found by journalists to be working in the NHS or even the Home Office,[33] and in 2009, the Attorney General was fined for employing a housekeeper who did not have the right to work.[34] Inevitably, many such 'illegal' workers are paid below the minimum wage and lack the protections of trade unions or the health and safety legislation. This indeed is often what makes them popular with employers. Particular concerns in the agricultural industry led in 2004 to regulation of 'gangmasters', who engage casual labour for farms and similar enterprises, following the deaths of a number of Chinese cockle-pickers in Morecambe Bay.[35]

Employment in the United Kingdom, as opposed to self-employment, is taxed at source. In addition, National Insurance (NI, or social security) contributions are also deducted at source in the 'Pay As You Earn' (PAYE) system. In practice, the only centralised identification a person required to take up employment until the past decade was a NI number. NI numbers were easily available to anyone on application until November 2005. This practice was curtailed after it was realised that it gave an appearance of legitimate status to those without it, though to an extent that had to be reversed because of the ambiguities surrounding various statuses,

---

[33] www.dailymail.co.uk/news/article-1240204/Jobs-illegals-Home-Office-dozens-NHS-public-bodies-break-immigration-laws.html.

[34] http://news.bbc.co.uk/2/hi/uk_news/magazine/8268603.stm.

[35] http://news.bbc.co.uk/2/hi/uk_news/england/lancashire/3464203.stm; Gangmasters (Licensing) Act 2004.

especially temporary admission. The centralisation of tax offices also began during that decade, together with the cross-referencing of NI and tax records. It used to be possible and indeed easy for anyone, not only for those without immigration status, to obtain an identity, or indeed several, by merely applying for an NI number. Many people, both workers and employers, erroneously believe that possession of an NI number constitutes proof of the right to work.

Social security benefits

As well as the NHS, the immediate post-war era saw the introduction of a comprehensive social security system in the United Kingdom, on a model suggested by the economist William Beveridge. Whilst the sufficiency of benefits might attract as much criticism as the efficiency of their administration, until August 1994 entitlement to social security benefits was established by residence, not by status. To claim, a person needed to be over eighteen, to have no income or an income below the 'applicable amount' and not to have remunerative work.[36] The Income Support (General) Regulations 1987 stated that the 'applicable amount' for a 'person from abroad' was nil.[37] Presence in the country was sufficient for EU nationals to claim welfare benefits before 1994, but others had to be lawfully present.[38] However, it was not clear what the scope of 'lawful presence' was, and there was in any event no usual way of proving status: most people, most of the time, claimed social and civic rights on the basis of presence and their own say-so, until the change of culture that began with the 1993 Act.

The first big case on the deliberate withdrawal of social and civic rights as part of effective immigration policy was *JCWI* v. *SSSS*, where Simon Brown, LJ, as he then was, decried the withdrawal of welfare rights from asylum seekers, describing it as a 'sorry state of affairs'.[39] On the legal issue of giving asylum seekers the choice between subsistence and abandoning their asylum claim, he said that this was such a grave step that it could not be made in secondary legislation, but only by Parliament in primary legislation. The subsequent Acts of Parliament might be considered a response to that assertion.

---

[36] Section 124 Social Security Contributions and Benefits Act 1992.
[37] SI 1987/1967, Sch. 7, para. 17. There were stated exceptions, such as persons from the European Union, refugees and those granted Exceptional Leave to Remain.
[38] *R(SB)* 25/85 (*Commissioner* v. *G.H. Hallett*), www.rightsnet.org.uk/pdfs/rsb/25_85.pdf.
[39] See n. 18 above.

In 1994, a requirement of 'habitual residence' was added.[40] This was a fundamental cultural change, made by statutory instrument – that is, administratively rather than by Parliament, as had been deprecated by Simon Brown, LJ in the *JCWI* case.[41] The mischief it was reputed to redress was that of 'benefit tourism' – the claiming of welfare benefits by foreigners intent on merely living as easily as possible off the resident population.[42] Whether or not the feeling was a creature of the media, it was certainly perceived, as Lord Hoffmann said, that: 'Voters became concerned that the welfare state should not be a honey pot which attracted the wretched of the earth.'[43]

The House of Lords looked particularly at how one establishes a new 'habitual residence' and how long it takes to do that, in *Nessa* v. *Chief Adjudication Officer* (1999).[44] Here Lord Slynn suggested that 'habitual residence' could be established by '[b]ringing possessions, doing everything necessary to establish residence before coming, having a right of abode, seeking to bring the family, "durable ties" with the country of residence, and many other factors ...'. The difficulty that even very senior judges had with the term suggested to one commentator that the term was 'formulated with more thought for political expediency than for legal practicality'.[45]

So far as asylum seekers were concerned, the Immigration Acts from 1993 onwards contained various provisions restricting welfare payments to them, or requiring them to be made by vouchers rather than cash.[46] After the *JCWI* case, a further major clash between the Home Secretary

---

[40] Income-Related Benefit Schemes (Miscellaneous Amendments) (No. 3) Regulations 1994 (SI 1994/1807). See M. Adler, 'The Habitual Residence Test: A Critical Analysis', *Journal of Social Security Law*, 2 (1995), 179.

[41] See n. 18 above. For problems with the related concept of 'ordinary residence', see CIS/3197/2004 Rowland 15 March 2005, where Commissioner Rowland refused to allow an appellant to give up, allowed his appeal and refused to allow him leave to withdraw the appeal should he wish to do so.

[42] See, for example, the discussion in CH/2321/2007, para. 10.

[43] *R (Westminster City Council)* v. *National Asylum Support Service* [2002] UKHL 38, 1 WLR 2956. *The Wretched of the Earth* is the English title of Franz Fanon's 1961 work *Les damnés de la terre*, on the Algerian fight for independence from France.

[44] [1999] 1 WLR 1937.

[45] P. Larkin, 'Migrants, Social Security, and the "Right to Reside"', *Journal of Social Security Law*, 14 (2007), 65.

[46] A provision brought in by the Asylum and Immigration Act 1996, subsequently abandoned and then returned to. See A. Eagle *et al.*, *Asylum Seekers' Experiences of the Voucher Scheme in the UK – Fieldwork Report*, (2002) www.homeoffice.gov.uk/rds/pdfs2/asylumexp.pdf.

and the judiciary came with an appeal against the effects of section 55 Nationality, Immigration and Asylum Act 2002, whereby asylum seekers who did not make their asylum claim at the port of entry would not be supported at all. This provision was eventually held to be unlawful in the case of Q.[47] This heralded a protracted and more general dispute between the government and the judiciary which was given wide publicity and even attracted some academic legal commentary.[48] The issue itself was the withdrawal of support for asylum seekers who did not claim immediately on arrival in the country.[49] The Asylum (Treatment of Claimants, etc.) Act 2004, in its original form, would have provided for the removal of the right of asylum seekers to seek judicial review of their cases through the courts, but the general and judicial protest was sufficient for that clause to be removed. The remainder of the 2004 Act still, however, contained some of the harshest provisions, including rules effectively preventing many foreigners from marrying, later deprecated by the House of Lords, and provisions removing rights to welfare benefits even for families with children which were too harsh even for the public taste, and were not used.

On 1 May 2004 a requirement, further to that of 'habitual residence', of a 'right to reside' was introduced.[50] Moreover, a person could not be 'habitually resident' without the 'right to reside'. In July 2007, the Court of Appeal considered this in *Abdirahman* v. *SSWP* (2007).[51] It found that a person might nevertheless be lawfully resident in the United Kingdom without having a 'right to reside'. A substantial group excluded by the rules were asylum seekers, who had no right to reside unless and until they had

---

[47] *R (on the Application of 'Q' and Others)* v. *SSHD* [2003] EWCA 364.

[48] *R* v. *SSHD ex parte Q* [2003] EWHC 1941 (Admin); Richard Rawlings, 'Review, Revenge and Retreat', *March Law Review*, 68 (2005), 378.

[49] Convention on the Status of Refugees 1951 Article 31 requires that no penalties be visited on refugees for unlawful entry provided they present themselves to the authorities without delay. In *Shire* v. *SSWP* [2003] EWCA Civ 1465, for example, Woolf, LJ considered that explanations of a delay of two days after arrival through an agent from Yemen were insufficient. The issue of presentation without delay was not, however, new: see also CIS/4439/1998 Commissioner Rowland, 25 November 1999, which, however, concerned a dispute as to whether a claim had been recorded at all.

[50] Social Security (Habitual Residence) Amendment Regulations 2004 SI 2004/1232; Income Support (General) Regulations 1987 Reg. 21 (3g); Housing Benefit (General) Regulations 1987; Council Tax Benefit (General Regulations) 1992; State Pension Credit Regulations 2002.*Yesiloz* v. *London Borough of Camden and Secretary of State for Work and Pensions* R(H)7/09, upheld Court of Appeal *Yesiloz* v. *LBC and SSWP* [2009] EWCA Civ 415.

[51] [2007] EWCA Civ 657.

been recognised as refugees by the Home Office, who were notoriously dilatory at doing anything.[52]

A particular aspect of the position of asylum seekers in the United Kingdom was dramatically altered at the end of 2005, in a way which looked at first advantageous to them, but whose overall effect is seriously deleterious.[53] Asylum seekers used routinely to be given the status of 'temporary admission'.[54] This allowed them to be physically present in the United Kingdom without contravening immigration rules, but was not leave to enter the United Kingdom as such. If their asylum claim was decided favourably, they would until August 2005 be given Indefinite Leave to Remain which, for most practical purposes, was indistinguishable from citizenship.[55] Perhaps half a million people lived, and maybe still live, in the United Kingdom with the non-status of temporary admission, which was not confined to asylum seekers.[56] The lack of status was unimportant until the rules as to permissible working began to be enforced after 1996 and the rules as to claiming welfare benefits changed in 1994 and 2004. The decision in *Szoma* was that those on temporary admission were 'lawfully present' for the purposes of certain bilateral treaties, but the issue had to be fought out in numerous smaller social security cases.[57] However, in the course of the *ratio*, the case also held that an asylum seeker was not a refugee until accepted as such by the Home Office. Making this acceptance constitutive rather than declaratory of refugee status was a departure from international norms as well as previous domestic law.[58]

During the period covered by this study, nationals of Eastern Europe were affected particularly by these rules. Asylum seekers were often nationals of the accession states. Some might then have qualified for benefits as EU workers, so there followed a series of tribunal and court decisions considering the interrelation between domestic welfare legislation and the definition of 'worker' imported by Council Reg. 1408/71 for

---

[52] See the remarks of Lloyd, LJ, para. 19, where he does not distinguish between refugee status, which is not an immigration status, and the immigration status it brings; at the time of the case, that was five years' leave, but this was a recent change from the previous Indefinite Leave to Remain.

[53] *Szoma* v. *DWP* [2005] UKHL 64.   [54] Para. 21, Sch. 2 Immigration Act 1971.

[55] This changed from August 2005, after which they were generally given five years' leave, which still brought the right to work and claim benefits.

[56] No one really knows how many: see HC Home Affairs Committee, Immigration Control HC 775-III (*Fifth Report*, Session 2005–2006), Ev. 149.

[57] See, for example, CIA/1773/2007, in respect of a Turkish national whose asylum claim had been rejected, as were all her other claims.

[58] See Sawyer, 'Elephants in the Room'.

any EU citizen.[59] After *Abdirahman* in 2007 it was clear that temporary admission did not amount to a right to reside, which required 'more than a mere right to be present'. A favourable decision on an asylum claim – not precluded by accession – would have a profound effect on an EU non-worker. Nevertheless the Home Office tended to abandon all asylum claims by those from accession states. 'This is yet another case where the immigration authorities appear to have discontinued action on the claimant's asylum claim merely because he had been a citizen of the European Union when mere citizenship was not enough to confer on him a right of residence', said a judge in one case, and in another: 'If social security entitlement is to be linked to immigration status, it is necessary for the immigration authorities to make the necessary decision when they have been requested to do so.'[60] The effect of the Home Office practice was to exclude refugees from Eastern Europe – often Roma – by a form of administrative abdication.

Home Office practice also excited judicial criticism elsewhere. A remarkable number of people entitled to Jobseeker's Allowance, a particular benefit for unemployed persons who nevertheless qualified as 'workers', were wrongly told by benefit officers to apply for Income Support, a benefit for those without other means but whose availability was much more restricted.[61] Those who did not qualify might however still be refugees – but not for the purposes of welfare benefits, if the Home Office failed to deal with their claim.

[59] See, for example, CIS 3789/06 Commissioner Howell 23 September 2008; CIS/3216/2006 and CIS/4345/2006 Commissioner Rowland 22 August 2008; CIS/185/2008; CIS 868/008 Commissioner Howell 24 September 2008; CIS/3505/2007 [2009] UKUT 25 (AAC) UTJ Jacobs; CIS/0408/2009 *PM* v. *SSWP* UTJ Jacobs [2009] UKUT 236 (AAC). A notable proportion of claimants are ethnic Somalis. For the experience of a Somali national, see CIA/2702/2000.

[60] Per Rowland in CIS/1773/2007, para. 12, and in CJSA/2687/2007 [2009] UKUT 208 (AAC) para. 16 (where a Lithuanian national's asylum claim was never determined). See also R. Sales, 'The Deserving and Undeserving? Refugees, Asylum Seekers and Welfare in Britain', *Critical Social Policy*, 22(3) (2002), 456.

[61] See, for example, CIS/593/2009 *SSWP* v. *CA* [2009] UKUT 169 (AAC) Poynter, DJ: 'This is yet another one of those unfortunate and avoidable appeals in which a claimant who was entitled to, and receiving, jobseeker's allowance has been advised by Job Centre staff to claim income support instead and then found that she is refused … because she does not have a relevant right to reside in the United Kingdom' (para. 1). 'This appeal is just one example of a problem which, in my day-to-day experience … is occurring regularly and frequently … there is something unattractive about advising a claimant who is properly receiving jobseeker's allowance … to claim income support instead and then, once she has done so – and has given up her right to jobseeker's allowance – telling her she is not entitled to income support. Claimants are certainly left with a strong and justified sense of grievance when that happens' (paras. 16–17).

Setting up a business

There are no restrictions on running a business in the United Kingdom that depend on national or immigration status. EU citizens have the right to establishment. It is possible for others to obtain immigration status on the basis of being a wealthy person who will employ people in the United Kingdom, and this status may be enlarged over time into settlement and citizenship, but this is not guaranteed. Mohammed Al-Fayed, who bought the famous London shop Harrods, has famously been unable to secure a British passport.[62]

There might be practical difficulties in setting up a business if a lack of official immigration status means that one has problems obtaining appropriate references or banking services. These problems can be got round by having sufficient private wealth to obtain immigration permission on the basis of being an investor, or by operating through friends or through limited companies where others are willing to give any necessary guarantees.

More complex is the situation of someone who seeks social security benefits based on a past period of self-employment, where that self-employment is also relied on to establish a 'right to reside' (see above, p. 172). For example, a Czech interpreter who claimed to have established a right of residence as a self-employed person, and thus to be entitled to Income Support, had to go to appeal to establish his rights because of errors made by the public authorities.[63] It was asserted, wrongly, by the Secretary of State that the registration of foreign workers was required for them to bring themselves within the definition of self-employment. The previous tribunal had wrongly accepted the Secretary of State's word for that without requiring reference to the authority for it, which did not exist.

Working in public services

Much public service working in the United Kingdom, through local councils or in schools, operates in the same way as private employment, so that entitlement to work in the United Kingdom has to be shown. The same applies to the lower reaches of the central government civil service. However, there is a test of nationality – for example, for the judiciary – and

[62] *Fayed* v. *SSHD* [1997] 1 All ER 228.
[63] CIS/3213/2007 [2009] UKUT 58 (AAC) Rowland.

appointment to more elevated civil service ranks may be subject to a nationality test that includes previous generations. In a society that has a tradition of assimilation but not of paperwork, this can mean an unexpected inability to take up a senior post through a paper trail that goes cold very quickly or reveals that a parent never regularised their status in the United Kingdom. The scope of this is limited in numbers but it can be devastating to individuals. For most people, however, working in the public services is no different from elsewhere.

Access to the courts and justice systems

The 'Immigration Acts'[64] of the 1990s were part of a general campaign to change legislative culture and exclude those without status. The Bill that became the 1996 Act was brought in, according to the Home Secretary, Michael Howard, to 'strengthen our asylum procedures so that bogus claims and appeals can be dealt with more quickly; ... to combat immigration racketeering through stronger enforcement, new offences and higher penalties; and ... to reduce economic incentives which attract people to come to this country in breach of our immigration laws'.[65] There is however no nationality or status qualification to being a party to legal proceedings in the United Kingdom.

The major inhibition is the inefficiency of the process and in particular its cost. Following cutbacks over the past two decades it is difficult to obtain legal aid, largely now because the terms of work are so detrimental to practising lawyers that relatively few will now take civil legal aid work at all. Criminal legal aid is still relatively easy to obtain for serious offences but for minor offences the ease of obtaining it varies depending on the current central approach to demonstrating financial need (unless one is in receipt of state benefits, which a person without immigration status is unlikely to be, this can be very awkward) and the efficiency of its local operation. Obtaining legal advice and assistance in relation to immigration matters is particularly difficult because this has been especially hard hit by legal aid cutbacks.

The Immigration and Asylum Act of 1999 ran to 170 sections and 16 schedules, setting up the Office of the Immigration Services Commissioner (OISC) and a system for the compulsory qualification of those giving immigration advice. The giving of such advice for reward of any kind without proper accreditation is now a criminal offence.[66]

---

[64] See n. 14 above.   [65] Hansard, 11 December 1995 Col. 699.
[66] Immigration and Asylum Act 1999 sections 84 and 91.

The main impediment that those of concern in this study were likely to find in relation to obtaining legal assistance would be the cost, since they were economically disadvantaged, but the effects of the lack of respect for, and impoverishment of, immigration work among UK solicitors should not be underestimated. In Oxford, a city with a high population of such people of concern and where much of the UK field work for this study was done, there was then only one firm of solicitors undertaking non-business-related immigration work on legal aid.

Marrying, founding a family and family reunion

Marriage in the United Kingdom has been regulated by the state since 1753.[67] Marrying a British citizen does not bring an automatic entitlement to enter or remain in the UK. However spouses are usually given permission to enter and they may apply for naturalisation as British citizens themselves after a shorter period than others.[68] Spouses are supposed to apply from abroad for admission as spouses, or fiancés for leave to enter in order to marry. However clearly if a foreign national who is lawfully within the United Kingdom for some other reasons marries a British person, they will acquire rights protected by Article 8 of the ECHR.[69] This route to settlement in the United Kingdom on the basis of marriage to a British person has attracted considerable concern for its potential for fraud.

The right to marry is itself protected by Article 12 of the ECHR. It was felt, however, that it was very easy to contract a 'marriage of convenience' or 'sham marriage', and with occasional media scandals about serial professional bigamists, usually women, in 1999 Registrars of Marriage were put under a duty to report such suspected marriages to the Secretary of State.[70] Nevertheless, the government found the potential for immigration fraud still to be too high, and introduced a procedure for a 'certificate of approval' to be fulfilled wherever a party to the marriage was subject to immigration control, but excluding Church

---

[67] The phrase 'common law marriage' in its popular usage of unmarried cohabitation is almost invariably misplaced.

[68] The marriage provisions now also apply to civil partnerships.

[69] This requires respect for family life and, while it does not guarantee that that family life will be carried on in any particular country, presents an obstacle to any authority trying to exclude the foreign national.

[70] Section 24 Immigration and Asylum Act 1999. All such provisions were subsequently also applied to civil partnerships.

of England marriages.[71] This was challenged by Mohmoud Baiai and
Izabela Trzcinska in the High Court,[72] the Court of Appeal[73] and up to
the House of Lords,[74] where it was held that the process was 'an arbitrary
and unjust interference with the right to marry'.[75] The scheme had to be
modified and, part of the unfairness being the high fees required, repayments had to be made; fees were suspended from 9 April 2009. The issue
remains, however, of concern to both the government and the media.

These rules did not affect the founding of a non-marital family, which
also attracts protection under domestic legislation and Article 8 ECHR.
If the relationship ends, in both cases if the foreign national has not been
registered or naturalised they also lose the benefit of any immigration status that was dependent on the relationship, and are liable to removal. This
will apply even if they have the care of British citizen children of the relationship and that removal means the British children are also effectively
expelled.[76] This is, however, more of a difficulty in founding a British family than in founding a family *tout court*, and given the current fragility of
British status it is not peculiar to those who are *de jure* or *de facto* stateless.
Certain forms of temporary status, such as work permits or student visas,
can carry the right to bring one's dependent family, and the European
rights of free movement include the right to family reunion in the receiving country, a right often interpreted generously in practice.

The position of minor children is, however, identified with that of their
parents. They have no *locus standi* in the immigration rules to claim family reunion, whether they are British citizens or hold some other status.
Unaccompanied asylum seeking minors are not returned but do not
have the right to seek the admission of their parents,[77] and they are often
returned to their 'home country' once they reach the age of majority of
eighteen years.

Obtaining decent accommodation

Many people in the United Kingdom find they have no enforceable
practical right to decent accommodation. There is legislation requiring

---

[71] Asylum and Immigration (Treatment of Claimants, etc.) Act 2004, sections 19–25;
Immigration (Procedure for Marriage) Regulations 2005.

[72] [2006] EWHC 823.   [73] [2007] EWCA Civ 478.

[74] [2008] UKHL 53.   [75] Per Baroness Hale of Richmond, para. 44.

[76] *M* v. *Islington LBC* [2004] EWCA Civ 235, *Jaramillo* (Application No. 24865/94) and
Sorabjee (Application No. 23938/94).

[77] Notwithstanding a statement to the contrary by Barbara Roche when she was Minister
for Immigration: *Immigration Asylum and Nationality Law and Practice* (2003), 41.

local authorities (councils) to provide accommodation to those who are in their area and connected with it who are homeless, and social housing is available to those in need. However, there is insufficient accommodation overall, much of it is in poor condition, and the allocation of social housing is a very contentious issue not merely for those with problems of status.[78] The widespread destruction caused by bombing in the Second World War, together with the degradation over time of poorly maintained Victorian housing, led to 'slum clearance' and the raising of cheap accommodation in new towns, large housing estates and tower blocks with no concierge arrangements. Owner-occupation is more necessary than merely desirable, but financially beyond the reach of many people, including couples, unless they have private means as well as a normal income. Private lettings were deregulated for families (but not businesses) under the Thatcher government in the 1980s, so there is no longer security of tenure, and tenancies are often nasty as well as short. Those without immigration status are particularly likely to be vulnerable because they are often without the demonstrable means to obtain any form of private housing: it is, however, generally an area which is unsatisfactory for many British people as well.[79]

So far as the stateless are concerned, they would historically have been included in those whom a local authority would try to house in accordance with its obligations under the homelessness legislation. Often such provision would mean housing families in bed-and-breakfast hostels where they might, for example, be obliged to stay out of the hostel for large parts of the day. Some priority was often given to asylum seekers as they would frequently be without local family support and resources. This could be controversial if they were perceived as knocking local people further down the queue. However provisions especially in sections 4–5 of the 1993 Act and section 9 of the 1996 Act relieved local authorities of their duty to house those without status by giving authority to central government to provide separate accommodation. Various strategies have been tried and commenced, such as dispersing asylum seekers to towns other than those in which they historically and habitually collected, especially ports of entry,[80] and building large accommodation centres. It was

---

[78] See, for example, the House of Lords case of R (on the application of Ahmad) v. Mayor and Burgesses of the London Borough of Newham [2009] UKHL 14.

[79] See for discussion, D. Cowan and M. McDermont, Regulating Social Housing (London: Routledge, 2006).

[80] For a critical assessment, see Audit Commission, Another Country (2000), www. audit-commission.gov.uk/SiteCollectionDocuments/AuditCommissionReports/NationalStudies/anothercountry.pdf.

announced in 2001 that ten of these would be built, housing 3000 asylum seekers, but the proposal proved difficult to realise.[81]

Renting and buying property

There are no legal rules that prevent a person from renting or buying property if they do not have a particular immigration status. However, residential property in most of the United Kingdom is very expensive, and if you need to obtain credit that will be more difficult if you do not have status. This is because, if you cannot persuade the lender that you are permanently established in the United Kingdom and it appears you are liable to leave or be removed, it is perceived as less likely that you will complete the repayments during the term agreed. If the loan is unsecured, the lender is therefore less likely to see the return of the money. Even if the loan is secured, the lender is therefore less likely to obtain the advantages of your paying interest over the period, which is the business of such lenders, and more likely to have to realise the security, which is undesirable and should be a last resort.

Consciousness of immigration status, let alone checking it, is a comparatively recent phenomenon. The fact that someone has bought a house on a mortgage in the past does not necessarily mean they had or have a regularised status.

Protection against detention and removal

The common law protection against detention is the right to move a writ of *habeas corpus*, which amounts to the only specific individual right, as opposed to liberty, in that system. It works by the claimant seeking a court order for her release, which will be refused only if the detainer can show lawful authority for the detention. The Home Secretary is as subject to this requirement as anyone else. However, the effectiveness of *habeas corpus* has been somewhat damaged by the availability and use of assertion, in cases of alleged terrorist plots, that to show the reasons for the detention would damage national security.

Immigration officers have considerable powers under the Immigration Act 1971 as amended to detain for breach of the immigration rules, and

---

[81]   The National Audit Office also published on this point: see, for example, *The Cancellation of the Bicester Accommodation Centre* (2007), HC 19 2007–2008, www.nao.org.uk/ publications/0708/the_cancellation_of_bicester_a.aspx.

especially as a prelude to removal from the country. They now wear uniforms, and 'front line' officers are armed, though not with firearms. The practice of making 'dawn raids', especially on families with children, is often deprecated, but continues. The United Kingdom Border Agency (UKBA) does advert to Article 5 of the ECHR, which protects the 'right to liberty and security of the person'.[82] It warns officers not to exceed their powers or to use them for inappropriate purposes, or they may be sued. Nevertheless, it is often felt that in relation to both detention and removal, those who might suffer abuses are not in a strong position to sue. In support of this view, there has been published research into practices that could have led to court proceedings but have not done so.[83]

With regard to removal, the ECHR would be likely to be of use to those of concern in this study. Article 3 provides that a person may not be subject to torture or inhuman and degrading treatment, and this has been part of the domestic law of the United Kingdom since October 2000. There have, however, been controversies about how that translates into the right not to be removed. The United Kingdom was at the forefront of making law at Strasbourg on the right of foreign nationals not to be removed to the risk of death or torture, or to conditions amounting to inhuman or degrading treatment where the person had a terminal illness.[84] The House of Lords decided in a domestic case in 2005 that a failure to provide support, especially for those making 'late' asylum claims, could amount to a breach of Article 3.[85]

Inheriting property

There are no restrictions as to nationality or immigration status in the United Kingdom about inheriting property, be it land or personal property (immovable or movable property). However, owning a house does not give a person a right, from the point of view of the immigration rules, to live in it, nor a right to remain in the country.

A person may make a UK will if they are domiciled in the United Kingdom. Domicile is largely a question of fact – where you live your

---

[82] See, for example, UKBA Immigration Directorate's Instructions, Chapter 31, Section 1 – Detention Policy in Port Cases, para. 2.1.

[83] See, for example, C. Granville-Chapman, *Harm on Removal: Excessive Force Against Failed Asylum Seekers* (London: Medical Foundation for the Victims of Torture, 2004).

[84] *Soering* v. *UK* (1989) 11 EHRR 439, *D* v. *UK* (1997) 24 EHRR 423, *N* v. *UK* (Application No. 26565/05).

[85] *Adam, Limbuela and Tesema* v. *SSHD* [2005] UKHL 66.

life – and a state of mind – where you believe you are based and intend to stay. It is thus perfectly possible to be domiciled in the United Kingdom while having no legal right to be there. Other, more artificial and specific rules as to domicile apply in relation to tax affairs but, again, they depend on physical fact rather than legal status.

Burial

Most people who die in the United Kingdom are cremated, but some prefer burial, especially if they have religious reasons for it. The right to burial is not contentious, save at the very broad level of public concern for the use of land, or at the specific level of those who wish to be buried in a particular religion, which may or may not accept them.

Empirical findings

The frequent ambiguity of status in the United Kingdom and the inconsistent treatment of those without it means that it is difficult to specify who falls within the definition of 'stateless', and it is of course difficult to find such people. The research team spent two months locating people who met the definition of *de facto* stateless person used in this study. They were identified eventually through refugee and social service organisations, who were asked for initial introductions to potential participants who might be classified as effectively stateless, although it was only during interviews that the team was able to verify their status. In order to build up a base of contacts, research assistants volunteered from October to December 2007 in social service organisations where they established personal relationships and built up trust with potential participants, some of whom agreed to take part in the research and introduced the team to other participants. Organisations central to this study were Oxford Asylum Welcome (OAW), Open Door Session (ODS), which is sponsored by the East Oxford Community Centre and Oxford and Cherwell Valley College (OCVC), a college of further education.

The sample population included long-term asylum seekers and refused asylum seekers who had been in the United Kingdom on average over five years. Some of the participants interviewed were on temporary admission but others had not been given any status, or had lost status following a negative asylum application, and remained in the country without permission.

Two specific cases concerned participants who would perhaps be con-sidered *de jure* stateless in that they no longer had an effective link to their country of origin; their situation was further complicated because they had emigrated as children from a disputed area in Kashmir and, over more than a decade neither the British, nor Indian, nor Pakistani authorities had been able to establish their nationality. The majority of participants had a recognised nationality but could not call upon their home state for protection, because it was either engulfed in war and considered unsafe or because it refused to re-admit its own nationals. For these reasons, they were considered by the research team as *de facto* stateless.

Participants included men and women, although the gender balance was significantly tilted towards men, reflecting the general trends in asylum seeking in Britain. Participants originated from a wide range of countries although most were from countries in conflict that are among the 'top ten' of current asylum seeking populations[86] includ-ing: Afghanistan, Algeria, Chad, China, Congo Brazzaville, Democratic Republic of Congo, Eritrea, Iran, Iraq, Kashmir, Kosovo, Sri Lanka, Sudan, Tunisia and Uganda. Most were under thirty-five years of age but some were in their forties and one in his fifties. Some women were also interviewed. In most cases they had family in the United Kingdom but one had arrived on her own and her formal status was not made explicit to the research team.

The researchers relied on both individual interviews and focus groups, though some individuals participated in both. The researchers asked how a change in status – for example, having their application for asylum rejected – affected the participants in terms of their social and economic entitlements and their personal life. To evaluate the sense of personal loss, researchers sought to understand how the participants perceived and experienced their situation. Participants were asked questions aimed at eliciting which rights they felt were essential to everyday life; including the rights to work, to social security, to education and to healthcare, access to courts and to the justice system, as well as protection from deportation. The methodology was qualitative rather than quantitative, and was pri-marily illustrative, enabling the researchers to set out information on the issues addressed and to illustrate the ways in which people lived and man-aged in the United Kingdom without status.

---

[86] See *Asylum Statistics, United Kingdom 2007*, Home Office Statistical Bulletin, 11/08, www.homeoffice.gov.uk/rds/pdfs08/hosb1108.pdf.

The experience of healthcare in England

Access to healthcare in the United Kingdom for non-residents and non-EU nationals is a particularly controversial issue. In April 2008, just before the interviews were completed, the High Court had ruled that it was unreasonable for doctors to assess the immigration status of patients.[87] This had suggested therefore that refused asylum seekers could enjoy free access to the NHS, but this was later reversed by the Court of Appeal.[88] In practice, notwithstanding the rules and Guidance,[89] refused asylum seekers have often found it difficult to receive certain kinds of treatment, especially antenatal care (Anya 2007).

Those who managed to receive care, including HIV/AIDS treatment, were sometimes later billed for thousands of pounds.[90] Most of those interviewed, however, claimed that on the few occasions that they needed to see a doctor, they were treated well. In one Oxford focus group, the sentiment expressed was 'we cannot complain'. One participant, however, claimed he had to argue with a doctor over the cause of his injuries, which made him mistrustful:

> I had here problems for example with my GP. I broke my shoulder here in the UK and I went to see my GP. I told him that I broke my shoulder here and he did not want to believe me. He said I broke my shoulder in Chad. I have problems with my shoulders. I did a lot of sport as a child and I broke my right shoulder in Chad and since then it is loose and it gets out a lot of times, but I broke my left shoulder here in the UK and I explained that to my GP but he did not listen. I don't know why. But he didn't want to believe me. I am sure if it would have been an English guy he would have believed me. There I felt disadvantaged. (ODS, 4)

However, generally the view of the participants of their access to healthcare was favourable, notwithstanding their lack of status. One man who had been hospitalised after a stroke claimed that he was treated just like other patients even though he has no right to remain in the United Kingdom (ODS, 3). One woman who gave birth to a baby in the United Kingdom claimed that healthcare had saved her life (OAW, 4).

---

[87] See *A, R (on the application of)* v. *West Middlesex University Hospital NHS Trust* [2008] EWHC 855 (Admin).

[88] See *YA, R (on the application of)* v. *Secretary of State for Health* [2009] EWCA Civ 225 (and n. 29 above).

[89] See n. 30 above.

[90] S. Hargreaves and A. Burnett, 'UK Court Decision: Healthcare and Immigration', *The Lancet*, 317 (31 May 2008), 1823.

Treatment for mental health problems was, however, a different story. Although several participants complained of depression, anxiety and traumas linked to their situation of exile, none mentioned receiving any treatment. One case worker later mentioned that some teenagers had received medication. Some saw doctors as complicit in their denial of status, as recorded by one teenager:

> I didn't have documents to prove my age, so they began to doubt about it and they sent me to a doctor in London. The doctor couldn't establish my age and he said I could be 15, 16, 17 or 18. So the Home Office said that I was 18 and case closed. But by that time I was just 16. (OCVC, 4)[91]

Education

Few participants interviewed had school-age children, unsurprisingly, given the profile of the population. Those that did felt that education was a critical means of integration and they were overwhelmingly positive about the quality of education offered. Other participants who were of the age to be in further education themselves cited the excellent care they received from teachers and lecturers, though there were occasional problems. One seventeen-year-old noted that he had been subject to racism and teasing on account of his status:

> I remember one day in college when the teacher asked me about my background and I innocently told him in front of the class that I was an asylum-seeker and that I wanted to become a refugee. Everyone in the class began to laugh, even the teacher did, and I felt very embarrassed. I felt very bad. (ODS, 4)

Participants who had arrived in the United Kingdom as minors and started their courses before the 2004 Asylum (Treatment of Claimants, etc.) Act came into effect enjoyed access to further education, including

---

[91] Queries over age, and medical evidence to enable a decision on age, are frequent in the United Kingdom and have given rise to considerable case law and literature. In *R (and others)* v. *Manchester City Council and others* [2009] EWHC 3542 (Admin) in which 'Justice Holman held that in such cases, courts must do more than determine whether or not the claimant is a child, but should make their own determination as to the young person's actual age or date of birth. This pronouncement would then be binding on the local authority. This is necessary in order to establish the date up to which the claimant will be considered a child, and will need to be accommodated or provided with services by the local authority under the Children Act 1989', in 'ChildRIGHT: Court Report – Age Assessments of Asylum Seekers', *Children & Young People Now* (9 March 2010).

award-bearing courses.[92] One nineteen-year-old interviewed spoke about his difficulties with English language studies and how this prompted him to leave college (ODS, 4). Others progressed well and found in particular Oxford and Cherwell Valley College to be a supportive place where they were given opportunities, including learning English and information technology:

> I had access to education from the first moment. I could come to college. I was able to study. I studied level 1 in IT, English, carpentry. IT level 3. Study was one of the good things when being without status. (OCVC, 5)

Some participants with little official paperwork required help with enrolments:

> I study computing, but I would like to do my A levels in Public Services and later become a Policeman, but before I can do that I need to have my papers, if not it will be impossible. I had even problems to enrol here in the Cherwell Valley College. I had to start in January due to problems with my paperwork. (OCVC, 2)

University and vocational education proved more elusive, especially once participants looked outside the Oxford further education college described above. For example, one woman described how she had been offered a place at Manchester Metropolitan University to study Health and Social Care but was treated as an overseas student. Even though she claimed to be seeking asylum from a poor Central African country, because she was classified as an overseas student the fees were £6,000, which she simply could not afford. (LON, 1)

Others spoke about how they were thrown off vocational courses including apprenticeships once they turned eighteen, after which point there were simply no more opportunities:

> I started a bricking apprenticeship, but they kicked me out because I haven't got any documents. I stayed there for six weeks; I had to get up very early in the morning to get there. I made a lot of effort … I had to get two buses to get there. I was there every day from 8 till 5 and then they told me that I had to go. (OCVC, 1)

Employment

The right to work dominated most interviews. All participants noted that the denial of the right to work had left them dependent and increased

[92] See sections 8–13 on the treatment of claimants and in particular the cancellation of benefits.

their vulnerability. As one Afghan man reported, 'if you work you do not have to ask for housing and for benefits' which was desirable since surviving on benefits was simply not possible. This theme was picked up by a Congolese woman who also noted the aggregate benefits that followed the right to work:

> The thing is that we need to get the right to work. If we could do that, we could look after our own [sic] without relying on the Government … If I start working here, I'm gonna start paying my taxes, and where will the taxes go? It ain't gonna be to Congo. We've been living here for so long, so why can't we contribute to society? (LON, 1)

Instead, however, participants spoke of extended periods of idleness. Though it was suspected that some would have worked on a casual basis, no information was given and instead participants expressed their frustration at their lack of entitlements to work:

> I can't really do anything. I am just wasting my time. At my age, this should be a time to work; this is the age for doing this. (OCVC, 1)

Another admitted that he too was now idle, having been turned down for jobs on the grounds that it would be illegal to employ him.

Several participants responded to questions about the right to work by explaining the difficulties of living without status and above all without documentation and hence any potential entitlements:

> I met a lot of people, and they said to me that they would get me some work, but I have no documents so I cannot work. I can't even drive. I cannot get a driving licence without papers. I cannot even get the support money that I got when I was under 18. (OCVC, 1)
>
> When you don't have documents you can't do anything, anything. Without papers you have no future, you are stuck, you are blocked. It's like being in prison without knowing when you are going to go out. (OCVC, 2 BB)

The contrast between the above situations and that of a Kosovar who had recently been granted asylum was startling, not least because he claimed he was able to take control over his life and felt that 'anything was possible'.

No participants spoke about setting up businesses and there was no consideration of eventual self-employment in the future. Rather participants' aspirations were expressed in terms of securing work in occupations that were in high demand, including construction, or training for professions such as engineering (OCVC, 6).

Renting and buying property

One of the few benefits available to refused asylum seekers is a statutory provision which was introduced under the Immigration and Asylum Act 1999 and exists for those who are destitute and temporarily unable to leave the country (Section 4 support). This amounted to 35 pounds per week paid in vouchers and short-term accommodation. However, not everyone interviewed knew this was available:

> They rejected my case, they sent me to Oxford and since I got here I haven't received any help. Because they said I am over 18, I didn't get any housing; no monetary support; no documents. I live with my friends from Afghanistan and Iran. (OCVC, 4)

Those that mentioned their housing allowance also recorded that it was not sufficient. Moreover, the quality of housing was often criticised as cold, damp and poor, requiring heating, which placed the participants under an even greater burden. One African interviewee claimed that his house leaked (ODS, 3). An East Asian interviewee who had a baby spoke of similar conditions and commented on this size of her apartment and the fact that it was often cold. The costs of heating were mentioned by several who felt it was prohibitive:

> Yeah, you have to pay the bills (gas, electricity), that's why I don't put the heater on because I don't have the money. I am cold, but I don't put it on because it is too expensive. I just put it half an hour and that's it. We have the heater always off, we turn it only on if someone comes to visit. 46 pounds is not enough for shopping, the bills, for water, clothes [and heating]. (FG, 1)

Others spoke of their social conditions and in particular the fact that they lived in overcrowded households, in part because of the cost of housing in the United Kingdom. One participant who had younger siblings described living in a council house with a large family:

> Our life is difficult. We live in a 3 bedroom Council house and we are 8 altogether. I share a room with my brother, my younger brothers and sisters are in another room, and my father in another room. (OCVC, 1)

Another participant added:

> There is a big housing problem here. Housing is very expensive here. We live 6 in a 3 bedroom council house and we just moved in the summer to this bigger house. From 2001 to 2007 we lived in a 2 bedroom house, which was even worse. We asked for a bigger house in 2004 and they gave

us this new house in 2007, three years later. Everything is so slow here. (OCVC, 2)

The statements made by the participants however often appeared to reflect the situation of those living in poverty in the United Kingdom. This can also affect British nationals, as noted by one man who had been refused asylum and who was unable to return to his country of origin. He spoke about how he was now dependent on a Catholic charity for his accommodation and sometimes food:

> I have nothing. I get no support from the Home Office. Now I live in Francis House here in Oxford. They arranged a little room for me. I live with two other asylum seekers, one from Congo and the other one from Afghanistan and two other British people. Life is very hard, but the Franciscans are nice people. They give me sometimes food, and they help me also with the travel costs to report to the Police in London. I eat there sometimes, sometimes here in Open Door; it's just a struggle. I get sometimes support from my Iranian friends. They help me when they can. (ODS, 5)

Similar accounts were provided by other interviewees who spoke about living with friends and from charity. Most participants were dependent on either very limited welfare benefits that were available to families that had under-age children or through charitable relief. For example, one family of four children and two parents relied solely on £30 per week from a local refugee charity in Bolton called BRASS and the support group that was set up to lobby for them to be allowed to stay in the UK (LON, 1). Another admitted: 'I live from charity, from places like Asylum Welcome and Open Door. Sometimes I struggle to get food but my friends or these organisations give me always a hand.'

In addition to the poor quality of housing and the need to rely on charity, participants spoke at length about what it was like living in often high-crime neighbourhoods with no effective law enforcement. One man originally from Afghanistan told of his situation being burgled twice:

> Shortly after I moved to my first house, my neighbour, an English man, broke into my house and tried to get my wallet. I fought against him, I bite [*sic*] his hand and he couldn't get my wallet. I didn't know what to do. It was a scary situation. I didn't have the Police number to call them. In my second flat some guys entered again my house and they stole my mobile phone. They entered and when I was about to call the Police they took my mobile phone and they escaped. They were 4 male, I couldn't do anything. All this was not nice. (OCVC, 6)

Others also described the dangers of living in state-subsidised housing in areas where there was a mixed population and asylum seekers were at risk of attack:

> I got a city council flat in [East Oxford] and when I got there, after a few days a street gang attacked me. They called me green cardy (because in the US immigrants have a green card) and they began to chase me. I was with a friend and we had to run for our lives. (ODS, 4)

Again, however, elements of these situations are not specific to those without status, but can also apply to British people.

Family reunion and related family matters

For participants that had families, both younger siblings and children of their own, there was a sense that the state had invaded their family lives. Some older participants explained how, following a negative asylum decision, the state took over intimate areas of their family life which traditionally fell under their responsibility. The break-up of family structures was among the most painful effects of their loss of status and cut to the core of their sense of dignity. One man who claimed to have been tortured in Iran explained that from the moment he entered the United Kingdom he was unable to re-establish regular communication with his children. His account was among the most painful, but he was far from alone. Other participants provided distressing accounts of how their families were pulled apart.

The Iranian described how, even as he got geographically closer to his family, he was still distanced from his children. He explained his situation:

> I couldn't stand the situation [in Iran] anymore and in January 2006 I sent my children to Britain by plane two months in advance and I came on the road. I didn't want to come back to this country, but I was told that when you try to enter Europe again it is always better to go to the first country because they have your fingerprints and they can deal with your case. I applied for asylum but the Home Office has rejected again my application. I am desperate; I don't know what I can do. I cannot have my children with me. They [now] live in Manchester with an English family. I just see them now and again and when I go there I cannot even go to their house. I see them always in the city centre. The family told them not to tell me where they live, so I stay there a couple of days and then I come back to Oxford. (ODS, 5)

For other participants, the effects of stress resulted in the fracturing of family relationships and personal loss, as reported by a Congolese woman:

> When the benefits were removed for the 18 months between the appeal failing and the case being reopened, the Council tried to evict my family from the house and take the children into care. We were re-located to Liverpool where we were removed from friends and the children were taken out of their schools. As a result of all the stress, my pregnant mother lost her baby. (CON, 1)

One further episode illustrates the way in which state policies have contributed to families disintegrating, while the state has struggled to deliver a consistent response to refused asylum seekers and their children. In summer 2004, Thames Valley Police officers and the UK immigration authorities arrested a number of declared Pakistani refugee families in Oxford as part of 'Operation Iowa'. The incident led to a criminal trial and an immigration inquiry which resulted in the cancellation of refugee status and subsequent withdrawal of state protection that had been given to a group of children. What complicated the matter was that the families concerned claimed not to be Pakistani but in fact Kashmiri, their nationality status having been disputed by the British, Indian and Pakistani governments. Although Kashmiris born in India are entitled to the same rights as citizens, India has consistently denied citizenship to Punjabi Muslims[93] who have been living in Kashmir for more than sixty years. The situation has been further complicated by the geography of Kashmir, the history of conflict in the region and domestic politics in the disputed territories.[94]

---

[93] India amended its Citizenship Act of 1955 and Citizen Rule of 1965 so as to authorise the district magistrate of Jaisalmer to grant Indian citizenship to Pakistanis who had been living in the border district for the last five years. This effort was aimed at some of the Kashmiri Pandits who represented approximately 12 per cent of the population in the Valley in 1947 but since 1989 had been expelled (as many as 300,000 families had been forced out) (M. Lynch, *Lives on Hold: The Human Cost of Statelessness*, Washington, DC: Refugees International, 2005). In 2003, the Ministry of Home Affairs requested states to provide identity cards to displaced Kashmiri Pandits with the aim of regularising the situation of at least 50,000 displaced persons, who were not registered as 'migrants' when they left the Kashmir Valley after 1990. However, for over 100,000 Punjabi refugees who fled to Jammu and Kashmir from the neighbouring Sialkot district of Punjab province (now in Pakistan) in 1947, both they and their descendents have been denied the right to citizenship in India; their exclusion has been a source of recent protest and unrest.

[94] In spite of large demonstrations, the State Assembly of Jammu and Kashmir nonetheless rejected a bill in May 2007 seeking to grant citizenship and other rights for the refugees of West Pakistan in the Jammu and Kashmir State. See Internal Displacement Monitoring

The refugees who settled in Oxford claimed to be from Kashmir, though they had ties to Pakistan and their ancestral home was described to the author as 'Sialkot'. Yet, their specific nationality status became an academic matter following 'Operation Iowa' which brought the families to court and began a process whereby their rights to remain in the United Kingdom were called into question.[95] In the criminal case *R* v. *Faruq and Others (Operation Iowa)* (2005), the Crown Prosecution Service (CPS) claimed that there had been a conspiracy to contravene the Immigration Act by bringing relatives into the United Kingdom under false pretences and then falsely claiming asylum as a prelude to fraudulently claiming benefits from government departments and local authorities.[96] As a result of this criminal hearing, the Home Office then revoked the status of several of the parties concerned, including the children of the families involved in the criminal act. It was argued that if the families had lied during their asylum application, then other information could no longer be considered credible, including the ages of some of the children. Some families were removed.

Interviews conducted in winter 2008 with some of the older children of family members revealed the extent to which the governmental action undermined their well-being and personal identity. As one commented, 'there is something missing from me. I have no ID card. I cannot show to anyone who I am' (OCVC, 1). Another put it simply: 'my identity is missing. Everyone has their identity' (OCVC, 2). Sadly, the plight of the two Kashmiri interviewees remained unchanged. Both continued without status and lead a precarious existence where they depend on charitable organisations and the goodwill of professionals.

Access to courts and the justice system and freedom from detention

Participants spoke of an ambivalent relationship with justice sector institutions, including courts and the police. Although several had found help

Centre (IDMC), 'India – Jammu and Kashmir: Displaced due to 1947 Partition of Indian Protest in Jammu to Demand Citizenship' (Geneva: IDMC, 2007), www.internal-displacement.org/idmc/website/countries.nsf/(httpEnvelopes)/f6e66d867c1f56b3c12572 c30054b7b4!OpenDocument&Click=.

[95] See 'Lesson Learned', *Oxford Mail* (Friday 23 July 2004a), http://archive.oxfordmail.net/2004/7/23/10133.html, and 'Meeting to Discuss Grievances over Coverage', *Oxford Mail* (Thursday 12 August 2004b), http://archive.oxfordmail.net/2004/8/12/9616.html.

[96] See website of John Black, QC (n.d.), www.18redlioncourt.co.uk/index.php/barristers/black/125.

through local law firms and social service organisations that could put them in touch with lawyers, many were frustrated with the system. One participant described how over a six-year period he had had eight different solicitors: 'It is always the same story. They say they will help, but after a while they are not interested in the case' (ODS, 3). Others, though frustrated with the length of time and lack of information from the Home Office, felt that they had access to legal assistance and the legal system.

Opinions on the role and effectiveness of the police, however, were less positive. Though participants did call the police when threatened, as mentioned above, none felt that the police protected them. A participant who had been attacked by a street gang hostile to asylum seekers had sought police assistance, but not found the results entirely helpful:

> When I was running I called the Police from my mobile but they did not turn up. I got safe home but it was a scary situation and the Police didn't do anything. I called several times from my home but they just gave me a hard time. They didn't want to believe me. I think a lot of policemen are hypocrites. They don't like foreigners. The Police just acted when I spoke with Asylum Welcome, they called the Police and just then two Police officers came to my house to ask about the problem. After that they caught one of the leaders of the gang, but that was even worse. The gang realised that I was the one that went to the Police and they were all the time after me. It was very scary. I had always to run away and hide from them. (ODS, 4)

However, he devised his own solution:

> After a while I found out about the name and the address of the gang leader and I went to see his mum. He is also a black guy like me. I spoke to his mum and I told her everything about her son. I told her that I didn't want to go to the Police again, that I just wanted to do my own thing. I told her that I am a peaceful guy and that I don't want problems with her son. After this, I never had problems again with the crew. The mum of this guy solved the problem, but not the Police. A lot of policemen are just hypocrites. They discriminated me because of my origins. When they attacked me they never turned up. You cannot rely on them. (ODS, 4)

Several participants were concerned about the constant surveillance by the police, which they interpreted as the face of the state: the police were a source of both authority and fear. Encounters with the police also carried a sense of shame and embarrassment:

> I was stopped twice by the police. They stopped me and searched me and they took my details. I felt so bad, I was surprised. Why are they stopping me? I haven't done anything. (OCVC, 1)

Most mistrusted the police, fearing arrest and deportation. One interviewee put it simply – 'I am afraid of the Police coming home and deport me' (OCVC, 6). Others spoke of evasive tactics to avoid contact with the police:

> Before when I didn't have status I tried always to stay at home after 8 o'clock, because you never know, you might get into trouble, some people just come and disturb so it's better to stay home, to find something to stay home. Now is good, last night I was out, so now, with status, it's fine. (OCVC, 5)

> You just run away. You have to, if you haven't got an ID is always better to stay away from the Police. (OCVC, 4)

Another commented on the way in which removals were conducted, which he believed to be general practice:

> Sometimes they come at 4 o'clock in the morning when you are in bed and they take and they deport you. They just come to your flat and they catch you there. They have your address and they know that you have been refused. (AB)

8

Non-citizens in Slovenia: erasure from the register of permanent residents

JELKA ZORN

For me, the most important right is the right to dignity, and that your dignity is not trampled in such a banal and total way.

(Iztok)

We came here to work, to earn our living fairly, and then we were erased. Maybe we were too kind and prepared to take any kind of job and this was turned against us. They wanted to get rid of us – by humiliating us.

(Slavenka)

I would like to stress again that I belong to this country, to Slovenia; this belonging is hundred per cent. This is how I feel. I perceive Slovenia as my home country despite the fact that I was born in Bosnia. I was educated in Slovenia, and my Slovene vocabulary is better than my Bosnian, my family is here, I have lost my ties to Bosnia. Once I lost my status [in Slovenia], as a foreigner I couldn't do anything, I felt redundant everywhere.

(Ivan)

Introduction

The present territory of the Republic of Slovenia has been the scene of an eventful, but notably fast-paced history of political formations: a Slovene born in 1919, for example, has lived in several states: the Kingdom of Serbs, Croats and Slovenes (1918–31), the Kingdom of Yugoslavia (1931–41), the Socialist Federal Republic of Yugoslavia (SFRY, 1945–91) and the Republic of Slovenia (1991–). Each of these transitions brought about problems rooted in the particular epoch and geo-political configuration. During the most recent transition period, from the SFRY to the sovereign state of Slovenia, it was citizenship designation, and not the change of state borders, that resulted in *de facto* statelessness. Persons who became stateless had their personal documents destroyed or invalidated in 1992, and thus their permission to stay was denied. The war in Croatia and Bosnia and Herzegovina aggravated the situation, since these newly produced non-citizens could not travel to war zones in order to obtain the foreign passports which the new state of Slovenia demanded of them when they tried to escape their *de facto* stateless situation.

In 1991 Slovenia seceded from the SFRY. At the outset, the Slovene independence process seemed highly democratic, transparent and respectful of human rights and minorities. However, ethno-nationalist sentiments found their way into citizenship and aliens policies, which not only left 25,671[1] long-term immigrants from other republics of the former Yugoslavia without citizenship of the new Slovene state, but also deprived them of their rights and status as legal aliens. Only a decade after the initial act that rendered them *de facto* (not necessarily *de jure*) stateless, they began a collective struggle for recognition, naming themselves the Erased to call attention to the fact that they had been literally erased from the register of permanent residents.

The fieldwork research on statelessness in Slovenia is based on twenty-five interviews with persons erased from the register of permanent residents.[2] The interviewees were chosen using the 'snowball' method.[3] Many of these persons have been active in the struggle of the Erased in some way or another, or at least present at some of the public events organised by the two associations of the Erased. These associations represent a loose-knit network of erased persons struggling to present their point of view and demand rights. Although their lives deteriorated significantly due to the erasure, it should be noted that not all of the 25,671 persons affected by this act suffered consequences of gravity and duration comparable to that suffered by those whose experiences are presented here. Or, even worse, many did not manage to return to Slovenia until today: short visits to relatives in Bosnia and Herzegovina or Serbia in 1991–2 turned into permanent exile and years of war refugee experience.[4]

Before each interview, respondents were contacted by phone and asked if they would be willing to be visited and interviewed. The

---

[1] Ministry of the Interior's Press Conference (27 January 2009), www.mnz.gov.si/nc/si/splosno/cns/novica/article/12027/6214/, accessed 1 February 2009.

[2] Interviews were conducted by a group of nine students of social work from the University of Ljubljana under the author's supervision.

[3] Those who were interviewed for the purpose of this study further arranged contacts with other erased persons.

[4] Interviews with the Erased conducted in Bosnia and Herzegovina, Novi grad by the author on 15 September 2007.

respondents were mostly men (eighteen out of twenty-five) in their fifties. Four persons were in their late thirties, and one was in his seventies. One man and two women were born in Slovenia, others were born in Bosnia and Herzegovina and other parts of the former Yugoslavia (Serbia, Kosovo, Macedonia). Most of them had moved to Slovenia in the 1970s. One woman is of Bosnian Roma descent. All the respondents were erased from the register of permanent residents in 1992; at the time of the interviews (winter 2007–8) most of them possessed personal documents and a permit to stay in Slovenia. Sixteen of them had also received Slovene citizenship. One woman was still without a permit to stay in Slovenia at the time of the interview, and she feared detention and deportation.

The content of the interviews reveals two main reasons behind these persons' decision to participate in the research: they had already secured some sort of status in Slovenia, and they held the government, and not themselves, responsible for their erasure. These two reasons were probably decisive in most respondents' decision to participate. This needs to be mentioned because public depictions of the Erased are usually extremely negative (enemies of the nation and the state, war profiteers, etc.), and many that had their personal documents invalidated in 1992 do not wish to identify with the term 'Erased' nor to discuss their experience. However, it was not until 2002 that this problem was given a name and the issue of the erasure became publicly known. Since the formation of the Association of Erased Persons of Slovenia in 2002, this problem has drawn a great deal of public attention, both positive and especially negative. Despite stigmatisation by the media, respondents were prepared to share their experiences and views, which could be considered a form of struggle for their rights, seeking recognition of their experiences and respect for their opinions.

For example, in his interview, one man illustrated how the stigmatisation of the Erased resulted in losing his best friend:

> Only once did I attend a protest. I would never do that again, I paid the huge price of losing my best friend ... He saw me on TV. I was asked if I would claim any rights. I said that I only demanded the pension which I had earned. I would not sue the state – the dispute I have is not with the state, it is with the Pension and Disability Fund. We used to be best friends. Now we are not any more. This really hurts me. He resented me for being erased. (Milenko)[5]

---

[5] All interviewees' names have been changed unless otherwise indicated.

Most of the respondents provided a detailed explanation of how they realised that they had been put in the position of persons without permission to stay at their home address in Slovenia and how this affected their
self-perception, reactions from those around them, the implementation
of various rights and their ability to access public services. In this chapter,
the main emphasis will be placed on the issue of the (in)accessibility of
rights. In many cases, these persons were denied the right to employment
or a pension, public service benefits, healthcare (including the chance to
take out health insurance), the right to cross state borders, the right to
possess a Slovene driving licence, etc. They were denied their share of collective property during the reform of ownership. Furthermore, they were
vulnerable to detention, deportation and other forms of police treatment.
They were often brought before misdemeanour judges and fined for their
'illegal' stay in the country. Although the situation of illegality into which
they were cast was not their fault, since it was the Ministry of the Interior
which had erased them from the register of permanent residents, they
were the ones who had to pay all the fines. Other expenses, such as notarised translations of various documents, administrative fees and solicitors' services, were also mentioned by the interviewees. Before discussing
the situation of survival without any legal status in the country, an explanation of how the erasure from the register of permanent residents came to
be administratively possible and practicable will be given.

Secession and overall initial determination of citizens in the new state

With the disintegration of the SFRY in 1991, Slovenia became the
first republic to establish itself as an independent state.[6] The first legal
foundation of Slovene statehood was the Constitution of the People's
Republic of Slovenia of 1947.[7] The right to secede was defined in the 1974
Constitution of the SFRY.[8]

---

[6] The sovereignty of the Republic of Slovenia was declared on 25 June 1991 on the basis of
the Basic Constitutional Charter on the Independence and Sovereignty of the Republic of
Slovenia, *Official Gazette of the Republic of Slovenia*, No. 1/1991-1. The Republic of Slovenia
regards the day of its international recognition as 15 January 1992. The legal and political basis for recognition by the EC were opinions of the special commission headed by
Robert Badinter; the opinions were issued on 11 January 1992, www.mzz.gov.si/index.
php?id=13&tx_ttnews[tt_news]=22815&tx_ttnews[backPid], accessed 15 February 2008.

[7] I. Kristan, *Družbena ureditev SFRJ* (Ljubljana: Založba Obzorja Maribor, 1976), 50.

[8] Kristan, *Družbena ureditev SFRJ*, 85. The right to self-determination was stipulated
in Part I of the Basic Principles of the Constitution. For the SFRY Constitution, see

In the framework of the SFRY, the ethno-cultural boundaries of the Slovene nation, so to speak, coincided with its political borders: with Slovenes making up 94 per cent of the population, Slovenia was the most ethnically homogenous Yugoslav republic until the early 1970s.[9] Economic immigration from other Yugoslav republics during the 1970s and 1980s became an important factor of ethnic de-homogenisation.[10] According to the 1991 census, 88.3 per cent of residents identified themselves as ethnic Slovenes,[11] meaning that approximately 10 per cent of the population had immigrated from other areas of the SFRY (Croats, Serbs, Muslims, Bosnians, Albanians, Macedonians, Montenegrins).[12]

In 1991, the initial overall determination of Slovene citizens was defined by Articles 39 and 40 of the Citizenship of the Republic of Slovenia Act.[13] The provisions of this Act derived from the 1974 SFRY Constitution and subsequent citizenship laws, which stipulated two layers of citizenship,[14] although the existence of registers of citizenship statuses at the level of the republics dates back much further.[15] According to the 1974 Constitution, every Yugoslav citizen was simultaneously a citizen of a republic.[16] On the basis of this Constitution, new federal and republican citizenship Acts were introduced in 1976.[17] Citizenship of a republic was an

---

http://sl.wikisource.org/wiki/Ustava_Socialisti%C4%8Dne_federativne_republike_ Jugoslavije_%281974%29/Temeljna_na%C4%8DDela, accessed 15 February 2008.

[9] Kristan, *Družbena ureditev SFRJ*, 86.

[10] Statistical Office of the Republic of Slovenia, *Population Census Results* (2003), www.stat. si/popis2002/en/rezultati/rezultati_red.asp?ter=SLO&st=7, accessed 6 December 2007.

[11] 0.2 per cent identified as members of the Italian minority, 0.4 per cent as Hungarians and 0.5 per cent as Roma; however, these groups are considered as autochthones minorities by the Constitution of the Republic of Slovenia, Articles 64 and 65. Roma are, however, also among the immigrant population.

[12] 7.3 per cent of residents identified themselves as Croats, Serbs, Muslims, Bosnians, Albanians, Montenegrins, or Macedonians; 0.6 per cent as Yugoslavs (which was perceived as a transnational concept); 0.5 per cent of the population did not wish to declare their ethnic belonging and for 2.2 per cent there is no data. Statistical Office of the Republic of Slovenia, *Population Census Results* (2003).

[13] Citizenship of the Republic of Slovenia Act, *Official Gazette*, No. 1/1991. In English, see www.mnz.gov.si/fileadmin/mnz.gov.si/pageuploads/EN/enDUNZ/ZDRS-Eng.doc, accessed 15 February 2008.

[14] Article 249 (Chapter Relations in the Federation) of the Constitution of the SFRY (1974); Citizenship of the SFRY Act, *Official Gazette of the SFRY*, No. 58/76 and Citizenship of the Socialist Republic of Slovenia Act, *Official Gazette of the SFRY*, No. 23/76.

[15] On the basis of the Citizenship of the Federal Peoples' Republic of Yugoslavia, issued on 25 November 1946, the Instruction to Run a Register of Citizens of the Peoples' Republic of Slovenia was issued, *Official Gazette of the Peoples' Republic of Slovenia*, No. 42/47.

[16] Article 249 (Chapter Relations in the Federation) of the Constitution of the SFRY (1974).

[17] Citizenship of the SFRY Act, *Official Gazette of the SFRY*, No. 58/76 and Citizenship of the Socialist Republic of Slovenia Act, *Official Gazette of the SFRY*, No. 23/76.

administrative, obligatorily ascribed status and a formal precondition for obtaining federal citizenship,[18] but was generally unknown to the citizens of Yugoslavia. It seems that citizenship of a republic served no practical purpose: for Yugoslav citizens, and that for them it had no legal consequences.[19] It became relevant only once the SFRY had begun to come apart. In the successor state Slovenia, it was applied as an initial criterion for the overall determination of the citizenship population.[20] Article 39 of the Citizenship of the Republic of Slovenia Act states:

> Any person who held citizenship of the Republic of Slovenia and of the Socialist Federal Republic of Yugoslavia in accordance with the existing regulations shall be considered a citizen of the Republic of Slovenia.

For long-term residents of Slovenia who were not considered citizens of the Republic of Slovenia (immigrants from other republics of the SFRY), Article 40 defined the conditions for obtaining Slovene citizenship:

> A citizen of another republic that had registered permanent residence in the Republic of Slovenia on the day of the plebiscite of the independence and sovereignty of the Republic of Slovenia on December 23, 1990, and has actually been living here, shall acquire citizenship of the Republic of Slovenia if, within six months of the entry into force of this Act, he/she files an application with the administrative authority competent for internal affairs of the community where he/she has his/her permanent residence.

Post-secession applications for Slovene citizenship (1991)

The six-month window for submitting citizenship applications expired on 15 December 1991. More than 174,000 persons, or 8.7 per cent of the total population, of which approximately 30 per cent had been born in

---

[18] L. Šturm, *Upravnopravne institucije: izbrana poglavja*, 3rd edn. (Ljubljana: Law Faculty, 1984), 14.

[19] Some of the deputies of the Assembly of the Republic of Slovenia, when discussing a new citizenship law of the independent Republic of Slovenia, emphasised that the institution of republican citizenship was generally unknown to residents of Slovenia and also that records were not really kept in order. *Transcripts of the National Assembly Sitting No. 19*: 9, 15, 21, 22, 30 May and 3 and 5 June 1991. See also Zorn ' "We, the Ethno-Citizens of Ethno-Democracy" – The Formation of Slovene Citizenship', in J. Zorn and U. Lipovec Čebron (eds.), *Once upon an Erasure: From Citizens to Illegal Residents in the Republic of Slovenia* (Ljubljana: Študentska založba, 2008), 52 and B. Beznec, 'The Impossible is Possible: An Interview with Aleksandar Todorović', in J. Zorn and U. Lipovec Čebron (eds.), *Once upon an Erasure: From Citizens to Illegal Residents in the Republic of Slovenia* (Ljubljana: Študentska založba, 2008), 19.

[20] Article 39 of the Citizenship of the Republic of Slovenia Act, *Official Gazette*, No. 1/1991.

Slovenia, applied for citizenship on the basis of Article 40, and 171,125 became Slovene citizens.[21] Not all non-Slovene long-term immigrants were granted Slovene citizenship – some applications were rejected, and some people did not apply for various reasons. It is also important to stress that many intended to apply for citizenship, but were deterred by inaccurate information delivered by clerks at municipality centres. They were told that without a birth certificate it was not possible to apply. The law gave everybody a chance to apply. However, later they would be required to supplement their application by a specified deadline.

But how did immigrants understand the application specified in Article 40? My own fieldwork[22] and the work of several other researchers[23] has shown that actual and potential applicants understood it in a number of ways: many understood it instrumentally, as a basis of rights and duties; for some, its implications were symbolic. Those who expressed its symbolic undertones can be further divided into two groups: those who equated citizenship status with ethnic belonging ('Why should I become a Slovene, when I was not one') and those who understood it as a matter of subjugation ('I felt guilty, less worthy because I was not a Slovene … A request [for citizenship] was proof of your loyalty').[24]

Those who did not apply for citizenship listed a number of reasons. Some had received false information on the application procedure by employees of the Ministry of the Interior,[25] as already mentioned; others mistakenly assumed that they would automatically get Slovene citizenship as ethnic Slovenes – they had been born in Slovenia or had moved

---

[21] F. Medved, 'From Civic to Ethnic Community? The Evolution of Slovenian Citizenship', in R. Bauböck, B. Perchinig and W. Sievers (eds.), *Citizenship Policies in the New Europe* (Amsterdam: IMISCOE, Amsterdam University Press, 2007), 218.

[22] J. Zorn, 'Ethnic Citizenship in the Slovenian State', *Citizenship Studies*, 9(2) (2005), 135 and the interviews made for this study.

[23] Beznec, 'The Impossible is Possible'; U. Lipovec Čebron,'The Metastasis of the Erasure', in J. Zorn and U. Lipovec Čebron (eds.), *Once upon an Erasure: From Citizens to Illegal Residents in the Republic of Slovenia* (Ljubljana: Študentska založba, 2008), 71–88; B. Mekina, 'A Monument to the Erased', in J. Zorn and U. Lipovec Čebron (eds.), *Once upon an Erasure: From Citizens to Illegal Residents in the Republic of Slovenia* (Ljubljana: Študentska založba, 2008), 44; M. Muršič, 'The Erasure is Always and Everywhere', in J. Zorn and U. Lipovec Čebron (eds.), *Once upon an Erasure: From Citizens to Illegal Residents in the Republic of Slovenia* (Ljubljana: Študentska založba, 2008), 32.

[24] Beznec, 'The Impossible is Possible', 21, 20.

[25] N. Kogovšek, 'The Erasure: The Proposal of a Constitutional Law as the Negation of the Rule of Law', in J. Zorn and U. Lipovec Čebron (eds.), *Once upon an Erasure: From Citizens to Illegal Residents in the Republic of Slovenia* (Ljubljana: Študentska založba, 2008), 196.

to Slovenia as infants.[26] Another reason for not applying for Slovene citizenship could be the fact that, in the period of the six-month window for applying (from 25 June to 25 December 1991), Slovenia had not yet been internationally recognised as a sovereign state,[27] and also that not everybody supported secession:[28]

> I would have had the right to receive citizenship, but I didn't apply since I could not predict what would happen. Then, in 1991, I had been living in Slovenia for 48 years. (Milenko)

> I came to Ljubljana with my parents when I was one year old, in 1958. I was educated here, and worked and raised a family here. The last document [prior to the erasure] was my ID, issued in April 1991, just a year before the erasure took place. It should have been valid until 2001, but it was destroyed in 1992. I didn't apply for citizenship since I missed the deadline – I was in the hospital after surviving a serious car accident ... I have brothers and sisters. Myself and one of my brothers, we were erased, but my other siblings got Slovene citizenship. (Iztok)

> I was born in 1953 in Slovenia, my mother was a Slovene. She was a partisan and she met my father during the Second World War. He was a Serb but had been living in Croatia before he moved to Slovenia in 1946. He did his entire employment period here, in Slovenia. I had always perceived myself as a Slovene and I didn't apply for Slovene citizenship. (Mojca)

In either case, those who chose not to apply for Slovene citizenship believed that they would be entitled to rights as legal aliens on the basis of their permanent residence address in Slovenia. The subsequent erasure of all those who did not become Slovene citizens from the register of permanent residents, a total of 25,671 persons, was impossible to predict, despite growing anti-Yugoslav and anti-immigrant sentiments.[29]

Legal void of the Aliens Act

Besides the Citizenship of the Republic of Slovenia Act (1991), one of the fundamental laws of the incipient state was the Aliens Act of the same

[26] J. Dedić, V. Jalušić and J. Zorn, *The Erased – Organized Innocence and the Politics of Exclusion* (Ljubljana: Peace Institute, 2003); Muršič, 'The Erasure'.

[27] Beznec, 'The Impossible is Possible'.

[28] At the Plebiscite for the Slovene independence held on 23 December 1990, 93.2 per cent of eligible voters cast their vote, 88.5 per cent voted in favour of the secession. Government of the Republic of Slovenija, *Kronologija*, www.slovenija2001.gov.si/pot/kronologija, accessed 1 February 2008.

[29] Dedić, Jalušić and Zorn, *The Erased*; B. K. Blitz, 'Statelessness and the Social (De) Construction of Citizenship: Political Restructuring and Ethnic Discrimination in Slovenia', *Journal of Human Rights*, 5(4) (2006), 453; Beznec, 'The Impossible is Possible'; Lipovec Čebron, 'The Metastasis'.

year.[30] Drafts of both laws were discussed at the National Assembly in May 1991 and adopted on 5 June 1991; that is, twenty days before the independence ceremony. The Aliens Act defined, among other things, conditions under which a non-citizen could enter the country and obtain a visa or temporary or permanent residence permit; which documents were issued to aliens; and basic regulations for refugees and the forcible removal of aliens without permission to stay. Article 81 of the transitional provisions stipulated that for long-term residents who had been citizens of the SFRY and who did not obtain Slovene citizenship, the provisions of the Aliens Act were to take effect two months after the expiry of the time limit for applying for citizenship or upon the issue of a final decision (in the case of a negative decision on a citizenship application).

During the discussions on the content of the new legislation, Metka Mencin, a centre-left-wing deputy of the Assembly, proposed an amendment to Article 81 of the Aliens Act. This amendment stated that immigrants from other republics who would not apply for Slovene citizenship would be issued permanent residence permits based on a registered permanent residence address or employment in Slovenia. Although the government approved of this proposal, a majority of deputies in the Assembly voted it down.[31] It was said that this matter 'does not need to be regulated by the Aliens Act, but by agreements between countries'. However, such agreements were never to materialise.[32]

This meant that Article 81 of the Aliens Act did not define provisions for persons who became 'aliens' due to the secession. These persons had resided in the country legally – those who were old enough to vote were eligible to participate in the Slovene plebiscite for independence (23 December 1991). Some of these 'new aliens' were born in Slovenia.

The Constitutional Court of the Republic of Slovenia *post festum* defined this absence of regulation as a legal void.[33] This legal void was

---

[30] Aliens Act, *Official Gazette*, No. 1/1991-I (not valid from 14 August 1999).

[31] *Transcripts of the National Assembly Sitting No. 19*: 9, 15, 21, 22, 30 May and 3 and 5 June 1991. See also Dedić, Jalušič and Zorn, *The Erased*, 47; Mekina, 'A Monument', and J. Zorn, 'A Case for Slovene Nationalism: Initial Citizenship Rules and the Erasure', *Nations and Nationalism*, 15 (2009a), 280–98.

[32] Dedić, Jalušič and Zorn, *The Erased*; Beznec, 'The Impossible is Possible'; Mekina, 'A Monument', 44; Zorn, 'A Case for Slovene Nationalism'.

[33] Decision No. U-I-284/94 issued by the Constitutional Court on 4 February 1999, http://ius.info/Baze/Usta/B/USTA66656335.htm, accessed 15 February 2008, and Decision No. U-I-246/02-28 issued by the Constitutional Court on 3 April 2003, *Official Gazette of the Republic of Slovenia*, No. 36/2003, http://odlocitve.us-rs.si/usrs/us-odl.nsf/o/B9DD3A68DBF1FC03C125717200288C2F, accessed 15 February 2008.

abused in order to invent and implement a measure which resulted in the total exclusion of those residents who did not become citizens of the new state. In contrast, residence permits for foreigners with non-SFRY citizenship issued in the period of the SFRY continued to be valid in the independent Republic of Slovenia.[34] The Constitutional Court claimed that depriving legal residents of Slovenia of their statuses was in violation of the principles of equality before the law, trust in the law and legal safety.[35]

Erasure from the register of permanent residents

The actual act of administrative exclusion that would become known as the erasure took place on 26 February 1992: those persons who did not become Slovene citizens in 1991 were secretly erased from the register of permanent residents of the Republic of Slovenia by the Ministry of the Interior.[36] The official number of these persons is 25,671, which constitutes more than 1 per cent of the Slovene population. At first this measure was not publicly conspicuous, despite its severe consequences for individuals and their families. It was not until 2002, after nearly a decade, that this issue was publicly addressed and named the *erasure*, with its victims calling themselves the *Erased*.[37]

The Erased were not notified about the change of their permanent resident status, and they often found out that they had been erased solely by chance. Their Yugoslav passports became invalid on 26 February 1992, whereas Slovene citizens continued to use their Yugoslav passports until

[34] Third para. of Article 82, Aliens Act, *Official Gazette*, No. 1/1991-I (not valid from 14 August 1999).

[35] Decision No. U-I-284/94 on 4 February 1999 was followed by several decisions in which the Constitutional Court reasserted its opinion: Decision No. U-60/97 on 15 July 1999, Decision No. U-I-89/99 on 6 October 1999, Decision No. U-I-295/99 on 18 May 2000, Decision No. U-I-246/02 on 3 April 2003 and Decision No. U-211/04-21 on 2 March 2006.

[36] Dedić, Jalušić and Zorn, *The Erased*; Ministry of the Interior of the Republic of Slovenia, Odprta vprašanja o izvajanju zakona o tujcih. Ref. No 0016/1-s-010/3-91 (4 June 1992), document published in the daily newspaper *Večer* (25 February 2004); J. Zorn, 'Ethnic Citizenship in the Slovenian State'; Blitz, 'Statelessness'; V. Jalušić and J. Dedić, 'The Erasure – Mass Human Rights Violation and Denial of Responsibility: The Case of Independent Slovenia', *Human Rights Review*, 9(1) (2008), 93.

[37] S. Pistotnik, 'Chronology of the Erasure 1990–2007', in J. Zorn and U. Lipovec Čebron (eds.), *Once upon an Erasure: From Citizens to Illegal Residents in the Republic of Slovenia* (Ljubljana: Študentska založba, 2008), 222.

25 June 1993.[38] Individuals whose names were removed from the register of permanent residents of Slovenia did not receive any formal notice, meaning that there was no formal procedure for filing complaints; it was not clear how to express grievances, or to whom, and on what legal grounds complaints should be filed:

> I knew I was erased when my husband and I went to the municipal administrative centre to register our car. It was in April 1992. My documents, passport and ID, were taken away. I asked them why, but I got no reply. (Slavenka)

> At the administrative centre, at the department for personal status, I handed in my documents. Without saying a word, or giving any kind of explanation, a woman at the desk voided my documents. I just stood there with a dumbfounded look on my face, because I didn't know what this meant. They punched a hole in my passport and voided my personal ID with a stamp. I asked what all this meant and she said that I was not a Slovene citizen and that I should register myself at the Office for Aliens. Instead of going to the Office for Aliens, I rushed to the first solicitor I could think of, an acquaintance, and asked him for an explanation. He had no idea what was going on. He didn't know how to answer any of my questions, but he did say that under no circumstances should I register at the Office for Aliens, because then they could even go so far as to deport me out of the country if I found myself unemployed, or if some other reason came up. So I didn't register at the Office for Aliens. (Nada)

> I felt something wasn't right at the time. It was a time of hostility towards us, 'Southerners'. I left my job before I could be sacked. Then it came as a shock, when I went to the administrative centre to sign that I am my daughter's father because I am not officially married to my 'wife'. I signed and then her birth certificate came to our address by post. My wife and I were shocked to see that the box with the father's name was empty. After that, it took me and my solicitor two years to get my name registered in the birth certificate of my daughter. And, as many other erased persons had experienced, my documents were also destroyed. (Petar)

General characteristics of and eligibility for permanent and temporary residence permits

The Aliens Act stipulates that aliens who wish to stay in Slovenia for a longer time must obtain a residence permit. According to this law a residence permit means a permit to enter the Republic of Slovenia and to reside for a definite period of time and for a specific purpose, or to reside

---

[38] Article 39 of the Passports of the Citizens of the Republic of Slovenia Act, *Official Gazette*, No. 1/1991-I (ceased to be valid since 5 August 2000).

for an indefinite period of time.[39] A resident permit may be temporary (*the first permit is always temporary*, and never longer than one year) or a permit for permanent residence.[40]

An alien who wishes to reside in Slovenia must have a valid travel document (valid for a minimum of three months longer than the intended stay in Slovenia), as well as appropriate health insurance and sufficient personal funds, or guarantors, to support them during their stay, for a sum at least equivalent to the minimum income in the Republic of Slovenia.[41] On 1 January 2008, for example, this amount consisted of 213 EUR per month.[42] Temporary residence permits are issued only for specific purposes and for specific periods of time. Permits are issued for employment or to set up or run a business,[43] for family reunion (the basis is heterosexual marriage only), study or other educational activities, or for other reasons such as national interest and other international customs.[44] Permanent residence permits are issued without any restrictions regarding the duration and purpose of stay in Slovenia. An alien with this kind of permit for residence has the status of a long-term resident.[45]

From 26 February 1992 onwards, the Aliens Act was applied to the Erased. The Erased could initially apply only for a temporary residence permit. One of the obstacles that these newly designated non-citizens faced was a demand to be in possession of a valid passport of a foreign country. As already mentioned, Slovene citizens were allowed to use their SFRY passports until 25 June 1993, whereas long-term residents who did not become Slovene citizens were prevented from doing the same. Many among the Erased could not obtain the passport of a foreign country. There were various reasons for this – some had never resided in another republic of the SFRY and thus had no address outside Slovenia. Others would have needed to travel to their original home towns, but this was not safe or even possible because of the war conditions in the SFRY. Many individuals did not dare to leave Slovenia since they (rightly) believed that they would not be allowed to re-enter the country on their way back.

---

[39] Article 25 of the Aliens Act, *Official Gazette*, No. 107/2006.
[40] Article 26 of the Aliens Act (2006).   [41] Article 27 of the Aliens Act (2006).
[42] Ministry for Labour, Family and Social Affairs www.mddsz.gov.si/si/delovna_podrocja/ sociala/denarna_socialna_pomoc/, accessed 16 February 2008.
[43] To open a firm would not suffice. For example, a respondent with the pseudonym Ivan explained: 'As a foreigner I was allowed to open a firm, but I could not get an employment permit.'
[44] *Ibid.*   [45] Article 26 of the Aliens Act (2006).

When a residence permit was revoked, not only did this terminate the right to remain on the territory of the Republic of Slovenia but it also ended claims to a range of social rights, including healthcare on the basis of health insurance,[46] access to the educational system,[47] the right to work,[48] the right to start a business,[49] the right to inherit property (on the basis of reciprocity principle between the state of which an alien is a citizen and Slovenia),[50] the right to family reunion,[51] the right to social assistance on equal terms with citizens,[52] and the right to free legal aid.[53]

Agency of the Erased: endeavours to acquire legal alien status anew

Under the Aliens Act 1991, persons erased from the register of permanent residents had the right to apply for residence permits on the same footing as any other foreign citizen. Many of them, however, did not meet the criteria set forth in the Aliens Act: they could not prove that they had sufficient means to support themselves and basic health insurance because the erasure had deprived them of their former rights and benefits (jobs, pensions, health insurance, social benefits, etc.). It should be noted that family integrity is a possible *reason* for applying for one's first residence permit (which is always a temporary permit, as stated above), but is not an eligibility criterion.[54] It does not give a non-resident the automatic right to join his/her spouse who may be a Slovene citizen or permanent resident. Another obstacle was that erased persons had been stripped of their legal

---

[46] Health Care and Health Insurance Act of the Republic of Slovenia, *Official Gazette*, No. 72/2006.

[47] Constitution of the Republic of Slovenia (Article 57), Elementary School Act, *Official Gazette*, No. 81/2006; Gimnazije Act, *Official Gazette*, No. 115/2006; Higher Education Act, *Official Gazette*, No. 119/2006.

[48] Article 10 of the Employment and Work of Aliens Act, *Official Gazette*, No. 4/2006, English version, www.mddsz.gov.si/fileadmin/mddsz.gov.si/pageuploads/dokumenti_pdf/zzdt_upb1_en.pdf, accessed 17 February 2008.

[49] *Ibid.*

[50] Reciprocity Act, *Official Gazette*, No. 9/1999; Inheritance Act, Article 6, *Official Gazette*, No. 15/1976.

[51] Article 36 of the Aliens Act (2006). An alien who possesses a residence permit and would like to bring their family (a spouse and/or children, parents only if an alien is minor) must submit evidence of sufficient funds to support those immediate family members who intend to reside in the country.

[52] Social Assistance Act, *Official Gazette*, No. 36/2004, Article 5 (Beneficiaries).

[53] Free Legal Aid Act, *Official Gazette*, No. 96/2004, Article 10.

[54] Article 30 of the Aliens Act (2006).

status and thus the years they had spent in Slovenia did not count when applying for a new resident permit or citizenship. A substantial number of residents who were deprived of their legal status could not fulfil the conditions set forth in the Aliens Act or Citizenship of the Republic of Slovenia Act, meaning that they either remained in Slovenia 'illegally' or on the basis of a temporary residence permit or tourist visa, despite the fact that their homes and families were in Slovenia.[55] All the respondents reported numerous obstacles and difficulties when trying to newly arrange their legal status in Slovenia:

> It is not true what people say, that if somebody was determined to get their status back they got it. It is not true, because I really did everything I could, I knew a lot of distinguished persons and I was totally integrated into this life and society, but I didn't succeed in arranging anything. I was well-off and I didn't manage to arrange my personal documents and status in Slovenia. I was literally treated as somebody who had just entered Slovenia. Not to mention that I was active, as a volunteer, in sports and culture. This was not acknowledged at all, anywhere by anybody … I went to the administrative centre for aliens hundreds of times, but they always turned me away since they found my application to be incomplete. I was unable to provide a certificate stating that my permanent address is elsewhere [in Bosnia and Herzegovina], or proof that I have sufficient means for living. I was unable to deliver these documents.

> At the Office for Aliens, after my Slovene ID was destroyed, they explained that I have to go to the Bosnian Embassy (and at that time there wasn't one in Slovenia, but only in Italy), that I needed to get a Bosnian passport and a registered address in Bosnia. I tried to do that. I phoned the Embassy and they asked me if I had a permanent address in Slovenia. I said: 'No, because it was revoked.' 'Then you can't get Bosnian documents either, not through the Embassy.' So I went without. I didn't have either Bosnian or Slovene citizenship or personal documents, nothing. (Iztok)

> I had to apply for status since I was erased. At the administrative centre I was told that I need to bring a receipt, some proof that I was not registered as a citizen anywhere else. This was just one of the documents that I needed to bring in order to get some sort of status. In this period [1992–3] telephone lines didn't function, buses didn't drive to Serbia, trains didn't go to Serbia; Slovenia and Serbia – then Yugoslavia, were practically at war. There was no Yugoslav or Serbian Embassy in Slovenia. In these circumstances I started collecting documents; first I needed to have this document stating that I was not registered in Serbia. After six months I managed to get the document and I brought it to the central administrative

---

[55] Dedić, Jalušić and Zorn, *The Erased*; Blitz, 'Statelessness'; Beznec, 'The Impossible is Possible'.

office on Beethovnova street. This document had been really hard to get. When I brought it in, they first demanded a notarised translation. I got it done. Next time, I brought the translated document. The employee went to consult with her superior. She was gone for five minutes. I expected that my status would be finally resolved. I believed I shouldn't be left to become stateless, since I was not registered in Serbia either. My solicitor was also there. When she came out of that room she said: 'Sir, you brought a document issued in the so-called Republic of Yugoslavia, with whom we don't have any international relations. This document is invalid for us, we are not obliged to consider it.' When I heard this I was angry, because I saw that their aim was to make it impossible for us, former citizens, to arrange our status here. The aim was to deter us, the Erased. They wanted us to leave Slovenia … A few years later I had another experience. One of the conditions for applying for citizenship was the Slovene language test. I brought my secondary school diploma; I wasn't a brilliant student, but I had a 5 [the highest mark] in Slovene language. I showed this to the employee: 'Please have a look, here is proof of my knowledge of Slovene.' Of course, I spoke Slovene to her. She said that I would have to take the Slovene language test again. That this is the rule. Because she was so persistent in this Slovene language exam I suggested: 'OK, I'll take the Slovene language exam under the condition that you issue me a document which states that you consider this diploma, issued in the Republic of Slovenia, invalid, that you don't recognise it. If I get this receipt, I'll take the Slovene language exam.' Then she took my diploma to her boss. After five minutes she returned saying: 'OK, Sir, you don't have to take the Slovene language exam again.' My citizenship application was rejected anyway … It was rejected – because they didn't find anything else – on the basis of a breach of public order and peace. Once I was playing music too loud, it was in a pub I hired. This was the reason my citizenship application was rejected! I was getting depressed. (Josip)

The inaccessibility of rights

Erased persons not only lacked a valid personal document which they could use to identify themselves officially, but also the invalidation of their documents actually meant the revocation of their legal status in Slovenia. The consequence was the inaccessibility of all the rights associated with the (welfare) state, including the most basic rights, such as the right to stay in Slovenia, and with it the right to family integrity, and the right to employment. From the point of view of the state, if a person is not allowed to stay in the country, it follows that that person is not allowed to find employment, seek social assistance, drive a car, or take out health insurance. The Erased, however, were long-term immigrants or were born in Slovenia to immigrant parent(s); some of them perceived themselves as Slovenes. It was 'natural', or at least understandable, that they stayed in Slovenia despite the erasure. This situation of *de facto* statelessness brought years of anxiety, suffering and trampled dignity; as from 26 February 1992 they officially became 'unwanted' or 'redundant' and had to survive outside the boundaries of the (welfare) state while remaining physically present in its territory. The destruction of their legal identity, a 'civil death', as one of the interviewees described it, deeply influenced their whole lives – for some, the erasure even had fatal consequences.[56]

The following excerpts from the interviews illustrate life, or rather survival, beyond the margins of citizenship or legal alien status. Examples of the inaccessibility of rights, which occasionally include descriptions of survival strategies, have been organised into the following spheres: employment, pension, family relations, healthcare, issues of border crossing, expenses associated with the erasure and police treatment.

Employment

Owing to the loss of legal status in the country, the Erased were not allowed to seek employment. However, this does not mean that they did not work – on the contrary, many respondents reported that they had to work under extremely precarious conditions, with long hours and without the rights normally associated with employment. Their socio-economic situation deteriorated dramatically, which affected their entire families. The loss of social networks associated with work and feelings of trampled dignity stemming from discrimination negatively influenced their health. As Uršula Lipovec Čebron[57] noted in her in-depth study of the health situation of four Erased persons, employment had been a key anchor for their identity. In these and other research interviews,[58] many Erased emphasised that they were good workers. They had, after all, moved to Slovenia to work. In the former Yugoslavia, workers were perceived in terms of the (ideologically socialist) ruling class; most rights were based on employment, and being a worker brought (self-)respect. For the Erased who had been employed for years or even decades, the loss of employment

---

[56] S. Vasović, 'Deported to Death', in J. Zorn and U. Lipovec Čebron (eds.), *Once upon an Erasure: From Citizens to Illegal Residents in the Republic of Slovenia* (Ljubljana: Študentska založba, 2008), 190; N. Kogovšek, J. Zorn, S. Pistotnik, U. Lipovec Čebron, V. Bajt, B. Petković and L. Zdravković, *Brazgotine izbrisa: Prispevek h kritičnemu razumevanju izbrisa iz registra stalnega prebivalstva Republike Slovenije* (Ljubljana: Peace Institute, 2010).

[57] Lipovec Čebron, 'The Metastasis'.

[58] See also Kogovšek *et al.*, *Brazgotine izbrisa*.

not only meant the lack of a means of sustenance; often it meant the first step towards an identity crisis which took the form of depression.

How did people survive in a situation where their right to employment had been revoked? The following excerpts were chosen because they provide the most illustrative responses to this question. The first interviewee became homeless. The second one could not develop her artistic potential; she had to close down her business and work at two low-paying jobs just to survive. The other three lost their jobs or had to close down their business and were forced to find work on the black market. Teodor also reported that his employer abused his vulnerable position as a person without documents and still owes him payment.

> My situation was as follows: I had a severe car accident on 30 December 1990. I barely survived; I spent few months in hospitals, and couldn't walk for some time. My boss was supposed to employ me after the New Year, but then, because of this accident, he didn't. Afterwards nobody wanted to employ me. I was a waiter, a good one, I used to serve in posh restaurants. I had to work illegally, or beg. I was like a tramp: without a home, without a family (I became redundant without papers), without everything. Of course, I didn't steal, this I would not allow to myself. But I humiliated myself, I begged for bread … Becoming a foreigner, I didn't get any assistance, and I didn't have health insurance either. (Iztok)

> I had a difficult time surviving without any kind of status in Slovenia. For a living, I often performed with a music band *Romanoraj* – for some time this was my major means of subsistence. It wasn't a lot of money. At the time, we got about 50 Euros per person for performance. When business was at its best, we had four performances a month, and in between there were gaps when we didn't perform. But even this had to be done through somebody else contract and account. I couldn't collect my earnings. To get by I had also to work under the table as a bartender, even though my business has always been in culture and I had all the potential there only if I didn't had this citizenship complication … I wasn't allowed to be registered as an unemployed person at the Employment Office. I was required to bring in a citizenship certificate, which I didn't have. I had hoped that they would kind of forget about the certificate. Once I was invited for a job interview, but they required me to bring the citizenship certificate that I didn't have. It was terribly frustrating … At one point I weighed 43 kilograms. I had no money for food or clothes. One can always find something to wear. I remember, once I ate only potatoes for two weeks, which were given to me by a friend. His mother wanted to throw these potatoes away, because they had plants growing out of them. (Nada)

> I used to have my own construction company, but I lost it. I lost my health insurance, I lost everything – for twelve years I went without. (Slobodan)

I lost my permanent work in beer factory. I'd worked there for eighteen years. If I had stayed I would have thirty years of employment by now. Then I worked in different places [without employment status]. (Hajrudin)

I had many jobs, my former employer owes me seventeen salaries. He owes me 8,000 Euros plus interest. I'm fighting to get this. In this country I don't feel safe. (Teodor)

Pension

The right to receive a pension is based on previous work and paid taxes and is not conditioned by one's status as a citizen or permanent resident.[59] Nonetheless, many of the Erased could not receive a pension due to a lack of legal status in the country. Former employees of the Yugoslav People's Army form a large share of those who were denied a pension.[60] It is obvious that they have been constructed as a national enemy, regardless of their inactivity during the ten-day military conflict in Slovenia after state independence was declared in the summer of 1991. Owing to this injustice and to the fact that they had once shared the same employer and so knew each other, former employees of the Yugoslav People's Army were among the first to take up the fight for the rights of the Erased. Defenders of the politics of erasure (right-wing politicians, for example) have successfully presented the view that the Erased are exclusively Yugoslav military personnel who were 'justly punished' for their disloyal behaviour towards the Slovene nation. The right to receive a pension was denied to Milenko and Mitar, former employees of the Yugoslav People's Army, for example, and they reported that this ruined their life:

I am seventy four and this situation [of not receiving my earned pension] ruined my life. (Milenko)

Until today I still haven't got all my pensions. I manage to get, with the help of Krivic and another lawyer, citizenship in 2002. I retired in December 1991; however, I got my pension in the same year as citizenship, in 2002. Then my life started to become normal again. Because I didn't receive my pension I had to work hard ... Both my wife and I did physical work; we were paid in cash. Then I got used to always carrying around some money with me, because I never knew when I would be removed from the

---

[59] Pension and Disability Insurance Act, *Official Gazette of the Republic of Slovenia*, No. 106/1999.
[60] Mekina, 'A Monument'.

country … The whole family suffered. One who doesn't have this experience cannot imagine how terrible it is when you're denied something that is yours and you have to fight for it for over fifteen years. All these complaints and legal procedures exhausted me. (Mitar)

Family relations and how the situation affected children

Within the family structure, it often happened that only one parent was erased, although a number of combinations were possible. There are cases where the permanent resident status of all family members was revoked. 5,360 children and 5,008 persons aged eighteen to twenty-nine found themselves among the Erased.[61] These children and youngsters and those whose family members were erased exhibited a wide range of reactions. Some were supportive of their families, while others resented their parents and blamed them for their exclusion and poverty. The same applies to spouses. Some were supportive, and their relationship grew even deeper; for others, a situation in which a spouse had been denied the right to employment became a source of irresolvable conflict. This also applies to other people in the erased persons' environment: relatives, friends, neighbours, schoolteachers, etc. An erased person who will be referred to as Iavor reported that his wife and daughter were supportive, and that the whole family felt excluded and stigmatised:

> My wife was scared to tell their parents that I was erased. And I didn't want to play games. Once they were invited over to our house, I wrote above the door frame, using a magic marker: Here lives an erased person of Slovenia. Afterwards the relatives took it quite well. But it was difficult to erase the sign. (Iavor)

Nada and Elvisa, two mothers who had been erased, reported that exclusion from normal life had especially devastating consequences for their children. Nada's ex-husband got custody of their children. She reported that the social worker discriminated against her due to her lack of status:

> What actually happened was that I found myself in the situation of no legal status. My husband cleverly took advantage of these unfortunate circumstances. He filed for custody of our two children and won the suit. I couldn't even go to court, not even once, because I didn't get mail, or I couldn't pick it up from the post-office because I didn't have any valid

---

[61] This data was published by the Ministry of the Interior in 2009, www.mnz.gov.si/fileadmin/mnz.gov.si/pageuploads/2009/izbrisani-koncni_podatki.pdf, accessed 8 August 2009.

personal document to represent myself. A few months later, I found a notice that I failed to appear in court and that my husband gets custody of the children nailed to my door. My husband prevented us from having contact, and I didn't see my two children for eight years. It wasn't until I obtained documents that I could arrange visitation rights and see them. It is a sad story. My son told me that they tore up my letters right before his eyes … However, owing this whole situation I found myself in, I believe I couldn't have taken a proper care of my children; they would have suffered a great deal with me. (Nada)

Elvisa never regained the trust of her older daughter, who resented her mother for the poverty she had to experience as a youngster. Furthermore, Elvisa's father, who is himself a Bosnian immigrant in Germany, where he receives a pension, could not understand the issue of erasure; he blamed Elvisa and did not give her moral or material support:

The most horrible thing for me was that I couldn't take a proper care of my children. I couldn't arrange things for their schooling … In front of the whole classroom a teacher told my son 'from today you don't have lunch in school, your mother hasn't paid for three months'. And a child couldn't learn, he couldn't focus on school lessons, he only thought about his problems, how he didn't have winter coat, he went to school wearing a sweater, he couldn't have lunch in school, everybody did, only he didn't. He couldn't concentrate on school tests, he got bad marks. It was hard for children, because we were so poor. My son, his foot grew so fast and I didn't have money to buy him new sport shoes, his toe came out of his shoes and we walked from shop to shop and we both cried because we couldn't find something that we could afford … The eldest daughter, she also had problems in school, she argued with teachers and got only poor marks. She is bright but she barely finished primary school and she didn't meet the criteria to enroll in the secondary school for hairdressers. She started to be involved in all sorts of problem … She still doesn't understand it was not my fault. A neighbour has three children on her own, she was poorly paid like me, but her children got everything for school – the difference was that she had her personal document and I didn't have one. So she could claim different kinds of social benefits whereas I couldn't … I have no idea how we survived, one should ask my children how they survived; well, my eldest daughter hasn't really survived, because she still holds resentment, she is angry with me and with the whole world … I don't have my relatives, my siblings or my parents in Slovenia, I came as a young woman from Bosnia. I worked hard here …. My father lives in Germany and he couldn't understand my situation, he was angry with me, he would say: 'You don't know what problems are. Why don't you go to Bosnia, and you'll see … I know how people live in Slovenia.' He thought I was manipulating him to get some benefits from my relatives. (Elvisa)

Deterioration of health and access to healthcare

Exclusion on the level of the state led to exclusion from one's immediate surroundings, which resulted in feelings of powerlessness and stress.[62] These contributed to the development of various health problems, from diabetes to back pain and depression; several cases of suicide linked to the erasure were also reported. In cases where stress was exacerbated by the loss of (suitable) accommodation and an inadequate diet, health problems were practically unavoidable.

The first institution to address the health of the Erased was the Clinic and Consulting Centre for Persons without Health Insurance. The Clinic opened in 2002, ten years after the erasure.[63] Statistics from the Clinic significantly differ from those presented by other healthcare institutions. In its first year, the Clinic had 500 times more tuberculosis patients than the rest of Slovenia. Other diseases, such as pulmonary illnesses, circulatory problems (of both the heart and veins), gastrointestinal illnesses, acute problems of the central nervous system and depression, were also common. The Clinic treated two erased persons who had had their legs amputated because of narrow veins.[64]

Inspired by socio-cultural epidemiology (which statistically measures the health of a society in relation to the degree of social equality), Uršula Lipovec Čebron[65] interpreted the erasure as both a disease within Slovene society and a cause of the diseases of erased individuals. She showed the connection between factors that contribute to the development of a particular disease and the ways in which the Erased view their situation. Similarly, in the research discussed here, respondents saw a connection between their symptoms and the erasure:

> I lost sleep – literally [as a consequence of not receiving my pension]. Because of stress I got diabetes. My sight deteriorated to the point that I'm not able to read for more than five minutes. (Mitar)

> I lost too much weight. I have pains in my back. (Ana)

---

[62] Lipovec Čebron, 'The Metastasis'.
[63] The clinic was founded by the Ljubljana Healthcare Centre, the Municipality of Ljubljana, Slovene Philanthropy and Karitas. It is intended for all residents of Ljubljana who do not have basic health insurance (see www.pro-bono.ordinacija.net). Its annual reports show that, since the very beginning of its activities, the Erased have represented a high percentage of its users: roughly 22 per cent in the years 2002 and 2003, 46 per cent two years later and 20 per cent in 2006 (Lipovec Čebron, 'The Metastasis').
[64] *Ibid.*   [65] *Ibid.*

> I didn't have health insurance or money to pay to see a doctor. So I could not be medically treated, for ten years I went without. My health worsened and today I have a category three disability, but I don't agree, I should have been recognised for a category two.[66] My legs swell, I have open wounds in my feet, I can't see out of my right eye. My lungs are not OK, yes, I know, I should quit smoking. Only in 2002 the Clinic for persons without health insurance opened and then I could get medical help. (Iztok)

The health of the Erased was dually endangered: psychical pressure, sometimes combined with poor nutrition and unsuitable accommodation, resulted in various symptoms, for which medical treatment was denied. How did the Erased manage to survive such fatal exclusion from public services? Being *de facto* stateless, they were not able to take out health insurance (except insurance for tourists, which was short-term and expensive). The following excerpts from the interviews show three of the most common strategies for survival in a situation where one does not have access to public healthcare. The first interviewee relied on social networks; since the Erased were integrated members of Slovene society, it was not uncommon for them to turn to a relative or a friend who could help or medical staff whom they knew personally. Paying full price for medical services can be identified as the second approach. However, in a situation where one's right to work had been revoked and social assistance was denied, this option was rather difficult to undertake. In research on the consequences of the erasure conducted by Kogovšek *et al.* (2010),[67] one man reported that he was not allowed to see a doctor even when he offered payment for services. 'Suffering' can be identified as the third approach: the Erased did not manage to visit a doctor and went without any medical treatment whatsoever:

> When I needed an injection or medications, I arranged through my daughter-in-law – I went to see a doctor with her health insurance card. Or when I needed to repair my teeth, I used my son's health insurance card and went to see my son's friend, he is a dentist and has his own private practice. (Milenko)

> I had to pay for all health care services myself, and I couldn't get health insurance. I could only see a doctor if I paid. I had an expensive operation on my veins. In fact, I went into debt [to cover the costs of this treatment]. It happened that I went without electricity at home; I wasn't able to pay the bills, so they would turn it off. (Nada)

---

[66] There are three categories of disability in Slovenia – category one is for the severely disabled, and category three is for minor disabilities (Pension and Disability Insurance Act, *Official Gazette of the Republic of Slovenia*, No. 106/1999).

[67] Kogovšek *et al.*, *Brazgotine izbrisa*.

I didn't have health insurance. What did I do when I was ill? Nothing. I suffered. (Hajrudin)

Pregnant women were also among those who went without medical care: several women reported that they could not get medical check-ups for the entire period of their pregnancy and only went to the hospital for the delivery.[68] However, even delivery could not be taken for granted. In the following case, a newborn baby barely survived:

> My younger one was born in Ljubljana. At the time [1999] I didn't have health insurance, I didn't have papers. I went to the maternity unit, but since I had no insurance card, they sent me home despite the fact that my waters had started to break. I had no contractions, so they just sent me home; it was said that I was not yet been ready for delivery. I asked to be induced. They sent me home. My waters were breaking from Sunday to Monday afternoon, when I went to the maternity unit again. This time I was accepted and the medical personnel could not believe it. Immediately I got two bottles of infusion, so that the baby could have some liquid. Then I gave birth. The newborn was completely black, really black, he barely made it. I thanked God, my son survived and so did I. The medical personnel told me that I can sue for non-treatment when I first came to the birthing place. I said that I won't since they saved me, my son and I, we both survived I didn't want to file a complaint. (Sara)

Border crossing

One of the consequences of *de facto* statelessness concerns travel abroad. Many of the Erased have a personal history of immigration, and the revocation of residence rights resulted in a restriction of their right to enter Slovenia. Therefore, many erased persons simply would not risk leaving the country. In the interviews, respondents became especially emotional when they remembered how they could not visit their elderly parents and sick brothers and sisters or attend funerals in their home towns, which were located in foreign countries after Slovenia declared independence in 1991. They could not see newborn relatives (nephews, etc.).[69] It was not that they were prevented from leaving the country, but rather the knowledge that they would not be allowed to enter Slovenia on their way back which kept them inside the borders of Slovenia for years:

> My father still lives in Serbia. But for ten years I could not travel. When the Yugoslav Embassy opened in Ljubljana, only then I could receive my

---

[68] Lipovec Čebron, 'The Metastasis'; Kogovšek *et al.*, *Brazgotine izbrisa*.

[69] People from Bosnia and Herzegovina and Serbia needed a visa if they wished to travel to Slovenia. Visa criteria were strict, and at times travel was impossible due to the war zones in the territories of the former Yugoslavia.

passport, and since then I keep visiting my relatives. I couldn't go to my mother's funeral. For this I'll never forgive those who erased us. I was offered a one-way passport (to-go passport) when I asked at the local administrative centre to be given a document to be able to live normally. They replied: Go to Serbia to get a passport there. I knew that if I went I would not be allowed to return ... After ten years I could see my father and brothers again, and my mother had passed away in the meantime. In ten years time, I never crossed the border, I never left Slovenia. I was thinking about leaving, the pressure was unbearable, but I had a small kid, I couldn't just walk away, because they wouldn't let me in again. (Petar)

My brother died, I couldn't go to the funeral, my sister died, I couldn't go to the funeral. I couldn't go to Bosnia and Herzegovina. Actually I could, but then they would not let me in [back to Slovenia]. (Hajrudin)

I retired on 31 December 1991 [from the Yugoslav Army]. I couldn't get all the documents needed for my retirement in Slovenia, although I believed I should get the documents here, since I served my entire employment period in Slovenia. I had to get my birth certificate in Belgrade. In January 1992 I was on my way back home, but I was not allowed to enter Slovenia. For two days they kept me at the border. Those were two dreadful days ... afterwards I didn't dare to cross the border to travel outside Slovenia again because I was afraid I would not be let in again. I wasn't able to visit my sick father and the grave of my mother. (Mitar)

I haven't been to my home town for twelve years. In the meantime my mother died and I didn't go to her funeral. (Slobodan)

The author of this chapter also interviewed people in Bosnia and Herzegovina who had travelled there in 1991 or 1992 to get away from the military conflict in Slovenia or to visit their relatives. On their way back to Slovenia, they were stopped by border police and prevented from entering the country. Their holidays turned into permanent exile. While the war raged in their home towns, they sought refuge in refugee camps in Bosnia and Herzegovina and in Serbia. As of 2009, there were still families and individuals who were not able to return to Slovenia.[70]

Another problem pertaining to crossing the state border concerns obtaining various certificates and personal documents, such as a foreign passport, in order to become eligible for an alien's permit to stay in Slovenia. What legal options were available for travel abroad to acquire the required documentation? And how could one be expected to travel to his/

[70] Interviews with the Erased conducted in Bosnia and Herzegovina, Novi grad by the author on 15 September 2007.

her home town if military combat had paralysed municipal services and intimidated the whole village? Although Yugoslav passports remained valid until June 1993 for Slovene citizens,[71] the Erased persons' personal documents, including their passports, ceased to be valid from the day of the erasure (26 February 1992). Interviewees also reported that embassies of the newly formed states in the territory of the former Yugoslavia had not yet been opened in Slovenia. Even after these countries did establish embassies in Slovenia, they were often of little help to the Erased, since they could not prove their residence status in Slovenia. It was a vicious circle, difficult, at times even impossible, to break; many remained in a situation of *de facto* statelessness for years. It therefore comes as no surprise that there were people who opted to break the law and cross the border illegally:

> Let me return to the issue of acquiring personal documents in 1996. As already said, to be able to apply for Slovene citizenship I needed to be a citizen somewhere. In my case there was a possibility of having Croatian citizenship since I was obviously registered there due to my place of birth. I don't have any relatives in Croatia that I keep in touch with. Fortunately, my friend offered me help. She already helped me before, when I realised I was without status and she signed as my personal guarantor. Then she helped me with the border crossing issue. I entered Croatia illegally, because without a valid document I couldn't enter the country legally. At first, I had considered to cross a frontier through the fields, outside a border check point. Then my friend got up the courage and told me that she would give me a ride. On the Slovene side of the border I explained the policemen my situation. They were very clear that they wouldn't let me back without documents, and that I had to realise this. On the Croatian side we used our female charms on the customs officer. My invalid personal ID was tucked into my friend's passport. He quickly flipped through the passport, he saw that my ID was in there and didn't notice the stamp [saying it was invalid], so he let us pass. We managed to get to the Croatian side without any guarantee that I would be able to obtain Croatian documents and return to Slovenia. Because of this uncertainty, I didn't sleep a wink for two days. The psychological pressure was terrible; I was shaking. I had already suffered several years of being without documents, and the whole business with my ex-husband, who was hiding and taking advantage of the fact that I couldn't get at him. And now this. I had never committed even a misdemeanour in my life, and had never been convicted of anything. I'm not that kind of person and that's why crossing that border was something awful. (Nada)

---

[71] Passports of the Citizens of the Republic of Slovenia Act, *Official Gazette*, No. 1/1991-I (ceased to be valid since 5 August 2000).

Police control, detention and deportation

The Erased found themselves in a situation in which their very existence and residence in Slovenia was considered a violation of the law. According to the law, aliens without a permit to stay must not enter or must leave the country within fifteen days of the receipt of the negative final decision on their application. An alien who failed to leave the territory of the Republic of Slovenia was to be removed from the country.[72] This means that the Erased were liable to deportation from Slovenia. On 27 February 1992, the Ministry of the Interior issued instructions for local police departments regarding residents from other republics who did not obtain Slovene citizenship and who did not apply for a temporary or permanent residence permit: they were to be considered aliens without permission to stay, and thus subject to the Aliens Act. The police were to demand that they leave the country – to escort them to the border 'without any written decision of administrative authorities'.[73] This instruction allowed the police to not only implement the law, but to take it into their own hands and to rule on the Erased as illustrated by the following case:

> I got caught by the police at the restaurant where I used to work. We sat there at 7 in the morning, drinking coffee, when five policemen entered the restaurant. One of them approached me and asked for my documents. I replied I didn't have any. He didn't mind: 'It is OK, just tell me your name.' I told him my details and it was fine. They seemed to be finishing with us, when another policeman turned towards me and asked his colleague if I had documents at all. The other one replied that he already dealt with me, but the first one insisted and ordered me to go with them. They took me to the local police station and then they brought me before the misdemeanour judge. He issued a decision without an expulsion order. Despite this they put me back to police car and took me to the Detention Centre. It was Monday and they told me that on Wednesday I would be on the plane to Sarajevo. They didn't acknowledge the misdemeanour judge's decision. When they placed me in the Detention Centre I had the right to make one phone call. I called Mr. Krivic and he called my 'employer'. Then both came to get me out of detention. If they hadn't come, I would have been put on the plane to Sarajevo. This happened in 2002. Prior to this event I was successful in hiding, being invisible, I didn't make any

[72] Article 50 of the Aliens Act (2006).

[73] Ministry of the Interior, Instruction for implementation of the Aliens Act No 0016/4-14968, (1992), signed by Slavko Debelak, the Head of Office for Administrative Legal Matters of the Republic of Slovenia. Published by the weekly magazine *Mladina*, No. 9 (1 March 2004) www.mladina.si/tednik/200409/clanek/slo--izbrisani-matevz_krivic/, accessed 18 February 2008.

trouble for anybody, I would never steal. I avoided going to the centre of the town. (Iztok)

It has happened that the Erased were brought to the police stations, not for questioning, but for the police to show off their powers:

> For children it was not pleasant as they never knew if I'll return home or the police will stop me … I had my own way of self-defence when confronted by the police. When they brought me to the police station and kept me there for hours I didn't show any anxiety. I didn't make any comments. I think this made them even angrier. I didn't have to say anything because I didn't feel any guilt at all. I knew they would interrogate me and let me go. They have threatened me, that they will send me over to Bosnia. Once they kept me detained for twenty-four hours … Once the police came to my home in order to prove that I am the father of my children. I had to wake up my children, who were thirteen and nine at the time, to identify me as their father. I even have an official note on this event. (Slobodan)

The fact that the Erased were placed under the authority of the police does not imply that the police consistently exercised their powers, in the sense that every single stateless person would be detained and deported. Rather, it functioned as a *threat*, since the Erased were aware that they could be subjected to a police procedure at any time and that there was no institution in Slovenia to which they could turn for protection. This police regime rendered political action – that is, the struggle for one's rights – impossible. In this context, the police became the 'guardians' of legal status and the rights associated with it. Therefore, one could say that the harm inflicted upon the Erased was greater than the sum of individuals' pain. It made an impact on the whole of society, on its legal system and public services that should have implemented the principles of justice, equality and security of law. It also meant that the usual legal order did not apply to all: the Erased were criminalised without suspicion of a criminal offence. They were thus subjected to enormous psychological pressure:

> Being without status or Slovene documents, I was very scared. If I would see a policeman on the street, I would turn at the first street because I didn't know what would happen if they ran a check on me … I have heard stories where people got evicted from their apartments and deported from the country. I was surprised at how many people there were without documents. I kept quiet about it for some time, but once you start talking about it, you see that there are quite a few. (Nada)

> They took my permanent residence status and I couldn't obtain even a temporary residence permit. A police walked by my house, I hide myself on the roof or in the basement. This was such a psychological pressure!

> Then I ran away to Austria. There I had a friend who found me a job for three months. I didn't have any problems with Austrian police. (Teodor)

Most of the Erased interviewed by researchers had some kind of experience with the police; at the very least, as discussed above, they lived in fear of their control.[74] Unfortunately there were also cases of short- and long-term detention at the Aliens Centre and deportation from the country.[75] The cases of two erased persons, Ali Berisha and Dragomir Petronjić,[76] received attention in the Slovene media.

Ali Berisha was born to a Kosovo Roma family. He first moved to Slovenia in the 1980s. In 1993, he was detained and expelled to Albania (!), where he had never been in his life. He was returned to Slovenia, where he was detained again; however, this time he managed to avoid deportation by fleeing to Germany, where he reported himself as a Kosovo refugee. In 2005, he and his young family[77] had their asylum application refused. The family was supposed to 'return' to Kosovo; however, Ali Berisha felt more at home in Slovenia than in Kosovo, so he and his family came to Slovenia (where his last address had been prior to his erasure and refugee experience in Germany). As an erased person, Ali Berisha could not enter the country, so the family decided to ask for asylum. They were placed in Asylum Home, where they waited for their papers. The family had strong support from local and foreign activists. Amnesty International launched a campaign for their right to stay.[78] Nevertheless, the family got three deportation orders and was detained at the Aliens Centre twice. The third deportation order was realised and the Berisha family was sent back to Germany. The status quo has been maintained, and the Berisha family has not (yet) been sent to Kosovo.

---

[74] Dedić *et al.*, *The Erased*; Zorn, 'Ethnic Citizenship in the Slovenian State'; 135, R. Pignoni, 'The Story of Velimir Dabetič' and 'The Double Erasure of Ali Berisha', in J. Zorn and U. Liporec Čebron (eds.), *Once upon an Erasure: From Citizens to Illegal Citizens in the Republic of Slovenia* (Ljubljana: Študentska založba, 2008a, 2008b), 39 and 41; Vasović, 'Reported to Death'; Mekina, 'A Monument'; Kogovšek *et al.*, *Brazgatine izbrisa*.

[75] Dedić *et al.*, *The Erased*.   [76] These names are real.

[77] The Berisha family consists of Mr Ali Berisha, his wife, and their five children.

[78] See J. Zorn, 'New Borders, New Exclusions', in D. Zaviršek, J. Zorn, L. Rihter and S. Žnidarec Demšar (eds.), *Ethnicity in Eastern Europe: A Challenge for Social Work Education* (Ljubljana: Faculty of Social Work, 2007), 159; Pignoni, 'The Story of Velimir Dabetič', 39 and 'The Double Erasure of Ali Berisha', 41; and Amnesty International, *Slovenia: Amnesty International Condemns Forcible Return of 'Erased' Person to Germany* (2007), www.amnestyusa.org/document.php?lang=e&id=ENGEUR680022007, accessed 1 February 2008.

The second case reported by the Slovene press is even more depressing, as it had fatal consequences. In 1992 Dragomir Petronjić was stopped by the local police. As a result of the erasure from the register of permanent residents, he had no legal grounds to stay. He was brought before a misdemeanour judge, where he paid a fine for his 'illegal' stay. The police (and not the misdemeanour judge!) decided on and implemented his deportation. In the period of the fiercest combat in Croatia and Bosnia and Herzegovina, Petronjić – a Bosnian Serb – was handed to the Croatian police. What happened next remained a mystery for over fifteen years. His parents, his sister and his daughter actively searched for him, writing numerous letters to Croatian and Bosnian authorities. They feared he was dead, but they could not bury him and mourn. They did not understand why the Slovene police had expelled him, nor did they have any information on how he died. In 2007, the family found out that he had been killed shortly after his expulsion from Slovenia in one of the torture camps in Bosnia and Herzegovina. Despite the fact that his story has been brought to the public's attention, the policemen who decided to expel Petronjić have not been held accountable.[79]

Misdemeanour penalties and other expenses

> I had to pay for my illegal stay here. There was a judge, Janez, a large man, I will never forget him, he yelled at me when he realised I was without documents. 'At once, pack your stuff and get lost back to Bosnia.' 'How should I go without documents, there is a war zone there, my God, I can't go to Bosnia.' He didn't believe me, that my home town was in flames. Then there was a man who confirmed my claims about the war zone and he saved me. Otherwise I would have been expelled. (Hajrudin)

As noted above, when they encountered a person without documents, the police would bring them to the local police station and/or before a misdemeanour judge, or even take it upon themselves to expel them, as instructed by the Ministry of the Interior. Like the police, judges did not question the reason behind the 'illegal' stay of the Erased. One can assume that it must have seemed odd to fine individuals for having no legal status in Slovenia, despite the fact that their home address, their family relations and their fluency of the Slovene language reflected full integration into Slovene society.

---

[79] Vasović, 'Reported to Death'.

Various other expenses could not be avoided by the Erased, especially in the process of acquiring a permit to stay or citizenship. Prior to initiating legal procedures in Slovenia, the Erased needed to travel to their countries of origin in the territory of the former Yugoslavia in order to officially become foreigners. Travel costs and the acquisition of a foreign passport were not cheap:

> I needed to travel to Sarajevo hundreds of times. These expenses were huge. (Ivan)

Once the required foreign documents had been obtained, administrative fees for various certificates which were submitted as supplements to applications for resident permits or citizenship had to be paid. For those applying for citizenship, a language certificate had to be submitted, which meant that the applicant had to pay to take the Slovene language exam. For both citizenship and residence permits (except in cases covered by the Act Regulating the Legal Status of Citizens of the Former Yugoslavia Living in the Republic of Slovenia[80]), filing fees had to be paid when the application was submitted. Upon realising that legalising their stay at their actual home address turned out to be a complicated legal labyrinth, many erased persons hired a solicitor, incurring additional expenses for these services.

The following excerpts describe the various expenses that an erased person had to cover, from misdemeanour penalties and travel costs to administrative fees and notarised translations:

> I got my permanent residence status in February 2007. How many misdemeanour tickets I had to pay? I had to pay a lot. Police came, I didn't have documents. What did they do? They sent me to misdemeanour judge. I paid a lot. I didn't deserve this. I love this country. I've said this hundreds of times. I'll stay here. This is my second home … I applied for citizenship. I was required to bring many documents: birth certificate, certificate from Bosnia that I haven't been convicted, a proof that you have a place to live, and a job, a certificate of Slovene language knowledge, etc. All these documents I submitted with my application – and I paid fees. I didn't know that all these documents should be translated into Slovene. Therefore my application was rejected. Afterwards I got everything translated – it was expensive. I needed to pay administrative fees again when I submitted the application. I was rejected again because I didn't have employment. How could I have employment, if I didn't have papers? … Then I could get a permanent visa, I couldn't get citizenship. They asked witnesses to come to the Ministry to say that I have lived here all along.

---

[80] *Official Gazette of the Republic of Slovenia*, No. 61/1999.

They asked me at the Ministry, what if the witnesses demand reimbursement of their travel costs, how I would pay them? But they didn't demand anything. (Hajrudin)

It should be mentioned that a fee had to be paid for each document, and each document required a notarised translation (from Croatian to Slovene for Slovenes and *vice versa* for Croatians). That wasn't cheap. The fees in Croatia were high and everybody at the administrative units laughed at me and wondered why I was putting myself through this in the first place. They said that they were not pushing me back to Slovenia ... This whole matter had cost me a fortune, not including my work and time, just what I paid. I calculated that I had paid at least 2,300 Euros just for translations, administrative fees and travel expenses. It's a shame that I had to pay to have the electricity turned on, that I couldn't work legally, that I was exposed to certain dangers and surreal situations, that I didn't participate in sharing of collective property,[81] etc. And what about other material damages that cannot be proved easily? For example, the employment period that I lost (six years). Ironically I had to pay for the removal of my company from the register since I had to close it down. (Nada)

To summarise, the state doubly burdened the survival of households with an erased member(s): they had to cover various costs which other residents did not, such as administrative fees, fines, notarised translations, and the cost of medical care; at the same time, unlike other residents, they were not allowed to work or receive social assistance.

National anaesthesia

To borrow Hannah Arendt's words[82] it seems that only people of the same national origin or those completely assimilated and divorced from their origin could enjoy the full protection of legal institutions. This political 'closure based on citizenship'[83] led to the total administrative exclusion of those in-between, who were neither citizens nor ethnic Slovenes, but nevertheless long-term members of the polity:

One needs to be aware that such moments do play a part in history, especially in times of great uncertainty ... However, it is tragic and shameful that people have to go through this. I perceive it as an injustice, since it

---

[81] Nada mentioned she had not participated in sharing of collective property in 1992: when Slovenia became independent and property ownership was transformed from collective to private, each citizen received a certificate which he/she could invest in a stock of his/her own choice.

[82] H. Arendt, *The Origins of Totalitarianism* (New York: Schocken Books, 1951).

[83] R. Brubaker, *Citizenship and Nationhood in France and Germany* (Cambridge, MA: Harvard University Press, 1992a).

affected only people from the republics of the former Yugoslavia, and not other foreigners, from Western countries, for example. We came here to work, to earn our living fairly, and then we were erased. Maybe we were too kind and prepared to take any kind of job and this was turned against us. They wanted to get rid of us – by humiliating us. They [the authorities] should reflect on this situation. (Slavenka)

I don't understand why the erasure happened in the first place. It can be perceived as ethnic cleansing. Like during the Second World War, Nazis wanted to get rid of all Roma. (Ana)

They harassed us by phone. They called and said: 'You, Gypsy, when are you going to leave Slovenia for good?' (Mitar)

The narratives of the Erased suggest a question: why did their closest communities and public in general remain ignorant to their problems for over a decade? Or, to put it differently, why was there no room for a collective struggle, or even a discussion of the injustices that the Erased experienced, in the new democratic state founded on the principle of respect for human rights? The reasons for the invisibility of this mass violation of individuals' rights and breach of the rule of law are undoubtedly complex. Here, four reasons, which are tightly interwoven, should be mentioned:

(1) Legal and discursive division into 'Slovenes' and immigrants or 'non-Slovenes', which had been created already before the secession constructed the latter as cultural Other. Ethnic boundaries were preserved throughout the 1990s, which both enabled discrimination against the non-Slovenes and silenced the Erased as the most vulnerable members within this group.

(2) The surreptitious nature of the erasure individualised and isolated the victims: the Erased were not notified about the loss of their status and they could not know that they are not alone to be caught in bureaucratic labyrinths. Both this and the fact that they felt scared and redundant kept them isolated from one another and publicly invisible.

(3) An overall unemployment crisis beginning at the end of the 1980s and continuing into the first half of the 1990s overshadowed the issue of de facto statelessness. Mass unemployment was a result of the transition from socialist planned economy and collective ownership to a free-market neo-liberal economy and private ownership of the means of production.

(4) Governments' and media efforts to sacralise Slovene citizenship and the Slovene independence process also played a role in silencing the mass violation of human rights.

Conclusion

Full integration of all long-term immigrants into Slovene society was hindered by the surreptitious administrative rule of the erasure, whereby the legal category of an alien did not match the reality. This banal exclusion was to have very grave consequences.

On the basis of twenty-five in-depth interviews with the erased persons, and taking other studies[84] and reports[85] into account, it can be concluded that the following rights have been violated as a result of the erasure from the register of permanent residents: the right to security of law; protection of human dignity (these persons were made 'illegal' residents in their own homes); equality before the law; prohibition of torture; freedom of movement; protection of family integrity and parental rights and duties (some family members were detained and deported); the right to employment and an unemployment safety net; the right to receive a pension; the right to healthcare; the right to social assistance; the right to education; the right to purchase homes in the period of ownership transition.[86] The lives of many deteriorated: many were pushed to the brink of survival, having lost their health and social networks and were unable to visit their relatives in their countries of origin. Feelings of powerlessness, resentment towards the Slovene state and trampled dignity were not uncommon. Many children of the Erased experienced years of deprivation and stigmatisation.

The Erased and their lack of legal status figured in all reports of the Council of Europe and all accession reports of the European Commission, even as early as 1997 (Slovenia joined the European Union

---

[84] Dedić, Jalušič and Zorn, *The Erased*; Zorn, 'Ethnic Citizenship in the Slovenian State', 135; Blitz, 'Statelessness'; Beznec, 'The Impossible is Possible', 19; Lipovec Čebron, 'The Metastasis', 71; Zorn '"We, the Ethno-Citizens"', 52; Kogovšek *et al.*, *Brazgotine izbrisa*.

[85] Amnesty International, *Slovenia: Briefing to the UN Committee on Economic, Social and Cultural Rights*, 35th Session (2005); Commissioner for Human Rights, *Follow-Up Report on Slovenia (2003–2005): Assessment of the Progress Made in Implementing the Recommendations of the Council of Europe Commissioner for Human Rights* (Strasbourg: Council of Europe, 2006, https://wcd.coe.int/ViewDoc.jsp?id=984025& Site=CommDH&BackColorInternet=FEC65B&BackColorIntranet=FEC65B&Back ColorLogged=FFC679#P104_10139, accessed 21 December 2007; European Commission against Racism and Intolerance (ECRI), *Third Report on Slovenia*, adopted on 30 June 2006, made public on 13 February 2007 (Strasbourg: ECRI, 2007), www.coe.int/t/e/ human_rights/ecri/1-ecri/2-country-by-country_approach/Slovenia/Slovenia_CBC_3. asp#TopOfPage, accessed 9 December 2007.

[86] Article 117 of the Housing Act, *Official Gazette*, No. 18/91-I (not valid since 14 October 2003).

in 2004).[87] The Slovene Constitutional Court demanded, both in 1999 and 2003,[88] that the legal void contained in Article 81 of the Aliens Act be remedied through the re-registration of erased persons from the day of their erasure (26 February 1992). The Act Regulating the Legal Status of Citizens of the Former Yugoslavia Living in the Republic of Slovenia,[89] which came into effect in 1999, partly solved the problem of long-term residents without status. This law was adopted as a result of both European Commission accession reports and the 1999 decision of the Constitutional Court.[90] The majority of the Erased who had stayed in Slovenia were able to obtain permanent residence permits under this law (approximately 12,000).[91] Nonetheless, the law proved to be unsatisfactory: it was not retroactive; it excluded those who had been removed from Slovenia or prevented from returning; it excluded those who had permanently stayed in Slovenia but were unable to obtain a foreign passport (a person can be registered as a legal alien only on the basis of a foreign passport); and it only provided a three-month window for application.[92] On the whole, the law was not compliant with the 1999 Constitutional Court's decision.

The Slovene state's next attempt to resolve the issue of the erasure came in 2002 with the adoption of Article 19 of the Act Amending the Citizenship of the Republic of Slovenia Act:[93] 1,676 persons who had been erased from the register of permanent residence were able to acquire citizenship under the more lenient conditions of this Act.[94]

---

[87] European Commission, *Agenda 2000 – Commission Opinion on Slovenia's Application for Membership of the European Union* (Brussels: European Commission, 1997), http://ec.europa.eu/enlargement/archives/pdf/dwn/opinions/slovenia/sn-op_en.pdf, accessed 6 December 2007.

[88] Constitutional Court Decision No. U-I-246/02-28 issued on 3 April 2003, *Official Gazette of the Republic of Slovenia*, No. 23/2003.

[89] *Official Gazette of the Republic of Slovenia*, No. 61/1999.

[90] First reading of the Draft of the Regulating the Legal Status of Citizens of the Former Yugoslavia Living in the Republic of Slovenia, National Assembly Session 13 (Issue 6) on 21 April 1999. For transcripts of the Session, see www.dz-rs.si/index.php?id=97&cs=1&fts=ZUSDDD&mandate=2&unid=SZA2|3A2835888A0678B4C125675F002476CB&showdoc=1, accessed 10 June 2007.

[91] By 3 April 2003 11,746 Erased residents had obtained permanent residence permits on the basis of the Act Regulating the Legal Status of Citizens of the Former Yugoslavia Living in the Republic of Slovenia, 990 applications were still being processed by the Ministry of the Interior. See Constitutional Court Decision No. U-I-246/02-28 issued on 3 April 2003, *Official Gazette of the Republic of Slovenia*, No. 23/2003.

[92] Kogovšek *et al.*, *Brazgotine izbrisa*.

[93] *Official Gazette of the Republic of Slovenia*, No. 96/2002.

[94] Medved, 'From Civic to Ethnic Community?', 220.

In April 2003, the Court once again ruled in favour of the Erased, who had argued that the Act Regulating the Legal Status of Citizens of the Former Yugoslavia Living in the Republic of Slovenia was not compliant with the Constitution. Since then, 4,100 supplementary decisions have been issued retroactively by the Ministry of the Interior to those who had already obtained permanent residence permits.[95] However, a majority of the Erased continue to have a void in their residence statuses, they have received no compensation, and there are still erased persons without any legal status whatsoever. In February 2009 the Ministry of the Interior declared that they were determined to implement the Constitutional Court decisions and thus they started to issue decisions on permanent residence status retroactively, however, again only to those erased persons who had already acquired permanent residence or citizenship in Slovenia. The opposition parties submitted an interpellation on the work of the Interior Minister in the National Assembly. The interpellation failed and the Minister declared that she will continue her work not only of issuing specific decisions to the Erased, but also of fully implementing the Constitutional Court ruling, despite the pressures of both opposition parties and public opinion.

Despite the harsh exclusion of some long-term residents, Slovene nationalism was throughout the 1990s recognised as positive because the Republic of Slovenia was declared to have been founded on civic (as opposed to ethnic) principles and because Slovene nationalism was juxtaposed with the nationalisms of other nations from the former Yugoslavia. The Slovene nation managed to secure a reputation as a victim which had won its independence through the struggle for justice and human rights, and which was therefore incapable of seriously or systematically oppressing others.[96] In reality, a more sophisticated ethno-nationalism impregnated the state administration: the erasure constructed and humiliated the 'enemy' by diminishing political opportunities for self-presentation and disabling legal means for self-defence.

---

[95] Amnesty International, www.amnesty.si/clanek.php?id=324, accessed 12 February 2007.

[96] Dedić et al., The Erased, 10.

9

The statelessness issue in Estonia

RAIVO VETIK

The issue of statelessness has a very specific face in Estonia, where *de jure* statelessness is relatively common. Citizenship is itself a complex phenomenon, in which the relationship between the *de jure* and *de facto* aspects can take different forms. Soysal, for example, claims, that in the era of post-national membership in Europe, rights are no longer dependent on *de jure* citizenship, but on supra-national institutions, which emphasise the universality of rights, as opposed to their national character.[1] Hammar, on the other hand, claims that in modern states a large proportion of aliens is emerging, with no interest or opportunity to acquire citizenship. These people are the so-called 'denizens', to whom rather broad-scale rights and social benefits extend. Thus, they cannot be regarded regular aliens; nor, however, are they naturalized citizens.[2] Estonia represents an example of a state where a large number of long-term permanent residents do not own Estonian citizenship *de jure*, but whose social rights (*de facto* citizenship) do not differ remarkably from those of the Estonian citizens. However, this is not an example of a post-national condition described by Soysal, but that of a post-communist one, where the issue of massive denizenship has a specific history and meaning.[3] The goal of this chapter is, first, to discuss the formation and dynamics of massive statelessness in Estonia after the country regained independence in 1991; second, to outline the main aspects of the legal status of the stateless non-citizens as compared to the Estonian citizens; and, third, to report the results of several interview projects carried out by the author on how the non-citizens perceive

---

[1] Y. Soysal, *Limits of Citizenship: Migrants and Postnational Membership in Europe* (Chicago, IL: University of Chicago Press, 1994).

[2] T. Hammar, *Democracy and the Nation State: Aliens, Denizens and Citizens in a World of International Migration* (Aldershot: Ashgate, 1990).

[3] P. Järve and V. Poleschuk, *Country Report: Estonia*, EUDO Citizenship Observatory, European University Institute in collaboration with Edinburgh University Law School (2009), http://eudo-citizenship-eu/docs/CountryReports/Estonia.pdf

their statelessness and how they manage in the Estonian labour market, educational system and other areas of everyday life.

Emergence and dynamics of mass statelessness in Estonia

Estonia is a comparatively young state created in the unique historical situation at the end of the First World War. Taking advantage of the chaos of the German–Russian conflict, Estonia seceded from the Russian Empire and declared independence on 24 February 1918. The Tartu Peace Treaty with Russia was signed on 2 February 1920, which constituted the first *de jure* recognition of Estonia; recognition from major European powers followed within a year. However, on 28 September 1939, under threat of military intervention, Estonia accepted the so-called 'pact of defence and mutual assistance' with the USSR. On 16 June 1940, the USSR accused the Baltic states of violating these pacts and plotting against the Soviet Union, demanding unlimited entry of Soviet troops and the formation of pro-Soviet governments. Estonia capitulated, and a puppet government took office on 21 June 1940. After the German occupation during the Second World War, the Soviets returned and established the Soviet regime, which endured for the next half-century.

Before the Soviet occupation, according to the 1934 census, the Estonian population was composed of 88 per cent Estonians, 8 per cent Russians, and 4 per cent other nationalities. The Russians lived mainly in the border regions of Narva, Peipsi and Petseri. In 1945, the Soviet authorities changed the border, giving the regions of Estonia inhabited mostly by native Russians to the Russian Soviet Federal Socialist Republic (the RSFSR). This made Estonia a very homogeneous state, with Estonian speakers forming 97.3 per cent of the population. During the ensuing Soviet period, the number of non-Estonians increased over twenty-sixfold, from 23,000 in 1945 to 602,000 in 1989. At the same time the number of Estonians decreased from about 1 million in 1940 to 965,000 in 1989.[4]

These dramatic demographic changes were due to migration and differences in fertility rates, as well as to Soviet political and military measures. Estonian birthrates remained lower than those of non-Estonians throughout the Soviet era: the absolute number of Estonian births per year dropped by about 20 per cent during this period. The number of

---

[4] R. Vetik, 'Ethnic Conflict and Accommodation in Post-Communist Estonia', *Journal of Peace Research*, 30(3) (1993), 271.

non-Estonians in the population rose mainly because of immigration. Post-war immigration into Estonia resulted from a Moscow policy that aimed at mixing different nationalities in order to strengthen control over peripheral regions, as well as from the logic of socialist industrialisation, which tended to concentrate labour resources in certain areas.

In 1985 Mikhail Gorbachev came to power in Moscow and launched political and economic reforms that eventually brought an end to the Soviet Union. In Estonia open public protest against the Soviet regime began in the summer of 1987, when a demonstration demanded publication of the secret protocols of the Molotov–Ribbentrop Pact of 1939. In March 1990 the first partially free elections for the Supreme Council of Estonia were held. The Estonian Supreme Council immediately declared Estonia's status as an occupied country and announced that it had entered a period of transition leading to restoration of the Estonian Republic. The independence of Estonia was regained during the *coup d'état* in Moscow on 20 August 1991.

In February 1992 the citizenship law of 1938 was re-enacted with minor amendments by the Estonian Parliament, proceeding from the idea of legal continuity with the earlier Estonian Republic. The law was exclusive in the sense that it defined as citizens only those residents who were citizens of Estonia before Soviet occupation and their descendants. The law required two years' residence before a person was entitled to apply for citizenship, and a further one-year waiting period before the applicant could be naturalised. The law also included a requirement to take an oath of loyalty and it restricted certain categories of people from gaining citizenship, such as military officers and foreign intelligence personnel. In addition, the law required knowledge of the Estonian language, which effectively resulted in statelessness of the majority of non-Estonians living in Estonia at that moment.[5]

In 1995 a new Citizenship Law was adopted introducing some new conditions for naturalisation. According to the law a person had to meet a series of conditions to acquire Estonian citizenship. An applicant should have been residing in Estonia already before 1 July 1990, and possess a long-term or permanent residence permit at the time of submitting the request for naturalisation. If only one of these requirements was met, the person applying for Estonian citizenship must also have proficiency in the Estonian language on a day-to-day level; be at least fifteen years of age;

---

[5] R. Kionka and R. Vetik, 'Estonia and Estonians', in G. Smith (ed.), *The Nationalities Question in the Post-Soviet States* (London and New York: Longman, 1996), 129.

have lived in Estonia on the basis of a residence permit for at least eight years, at least five years of which on permanent basis; have knowledge of the Estonian Constitution and the Citizenship Act; have permanent lawful income sufficient to support himself or herself and his or her dependents; have a registered residence in Estonia; be loyal to the state of Estonia and take an oath: 'In applying for Estonian citizenship, I swear to be loyal to the constitutional state system of Estonia.'[6]

The citizenship law has been amended several times since, easing the requirements for obtaining citizenship for certain categories of non-citizens. For example, the waiting period for naturalisation has been reduced to six months and a simplified naturalisation procedure has been established for people with disabilities. Further, children who are younger than fifteen years may obtain citizenship without having to pass a citizenship examination, if their parents request it. In addition, stateless children who were born after 1992 may also obtain citizenship with a simplified procedure, if both parents are stateless.

If after adoption of the Citizenship Law in 1992 almost one-third of the population of Estonia were left stateless, then the situation has changed since then. By 2009 the proportion of stateless persons had decreased about twice – about 8 per cent were still stateless and 8 per cent were citizens of foreign states (mainly Russia). Thus, between 1992 and 2009 about 150,000 persons were naturalised in Estonia, while about 100,000 persons remained stateless non-citizens. The dynamics of the naturalisation process during the period can be illustrated by the data from the Citizenship and Migration Board in figure 9.1.

When comparisons are made with the policies of other EU countries, Estonian citizenship policy has been treated in the literature as being rather exclusionary in nature.[7] Such policy can be explained, first of all, by high level of perceived threat and mutual distrust between the Estonian majority and Russian-speaking minority in the country. This can be illustrated, for example, by the fact that while in the 1991 independence referendum a majority of Estonians voted for pro-Estonian independence, only 25 per cent of the Estonian Russians were in favour of it. Thus, only six months before the actual regaining of independence, Estonian society was fundamentally polarised over one of the most existential political

---

[6] Citizenship Act, *Gazette* I 12 (1995), 122.

[7] J. Niessen, T. Huddleston and L. Citron (in cooperation with A. Geddes and D. Jacobs), *Migrant Integration Policy Index* (London: British Council and Migration Policy Group, 2007).

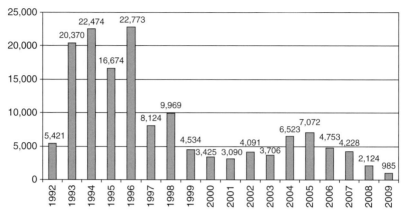

Figure 9.1   Persons who have acquired Estonian citizenship by naturalisation (1992–2009, 2nd quartile) *N* = 150,336
Source: Citizenship and Migration Board (2009).

issues, which inevitably evoked strong mutual fears regarding the future.[8] In addition, regular inter-state tensions between Estonia and Russia during the last two decades continued to strengthen mutual perceptions of threat, which is one of the most important obstacles for national integration in the country.[9]

Legal status of stateless non-citizens

Estonian law prohibits discrimination against people on the basis of, among other grounds, their ethnicity, language, origin, or religion. The Constitution of the Republic of Estonia stipulates as follows: 'The rights, freedoms and duties of each and every person, as set out in the Constitution, are equal for Estonian citizens and for citizens of foreign states and stateless persons in Estonia.'[10] However, both official social statistics as well as survey research indicate that discrimination against certain social groups does exist in, for example, the labour market and the educational system.[11] Nevertheless, as will be argued in this chapter,

---

[8] Vetik, 'Ethnic Conflict and Accommodation', 271.
[9] R. Vetik, *On the Boundary of Two Liberties* (Tallinn: Huma, 2007) (in Estonian).
[10] Constitution of the Republic of Estonia (Article 9).
[11] J. Helemäe, 'Self-Realisation at Work and Perceived Opportunities for it', in R. Vetik (ed.), *Integration Monitoring of Estonian Society* (2008) (in Estonian), http://ec.europa.eu/ewsi/UDRW/images/items/docl_9870_693007823.pdf and K. Kasearu and A. Trumm,

the situation of stateless non-citizens in Estonia should be viewed in the broader context of the situation of the whole Russian-speaking population, due to the fact that most immigrants arrived in Estonia during the Soviet period. Most instances of discrimination against stateless non-citizens are based not on their legal status but on cultural and other factors, which are related to their ethnicity.

The core legal Act regulating the status of stateless non-citizens in Estonia is the Law on Aliens, adopted in 1993, which refers to both citizens of foreign states and stateless persons as 'aliens'. The other key statute is the Law on Refugees, which was adopted in 1997. At the same time Estonia signed the Convention relating to the Status of Refugees of 1951 and its Protocol of 31 January 1967. The amendments to the Law on Refugees of May 2003 harmonised Estonian asylum procedures with the relevant EU legislation. The Law on Granting International Protection to an Alien was adopted in July 2006, following a report by the European Commission against Racism and Intolerance (ECRI).[12]

In general, stateless non-citizens in Estonia enjoy the same rights and free access to social protection as citizens. For example, aliens with any type of residence permit are protected by the Law on Social Protection,[13] the Law on the Social Protection of the Unemployed,[14] the Law on the Social Protection of Disabled People,[15] the Law on State Pension Insurance,[16] the Law on State Support for Families[17] and other related legislation. According to the Law on the Legal Chancellor, everyone has a right of recourse to the Legal Chancellor if s/he finds that a natural person or a legal person in some private law matter has discriminated against him or her on the basis of sex, race, ethnic origin, colour, language, origin, religion or religious beliefs, political or other opinion, property or social status, age, disability, sexual orientation or other grounds specified by law.[18]

'Material Well-Being and Satisfaction with Life among Estonians and Non-Estonians', in R. Vetik (ed.), *Integration Monitoring of Estonian Society* (2008), (in Estonian), http://ec.europa.eu/ewsi/UDRW/images/items/docl_9870_693007823.pdf.

[12] European Commission against Racism and Intolerance (ECRI), *Estonian Country Report*, www.coe.int/t/e/human_rights/ecri/1-ECRI/2-Country-by country_approach/Estonia/Estonia%20third%20report%20-%20cri06–1%20estonian.pdf.

[13] Law on Social Protection (Article 4).

[14] Law on Social Protection of the Unemployed (Article 2).

[15] Law on Social Protection of Disabled People (Article 3).

[16] Law on State Pension Insurance (Article 4).

[17] Law on State Support for Families (Article 2).

[18] Law on the Legal Chancellor (Article 19).

This section will discuss the following aspects of the legal status of stateless non-citizens in Estonia: access to employment, access to the educational system, access to the health system, right to set up business and to rent and buy property, right to work in the public service, right to residency and to family reunification, access to the courts and justice system and right to protection from detention and deportation.

Access to employment

The Constitution of the Republic of Estonia stipulates that an Estonian citizen has the right freely to choose his or her area of activity, profession and place of work. Citizens of foreign states and stateless persons who are in Estonia have this right equally with Estonian citizens, unless otherwise provided by law.[19] The Law on Employment Contracts prohibits unequal treatment on the basis of sex, race, age, ethnic origin, language proficiency, disability, sexual orientation, obligation of military service, family status, family life obligations, social status, representation of employees' interests, membership in employees' organisations, political opinion, membership in a political party, religious or other belief.[20] In May 2004, the Law on Employment Contracts was amended to include anti-discrimination provisions. This Law contains articles on discrimination at the recruitment stage as well as concerning matters such as salary levels, promotion, working conditions, termination of employment and training. The Law also defines direct and indirect discrimination and provides for a shared burden of proof in employment discrimination cases.

The Law on Employment Contracts guarantees the right to demand from the employer compensation for proprietary and non-proprietary damage resulting from any discrimination.[21] However, a person with whom the employer has refused to enter into an employment contract does not have the right to demand entry into such a contract. Provisions regarding a shift in the burden of proof are defined in the law.[22]

There is a requirement that all employees of the public sector and many employees of the private sector pass language tests if they have not graduated from Estonian-language schools. A special commission under the Ministry of Education has been set up to deal with the problems of the Estonian-language examination.

[19] The Constitution of the Republic of Estonia (Article 29).
[20] The Law on Employment Contracts (Article 9).
[21] Law on Employment Contracts (Article 103).
[22] Law on Employment Contracts (Article 144).

Non-citizens cannot work as state and municipal officials. However, they can be employed as non-officials for auxiliary services in state and municipal institutions. Estonian law additionally introduces a citizenship requirement for certain non-official positions. For instance, a non-citizen cannot be a rector of a publicly funded higher education institution, and also cannot be a bodyguard.

Non-citizens with temporary residence permits can be employed only if they have work permits. Work permits are not required for persons with permanent residence permits, prisoners, crew of trains and drivers of vehicles engaged in the carriage of passengers or goods[23] or for Soviet-era residents who applied for a residence permit before 12 July 1995 and were subsequently granted such a permit.[24] The Law on Aliens recognises the possibility of short-term employment (up to six months per year) without a work permit for members of certain occupations such as teachers, scholars or sportsmen.[25]

Access to educational system

The Republic of Estonia Education Act stipulates as follows: 'Children of citizens of foreign states and of stateless persons who reside in Estonia, except children of representatives of foreign states, are subject to the obligation to attend school.'[26] Children who attain seven years of age by 1 October of the current year are subject to the obligation to attend school. Students are subject to the obligation to attend school until they acquire basic education or attain seventeen years of age.[27]

In the Soviet period there were two parallel educational systems in Estonia – the Estonian-language system and the Russian-language system. Since 1991, when Estonia regained independence, several steps have been taken to create a unified educational system. One of the most important of these consists in the fact that since the academic year 2007 Russian-language upper secondary schools began a transition to Estonian as one of the languages of instruction. The aim of the reform is that, after the transition period, 60 per cent of all instruction in minority upper secondary schools should be made in Estonian. The prolongation of the transition period may be permitted by the local authorities to a school on an individual basis.[28] For smaller minorities in Estonia, mother-tongue

---

[23] Law on Aliens (Article 13 (4)). [24] Law on Aliens (Article 20 (2)).
[25] Law on Aliens (Article 13). [26] Republic of Estonia Education Act (Article 8).
[27] Basic Schools and Upper Secondary Schools Act (Article 17).
[28] Law on Basic School and Upper Secondary School (Articles 9 and 52).

education has been confined primarily to programmes outside regular school (that is, Sunday schools). There have been efforts to open minority private schools, but with modest success, due to the low numbers of students and lack of funding. Publicly funded higher education is available only in Estonian, with limited exceptions for certain groups. Thus, young people without good Estonian language may continue their studies in Russian-language private higher education institutions. However, these institutions do not normally have accredited programmes at MA or PhD level.

Access to health system

According to the Constitution of the Republic of Estonia everyone has the right to the protection of their health. An Estonian citizen has the right to state assistance in the case of old age, incapacity for work, loss of a provider, or need. Citizens of foreign states and stateless persons who are in Estonia have this right equally with Estonian citizens, unless otherwise provided by law.[29]

Thus, health protection is given to all legal residents in Estonia regardless of their legal status. Access to the health system is based on possession of health insurance. During the time that an alien is deemed to be a person insured by compulsory health insurance pursuant to the Health Insurance Act, and in cases provided for by international agreements, an alien need not have an insurance contract guaranteeing that any costs related to his or her medical treatment as a result of illness or injury will be met.[30]

In the case of asylum seekers, the initial reception centre will, as necessary, arrange for assistance, emergency care and medical examinations during asylum proceedings, and also for applicants for residence permits on the basis of temporary protection during those temporary protection proceedings.[31] The reception centre may permit an applicant to stay away from the reception centre overnight to receive medical care.[32]

Right to set up a business and to rent and buy property

The Constitution of the Republic of Estonia stipulates as follows: 'Estonian citizens have the right to engage in enterprise and to form commercial

---

[29] Constitution of the Republic of Estonia (Article 31).
[30] Aliens Act (Article 17).
[31] Act on Granting International Protection to Aliens (Article 12).
[32] Refugees Act (Article 9).

undertakings and unions. Conditions and procedure for the exercise of this right may be provided by law. Citizens of foreign states and stateless persons who are in Estonia have this right equally with Estonian citizens, unless otherwise provided by law.'[33] According to the law, a residence permit for undertaking business in Estonia may be issued to an alien who owns shares in a company or acts as a sole proprietor if the company or the sole proprietor is registered in the Estonian Commercial Register and if the business is necessary for the national interest of developing the Estonian economy and the settlement of the alien is important for the business. The fields – and, if necessary, the territory – of activities, are specified in the residence permit for business.

An alien may be granted a residence permit on the basis of business activities if he/she has invested in Estonia a capital sum of 1,000,000 kroons under his/her control in the case of a company, or has invested in Estonia a capital sum of 250,000 kroons under his/her control in the case of a sole proprietor. An alien who has been granted a residence permit for business so as to participate in the activities of a company may work only in the company specified by the residence permit in order to carry out managerial functions. If an alien has been granted a residence permit for business he/she cannot work in Estonia under the management direction of any other person. An alien who has been granted a residence permit for business must inform the Citizenship and Migration Board about any change in certain circumstances which form the basis for the issue of a residence permit: if the alien has difficulties in performing the obligations undertaken; or if the alien is not able to perform his/her obligations.

In general, aliens may peacefully enjoy their property rights in Estonia. However, there are a few restrictions established for sale and possession of weapons according to the Law on Weapons. According to the Law on Restrictions on the Transfer of Ownership of Immovable Property, ownership of a plot of agricultural or forest land whose size is more than 10 hectares may be normally transferred to an alien only with permission of the county governor.[34] Without a special governmental permission an alien who is not a citizen of the European Economic Area (EEA) cannot buy immovable property on islands (except for the four biggest islands) or in territorial units close to the state border.[35]

---

[33] Constitution of the Republic of Estonia (Article 31).
[34] Law on Restrictions on the Transfer of Immovable Property Ownership (Article 2).
[35] Law on Restrictions on the Transfer of Immovable Property Ownership (Article 3).

Right to work in public services

The Constitution of the Republic of Estonia stipulates as follows: 'Positions in state agencies and local governments shall be filled by Estonian citizens, on the basis of and pursuant to procedure established by law. These positions may, as an exception, be filled by citizens of foreign states or stateless persons, in accordance with law.'[36] However, at the moment such an opportunity is not foreseen in the Law on Public Service. The Language Law requires that all public servants and public sector employees, service personnel, medical professionals and sole proprietors must use the Estonian language, with their actual proficiency determined through examination. Non-citizens who have obtained at least primary education proficiency in the Estonian language are exempted from the requirement to pass a language examination.

Aliens have no right to stand as a candidate in elections in Estonia.[37] Estonian-language requirements for a candidate at national and local elections were abolished in 2001; nevertheless, Estonian is the only official working language in local self-government and councils.

Right to residence and family reunion

Residence permits in Estonia may be permanent or may allow for temporary residence of up to five years. A temporary residence permit may be received for employment or study in Estonia. There are rigid rules and procedures to ensure that a person can be permitted to come to Estonia to work only if the country is lacking a specialist ready to take the job on offer. For instance, before application for permission to invite a foreign worker is filed in the Labour Market Board, an employer has to conduct a public competition for the job in Estonia for at least two months, making use of the services of a state employment agency.[38] At the moment, all services provided for in the Law on Employment Service are available only to citizens, aliens with permanent residence permit and refugees.[39] Aliens with temporary residence permits (including Soviet-era residents who failed to receive permanent permits for various reasons) can use only two basic services: (1) information about the situation in the labour market and about possibilities for training for employment, and (2) employment mediation.

---

[36] Constitution of the Republic of Estonia (Article 30).
[37] Law on Aliens (Article 5).   [38] Law on Aliens (Article 13 (2)).
[39] Law on Employment Service (Article 5).

The situation of non-citizens is less favourable as compared with Estonian citizens regarding the right to family reunion – they are required to prove that their family reunion in Estonia is justified.[40] An application for a residence permit to settle with a spouse who resides in Estonia and who is an alien is considered to be unjustified if the alien who applies for the residence permit and the spouse for the purposes of settling with whom the residence permit is applied for do not prove that it is not possible for them to settle in the country of their common citizenship or in the country of citizenship or country of habitual residence of the alien who applies for the residence permit.

The Aliens Act specifies that annual immigration is not allowed to exceed a number equivalent to 0.01 per cent of the country's citizens and permanent residents. Citizens of the European Union, the European Free Trade Association (EFTA), the United States and Japan are exempted from the immigration quota. In line with a 2000 Supreme Court ruling, the immigration quota is also not applied to persons wishing to reunite with family members who were citizens or permanent residents of Estonia. An amendment to the Aliens Act in 2002 exempted spouses of Estonian citizens or foreigners with a residence permit, as well as minor or adult children, parents, grandparents, or wards of Estonian citizens or legally resident foreigners (who have resided in Estonia for at least five years), from the immigration quota.

A temporary residence permit may be issued to the following aliens to settle with a close relative who is an Estonian citizen, or to settle with a close relative who is an alien who has resided in Estonia for at least five years on the basis of a permanent residence permit: (1) to a minor child in order to settle with his/her parent; (2) to an adult child in order to settle with a parent if the child is unable to cope independently due to health reasons or a disability; (3) to a parent or grandparent in order to settle with his or her adult child or grandchild if the parent or grandparent needs care which it is not possible for him or her to receive in the country of his or her location or in another country and the permanent legal income of his or her child or grandchild who legally resides in Estonia ensures that the parent or grandparent will be maintained in Estonia; or (4) to a person under guardianship in order to settle with the guardian if the permanent legal income of the guardian ensures that the ward will be maintained in Estonia. A temporary residence permit may also be issued to aliens in cases under (1), (2) and (4) above if the close relative with whom an

---

[40] Law on Aliens (Article 12 (7)).

alien wants to settle has a temporary residence permit. Since May 2003 the officials of the Citizenship and Migration Board and Labour Market Board have had the right to enter a person's dwelling, with the owner's permission, for verification of the facts that are important for the issuing of a residence permit.

Access to courts and justice system, protection from detention and deportation

The Constitution of Estonia provides for the right to a fair trial. Trials are public, there are a judge and public assessors and defendants have the right to be present and to consult with an attorney in a timely manner. Defendants can confront or question witnesses against them and/ or present witnesses and evidence on their own behalf. Defendants and their attorneys have access to government-held evidence relevant to their cases. The law extends these rights to all residents, whether or not they are citizens.

The Estonian authorities do not provide a system of free legal aid for asylum seekers. The Estonian Refugee Council (ERC) provided such services until 2003, with the help of the United Nations High Commissioner for Refugees (UNHCR). As the UNHCR no longer provides the ERC with financial assistance, this NGO is unable to give legal advice to asylum seekers as it used to. However, all residents, whether citizens or not, can file a complaint with the Legal Chancellor about court findings and other issues.

Estonian law prohibits arbitrary arrest and detention. Under the Constitution, warrants issued by a court are required to make arrests. Detainees must be informed promptly of the grounds for the arrest and given immediate access to legal counsel, and there is a functioning bail system. A person may be held for forty-eight hours without being charged formally; further detention requires a court order. A person may be held in pre-trial detention for two months; this term may be extended for a total of twelve months by court order. Estonian law prohibits forced exile as well as restriction on the right of non-citizens to foreign travel, emigration, or repatriation.

Perceptions and effects of statelessness: empirical findings

The previous section revealed that the formal rights of stateless non-citizens in Estonia do not differ significantly from those of Estonian citizens. As discussed in the first section, this is mostly due to the historical and political context, in which mass statelessness began to be seen in Estonia at the beginning of the 1990s. The aim of the current section is to discuss what factors reproduce statelessness in Estonia and how statelessness status affects people's ordinary daily life.

In one of the research projects upon which the current analysis is based, ten in-depth interviews (lasting up to one hour) were carried out with stateless persons who also had children under fifteen years of age with undetermined citizenship. Of the ten interviews, five were carried out with respondents from Tallinn, two from Narva and one each from Jõhvi, Sillamäe and Kohtla-Järve. In Tallinn, people from different parts of the town were interviewed (three from Lasnamäe, one from Õismäe and one from the city centre area). Three of the ten participants had applied for Estonian citizenship through the naturalisation process, but had not been successful.

The basis for our sampling procedure was an anonymised list provided by the State Chancellery, which contained data about residents with undetermined citizenship who also had children under fifteen years of age. As at 24 January 2007, there were 125,799 persons with undetermined citizenship in Estonia, including 4,300 children under fifteen years of age who possess long-term residence permits as well as having both parents with an undetermined citizenship status. The list provided to us included 2,437 such cases. The gross sample was determined as ten times bigger, and the stratified sample ($n = 100$), chosen from the total population, was divided into strata on the basis of residence areas and the children's ages. In each stratum, simple random sampling was then employed.

The people included in the sample were sent contact letters, introducing the research and requesting their consent to participate. Eighteen people demonstrated their willingness to take part in the study, of whom ten where chosen for interview, according to the stipulated condition for residential variety, as well as accounting for variety in gender, age and status as a single or joint parent. The interviews in Tallinn and the Ida–Virumaa towns were carried out by Saar Poll research company interviewers on the basis of a previously prepared questionnaire, over the period 9 April to 28 April 2008. The interviews were recorded and subsequently transcribed. The second project upon which the current analysis is based was a focus group interview with five respondents, carried out in February 2010 in Narva. The respondents in the focus group included stateless non-citizens as well as citizens of Estonia and citizens of Russia. This project showed that the most immediate impact of being stateless had to do with the need to obtain a residence permit. While it is less of a major issue for the Russian-language population now, it was a burning problem at the beginning of the

1990s when the institution of temporary and permanent residence permits was introduced in Estonia. The focus group interview study with Estonian Russians carried out in Narva revealed that the respondents (age follows name) remained very critical about the institution as such:

> One morning we just figured out that we are living in a different state. Nobody asked if we wanted it, and such a transition was very difficult for us. (Tatiana, 39)

> We did not have any choice, they gave us a residence permit and that was it. First temporary and then permanent. Nobody asked, what is my opinion and it did not affect anything, you just take what they give. (Nikolai, 34)

The second most immediate issue related to statelessness status has to do with family reunion. The experience of the respondents in the focus group interviews proved to be diverse in this regard:

> I know a teacher, her husband lives in Ivangorod. He serves in the Russian army and cannot come to Estonia. They have visits at weekends. (Katja, 27)

> Many people have invited their parents and, I think, mostly there is no problem. It is difficult to say, but I know there are positive cases. There are also negative cases, however, but I do not personally know these people. (Denis, 27)

When discussing the impact of legal status on access to the labour market one needs to take into account the situation at the beginning of the 1990s in the context of transition to a market economy. Material well-being became highly problematic for most people in Estonia, irrespective of their citizenship status. However, in the process of the market reforms, a particularly deep recession hit certain branches of economy, such as the oil shale industry in the North-East of Estonia, where mostly Russian-speakers were employed. Thus, structural reasons at that time tended to move the Russian-speaking minority to lower positions in several segments of the Estonian labour market. Unemployment has tended to be higher among Russian-speakers compared to Estonians during the whole period of the last two decades, while the over-representation of minorities among the unemployed can be seen especially among persons with advanced levels of education.[41] Previous research reveals that the emergence of ethnic inequality in the labour market is a consequence of several factors, including the lack of Estonian citizenship and insufficient proficiency in Estonian language among non-Estonians.[42]

[41] Helemäe, 'Self-Realisation at Work'.
[42] Kasearu and Trumm, 'Material Well-Being and Satisfaction'.

According to the focus group study in Narva, the possibility of managing to get by in the current economic recession does not depend on a person's citizenship status – the respondents mentioned that networks of people are the single most important factor for the unemployed to manage. However, it was also mentioned that jobs in the public sphere are open only to persons with Estonian citizenship and that this kind of job is particularly valuable in the current economic conditions:

> They [in the public sector] have stable salaries in city government, police, etc. Also there is a career system in the public sector. Thus, in such cases citizenship status does influence chances to get a job, in all other cases there is no difference. If you have good recommendations and if you have shown yourself from [the] positive side, then in [the] private sector the passport does not matter. (Lidia, 34)

In the focus group study several questions were asked also about how legal status impacts stateless non-citizens' access to healthcare in Estonia. The respondents reported that they did not feel such an impact:

> My husband is unemployed and he is stateless. However, there is no problem in seeing a doctor and he has been served well, as a rule. And this is free of charge. (Lidia, 34)

However, there is other data in the literature revealing that in reality several health indicators for Estonian and Russian-language segments of society have been diverging during the last two decades. Estonia is known for the very low level of a number of health indicators compared to other EU member states, particularly average life expectancy, which was only seventy-one in 2007. Estonia is also distinguished by the fact that life expectancy varies to a great degree among various social groups, including ethnic groups. While life expectancy for men is shorter than for women in all EU states, the difference between men and women in Estonia is among the greatest in Europe, at 10.9 years.[43] The differences in life expectancy according to education are also high – an analysis of the data from the last (2000) census shows that life expectancy among twenty-five-year-old men with higher education was 13.1 years longer than that of men of the same age with only primary education; the corresponding difference among women was 8.6 years.[44] In addition, a comparison of

---

[43] R. Vetik, 'Why the Estonian Position in the human development index is not Improving', *Estonian Human Development Report 2007, Studies of Transition States and Societies,* 1(1), 3 (in Estonian).

[44] M. Leinsalu, D. Vågerö and A. E. Kunst, 'Estonia 1989–2000: Enormous Increase in Mortality Differences by Education,' *International Journal of Epidemiology,* 32 (2003), 1081.

the national mortality database and census data shows that from 1989 to 2000 the differences in life expectancy between Estonians and Estonian Russians increased from 0.4 years to 6.1 years for men and from 0.6 years to 3.5 years for women.[45] It is difficult to explain the emergence of such a difference; most probably it has to do with the different resources which persons can bring to deal with the problems of the transition period that Estonia has undergone.[46]

Education is one of the most important arenas for integration of the Russian-language minority in Estonian society, as education substantially shapes their labour market outcomes. In this context it is important to note that the shift to Estonian-language higher education at the beginning of the 1990s transformed Russian-language general education into an academic dead end, as the further choices of a Russian-language secondary school graduate became limited. This applies most of all to those Russian-speaking students whose Estonian language skills are insufficient to continue university studies in Estonian. Thus the Russian-speakers feel that besides the advantages that the transition to partial instruction in Estonian gives, there are also several significant risks, such as the threat of assimilation and a decline in Russian school students' exam results and thus inequality of opportunities for further education as compared to Estonian school students. Research data also indicates that Estonian Russians regard it as necessary that the shift to partial Estonian-language instruction should happen considerably sooner than it is now taking place according to the current regulations: they feel that it should happen not in secondary school, as is the case at present, but rather in pre-school or at the latest in primary school. Thus, research data shows that studying partially in Estonian does not have a negative reception from the Russian-speaking population; however, fears and a sense of threat have been provoked by a poorly prepared transition to partial Estonian language instruction.[47]

The focus group study in Narva confirmed that knowledge of languages has the most significant impact on the educational choices of Estonian Russians. Poor knowledge of the Estonian language strongly diminishes their educational opportunities. However, it does not exclude at least trying:

---

[45] M. Leinsalu, D. Vågerö and A. E. Kunst, 'Increasing Ethnic Differences in Mortality in Estonia after the Collapse of the Soviet Union', *Journal of Epidemiology and Community Health*, 58 (2004), 583.

[46] Vetik, 'Why the Estonian Position'.

[47] E. Saar, 'Education', in R. Vetik (ed.), *Integration Monitoring of Estonian Society* (2008).

I entered university this year. I am [a] citizen, but I was not asked about it, so I do not know if it had any impact on my reception. I entered the Estonian-language programme, but I do not speak Estonian. We will see what will happen, I am positive. (Lidia, 34)

The focus group study also revealed that our respondents did not feel any impact on educational opportunities related to a person's legal status. However, we also learned that citizens of Russia and stateless respondents consider universities in Russia as an opportunity for continuing their education. Those respondents who discussed such an opportunity indicated that there were also problems in this regard:

It is very difficult to get into a university in Russia as there are different programmes. In Russia the programmes are much stronger, particularly in science, so it is very difficult for us. (Tatiana, 39)

The in-depth interview study described above offered four main explanations for the persistence and widespread nature of statelessness among Estonian Russians. The first of these was an emotional aversion to applying for citizenship related to the fact that many Estonian Russians feel that, similarly to ethnic Estonians, they should have automatically been granted citizenship after independence was restored in Estonia:

We have not applied, and do not intend to apply for citizenship in the future. I was born here and have lived here for over forty years. I have already two children here. And I consider applying for citizenship a too big humiliation for myself. No such thing exists in any other state of the European Union. (Male, 41, Jõhvi)

Many of those interviewed could have sought citizenship but chose not to, for a variety of reasons. Earlier studies suggested that many people lacked accurate information about citizenship application procedures.[48] Our study suggested that unwillingness and confusion was centred at least as much on the conditions to be met:

One has to go to the migration centre. Submit the documents there. There are also many brochures. In Narva there is the migration centre, all the documentation is accessible and also hung on the wall. (Female, 36, Narva)

---

[48] S. Aspal, K. Kallas and K. Kasearu, in M. Lauristin, K. Korts and K. Kallas (eds.), *Integration Strategy 2008–2013* (Tartu: University of Tartu Institute of Baltic Studies, 2008), 54; K. Kallas, *Integration Strategy 2008–2013 – Final Report of the Feasibility Study* (Tartu: University of Tartu Institute of Baltic Studies, 2008), Part IV, Legal and Political Integration, 19.

One lady came and told me that there is no sense in going. A large sum had to be paid and she was told that she is a non-citizen and has no right. (Female, 44, Tallinn)

I actually don't even know [what one should do to apply for Estonian citizenship]. I have not even taken an interest in that, because I can't speak Estonian, and that's exactly the reason why I don't know. (Male, 28, Kohtla-Järve)

There were, however, also concerns about the language test, both because of the difficulty and the expense of learning Estonian:

Estonian language courses cost an immense amount of money. I cannot afford myself to pay 1500–2000 Crowns per month for it, because I have two children and one of them, besides, is ill. And so unravels a vicious circle: if I do not know Estonian, I cannot find a well-paying job, and therefore cannot pay for the courses. (Female, 37, Tallinn)

I cannot speak Estonian sufficiently to pass the language exam. Estonian is very hard to learn, because there are so few contacts between the two ethnic groups in our country. Some people do communicate in Estonian at work, but I worked at a place where everybody was Russian. So, I use Estonian only at shops, about 5–10 minutes per day. But this is not sufficient … We have not been provided with proper conditions for studying Estonian. That is the first reason why I have not applied for Estonian citizenship. (Female, 37, Tallinn)

People don't know [the] Estonian language. And not everybody also manages to. I am twenty-nine years old, but I don't believe that I can learn it. If there were more Estonians at work or around, then yes, maybe. Even though there are also Estonians at work, I mostly communicate with Russians. (Male, 28, Kohtla-Järve)

Some people were comfortable as being stateless and considered that the lack of Estonian citizenship did not affect their everyday life. It was apparent from the interviews that the fact that 'one could manage' in Estonia without citizenship was considered one of the reasons for statelessness. We encountered the following answers to the questions, of whether not having Estonian citizenship affected their life:

He [the respondent's husband] does not intend to apply for Estonian citizenship, because he knows that he already came here at a more mature age and cannot learn [the] Estonian language in any way. He doesn't apply for some other state citizenship because he also feels comfortable with the gray passport. My husband does not feel that he is discriminated [against] here in any way. And he has also not encountered that. He has his own business here. He is very loyal to Estonia, but as his business here is doing well and the lack of citizenship does not bother him, he does not feel that applying for some country's citizenship is necessary. (Female, 33, Tallinn)

At employment or otherwise, there is not really a difference: everybody is treated the same. But deep down there is still the feeling of not being similar to others. (Female, 44, Tallinn)

I think that those people who want citizenship, do everything to receive it, but those who do not wish for it, will never get it. Citizenship is not important to some, because they are satisfied with their lives and have also a good income. So – they don't even have time to think about citizenship. (Female, 33, Tallinn)

Conversely, some Russian-speaking non-citizens were sometimes reluctant to put forward their citizenship applications because they felt they were 'nobodies' or 'second-rate' persons in the eyes of the Estonians or the state:

I have already applied for citizenship of Russia, for I will no doubt receive it without problems, just like that. I actually do not care which citizenship I receive. If I had lived long in the USA or England, I could have already become an American or Englishman. But our situation with these 'wolf' passports is atrocious. They have already done such a big deal out of their nationality, that we are like flies to them with these gray passports. We were simply segregated already in the beginning. (Male, 41, Jõhvi)

The second reason why I do not wish to apply for citizenship lies in the fact that I do not want to become a so-called 'second-rate' citizen. Because I will be considered as this person who has become a citizen through naturalisation. But why acquire citizenship then? (Female, 35, Tallinn)

Our data reveals that connection with Russia could be another reason for not seeking Estonian citizenship. Applications for Russian citizenship have increased recently in Estonia as the Russian government had been active in popularising Russian citizenship and obtaining Russian citizenship could thus be seen as easier than obtaining Estonian citizenship:

I think that people have already understood that nobody will change the laws anymore and they will not obtain citizenship. They know that they will not pass the language exam and will take Russian citizenship. They will at least have some citizenship then. It can be observed that things are improving in Russia and people will become interested in Russian citizenship. Some also have relatives in Russia. (Female, 33, Tallinn)

Being a non-citizen is very difficult. Also, some people have relatives in Russia. Some take Russian citizenship because they have strived, but not succeeded in obtaining Estonian citizenship. Some elderly people take Russian citizenship only because they are unable to learn the language. (Female, 35, Tallinn)

Besides the fact that an applicant did not have to learn Estonian, Russian citizenship would mean easier travel to Russia to visit relatives:

Many have close ones in Ivangorod: earlier it was all like one town [Ivangorod and Narva]. In order to not apply for a visa each time, people choose Russian citizenship. (Female, 36, Narva)

Maybe, because it is cheaper and for business as well. The cigarettes and lots of other things, like children's clothes, are cheaper there. This is how many people probably reason. On the other hand, many have relatives on the other side. I also have relatives there. If you want to visit, you need to apply for a visa and so on. (Male, 41, Jōhvi)

As mentioned above, a simplified procedure is available for stateless parents to acquire Estonian citizenship for their minor children. According to Article 13, section 4 of the Citizenship Act, simplified naturalisation can be sought in respect of minors under fifteen years of age who were born in Estonia after 26 February 1992. Naturalisation may be applied for by parents, single parents or adoptive parents, who have (by the time the application is submitted) legally resided in Estonia for a minimum of five years and who are not considered citizens by any other state (for example, persons with undetermined citizenship). Nevertheless, there are still parents who do not make use of this opportunity. Analysis of the reasons behind this reveals that these are mostly pragmatic: some parents do not wish to take responsibility for such decisions, preferring to wait until the children become of age and decide for themselves which citizenship to choose. Other parents mentioned that they are not sure about their children's educational plans – if people wish their children to be educated in Estonia, then as a rule, they apply for Estonian citizenship for their children; but if they think that their child can more easily (due to the mother tongue) or more efficiently (because the Estonian education level is considered to be low) continue to study in Russia, then they tend to prefer to wait. For example, one respondent said:

My son wants to go to Russia to study and it is hard to do that with Estonian citizenship. I wanted to acquire double citizenship, but I was not able to and have to apply again. The language barrier is also a big problem. It is easier for him to study in Russia than in Estonia. (Male, 41, Jōhvi)

The obligations that came with citizenship could also mean that it compared unfavourably with statelessness, given that this brings few immediate disadvantages in Estonia:

> My second child is a boy. And I don't wish that somebody would send him to the army, be it Estonian or Russian, to fight in some strange places without his consent. I want to leave him the right to decide himself, what state's citizenship he wishes, as he will soon be fifteen years old ... Maybe, if our future was more visible and life was more stable, I would have done it long ago. I would have taken that responsibility. It is easier to obtain citizenship than to change it. (Female, 37, Tallinn)

> I have thought about the blue passport, but what happens then, when he is seventeen years old. I wouldn't want my child to serve in this country's army. Let's see what will happen to this country in ten years. (Female, 24, Tallinn)

The ambiguities of *de jure* statelessness in Estonia

The main peculiarity of the issue of statelessness in Estonia consists in the fact that legal status does not seem to have a very noticeable impact on how people manage in their everyday life. The data of the research reported in this article clearly support such a conclusion. However, most of Estonian Russians, and particularly those without Estonian citizenship, are not happy with the policies the Estonian state has been pursuing. The obligation to go through naturalisation only due to the fact that 'the rules of the game' were changed in Estonia at the beginning of the 1990s is viewed as demeaning by those who have lived in Estonia most of their lives. Perceptions of unfairness as well as difficulties in learning the Estonian language and passing the citizenship examination are the main reasons for the stateless non-citizens' refusal to acquire Estonian citizenship. The most common view among Estonian Russians is that at least those who were born in Estonia should receive citizenship automatically. Such a position is supported in surveys by also about half of ethnic Estonians.[49]

One could argue that the long-term statelessness of a remarkable share of the permanent residents in Estonia is damaging to the Estonian national interest.[50] The citizenship policy needs reconsideration as the challenges that the Estonian state is facing have changed considerably,

---

[49] R. Vetik *et al.*, 'Introduction and Trends', in R. Vetik (ed.), *Integration Monitoring of Estonian Society* (2008), www.meis.ee/raamatukogu?book_id=196 (in Estonian).

[50] Vetik, *op cit.*, *On the Boundary of Two Liberties*.

compared to the time when the citizenship regulation was adopted in the 1990s. The internal and external context of the citizenship issue is now completely different, as Estonia has become a member of the European Union and NATO. Analyses of the socio-economic and demographic trends confirm that the quality of human capital is becoming the main developmental problem for Estonia in an international comparison.[51] If the national interest of Estonia depends on successful adaptation in a rapidly globalising world, then an institution of citizenship should exist that both Estonians and Estonian Russians can identify with and which supports the realisation of the human potential of all people in Estonia. Engaging long-term permanent residents as part of the Estonian citizenry and creating favourable conditions for realising their capacities is one of the most urgent policy challenges currently facing Estonia.

[51] Vetik, *op cit.*, 'Why the Estonian Position'.

10

The *sans papiers* in France

ARNAUD LUCIEN, DAVID MARRANI
AND THE EDITORS

Being and becoming French

The original post-Revolutionary French Republican Constitution embodied a universalist ideal, making no distinction between French nationals and others.[1] There have been many versions of the Constitution since then, and that approach has long since gone. The current French Constitution[2] proclaims in its Preamble both the sovereignty of '*le peuple*' and the principles of human rights. Article 1 guarantees the equality of all citizens before the law, and political groups are guaranteed participation in politics under Article 4, but the context is that of an electorate of all citizens. It does not include non-nationals, who may have legal rights granted by the French Constitution to foreigners, sometimes in pursuit of international treaty obligations, but who may alternatively find that they do not even have the right to remain in the country.

Before the Revolution, France practised the *jus soli*, so that those born on the monarch's territory belonged to his sphere of power and were accordingly French nationals. The *jus soli*, associated with monarchical allegiance, was replaced after the Revolution with a *jus sanguinis* system, so that being French was connected instead with the French people. This, however, meant that the children of migrants born in France were forever foreigners, even down the generations (something they often preferred, as it meant they were not obliged to perform military service). Elements of the *jus soli* were therefore later reintroduced, at first for the third generation.

---

[1] Following the Revolution of 1789, the First Constitution was proclaimed in 1791 (Constitutional Monarchy). The First Republican Constitution was proclaimed in 1793.
[2] Currently that of 4 October 1958 as amended, see www.legifrance.gouv.fr/html/constitution/constitution.htm, accessed 20 April 2010.

Currently, France practises a system of 'double *jus soli*' combined with its *jus sanguinis* system. The 'double' refers to the requirement of two generations to establish French nationality on the basis of the *jus soli*. The double *jus soli* means that a child born in France to two foreign parents is French if one of those parents was born in France. Under the *jus sanguinis* system, a child may register as French if one parent is French at their birth, wherever they are born; there is no limit to the number of generations through which this can pass. A person born in France will also become French at the age of eighteen if then still resident there, unless they decline the citizenship. Naturalisation is theoretically possible for foreigners after five years' residence in France, but is notoriously difficult and slow save for spouses of French nationals, who used to benefit from a quick and simple system of naturalisation by declaration, though this was more recently restricted.[3]

French nationality law has also had phases during which it positively rejected its residents of foreign origin, even if they had become French. Between 1915 and the end of the Second World War, France passed a number of laws allowing for the withdrawal of nationality from naturalised citizens. The current law allows that a person can also be deprived of French citizenship if they commit certain crimes within ten years of naturalisation. French nationality can be renounced, but not so as to leave a person stateless.

Following the Liberation in 1945, France had a deliberate policy of encouraging naturalisation, but among those of European origin. France's shedding of its colonies in the later twentieth century presented other issues. Algeria was a part of France (that is, not a foreign colony) and her population was and is largely Muslim North African. In 1962, following Algerian independence, the Evian Accords provided that Algerians aged over eighteen and living in France could become French citizens if they made a 'declaration of acceptance' of the French Republic. This was, however, politically unacceptable to many Algerians, so those who lived in France often did so effectively as *de facto* stateless persons. The requirement of the 'declaration of acceptance' was abandoned in 1967, so that the only requirement was five years' residence in France. The population

---

[3] Loi 2003–1119 of 26 November 2003, *Journal Officiel de la République Française (JORF)* 27 November 2003, 20136; Loi 2006-911 of 24 July 2006, *JORF* 25 July 2006, 11047. Dual citizenship is allowed, although occasionally France's signing of the Council of Europe Convention of 1963 on dual citizenship, and attempting to avoid it, is adverted to where convenient.

affected was, however, that which now often finds itself marginalised by policy considerations.

The anxiety to include resident foreigners as part of the French citizenry takes a strongly cultural Republican form, and is involved with the widely known debates over *laïcité*, or secularism. The *laïque* model ostensibly seeks to include all individuals as equal members of the citizenry; it is possible, however, to see it as being prepared to exclude those to whom the French conception of *laïcité* is itself unacceptable. The apparently neutral and inclusive principle of *laïcité* lies behind the prohibition of the hijab in schools,[4] where it may however alienate the Muslim community. The cause of the resulting tensions is attributed in some quarters to insufficient integration and assimilation by that community.

French nationality law reflects these tensions. The liberal rules allowing Algerians to become French citizens themselves led to perceived problems, especially the phenomenon of those who were 'français sans le savoir et sans le vouloir' (French without knowing it or wanting it). Children born in France to parents born in former colonies or overseas territories were automatically French at birth following changes to the law in 1973.[5] Almost contemporaneously, however, as in Germany, labour immigration was halted, and there were attempts to repatriate large numbers of Algerian nationals. Ten years later, the *titre unique* (ten-year residence permit) was created.[6] By this time, nationality law had become a contentious political topic, with the rise of unemployment and of the far right in France, which particularly opposed the policies of naturalisation. Restrictions on immigration, however, meant that residents might wish to naturalise in order to secure their position. Since the 1970s there has been substantial non-European immigration. From the 1990s, almost half those seeking to naturalise were from North Africa, and many of those seeking to naturalise have been received in a relatively hostile climate.

In 1993, nationality law was restricted so that the double *jus soli* rule no longer included those claiming through a parent who was born on an independent, formerly French, territory outside France. The application of the double *jus soli* to children born in France to parents who had been born in Algeria before independence in 1962 applied only where the relevant parent had been living in France for five years at the time of the birth, notwithstanding that Algeria had, before independence,

---

[4] Especially after Loi 2004-228 of 15 March 2004, *JORF* 17 March 2004, 5190.
[5] Loi 73-42 of January 9, 1973, *JORF* 10 January 1973, 467.
[6] Titre unique de séjour et de travail, Loi 84-622 of 17 July 1984, *JORF* 19 July 1984, 2324.

been part of France rather than a French foreign territory. Access to French citizenship for children born in France to foreign parents was also restricted, making it possible only if they recorded a formal declaration to that effect between the ages of sixteen and twenty-one. The waiting period for spouses before they could naturalise by declaration was increased from six months to two years. Nationality law became part of the 'code civil'.[7]

These restrictions led to certain endemic forms of statelessness, particularly among French-born young people who did not realise they were not already French, and so failed to make a declaration adopting French nationality before it was too late. Some also had difficulty establishing five years' continuous residence immediately preceding the declaration. In 1998, the law was revised to include further liberal reforms, especially for children born in France to foreign parents, with certain provisos.[8] For the children of Algerian parents, the 'double *jus soli*' was reinstituted and the timeframe for the five years' residence condition was broadened.[9]

In 2003, two laws were passed. One (Loi 119 of 26 November), as well as dealing with some nationality issues, claimed to ensure the proper welcoming of desired immigrants by embedding stronger methods for excluding the undesired, such as the creation of databases and provisions for fingerprinting. The other (Loi 1176 of 10 December) reformed the asylum process. In effect, so far as naturalisation and immigration were concerned, the law became more restrictive. Whereas the waiting period for spouses seeking to naturalise had previously been one year, it was now increased to two years, and language tests for foreign spouses were introduced. There were more investigations as to the nature of marriages, designed to find and deter marriages of convenience. There were already numerous requirements for the naturalisation of the many unaccompanied foreign children in France; these were also tightened up. Whereas until 2003 such children were able to naturalise by declaration, this provision was now restricted to those under fifteen. Those over

---

[7] Chapitre III *Code civil*, see www.legifrance.gouv.fr/affichCode.do?cidTexte=LEGITEXT0 00006070721&dateTexte=20100422, accessed 20 April 2010.

[8] It applied to: (1) those between the ages of thirteen and sixteen who could have a parental declaration made for them; or, those who (2) could make their own declaration between sixteen and eighteen; or (3) those who could claim French nationality if they had been born and lived in France until they were eighteen.

[9] Article 21-7 *Code Civil*. A further transformation has been the amendment of Articles 76 and 77 of the French Fifth Republic Constitution in 1998, which created the citizenship of New Caledonia.

fifteen had to wait an additional five years, their fate described as 'floating between illegal status and general social exclusion'.[10]

The changes to citizenship policy in France reflect a broad transformation in attitudes towards the admission of foreigners and the acceptance and integration of foreign nationals generally. The current management of immigration shows a more concerted attempt to restrict demographic changes as a result of migration, as determined by the perceived needs of the French state and people, hence the policy of selective immigration or 'immigration choisie', as described by Sarkozy. Since 2008 this policy has been developed by the introduction of *contrat d'accueil et d'integration* (reception and integration contract).[11] The idea behind the use of such contracts is that France should only accept immigrants considered to be 'useful' to the French economy and who can demonstrate their ability to assimilate in the French culture. Only those who can show the ability to assimilate – in effect by already having been assimilated or being on the route to assimilation, are then able to naturalise. In 2008, a Moroccan woman was refused naturalisation on the grounds of having failed to assimilate sufficiently (*default d'assimilation*), because she wore a burqa or niqab.[12] This court in this widely publicised case referred to her religious practices which, it was claimed, were incompatible with accepted French values of gender equality.[13]

Naturalisation procedures have also included a greater emphasis on the cultural dimension. Although language tests for applicants were introduced after the Second World War,[14] in 2003 and then again in 2005 the language qualifications were strengthened by means of additional citizenship tests which required that applicants understand the rights and responsibilities of a French citizen. Since 2007, the *contrat d'accueil et d'integration* has codified the requirements of language and civic knowledge for foreigners wishing to settle in France. Linguistic ability is now assessed by interview, though it is unclear how consistently this works. The procedure is carried out through local government, with some

---

[10] P. Weil, A. Spire and C. Bertossi, *Country Report: France* (2009), www.foyer.be/IMG/pdf/EUDO-2009-France-linked.pdf.

[11] See, for example, the Appel No. 09VE00358, 19 January 2010, Cour Administrative d'Appel de Versailles. Here a Malian man born in 1964, who had been in France since 2001, appealed against the refusal of a *carte de séjour*.

[12] An all-covering long dress, or a veil covering all of the face except the eyes.

[13] In *Mme M*, the *Conseil d'État* referred to the 'pratique radicale de sa religion, incompatible avec les valeurs essentielles de la communauté francaise, et notamment avec le principe d'egalité des sexes' (No. 286798, Séance du 26 mai 2008, lecture du 27 juin 2008).

[14] See Ordonnance 45-2658 of 2 November 1945, *JORF* 4 November 1945, 7225.

regional variation.[15] The decentralisation of the French state[16] has resulted in regional variation in the treatment of non-nationals, with those in big cities generally faring worse.

Rights of undocumented residents in France

For those who are not accepted as French, or as legitimate residents, and who are living in France without permission, there is a complex legal framework that is itself in the process of change, already under way when this study was undertaken.

Refugees and the de jure stateless

France has a well-developed system for the recognition of refugees. The principle of asylum is recorded in the Constitution,[17] and France is also a party to the 1951 United Nations Convention on the Status of Refugees.[18] France's long-standing tradition as a place of sanctuary (*Terre d'accueil*) was codified by the *Code de l'entrée et du séjour des étrangers et du droit d'asile* (CESEDA) (Code on entry and reception of foreigners and the right to asylum) and given specific constitutional recognition by a ruling of the French constitutional court.[19] France is also a signatory to the Conventions on the Reduction of Statelessness, and the constitutional court has further affirmed its commitments to prevent and reduce statelessness.[20]

There is no provision within domestic law that deals specifically with the situation of non-nationals claiming recognition of their status as stateless persons, but stateless people who are determined to be refugees may be given ten years' residence after which they have the right to naturalisation. There is also a system of subsidiary protection for those who are not refugees as such but cannot return to their countries of origin because it would be unsafe for them to do so. In such cases, people are granted a one-year renewable permit, with the right to work. It should be noted that

---

[15] www.interieur.gouv.fr/sections/a_1_interieur/le_ministre/interventions/conference-presse-immigration, accessed 25 May 2007.

[16] Article 1, 'La France … Son organisation est decentralisée'.

[17] Preamble to the 1946 Constitution, para. 4; 1958 Constitution Article 53-1.

[18] Ratification authorised by Loi 54-290 of 17 March 1954; ratification of the Protocol of 1967 by which the 1951 Convention was applied to future refugees was authorised by Loi 70–1076 of 25 November 1970.

[19] Cons. Const., Décis. 79-109 DC, 9 January 1980, RJC 1–74, *JORF* 11 January 1980, 84.

[20] Cons. Const., Décis. 93-325 DC, 13 August 1993, *JORF* 18 August 1993, 11722.

asylum seekers whose cases are undecided after one year also have the right to work.

Statelessness determination procedures are organised as follows. The French *Office Français de Protection des Refugies et Apatrides*[21] (Office for Protection of Refugees and Stateless) (OFPRA) is responsible for examining claims and determining the status of applicants.[22] In some instances, where someone is found under the respective conventions to be both a refugee and statelessness person, a non-national has the status of *réfugié-apatride* (refugee – stateless person). If a non-national is granted the status of stateless person, he or she will be placed under the protection of the OFPRA,[23] his or her personal and administrative status governed by French law. The stateless person will receive a temporary permit called a *carte de séjour temporaire, mention vie privée et familiale*. This document also permits the holder to work and, if the claimant shows that he has spent three years living in France, he may be granted a ten-year temporary residence permit. These remarks about the entitlements of stateless persons apply, however, only to the *de jure* stateless.

There are many non-French people who have made a life in France without permission to be in the country. If they are not recognised as refugees and they do not have permission to live in the country then, as they cannot provide any documentation to demonstrate that they are entitled to remain, being undocumented they are known as the *sans papiers* ('without papers').

The sans papiers: *resistance and response*

The policy of removing rather than regularising those living in France without permission caused considerable tension. With the repeal of the earlier principle of automatic regularisation after ten years of continuous residence in France (established in 1998), the fate of many non-citizens became most uncertain. The policy of removals was stepped up even though the Minister of the Interior noted that it would be quite inconceivable for many people to return to their country of origin.[24] Enforcement of

---

[21] Hereinafter referred to as OFPRA.

[22] This follows from the first article of the Convention of New York, September 28, 2004, the CESEDA and the 14 August 2004 Décret.

[23] Article L721-2 and -3 CESEDA.

[24] He stated 'Cependant, j'ai bien conscience que le retour dans le pays d'origine après 10 ans de séjour illégal en France est parfois inconcevable' ('I am conscious that returning to the country of origin after staying illegally for ten years in France is inconceivable'),

the stronger removals policy was met with resistance by the *sans papiers*, who proved to be relatively well organised. A protest by the *sans papiers* in 1996, involving the widely publicised occupation of the church of Saint-Bernard in Paris, was followed by confirmation by the *Conseil d'Etat* that the French administration could regularise the status of foreigners.[25]

The idea of regularising families with school children appears to contradict the general policy of immigration control but, as a result of strong media coverage of the families concerned, a *circulaire* of 31 October 2005 proposed a moratorium until the end of the school year 2006. At the end of June 2006 the Minister was confronted by increasing tensions over the stricter policy of removing the *sans papiers*. Watch committees were organised and a system of 'godparents' set up to provide accommodation for, and look after, children who were liable to be removed with their parents.

The Minister of the Interior then drafted two new *circulaires* concerning the undocumented foreign families with school children. The *circulaire* was part of a corpus of new norms attempting to create a balanced immigration policy and completed the earlier 2005 *circulaire*. The *circulaire* of 13 June 2006 applies to families (including single-parent families) with at least one child at school since September 2005: in addition, the French Home Office issued a *circulaire* (also on 13 June 2006) in which the Minister set up conditions for the (exceptional) regularisation by *Préfets* of school children and their families if they had been resident in France for at least two years by 13 June 2006. They also had to fulfil the following conditions:

- Have at least one child in school
- Have a child born in France or resident in France since the child was 13
- At least one parent had to contribute to the maintenance and education of the child
- The family needed to show a real will to integrate into French society, particularly by attempting to master the French language
- Not have any links with the country of which he or she is a national.

The general principle behind the policy was to encourage families to return to their country of origin. If they decided to return, financial support was offered (available from 2005 onwards). The amount of money offered was

---

www.interieur.gouv.fr/sections/a_l_interieur/le_ministre/interventions/reunion-prefets-24-07-067570/?portal_status_message=psm_status_changed, accessed 25 May 2007.

[25] Cons. Const., Décis. 93-325 DC, 13 August 1993, *JORF* 18 August 1993, 11722.

raised by the new *circulaire* from €150 to €2,000 for an adult, €3,000 for a couple, €1,000 per minor child up to three children, then €500 per extra child. The amount varied if families were prepared to return before 13 August 2006. Indeed, the *circulaire* of 14 June 2006 offered more attractive sums for people to return.[26]

In addition, a new scheme was introduced allowing families to remain in France on an exceptional and humanitarian basis. In such exceptional cases, if families did not accept to go back to their country of origin, these undocumented foreigners could be granted a temporary permit (*carte de séjour temporaire mention vie privée et familiale*) provided they met six conditions:

(1) The family had been in France for at least two years
(2) A child had been at school at least since September 2005
(3) The child was born in France or had arrived in France when he was very young, at the latest when he was thirteen
(4) The family's life was essentially in France and not in the country of origin
(5) The parents contributed effectively to the maintenance and education of the child
(6) The family had shown a real wish to integrate into French society.

On the application of the *circulaire*, the Ministry described four types of situation:

(1) Foreigners outside the scope of the *circulaire*, but otherwise still within the normal scope of French legislation on foreigners; such as people regularly on the French territory waiting for family reunion or a spouse on the territory with irregular status (asylum seekers, single persons or couples without children, foreigners returned to France under the 'Dublin Convention', … etc.)[27]

---

[26] €4,000 for an adult, €7,000 for a couple, €2,000 per child up to three children then €1,000.

[27] The original 'Dublin Convention' (Convention Determining the State Responsible for Examining Applications for Asylum lodged in one of the European Community States) was made in 1990 and came into force in 1997. The intention was broadly that asylum seekers should be able to make only one asylum claim within Europe, in the first European country in which they landed. This was superseded in 2003 by 'Dublin II', neither a Convention nor made in Dublin but Council Regulation (EC) No. 343/2003, made by the European Council of Ministers, and Commission Regulation (EC) No. 1560/2003. The system is implemented through the international electronic information network, 'DubliNet'. This is a central piece of EU legislation which determines the EU member

(2) Foreigners within the scope of the *circulaire*, i.e. families irregularly on the French territory with children at school, who could fulfil all the criteria: these would be documented

(3) Foreigners generally within the scope of the *circulaire*, but who could not fulfil the first criteria (i.e. this recognises the first two criteria as the most important): these would not be documented

(4) Foreigners within the scope of the *circulaire*, i.e. families irregularly on the French territory with children at school, who could claim to meet the first criteria, but not the one regarding integration: these would not be documented during the summer 2006 but might be in exceptional cases considered under the new legislation.

Problems with the new framework

In July 2006, the Association RESF (*Réseau éducation sans frontières*) officially contacted the agency HALDE (*Haute autorité de lutte contre les discriminations*) about inconsistencies in the processing of regularising applications by *Préfets*. One essential point of concern was the requirement that non-nationals must not have any link with the country of origin to be granted documentation on the grounds of exceptional and humanitarian protection. Many members of the French Parliament brought a 'still-born' motion to the *Assemblée nationale* on 21 September 2006 asking for the creation of an enquiry commission on the implementation of the *circulaire*.

In April 2007, the migrant and refugee assistance NGO Cimade presented a report based on an internet survey about the application of the *circulaire*.[28] Essentially, it showed that how the *circulaire* was implemented depended on the locality in which the undocumented foreigners applied. In small towns, there were no major difficulties. In large areas, like Paris, Lyon and Marseilles, the *préfectures* had to deal with a larger quantity of applications and the process was more complicated. The report also highlighted several obstacles. First, access to the *préfectures* was often difficult for the applicants, and the list of documents requested varied. It was therefore particularly difficult in many cases to prove that the undocumented foreigner wanted to remain in France and had tried to obtain a *carte de séjour temporaire mention vie privée et familiale*. In

---

state responsible for examining an application for asylum seekers seeking international protection under the Geneva Convention and the EU Qualification Directive.

[28] www.cimade.org.

addition, certain *préfectures* refused to deliver proper application forms. The interview process was also unsystematic and limited to the state agent checking the documents brought by the applicants (although in many cases, the *préfecture* allowed the applicants to be helped by someone from an NGO). The decision made by the state authorities was generally negative when:

(1) The undocumented foreigner had a temporary permit
(2) The spouse of the undocumented was documented, because of the procedure of family reunion
(3) Foreigners had never previously had to regularise their status
(4) Foreigners had applied for a permit or were in an appeal process relating to a refusal of a permit
(5) Foreigners were acting as parents of a child, but were not the parents
(6) Foreigners were from the European Union.

The Cimade report also elaborated on the nature of the *circulaire*. Under French law, a *circulaire* is only a communication instrument between the central authority and the external services[29] and does not create rights for citizens. In the case of the *circulaire* of 13 June 2006, the Minister of the Interior was only informing the *Préfets* of what they had to do – the document was essentially his interpretation of the legislation on the matter.[30] Nevertheless, some elements of the *circulaire* had direct or indirect consequences. In the case of the *circulaires* of June 2006, because they were not treated as legally binding documents, refusals by the administrative authorities could not give rise to any form of judicial review.[31]

Political response

The newly elected president, Nicolas Sarkozy, attached great importance to the situation of foreigners, and placed this issue prominently on his

---

[29] Although since 1978 the Ministry is obliged to publish any *circulaire* issued, it is only an internal document.

[30] 'Circulaires' are issued by the administration to subordinate personnel. They are taken into account by judges and practitioners, even though the *Cour de Cassation* has often reminded them that they do not have the force of law. See C. M. Germain, 'Approaches to Statutory Interpretation and Legislative History in France', *Duke Journal of Comparative and International Law*, 13 (2003), 195, 200.

[31] According to the CIMADE report, many applicants complained about the lack of any explanation in the letters they received refusing them documents, but the authorities felt no need to provide an explanation of the reasons for the refusal.

agenda. One important development was the creation of a new ministerial department.[32] The rationale behind this was to accommodate right-wing elements among the electorate,[33] although it was also claimed that the creation of a specialised ministerial department would simplify the task of administration.[34] Next, Sarkozy appointed Brice Hortefeux as the new minister in charge of preparing and implementing policy which had previously fallen within the responsibility of the French Home Office and the French Foreign Ministry. The president's mission letter sent to the new minister[35] confirmed that the new department was dedicated to managing the migration flux and that France now had established an official public policy around this issue.[36]

The fight against immigration was recognised as an absolute priority. Removals had increased by 140 per cent from 2002 to 2006. The minister was clear: undocumented foreigners did not have the right to stay in France and could be sent back to their country of origin, voluntarily or not. Moreover, the situation of undocumented foreigners with children in the French education system did not mean that the right to be schooled should be considered as grounds for allowing parents to remain in France. At the same time, Hortefeux emphasised the importance of the *contrat d'accueil et d'intégration*[37] for migrants who could meet the relevant criteria. In contrast to those threatened with removal, migrants who could obtain the 'contract' would be on course to receive permits for ten years, and in the meantime the state would provide housing, education and training. Hortefeux also stressed that French identity was the cornerstone of integration.[38]

---

[32] *Décret n° 2007-999 du 31 mai 2007 relatif aux attributions du ministre de l'Immigration, de l'Intégration, de l'Identité nationale et du Codéveloppement*, JORF 125 1 June 2007, 9964 texte n° 11.

[33] Alain Badiou, in an interview given to *Le Monde*, mentions how this national signifier is a major point of crystallisation, and how the creation of a special ministerial department takes into consideration the issue of foreigners and attracts votes from the extreme right, Alain Badiou, 'L'intellectuel de gauche va disparaître, tant mieux', *Le Monde* (14 July 2007).

[34] Indeed, the new president reorganised many ministerial departments to create, in effect, a psychological impact in the major areas on which he wanted to focus. For example, he linked employment with public finance and ecology with development.

[35] 'Immigration: Brice Hortefeux s'explique', *Le Figaro* (1 June 2007).

[36] N. Sarkozy, 'Lettre de mission adressée à M. Hortefeux, Ministre de l'Immigration, de l'intégration, de l'identité nationale et du codéveloppement' (9 July 2007).

[37] www.ofii.fr/article.php3?id_article=63.

[38] See, for example, n. 12, the case of *Faiza M*.

Legislative response

A draft law on immigration, integration and asylum was presented for discussion by the French Parliament on 4 July 2007.[39] It was supposed to be the last of the reforms initiated by the first and second of the new *Lois Sarkozy*.[40] Chapter 1 concerned the immigration of families and integration,[41] and the draft law was presented as a means of helping migrants to become French nationals. The government commented that these conditions could be implemented under the EC Directive 2003/86/CE (22 September 2003)[42] on the right to family reunification.[43] The draft law reiterated that applicants needed to have knowledge of the French language – Article 1 requires that all migrants older than sixteen agree to learn French – and knowledge of the core values of the French republic.[44] In addition, it required that applicants have a minimum income and proposed a new *contrat d'accueil et d'intégration pour la famille* dealing with the rights and duties of parents in France.[45] Minor corrections based on the practice of current legislation were also implemented. Article 4.3 abrogated Article L. 211-2-1 of the CESEDA which in its last paragraph (introduced by the statute of 24 July 2006) made it difficult for a spouse of a French national, particularly someone undocumented, to apply for a permit.

A refusal decision to grant rights to remain on the territory could have immediate effect and notification of it would automatically cancel a non-national's status, thus creating an undocumented foreigner.

The government's moves against the undocumented *sans papiers* provoked a resistance movement, which in turn created a reaction from the French administration. However, the resistance did not come only

---

[39] Projet de loi relatif à la maîtrise de l'immigration, à l'intégration et à l'asile.

[40] Loi 2003-1119 of 26 November 2003, *JORF* 27 November 2003, 20136; Loi 2006-911 of 24 July 2006, *JORF* 25 July 2006, 11047.

[41] 94,500 resident permits were issued in 2005 on the basis of the right to family reunification. Family immigration was the largest type of immigration in France before students (48,900) and workers (13,650).

[42] Under Article 7, para. 2, the Directive states that member states may ask foreigners to conform to the administrative measures of integration set up under domestic law.

[43] This is also a matter of implementation of the Preamble, 1946 Constitution, para. 10, the constitutional basis for family reunification.

[44] According to the website of the Agence Nationale de l'Accueil des Étrangers et des Migrations (ANAEM), migrants have to be taught: human rights (including property, independence of judiciary, …), male–female equality, *laïcité* and dignity of the human being, www.anaem.fr/article.php3?id_article=499, accessed 14 July 2007.

[45] See under Article 3.

from NGOs and pressure groups. Eight left-wing mayors in the Hauts-de-Seine department, in the greater Paris area, informed Hortefeux that they would endeavour to protect the undocumented foreign nationals, *sans papiers*, regardless of whether this entailed passing the thin wall separating legal from illegal action. This declaration came after the minister ordered *Préfets* in every French *département* to remind the mayors that operations to support the *sans papiers* would not be tolerated.[46]

Between 200,000 and 400,000 foreigners *sans papiers* were living in France at the time and the numbers presented a problem for local government officials that had supported the regularisation. The government hit back by issuing the 2006 *circulaire* in which it fixed limits on quantity and time to apply for regularisation, thus overcoming the impossibility of regularising so many thousands of *sans papiers* at one time.

Finally, the parliamentary debate on the draft law (*Projet de loi relatif à la maîtrise de l'immigration, à l'intégration et à l'asile*) proved to be extremely controversial, with deputies adopting an amendment to the bill aimed at removing the ban on statistics based on ethnic background, where French law had authorised the classification by nationality but not by race or ethnicity.

Rights of the undocumented in France

Right to work

The French Fifth Republic Constitution, through its Preamble integrating the Preamble of the 1946 Constitution, enshrined its socio-economic rights. Para. 5 states that no one may be discriminated against on the basis of their origin. It is therefore a constitutional right to be protected against discrimination based on being a national or a non-national. The decision of the constitutional court DC 99-423 of 13 January 2000 affirmed this principle.[47] A stateless person will be given a document called *Carte de séjour temporaire* with a special condition: *Vie privée et familiale* which may enable him to work. If the claimant shows that he or she has been living in France for three years, he or she will be able to benefit from a document called *carte de resident* for ten years (Article L314-11 9°) which also grants rights to work.

---

[46] 'Des maires refusent d'obéir aux préfets sur les sans-papiers', *Le Monde* (Paris) (13 September 2007).
[47] Cons. Const., Décis. 99-423 DC, 13 January 2000, *JORF* 20 January 2000, 992, Rec. 33.

Healthcare

Para. 11 of the 1946 Preamble highlights that the Nation guarantees health protection to everyone:

> It shall guarantee to all, notably to children, mothers and elderly workers, protection of their health, material security, rest and leisure. All people who, by virtue of their age, physical or mental condition, or economic situation, are incapable of working shall have to the right to receive suitable means of existence from society.

This right is also codified under the *Code de la Sécurite Sociale*.

However, these rights are limited by subsequent interpretation. A non-national may be part of the *Sécurite Sociale* system but only under certain conditions organised by statute law. Indeed, the general issue is whether or not she or he is regularly documented in regard to the relevant legislation. Accordingly healthcare is not a universal right in France.[48] Undocumented non-nationals may only be allowed medical care under a special regime, *l'aide médicale*. The Finance Act for 2003[49] grants *aide médicale* (medical assistance) to undocumented non-nationals who have been in France for three months. The situation is better for children, however, who are not bound by this restriction since the *Conseil d'État*[50] ruled that it was illegal under Article 3 of the International Convention on the Rights of the Child to withhold access to medical care. Consequently, non-national children may seek medical care regardless of residence status.

Social security support

Under Article L311-2 *Code de la Sécurite Sociale*, it is impermissible to discriminate based on nationality, but non-nationals must work to receive social security benefits. Under Article L311-7 *Code de la Sécurite Sociale*,[51] all social benefits from the *Sécurite Sociale* are open to all

---

[48] Under Article L161-25-1 and 2 *Code de la Sécurite Sociale*, non-nationals have a right to benefits such as health insurance, maternity insurance and death insurance; Article L115-647 *Code de la Sécurite Sociale* states that the non-national has to be regularly documented. This is based on a condition of lawful residence that can be proved as per article D115-6 *Code de la Sécurite Sociale*.

[49] Article 97 (1) Loi 2003-1312 of 30 December 2003, *JORF* 31 December 2003.

[50] CE (*Conseil d'État*), 7 June 2006, *Association Aides et autres*, com. Aubert, AJDA, 22/2006, 1189.

[51] Loi 98-349 of 11 May 1998 Article 41 I, *JORF* 12 May 1998.

non-national workers and their beneficiaries, *ayant droits* (appropriately entitled), but these are strictly linked to lawful residence (this condition does not apply to pensions). Non-nationals must reside in France
for at least three months continuously. This benefit is not applicable
to non-national asylum seekers, and under Article D374-6 *Code de la
Sécurite Sociale* social services are obliged to check that non-nationals
are documented before issuing benefits. Accordingly these benefits are
not available to the *sans papiers* and other stateless persons who are in
effect irregular migrants.

Under Article L512-2 *Code de la Sécurite Sociale*,[52] families with children may receive benefits under certain conditions: they need to prove
their residence and their children must have been either born in France
or have regularly entered the French territory via the family reunification procedure (*Livre IV* CESEDA) or be children of refugees.[53] Similarly,
under Article D512-1 *Code de la Sécurité Sociale*[54] a non-national (including a child of a non-national older than eighteen) may receive social
benefits if he or she can prove to be documented.[55] Article D512-2 *Code
de la Sécurité Sociale*[56] states the same but for child beneficiaries of the
non-national.[57]

---

[52] As modified by Loi 86-1307 of 29 December 1986 Article 7 I, *JORF* 30 December 1986
and Loi 2005-1579 of 19 December 2005 Article 89, *JORF* 20 December 2005.

[53] Permit of 10° Article L. 313-11 CESEDA; or Resident Permit of Article L. 313-13
CESEDA; or Resident Permit of Article L. 313-8 or 5° Article L. 313-11 CESEDA; or
Resident Permit of 7° Article L. 313-11 CESEDA if children have entered France with
their parents and their parents hold a Resident Permit card.

[54] As inserted by Décret n° 2006-234 of 27 February 2006 Article 1, *JORF* 28 February
2006.

[55] Documents similar to those listed under Article D161-25-2. There are: Permanent,
Temporary or Algerian Resident permit, or acknowledgement of request for renewal
of these; three months' Temporary Resident Permit with mention: '*reconnu réfugié*';
acknowledgement of request for a Temporary Resident Permit with mention: '*étranger
admis au titre de l'asile*' valid for six months renewable; acknowledgement of request
for refugee status with concessions valid for three months, renewable; Temporary work
permits (less than three months); Temporary resident authorisation together with temporary work permit.

[56] *Ibid.*

[57] The list of documents is slightly different: birth certificate attesting birth in France, certificate of medical control from ANAEM, after the beginning of the family reunification
procedure; family booklet delivered by OFPRA or birth certificate prepared by OFPRA
when a child is a refugee or stateless family member. When a child is a refugee or stateless
family member, the birth certificate is given with the ruling of a court giving care of the
child to the non-national seeking social benefits; visa given by the consulate naming the
child of a non-national with Resident Permit of Article L. 313-8 or of 5° Article L. 313-11
CESEDA; certificate delivered by the *Préfet* that the child has entered French territory

Right to marry and found a family; family reunion

France respects her obligations under the ECHR, including those relating to family life as recorded under Article 8. However, since the introduction of the 'immigration choisie' policy requires the admission of workers, not family members, there are some important challenges to the way in which the above rights are respected.

The right to marry is protected by the Preamble to the 1946 Constitution, para. 4,[58] and has been affirmed as a constitutional fundamental right under the 1993 *Décision*.[59] The right to marry cannot be dependent on the legal status of the non-national, however; the right to marry does not grant the right to live on the national territory[60] and the French administration examines marriages in case of fraud. Marrying someone with the aim of becoming a French citizen is a criminal offence punishable by a fine of 15,000 Euros and five years in jail.[61]

The legal basis for family reunification is provided in para. 10 of the Preamble to the 1946 Constitution, which states: 'The Nation shall provide the individual and the family with the conditions necessary to their development.'[62] *Le regroupement familial* forms the *Livre IV* CESEDA and since the case of *GISTI* in 1978,[63] this has been understood as a general principle of law which was in 1993 interpreted by the *Conseil constitutionnel* as the right to live a normal family life.[64] This principle was developed more precisely in a ruling from 2005: '*La procédure de regroupement*

---

with parents who are documented under 7° Article L. 313-11 CESEDA or 5° Article 6 Franco-Algerian agreement of 27 December 1968 as modified; Resident Permit delivered to sixteen- to eighteen-year-old non-national under Article L. 311-3 CESEDA. Under Article L524-1, benefits attributed to single-parent families may qualify for these benefits under the condition of lawful residence.

[58] Décis. Comm EDH (Commission Européenne des Droits de l'Homme), 8 February 1972 n° 5269/71, *X et Y c. Royaume Uni* Annuaire 15, 564.

[59] Cons. Const., Décis 93-325 DC, 13 August 1993, *JORF* 18 August 1993, 11722.

[60] CEDH (Cour Européenne des Droits de l'Homme) (ECtHR), 28 May 1985, *Abdulaziz, Cabales et Balkandali c. Royaume Uni* Rev. Conv EDH (*Abdulaziz, Cabales and Balkandal* v. *UK* (1985) 7 EHRR 471.

[61] Article L623-1 CESEDA.

[62] In addition, under Article 8 ECHR, the Strasbourg Court considered that the right for parents and their children to live a normal family life implied a right to family reunification. CEDH Olson 24 March 1998 n° 81, Eriksson 22 June 1989 n° 71, Margareta et Rose Anderson 25 February 1992 n° 91.

[63] CE 8 December 1978, n° 10097, Groupe d'Intervention et de Soutien des Travailleurs Immigrés *et al.* (GISTI): Rec. CE, 493.

[64] Cons. Const. 13 August 1993 n° 93-325 DC: Rec const. 224 RJC I-539 and Cons. Const. 15 December 2005 n° 2005-528 DC, *JORF* 20 December RFD Adm 2006 note Schoettl.

*familial est une garantie légale … du droit des étrangers établis de manière
stable et régulière en France à y mener une vie familiale normale…'*[65]

Family reunification itself was not regulated until 1976, when a statute was passed which allowed non-nationals to be joined by their families, under certain conditions.[66] Under Article L411–1 CESEDA,[67] and
amended on 24 July 2006, any non-national who has regularly resided
in France for eighteen months may apply for family reunification. The
family must prove sufficient financial resources, decent accommodation
and the family must not already be on French soil. The authorisation to
enter the French territory is given by the representative of the State in
the *département*, the *Préfet*, after verification of the conditions of accommodation and of financial resources. Family reunion cannot be considered for common law partners (*concubins*) and may not be successful if a
divorce procedure is filed. Finally, family reunion can only apply to children if they are under eighteen.[68] However, generally the undocumented
cannot benefit from these provisions.

Right to accommodation

According to the *Loi Besson*, every *personne défavorisée* (disadvantaged
person) can be protected and therefore get decent accommodation. The
notion of 'decent accommodation' is defined by the *Loi relative à la solidar-
ité et au développement Urbain (law on solidarity and urban development)*[69]

---

[65] Cons. Const., Décis. 2005-528 DC, 15 December 2005, para. 15.

[66] Article L411-5 'Le regroupement familial ne peut être refusé que pour l'un des motifs
suivants:
  1 Le demandeur ne justifie pas de ressources stables et suffisantes pour subvenir aux
  besoins de sa famille. Sont prises en compte toutes les ressources du demandeur et de
  son conjoint indépendamment des prestations familiales et des allocations … Les ressources doivent atteindre un montant au moins égal au salaire minimum de croissance
  mensuel
  2 Le demandeur ne dispose pas ou ne disposera pas à la date d'arrivée de sa famille en
  France d'un logemùent considéré comme normal pour une famille comparable vivant
  dans la même région géographique
  3 Le demandeur ne se conforme pas aux principes fondamentaux reconnus par les lois
  de la République.'

[67] 'Le ressortissant étranger qui séjourne régulièrement en France depuis au moins dix huit
mois, sous couvert d'un des titres d'une durée de validité d'au moins un an prévus par le
présent code ou par des conventions internationales, peut demander à bénéficier de son
droit à être rejoint, au titre du regroupement familial, par son conjoint si ce dernier est
âgé d'au moins dix huit ans et les enfants du couple mineurs de dix huit ans.'

[68] CE 29 June 1990 GISTI JCP 1991 II 61.

[69] 'Le bailleur est tenu de remettre au locataire un logement décent ne laissant pas apparaî-
tre de risques manifestes pouvant porter atteinte à la sécurité physique ou à la santé et
doté des éléments le rendant conforme à l'usage d'habitation.'

and a 2002 *decret* (decree). Decent accommodation entails housing that is connected to electricity, water, heating, with proper sewerage, a bathroom and a specified floor area (16 m² for two persons, 25 m² for three persons, 34 m² for four persons, and 43 m² for five persons). According to Article L 512–1 of the *Code de la Sécurité Sociale*,[70] stateless people who are documented are entitled to family housing. There are therefore substantial rights in relation to housing generally, but the principal issue concerning obtaining decent accommodation is discrimination.

Right to rent or buy property

An undocumented person has problems beyond that of insufficient resources in trying to obtain accommodation privately. It is difficult either to rent privately or to borrow money if one is without the proper papers. However, many migrants do benefit from community and other connections which enable them to obtain accommodation privately within their own spheres of contacts.

Right to education

The Preamble to the 1946 Constitution, para. 13 highlights that the Nation guarantees equal access to education for everyone.[71] This right is further affirmed in the 1989 Convention on the Rights of the Child, to which France is a signatory. Thus national and non-national children have the right to public education. Furthermore, between six and sixteen years old, education is compulsory.[72] Children of foreign origin must go to school but problems may arise for children younger than six and older than sixteen.[73]

The registration of children is not dependent on documentation and by law schools may not request such documentation.[74] Furthermore, the

---

[70] 'Toute personne française ou étrangère résidant en France bénéficie pour ses enfants des prestations familiales ... et par conséquent de l'allocation de logement familiale.'

[71] 'The Nation guarantees equal access for children and adults to instruction, vocational training and culture. The provision of free, public and secular education at all levels is a duty of the State.'

[72] *Livre* I, Titre III, Ch. 1 *Code de l'éducation*, www.legifrance.gouv.fr/affichCode.do?cidTe xte=LEGITEXT000006071191&dateTexte=20100422, accessed 20 April 2010.

[73] Article L 131-4 *Code de l'éducation*.

[74] Under the combined statute law of the 1945 Ordinance and ruling of the *Conseil d'État*, together with the *circulaires* of 6 June 1991 and 20 March 2002, no one may demand to see permits, and should not consider the age of the student when registering a child in a primary or secondary school or higher education institution.

Conseil d'État ruled that a decision to deny access to education to a child aged between the ages of sixteen to eighteen must be justified.[75] One source of the problem appears to be the delivery of the registration certificate by the local mayor for children between three and six going to *école mater-nelle* (nursery school). Such registration certificates must be presented to the school director before a child is allowed to enter the school.[76]

Under article L. 313–7 CESEDA,[77] a temporary resident permit '*étudi-ant*' (student) may be granted to a non-national in secondary education or higher education if he or she can prove sufficient resources. The French administration has discretionary power to grant the same resident permit without the resources condition if the non-national has been studying in France, without interruption, since he or she was sixteen, and is now in higher education, and entered France lawfully.

Many examples of specific cases of *sans papiers* with children in school have been reported in the media. In May 2007 *Libération* reported the case of Amadou Meite from the Ivory Coast, a father of four children, two of which were living in France (including one in primary school). He was living with, but not married to a documented spouse, and was asked to attend a meeting at the *préfecture de police de Paris* where he was arrested and removed. Similarly, the Doumbia family from Mali – parents and four children, with two in France including one in primary school – were also detained (though-immediately removed[78]). There is also the case of Meï Zhu Pan and Long Pan, a Chinese couple with three children, who arrived in France in 1999. The couple were put in a detention centre while the children were hidden by activists of the RESF.[79]

Right to vote

In 1981, the President François Mitterrand promised foreign nationals the right to vote, but this was never implemented.[80]

---

[75] CE, 23 October 1987, *Consort Metrat*. AJDA 1987, 758.

[76] Article L113-1 *Code de l'éducation*.

[77] Loi 2006-911 of 24 July 2006 *relative à l'immigration et à l'intégration*, JORF 25 July 2006, 11047.

[78] C. Coroller, 'Paris: expulsions quotidiennes dans le XXe, Série de reconduites à la frontière de *sans-papiers* aux enfants scolarisés', *Libération* (Paris) (12 May 2007a), www.liberation.fr/actualite/societe/253342.FR.php, accessed 25 May 2007.

[79] C. Coroller, 'Paris: sans-papiers arrêtés, enfants cachés', *Libération* (Paris) (25 May 2007b), www.liberation.fr/actualite/societe/256008.FR.php, accessed 25 May 2007.

[80] Parti Socialiste (1981) 110 propositions pour la France. Élections présidentielles, April–May 1981, www.port.ac.uk/special/france1815to2003/chapter12/documents/filetodownload,18211,en.pdf, accessed 20 April 2010.

Protection from detention and deportation

Protection from detention and deportation is covered in Articles 3[81] and 5 of the ECHR, as discussed in previous chapters of this volume. For claims relating to the status of stateless, claimants who do not agree with a decision can take their case to French administrative courts. However, they cannot appeal or delay as to removal *(Reconduite à la frontière)*.

France has more recently instigated a stronger policy of removals. Being an illegal or undocumented migrant in France is punishable by a prison sentence of a year or a substantial fine: in 2003, for example, 5,606 such migrants were convicted and 3,997 of those were imprisoned. There is criticism, however, that such figures do not capture the magnitude of removals and that in fact the number of people removed is far greater.

Access to the justice system

Those seeking asylum are provided free of charge with legal assistance, and the rules as to detention without process are strictly enforced in France. Access to the courts and to the legal justice system are granted by the French authorities and organised via the *Aide juridictionnelle*, the equivalent to legal aid. As stated by the *Conseil constitutionnel*, the right to asylum is a constitutional principle which allows one to exercise of the right to defence. For this reason, non-nationals seeking asylum may stay temporarily on French territory until a final decision has been made:

> Considérant que le respect du droit d'asile, principe de valeur constitutionnelle, implique d'une manière générale que l'étranger qui se réclame de ce droit soit autorisé à demeurer provisoirement sur le territoire jusqu'à ce qu'il ait été statué sur sa demande; que sous réserve de la conciliation de cette exigence avec la sauvegarde de l'ordre public,

[81] The French Republic has rarely been found guilty of violation of Article 3. In relation to deportation, the ECtHR in *Dahlia v. France* (19 February 1998, deportation of an Algerian convicted of crime), and *HLR v. France* (29 April 1997, deportation of a Colombian convicted of crime), held that there was no violation of Article 3. The ECtHR in *Gebremedhin v. France* (26 April 2007) held that there was a violation of Article 3. Para. 41 explained that the emergency summary procedures that may be used against the administrative decision of refusal to enter the territory (*référé devant le président du Tribunal Administratif*) were not effective remedies. The French mechanism here was considered similar to the Belgian one (*Conka v. Belgium* 5 February 2002). Para. 67 notes that in *zones d'attente* (waiting areas), the remedies were ineffective because the possibility to postpone the application of the decision (that exists in French administrative law) could not be activated properly in these areas. The Court held that France was in violation of Articles 3 and 13.

> l'admission au séjour qui lui est ainsi nécessairement consentie doit lui
> permettre d'exercer effectivement les droits de la défense qui constitu-
> ent pour toutes les personnes, qu'elles soient de nationalité française,
> de nationalité étrangère ou apatrides, un droit fondamental à caractère
> constitutionnel.[82]

Recent developments have brought new help to non-national workers. Under Article L341–6-2 CESEDA,[83] unions may bring an action on behalf of non-national workers (they have the right of *locus standi* under Article L341–6-1). Further under article L341–6-3, registered associations fighting against discrimination may request unions to petition against employers of non-national workers.[84]

Right to burial

The right to burial is not regulated any differently for non-nationals or the stateless in France. The right to burial is not explicitly defined for non-nationals. The death must be declared to the civil services of the local authority *Commune*, the *officier d'état civil*, a civil servant will then issue a death certificate. Non-nationals above eighteen and stateless have the right to prepare the conditions of their burial in accordance with their own religion.

Empirical findings

Interviews were conducted in two phases and across two main locations in October 2007 in Paris and from December 2007 to January 2008 in Toulon ($n = 18$). According to the *Office Français de Protection des Réfugiés et Apatrides* (OFPRA, the French Bureau for the Protection of Refugees and Stateless), there were 175 applications for the status of stateless out of 32,132 total claims (asylum and stateless) in 2007. This figure, however,

---

[82] 'Taking into account that the right to asylum, the principle of constitutional value, generally implies that the foreigner who claims this right is provisionally authorised to
remain in the territory depending on the conditions of his request; and provided that
this demand can be reconciled with the protection of public order, once leave to remain is
consented s/he must be allowed to exercise his/her rights of defence which constitute for
everyone, whether French national, foreign national or expatriate, a fundamental right of
the constitutional character', see Cons. Const., Décis 93-325 DC, 13 August 1993, *JORF*
18 August 1993, 11722.

[83] Modified by Loi 81-941 of 17 October 1981 Article 6, *JORF* 20 October 1981; Loi 2005-
882 of 2 August 2005 Article 89 I, *JORF* 3 August 2005, entered into force 1 January
2007.

[84] Modified by Loi 81-941 of 17 October 1981 Article 7, *JORF* 20 October 1981; Loi 2005-882
of 2 August 2005 Article 89 I, *JORF* 3 August 2005, entered into force 1 January 2007.

only captures a fraction of those living without status in France and the number of *de facto* stateless is considerably larger.

The sample population included men and women of different ages and with different statuses including migrants who had overstayed, asylum seekers and refugees. The participants originated for the most part from Afghanistan and North Africa. In order to access stateless populations, the research team relied on assistance from the three main organisations which provide help to undocumented migrants: (1) *France Terre d'Asile*[85]; (2) GISTI (Groupe d'Information et de soutien des Immigrés)[86]; and (3) CIMADE (Comité Inter-Mouvements des Évacués).[87] Although many other organisations exist, it is often difficult to reach them because these are run underground by the *sans papiers* themselves.[88] However, the research team found that one introduction often led to another, not least because the sample population, especially in Toulon, was interwoven and this facilitated the research process.[89]

In Paris interviews were conducted with undocumented migrants and irregular migrants as well as overstayers. Interviews were conducted mostly in French, though on one occasion in English. All of the participants recorded that they had left Afghanistan for Iran before travelling on to Greece. They claimed they had been threatened by the police who

---

[85] *France Terre d'Asile* was created in 1971 to emphasise the exercise of the right to seek asylum and to survey the legal and administrative evolution of the rights of refugees and asylum seekers. *France Terre d'Asile* has twenty-six *entres d'accueil* in France. In addition to providing advice and information, it provides social and administrative assistance and emergency housing for asylum seekers (more than 2,000 places are available) through the CADA (Centres d'Accueil pour Demandeurs d'Asile).

[86] GISTI was created in 1972 with the help of CIMADE. This organisation also provides legal information to undocumented migrants.

[87] CIMADE aims to provide solidarity to those who are oppressed and exploited and to ensure their protection, without consideration of nationality, ethnic or racial origins, political or religious positions. Created in 1939, most of its activities today consist in providing free legal advice to undocumented migrants.

[88] Other organisations include: *Collectif des sans papiers de Marseille; Collectif Arabe des Sans papiers Demandeurs d'Asile Sans droits & Précaires; Collectif multitude; 9ème Collectif; Collectif de soutien des exilés du Xème arrondissement de Paris; Collectif des sans papiers du 11ème; Collectif des sans papiers du 19ème; Collectif des sans papiers kabyles; Sans papiers de l'église Saint-Bernard; Collectif sans papiers-immigration de la CGT; Collectif des étudiants sans-papiers (CESP); Réseau pour l'autonomie des femmes immigrées et réfugiées (RAJFIRE); Comité d'action inter-associatif 'Droits des femmes, droit au séjour – Contre la double violence'; Ouvriers sans-papiers de l'Association populaire d'entraide.*

[89] For example, it was noted that the *sans papiers* are organised like a network, by communities, and they always know when a family arrives. As one participant explained, the most recent family to have arrived prepares the meal for the next arrivals (SW).

arrested some of them and took their fingerprints. When the research team met them, they were living and sleeping in a park close to the Canal Saint-Martin. The research team also interviewed five undocumented North Africans from Algeria (Kabyle) in the area around the Gare du Nord and the metro station Barbès-Rochechouart. Some had left Algeria because they felt threatened there by the state authorities; for the others, their aim was to find work in France as in Algeria they could not find any. As one participant noted, 'here I am paid 70 or 80 € for a day, I can send some money to Algeria. In Algeria, there is no work at all, and I am scared for my children' (H42).

In Toulon, an Algerian friend introduced the lead researcher to people whose status was considered irregular in French law. The research team met five overstayers and undocumented migrants (all from Algeria). As in Paris, some of the Toulon-based participants had come because they felt threatened in their countries but most simply wanted to find work in France. Their statuses were also quite different from each other: one of them had just got married, though he is applying for French citizenship. One of them has the status of foreign student but is working illegally in a restaurant. Thanks to the organisation *France Terre d'Asile*, the lead researcher had the opportunity to interview three additional asylum seekers in Toulon because, according to the head of the organisation, all of them felt as if they were stateless even if their status is not understood as such by the French authorities. The researcher also interviewed a social worker based in *France Terre d'Asile* to learn more about the conditions facing undocumented people and to fill in some gaps that had been left as a result of the participants' refusal to answer some questions. It should be noted that given the heightened tension surrounding the 'lois Sarkozy' – namely, the restrictive laws and practices introduced by the Sarkozy presidency, and the activist nature of the new ministerial Department of Immigration and National Identity (*Départment de l'Immigration, de l'Intégration, de l'Identité nationale et du codéveloppement*), which has stepped up removals – many people interviewed were wary of the research project – in Paris the lead researcher was mistaken for a policeman – and as a result participants did not want to give any names and often refused to answer certain questions.

Health

The question of health did not come up directly, no doubt because the participants were generally young and in good health. However, it did come up in terms of the negative effect that living without status had on the participants' mental well-being. Several respondents expressed frustration with their status and the restrictions it placed on them.

Education

The theme of education did not come up during conversations. Most simply did not have children and, concerning their own ambitions, work rather than further study dominated discussions.

Employment and integration

The primacy of work was repeatedly stated as the participants' main source of concern since this right represents a key for integration, even for those who do not have any place to live. Contrary to the common thought in France, the undocumented migrants interviewed all claimed that they are not asking for the right for social care or any other help provided by the state but simply the rights to work and to be protected from detention. As one participant stated, 'What we only want is to work … Like I said, we only want to work, we don't care about sleeping outside, having nothing, the only thing we want is the right to work' (AP). Others, when asked which right was most important to them said, 'for me work is the most important right' (X25), a view which was supported by many. One man reported that he would like citizenship simply to stay in France and that in his mind citizenship was the key to integration since it gave one access to work:

> My current status doesn't allow me to work full time, though I don't have much resources and it's difficult for me to get access to decent housing. In my personal life I feel like a low status individual, because the police often arrest me to verify my documents and because, I am obliged sometimes to work as an illegal worker. (C29)

Being refused the right to work also negatively affected their private lives, as one commented:

> I can't do anything, can't go to the restaurant, can't buy a car or a scooter, sometimes one of my friends lend me his motorcycle, but it is dangerous, there is no insurance and if I have an accident it could be very serious. (S28)

If work was considered an essential route to integration, language also figured. The lack of language affected Afghans more than other groups who could access a European language. Many participants could not read or write and as a result suffered from a lack of information which prevented them from benefiting from their rights. Many explained that they felt like they were '*deuxième zone*' [second-class] individuals, and noted that their personal identity was sharply linked with the recognition – or rather non-recognition – of their legal status.

Renting and buying property

The issue of accommodation and decent housing came up largely in discussion about the economic situation of participants. All of them want to have decent housing, as one informant (SW) said, however, the lack of financial resources made this very difficult for a number of participants. One North African participant explained:

> Practically, I don't benefit [for] the same rights, for example it is very difficult to rent a flat. Owners are not confident in people like me, earning not much money and coming from Algeria, and having no guarantee for the rent. (C29)

Others described how they managed on the limited benefits they were able to receive. One man recounted how people managed on 3 € per day – the daily amount one can receive from the CADA (*Centres d'Accueil pour Demandeurs d'Asile* [centres for Asylum Seekers]) and which can be used towards the costs of housing, electricity and gas, in addition to food or clothing. He explained that given their poor economic situation, 'one or two illegal migrants had to resort to prostitution to survive' (SW).

Family reunion and related family matters

The issue of family reunion was particularly contentious, given the introduction of tough policies over the past five years. However, it should be noted that many participants had, themselves, been in France for many years and were single. Given the large presence of their co-nationals in France, there was the possibility of eventual integration. Overall, however, participants talked about the need to send money rather than to try to bring family across to France. In the case of those who wanted to establish a family in France, the lack of financial means always spelled difficulty in establishing and maintaining relationships. As one young man commented:

> I can't do anything, I have sometimes some girlfriends, but it can't last as I don't earn much money, and I can't live everybody's life, having an apartment, a car ... I can't found a family. (SW)

Access to courts and justice system and freedom from detention

Most of the participants interviewed claimed to be frightened by the police and treated all the justice sector institutions as if they belonged to one body: in their minds, the Ministry of the Interior, the Department of Immigration and Identity, and police were one and the same body. Every administrative procedure was considered to be a threat, characterised by the possibility of arrest or detention. As one participant admitted:

> The problem is that I can be arrested by the police and be obliged to go travel back. I can't work or even have a family life ... I must always be careful ... I am always frightened when I see the police. (F31)

One Afghan described his pervasive sense of insecurity: 'They took our fingerprints. We can't do anything because we can get arrested by the police. We don't have any permit to work' (AP). An Algerian added, 'I am always careful with the police as I don't want do be jailed, and then go back to Algeria. Each time an employer ask me [for] my documents I prefer leaving the job' (M27). Another offered his own analysis of the situation, claiming that 'since Nicolas Sarkozy became Minister and then President, I feel like the police is more looking at me ...' (C29). For this reason, a third participant offered the following blunt remark: 'I just have a view on Nicolas Sarkozy, I hate him' (A33).

In Toulon some commented that the 'bureau des étrangers' was 'very severe' (C29). One participant claimed that this state agency regularly flouted French law:

> The services of the prefecture of Toulon are well known for their [failure] to observe the proper observance of the legislation. We are used to excess of power from the civil servants dealing with migrants. The families are not well informed though they don't claim for their rights despite their right for the 'aide juridictionnelle', a free judicial assistance provided by a lawyer. The matter is that they can't benefit from a fair procedure to recognise their status and rights. (SW)

The theme of bureaucratic interference and indifference to the law was picked up by another participant who claimed that even French friends of his had difficulty obtaining identity cards. In his case, noting that he could not acquire the necessary documentation, he opted to work illegally in a restaurant owned by an uncle (A33).

11

Analysis: the practical and legal realities of statelessness in the European Union

BRAD K. BLITZ AND CAROLINE SAWYER

The issue of statelessness in Europe

The variety of situations in which stateless people in the four countries studied in this project find themselves all have a place in the context of the conceptual, legal and political frameworks presented in the opening chapters of this book. Those situations represent the modern face of 'rightlessness', as discussed by Hannah Arendt,[1] and there are both similarities and differences among the legal and social deprivations facing the various populations of undocumented and excluded people within our definition of the stateless. The starting point for this chapter is a review of those populations, and an attempt to highlight the ways in which their situation is distinct from that of citizens or those with a regularised status. We then consider how the status and experience of statelessness in Europe has developed since the time of Arendt's discussion, whether because of political or legal developments, in the context of the findings of the country studies.

The way in which people tend to become effectively stateless, at least in Western Europe, has changed since Arendt's time, and the country studies reflect the contrasting ways in which people may now find themselves establishing their lives in countries that do not accept them as citizens or members. Some of the populations considered in the research were migrants, whether lawful immigrants whose permission to remain had changed or expired, refused asylum seekers, or simply those who had arrived clandestinely and without permission. This was especially the case in France and the United Kingdom. However, in the two new EU member states there was more similarity to Arendt's populations, in that the people sampled had not migrated in search of work or safety, but had

---

[1] See chapter 2 in this volume.

found themselves without status in the country that had long, sometimes always, been their home. Many were descendants of former migrants – for example, in Estonia, where ethnic Russians and others had been drawn into the territory during the time of the Soviet Union, when Russia as the dominant member was experienced as an occupying power. After independence, Estonia then often regarded ethnic Russians connected with the military as foreigners rather than Estonians (and, indeed, they largely maintained their own culture and language). However, even this definition is not clear in all cases and, in the context of Slovenia, the populations sampled less often obviously meet the definition of being foreign nationals who had settled in the country.

The case of Slovenia is a particularly good example of how the definition of a citizen may itself be in question. Although they may have been associated with Croatia, Serbia, Bosnia and other now-independent states carved from the former Yugoslavia, on the basis of ethnicity or place of birth, until the erasure, the nationality status of the participants in Slovenian study was not an issue either on a day-to-day basis or in more formal relations with the state. In contrast to Estonia, where nationality *per se* only became relevant in the context of the political restructuring post-1991 and there was a loss of citizenship as such, in Slovenia similar historical and political developments led to a reordering not of citizenships but of resident populations. The unifying Yugoslav citizenship disappeared, putting emphasis on the formal citizenship of what became the independent states. What the Erased lost was their non-citizen resident status in Slovenia as their country of residence. This led to their loss of the means of living their daily lives, and their physical departure was supposed to follow. A lesser formal lack of status in Slovenia therefore led to much greater practical consequences for the individuals involved. The 'Erased' of Slovenia lost the incidents of citizenship to a much greater extent than the *de jure* stateless ethnic Russian population of Estonia. Hence, citizenship *per se* cannot be the dominant concept in our analysis. Rather, the research suggests that it is the experiences of people who are deprived of the rights of citizens which better characterise situations of statelessness. This position links, too, to the assertions of scholars such as Arendt and Weis[2] that *de facto* and *de jure* statelessness should be dealt with together, as part of the same phenomenon.

---

[2] P. Weis, *Nationality and Statelessness in International Law* (Alphen aan den Rijn: Sitjhoff & Noordhoff, 1979); 'The Convention Relating to the Status of Stateless Persons', *International & Comparative Law Quarterly*, 10 (1961), 255.

The core of this research project was therefore an investigation of the rights enjoyed by *de jure* and *de facto* stateless people, and of those they most clearly lack. Such rights are set out variously in international and European legislation as well as at the domestic level in the different jurisdictions. The effectiveness as well as the content of the different kinds of legislation varies; international treaties tend to be less immediately useful to the individual, but their existence contributes to the general discourse on human rights. European rules, both EU Treaty provisions and human rights elaborated in Council of Europe conventions, may be more useful; they certainly indicate the regime which ought to unify the positions of the stateless populations of Europe. Domestic regimes, both formally and in practice, vary widely, however, and this study considers the scope of those variations to present and investigate the scope of experiences of statelessness in Europe today. What it suggests most obviously is the inadequacy of law – both in the sense that the law as it exists often does not address the issues of basic everyday human rights or does not make those rights enforceable, and in the more general sense that, as a consequence, the relevance of the discourse of law is itself brought into question. Often, however, the issue is the mismatch between what laws have been framed to do and popular belief.

The framework presented in this chapter considers three sets or bundles of rights consisting of (1) basic rights, (2) social rights, and (3) political rights. Much of the research concentrated on basic rights – above all, the rights to work, housing, education and family reunion, because these directly touch the lives of citizens, migrants and those with irregular or no status, across the European Union. Social rights were also considered – social participation through business and communal activities are critical for the social integration of anyone, irrespective of their immigration or nationality status. Indeed, it is precisely such activities which may guard against the ills of social exclusion and poverty, whence their relevance to the broader European project. The notion of political rights introduces a degree of controversy, not least because voting and holding office are seen as the foremost indicators of membership in the state. However, even informal rights to participation have a place in discussions regarding contemporary forms of exclusion on the basis of nationality and immigration status. As noted in chapters 2 and 3, participation is seen as an increasingly recognised means of realising social rights and empowering people, a point Krause raises particularly in her brief discussion of the *sans papiers* in France in chapter 2. Thus, the focus on the three bundles of rights frames the discussion about the ways in which stateless people live and also serves to illustrate how their lives differ from those of full citizens. It also enables a comparison of some of the mechanisms by which policies are enforced: it is striking that the implementation of rules and policies which destroy lives often comes about through minor administrative or bureaucratic processes whose banality belies their catastrophic effects.

For the purposes of comparative research, there are also several relevant points to be drawn from the social and political theories discussed by Krause and Gibney in chapters 2 and 3. Arendt first emphasised how the relationship between the individual and the state is both a mediating institution which determines access to rights and also a potential route for the violation of human rights. The practicalities of that relationship remain the central focus for investigation, whatever the precise terms of its formalities. The rights to protection and participation are essential characteristics of citizenship and thus the deprivation of these rights puts one effectively outside the state, whether one has another (ineffective) nationality or no nationality at all. As Krause and Gibney note, the deprivations may take the form of being denied the right to a home, to government protection, to participation in political life and to a place in the world from where one can seek redress for wrongs. Such concrete deprivations can best be illustrated by reviewing the context in which stateless people live and the rights which they enjoy, or lack.

What statelessness means

Statelessness appears differently in each jurisdiction, both as a legal construct and as it is experienced by those who are without an effective nationality. In the United Kingdom, following changes to a less inclusive formal citizenship system in the early 1980s, there has for almost two decades now been a strong and deliberate policy of increasing social exclusion for the undocumented. The legal status of most of those who are undocumented or irregular in the United Kingdom is not *de jure* but *de facto* stateless. Some are from areas with strong community and other links to the United Kingdom stemming from the former colonial era, such as those from the Indian subcontinent; most in any event go to live within established communities. They may arrive as refugees in the sense that they are leaving untenable conditions of life, even if they are not recognised or recognisable as refugees within the meaning of the 1951 Convention. While the presence in the United Kingdom of an existing established community from their country of origin is often a strong draw, this rarely leaves them well placed to manage their lives without any place in the wider society. Such communities are rooted, for example, in Somalia or Afghanistan, where the coherence of state organisation has crumbled and expectations of national protection are necessarily low. People leave for the United Kingdom more as a result of 'push' factors than 'pull' factors, and arrive in communities that lack financial and economic power. While physical, often forced, removal of unwanted migrants does happen, many undocumented people are not removed but live in an atmosphere of insecurity and fear that they may be. Normal public services such as healthcare are sometimes provided, but are unreliable. For example, accommodation is rarely satisfactory, even if often because such people are without funds rather than because of a lack of formal status. However, social provision can be patchy for everyone in the United Kingdom. Many undocumented people are obliged to live on charity in the longer term, rather than hoping to be able to claim benefits or work. Thus, even if their stay turns out to be long term or even permanent, they are unable to live a reasonable life for protracted periods, and may feel hopeless. The lack of access to education and training for a population mostly of young men means that as well as having insufficient resources to enjoy their present, they also lack the ability to plan and work towards a settled and productive future. There is every indication that UK government legislative policy will continue to build exclusion into all public service systems, and that any identity card system (if one is ever to be made to work) would be a strong tool to that end. While formal citizenship is still often obtainable on a generous basis, the general structure of the system is hardening. Of greater significance to the present study, however, is the more rapidly – if still patchily – hardening system of social exclusion, so that those who are not citizens or desired immigrants can no longer meld into the social fabric as before.

In France, the stateless and undocumented population is rooted largely in countries with which cultural or personal ties are retained. Sometimes the *de facto* stateless may be French-born or would otherwise consider themselves to be French. The former status of Algeria as an internal French department lends credence to the idea that those rooted in North Africa may consider themselves to be as French as those who have been based in the mainland of France for generations, and legal policy on the French citizenship of those of Algerian origin also reflects that ambiguity. For all the publicity of recent years about Sarkozy's harder-line policies in particular, the treatment of the French authorities of the stateless population is generally less harsh than that in the United Kingdom, though there are indications that formal applications for permits or naturalisation are more difficult to obtain in the big cities than in less urban areas. Part of the reason for this is the organised nature of the resistance to exclusion, both among the undocumented, or *sans papiers*, themselves and among the general public. This itself may stem from the clarity of the changes, which in turn appears to be rooted in a historical clarity of status which contrasts with the United Kingdom. Being without state protection in France manifests itself mostly as fear of contact with police and removal, rather than practical difficulty in making a life. Such difficulty also exists, and as in the United Kingdom it is unclear how much this is a result of the statelessness and how much a result of being economically disadvantaged. Poverty and lack of opportunity can also be found among the French. Nevertheless, it is mitigated for the stateless in France, by comparison with the United Kingdom, by a much greater sense of empowerment and a right to object to perceived injustice. Media attention in France has been much less hostile than in the United Kingdom and has focused as much on debates about the nature of French republicanism as on perceived economic threat, as in the United Kingdom. The debate in France has had a strong religious and cultural emphasis, since most of the undocumented or unwanted are Muslims whose lifestyle may look inconsistent with the French policy of *laïcité* (albeit often taking a surprisingly Catholic form). The issue addressed here is therefore entangled with an existing domestic issue about established communities whose formal citizenship is not in question. While in this study the cohort of interviewees in France was older and more established than that in the United Kingdom, this in turn is a symptom of the history of legislative policy. The history of a substantial disenfranchised North African population in France began earlier than the substantial, and more varied, population that makes up the classic stateless cohort in the United Kingdom. The coherence and rootedness of the *sans papier* population in France may also explain why it has much greater support from organised bodies and third-sector organisations such as *Terre d'Asile*. The stateless population of France has better access to employment than in the United Kingdom. Even if the employment is not legal, there is relatively little obvious exploitation compared to what happens in, say, Slovenia (which is a better comparison to the French cohort in terms of age and employability).

The situation in Slovenia is, however, historically very different from that in France and the United Kingdom. The legal structure of statelessness is heavily linked to the transition from being a state within Yugoslavia to being an independent and self-determining post-Soviet-era country. It is closest to the phenomenon of statelessness discussed by Arendt, in that those involved experienced a thoroughgoing removal of status and practical rights from those who previously had them (rather than not granting citizenship rights at all, as in the United Kingdom and France). There was also a deliberate state structure to the implementation of the policy, and both ministerial and lower-level state policies including the destruction of documents. As with the ethnic re-ordering of the Holocaust as discussed by Arendt, there was an attempt to abandon or wipe out a previously acknowledged and accepted part of the existing population (albeit short of killing them), instigated and carried out by the state. The 'Erased' were generally those who were nationals of another Yugoslav constituent state who had permanent residence status in Slovenia where they had led settled lives. What was removed was not their citizenship but their residence status and acquired rights. In theory, or in formal terms, they were not *de jure* stateless. In the sense that they were no longer able to live full lives or exercise citizenship rights in the country in which they had made their lives they were, however, experiencing a strong form of *de facto* statelessness, in that rights previously held – notably, property rights – were actively withdrawn. What links the phenomenon more strongly to that observed by Arendt is the prevalence of Roma (Gypsy) people in the population of the Erased. Even if this may be explained by the existence of a substantial Roma population in that geographical area it would surely have uncomfortable resonances even without the concomitant resurgence of anti-Roma activity and heightened nationalism across Europe in the wake of the fall of the Berlin Wall and the re-ordering of Eastern Europe afterwards.

Estonia has at least a superficial similarity with Slovenia as a small former component state that has seceded from a larger and more powerful communist-era agglomeration. Where Slovenia, however, sought its own identity in breaking away from the rest of Yugoslavia (including dealing with an earlier past as a constituent state of the Austro-Hungarian empire, and thus richer and more westward-looking culturally than most of the Yugoslav population), Estonia was formerly an internal part of the Soviet Union whose dominant power, Russia, had implemented an ethnic minority community within the state of Estonia itself. Where Slovenia in effect took the opportunity to exclude a weak minority population on independence in 1991, a clear political imperative led to the exclusion from Estonian citizenship of those whose residence in Estonia was connected to the former dominating power of the Soviet military. This meant families as a whole, but they were not, however, physically excluded.

A substantial *de jure* stateless population, often not of migrants but of those who were Estonian-born, was thus created. Perhaps, had they not been connected with a major regional power, their position might have been as precarious as that of the Roma of Slovenia. However, the apparently extreme condition of *de jure* statelessness was mitigated by practice. This study shows in particular how the according of the incidents of citizenship is more important in daily life than formal citizenship itself. In Estonia, as in the other Baltic states of Latvia and to a much lesser extent in Lithuania, an established form of statelessness has developed which itself has a form of documentation and carries practical rights which allow the *de jure* stateless to make a life in a way that the merely *de facto* stateless elsewhere cannot. It is notable, if ironic, that among the countries considered in this study, Estonia was the only one not to have ratified the UN Conventions on statelessness, but also the only country with a substantial population to whom they might relate. The other countries had ratified the Conventions, but had populations that were *de facto* rather than *de jure* stateless and who therefore fell outside the Conventions. In Estonia, apparently without the protection of citizenship status, the stateless population was formally in the worst situation so far as formal status was concerned, but with the most solidly established system of documentation and rights notwithstanding that lack of status. Despite a high level of formal disadvantage, the actual day-to-day formal difficulties of statelessness in Estonia are relatively minimal.

The legal regimes of statelessness differ considerably across the countries studied, and across Europe itself. Statelessness is a different formal phenomenon in different jurisdictions. It is described differently and its immediate roots and causes are often different. But its common factor is that it hurts above all as a lack of basic state protection and a lack of defence from the arbitrary or unjust wielding of state power. The visible face of it is an inability to make a life physically, by working or obtaining benefits to subsist and establish a place in society. If the four countries studied here were ranked according to the severity of the impact of statelessness, it would not be formal citizenship or nationality rights that mattered, but legal and social rights. In terms of social acceptance or exclusion at the practical level, broadly speaking, Estonia is the most accepting (despite being the only country with a substantial *de jure* stateless population); followed by France, where nationality legislation is heavily restrictive for those with a non-mainland-French heritage but there is a strong sense of Republican justice and human rights, and there have been protests and activism among the general citizenry in support of the *sans papiers*. Then comes the the United Kingdom, where acceptance and belonging by residence and choice are giving way to a new system of entitlement, yet to be fully established; with Slovenia, and her record of the erasure of unwanted residents, at the bottom.

The resonance with Arendt's characterisation of 'the right to have rights' is clear. Without a claim to citizenship and belonging, people can only hope for support and protection. Whether they get it depends on the prevailing mood of the country, and their position is fragile. To an extent, everyone's position is fragile: the law is only a game that everyone plays, and some laws are easier to ignore, or to change, than others. Thus in the United Kingdom the legal system previously recognised all those present and making a life as belonging for the purposes of practical, day-to-day support, but it has gradually changed to one more focused on the exclusion and removal of those who belong under a different system. These changes began with the exclusion of most British nationals born overseas, moving through the exclusion of some people born in the United Kingdom to the exclusion of many who have established lives there. The loss of rights has been gradual but rapid, and though much vaunted in the media its results are often not explicit or expected. In France, an established system of nationality and citizenship has seen clear and variable moves to deal with the end of colonial and quasi-colonial rule. The concept of a laïque state has been faced with a Muslim community whose practices rub up against those of the largely Catholic dominant community. A system of rights rooted in universalism but fed through a strongly felt ideal of the national, cultural state has thus thrown up a number of contradictions, especially in the modern era of multiculturalism. In Eastern Europe, the breakdown of the old order has led to a much clearer, more blatant withdrawal of rights from certain cultural, national, or ethnic groups. In Estonia the exclusion has been formal, from the national group which has the right to have rights, but the rights themselves – the practical rights such as the right to work – are accorded nevertheless. In Slovenia, the exclusion has been more physical and practical. The essence of the 'erasure' was from practical, not formal, citizenship. Even without a loss of citizenship it could lead to poverty or even physical exclusion, as where people left the country to visit friends and found themselves unable to return home. The situation of the stateless, whether *de jure* or *de facto*, in all four countries is linked by the sense for the individuals involved of uncertainty in the face of potentially arbitrary state power. There is a sense and a logic in this, since they have few formal and enforceable legal rights. Any rights they do claim may be negated by their threatened or actual expulsion from the country itself, and that threat may act as a deterrent to claiming those rights, for fear of exciting that expulsion. What connects the current situation in all four countries, and ought to make all the difference, is the development since Arendt's time of international and regional law and the norms they both embody and may enforce. The rights Arendt talked of people having the right to – those that make everyday life feasible – ought not now to depend as before on the right of nationality and citizenship. The fundamental everyday rights are believed to be fundamental universal legal human rights, available to all.

The flaws in the universalist ideal, and especially the strong and explicit reality of those flaws, are shown up in this study. Rights in international law may lack enforceability, as often with the apparent rights under the International Covenants of the 1960s, reflecting principally a more general policy or aim at the governmental level, as discussed in chapter 4, or perhaps a desire to attain or maintain a certain place in the international community. The establishment of such international rights does, however, as discussed in chapter 5, have a normative effect. They contribute to a broader sense of global responsibility of states towards individuals. Regional rights under European laws, which bind all the countries in this study, are much more enforceable in the legal sense, and so look much more like what lawyers regard as proper rights. These systems often grant wide rights, including to non-Europeans, and those rights are often enforceable by the individual. But, equally, those rights have serious limitations. Some of those limitations are internal and endemic to the regime in question. EU rights must be read within the context of the policies and treaties that have given rise to the concept of 'Fortress Europe', where those who are citizens of the Union (or, for the purposes of certain Agreements, of certain neighbouring countries), or family members of citizens or established workers, have relatively clear rights which are enforceable and generally respected. Other people, however, are subject to expulsion regimes that become ever more efficient through co-operation among EU states. The ECHR, with a longer and clearer record of protection of individual human rights, has proved to be very limited in its scope despite its enforceability where it does apply. The rights it protects are the negative rights of non-interference by the state rather than positive rights such as the right to shelter or subsistence, and it will prevent expulsion of a non-citizen – the archetype of a person with an Arendtian lack of the right to have rights – only in the most extreme circumstances. Even for those who remain, few Articles of the Convention are absolute. Many rights may be restricted in the name of public order, which can include the maintenance of a strong immigration (or anti-immigration) policy, and the person demanding rights may simply be physically excluded or expelled. Ironically, a person seeking to vindicate human rights within the European Union may invite expulsion merely by raising such rights and drawing attention to themselves. The apotheosis of the fragility of citizenship rights under the ECHR is, however, surely that even the expulsion of citizens is countenanced by it. The prohibition on the expulsion of a country's own nationals is not contained in the body of the Convention itself, but only in Optional Protocol No. 4.

Perhaps the most fundamental and unresolvable single concrete flaw in the establishment and practice of universal human rights – and one which is fundamental to international law and in sharp contrast to the evolution of liberal political theory – is the largely unquestioned ability of states to define their own nationals, on whatever basis they choose, including the freedom to change the rules and exclude groups who previously belonged. Similarly, states may change their immigration and residence policies. This is not new, but is fundamental to the idea of state sovereignty that underlies the international law system. The representation of any restriction on that freedom as imperilling public order links in an unfortunate way with the recurrent representation of foreigners as dangerous; some are, as are some nationals, but most are no more dangerous than the citizen population, except insofar as their status as foreigners may cause some to take fright. This concrete flaw is significant because it shapes the systems within which human rights operate and allows some people to fall outside these systems altogether. It is also significant because it allows people to be deprived of rights they previously had. It is noticeable in the cases of Estonia, and especially Slovenia, because there has been a fundamental change in the constitutional and legal regime that has carried with it a clear opportunity to re-draw or re-assert the human boundaries of the nation. The lack of restriction on such changes, combined with the lack of restraint on the exclusion and expulsion of non-nationals, means that there is no formal structural brake on the creation of new stateless populations and no prescribed sanction.

The ECtHR has put some restrictions on the scope of this problem. Cases on the rights of long-standing non-national residents have considered the human impact of such expulsions. It may be the perceived rights of other members of the non-national's family that make the difference, and that the impact of an expulsion on not only the person expelled but their family means that the expulsion itself is disproportionate even to the strong perceived right of states to regulate their own populations.

Nevertheless, even basic human rights remain far from universal, despite the widespread belief that long after the foundation of the ECHR there is a basic, necessary human rights regime in Europe. There is often a lack of popular agreement as to what the scope of reference of the phrase 'human rights' is believed to be, or which of the rights believed to be involved may be enforceable. Some people may relate the broad concept of 'human rights' to the dispossessed as an example of what they lack despite their lives based in Europe, while others may refer to it as the reason for their continued presence in a European country where they are not formally permitted to live. Rights that are believed to be universal and basic may not apply to everyone physically in Europe, notwithstanding the requirement in Article 1 of the ECHR to apply Convention rights to everyone within the jurisdiction of states parties, or they may apply but only for so long as they remain physically within Europe, with little prohibition on their expulsion, sometimes even if they are a country's own nationals. The right to have rights still largely depends on citizenship. Even citizenship itself is fragile, and it may not be enough.

Rightlessness today

The central concerns of Europe's stateless populations are economic, social and political. They also include psycho-social problems such as identity issues associated with the loss of a sense of home, protracted exile, displacement and insecurity broadly understood. In this setting, the emphasis is quite distinct from the general losses which Arendt describes and which are not tailored to elaborated rights, which are far more numerous than in her day.

The loss of home encompasses a range of ideas from the difficulties of renting, buying and leasing property to expulsion from a particular house or from a homeland. For the populations in this study, finding somewhere to live was generally an essentially economic and practical challenge. The research also illustrated an ideational dimension in terms of the construction and preservation of 'home'. In both Slovenia and Estonia, the idea of home is associated with nostalgia during the Socialist experiments that were the former Yugoslavia and USSR. Hence, 'home' has a different and broader meaning, not least because for stateless populations in such countries, they have remained in their physical homes (the Erased who were persuaded to leave Slovenia did not form part of the sample). Unlike the populations sampled in France and the United Kingdom, *de facto* stateless people in Estonia and the Erased of Slovenia have often never migrated.

Renting and buying property is problematic for all the populations sampled, though for different reasons. In Slovenia, the cancellation of status resulted in the loss of rights to social housing. It also meant the loss of jobs and hence put a great strain on people's abilities to obtain private accommodation. In practice, though many Erased persons who were married to Slovenes continued to enjoy access to accommodation, the situation was however much bleaker for those Erased who were divorced and for the former officers of the Yugoslav People's Army (JNA) among the Erased who were excluded from the right to social housing. In Estonia, non-citizens are required to obtain special permission to buy immovable property on islands (except for the four biggest islands) and in territorial units close to the state border with Russia. In practice, this means that they are unable to buy property in these regions.

In France, the problem of housing was not elaborated in great detail, though the lack of documentation and general mistrust of foreigners restricted the options available to the population sampled. Most participants appeared to resolve the housing challenges by drawing upon the strong ethnic/national links among the *sans papiers* communities. By contrast, the populations sampled in the United Kingdom had less access to ethnic community structures and the stateless populations were highly restricted in their opportunities for housing. In general there is no access to social housing and the costs of private housing are prohibitive. Participants explained that they were only able to get around these restrictions because either they had family members under eighteen, and as a result the family, including the interviewees, was entitled to state housing, or, as in the case of one Middle Eastern man, the only option was being housed by a charitable organisation.

The rights to marry and found a family differed among the four states sampled. These rights are compromised not only by state regulation but also by the generally poor economic situations of *de facto* stateless people. Again, the situation in Estonia was by far the best and non-citizens enjoyed the same degree of entitlements as nationals with respect to marriage and family associated rights. In the United Kingdom, though there are severe laws in place which curtail family reunion, most of the participants interviewed were single and this did not apply to them. However, one participant from Iran explained in great detail about how he was denied access to his children, how they had been taken from him and put into foster homes and how his family structure had been broken down. His account and claims of being deliberately distanced from his two children suggest that stateless people in the United Kingdom may not enjoy the full extent of their rights to family, as recorded under international and European law. The challenges to marry and found a family were most acute in Slovenia where the lack of documentation meant that some participants could not even assert their identities and claims to parenthood. Indeed, this was one area in which the loss of status impacted on the sense of identity and exacerbated their exclusion from mainstream society. The one clear outlier in our study in the case of the right to respect for private and family life, however, and one which relates most closely to the people described by Arendt, is the situation of the Erased. Their formal identities were sometimes destroyed to the extent that they were in some cases formally denied the opportunity to marry or have their names appear on birth certificates.

The right to work was fundamental to the situation of all the stateless populations, and often the most problematic. The right to employment in the public sector, more specifically the government sector, was generally not recognised in the four case studies, all of which included nationality-based criteria for access to such jobs. Estonia was one of the clear exceptions where stateless non-citizens still enjoyed a wide range of social rights, effectively almost comparable to Estonian nationals. The Erased of Slovenia reported loss of livelihood during the erasure. In France, the repeated demands for the right to work among the *sans papiers* interviewed indicate that regular work still remains highly problematic and even though they may find work in the informal economy, it is not sufficient. In contrast to France, the research in the United Kingdom recorded state intolerance of any economic engagement by stateless people. In this context, the United Kingdom appears among the more restrictive of states. The participants interviewed reported that they relied on charity, remaining idle and suffering psychological distress as a result of being prohibited from working and earning money. Whereas the *sans papiers* in France were vocal and agitated to defend their claims to work, the stateless populations in the United Kingdom were de-motivated and described feeling powerless. For the majority of stateless young people in the United Kingdom, their access to training and education now ends at eighteen.

The right to establishment was also compromised in Slovenia, France and the United Kingdom. In Slovenia, as well as often losing their jobs, the Erased were excluded from setting up in business for themselves, the roots of their problem being their lack of documentation and the difficulty of re-establishing themselves once their official documents had been destroyed. The loss of status also left the Erased vulnerable to exploitation and weakened their position in the informal economy. Many participants also noted that they had not been able to recover pension rights and monies lost during the period of the erasure. In France, there was little evidence regarding self-employment, again because it presupposed documentation. The findings were mixed: there were many suggestions that the *sans papiers* benefited from clandestinely run businesses, which were tolerated, though they were excluded from the formal economy for lack of documentation. A lack of status and documentation was increasingly a problem for those in the United Kingdom, who increasingly found obstacles in the way of engaging with economic and business life. As so often, however, things were better in this respect in Estonia. The Estonian stateless population enjoys the right to establish businesses and may participate in economic life, with few exceptions.

The loss of government protection is a defining characteristic of statelessness today. As with Arendt, the denial of protection is revealed in extreme situations, and above all the possibilities of detention and removal which perpetuate feelings of insecurity. As recorded by Ruth Rubio-Marin,[3] the practical obstacles to the enjoyment of rights for unlawful residents often include the dangers of exploitation and potential intervention from the state, namely detention and removal. Such fears are recorded in the case studies on France, Slovenia and the United Kingdom where the state repression is at first identified with police patrols, resonating with the Arendtian account. Participants described feelings of insecurity which they claimed was linked to their status as non-citizens. In Slovenia, the effects of the erasure had touched on almost every aspect of their lives, turning upside down the reality they had known. Interviewees spoke of feeling unsafe, not knowing what they could achieve or what was accessible to them, and also in the knowing that some Erased persons had been removed from Slovenia and were now unable to return. Similarly, participants in the United Kingdom and to a lesser extent France expressed feelings of insecurity. In the United Kingdom, this was in part linked to a loss of identity and the general context of perceived arbitrariness, as described in chapter 7. In France, the lack of documentation and the apparent permissiveness of the state in some situations had forced participants to seek ways of getting around the law, though they felt insecure when they came into contact with any law-enforcement bodies or officials. In Estonia, participants did not voice such concerns, though the deterioration in relations between the two main ethnic groups had created some cause for concern.

---

[3] R. Rubio-Marin, *Immigration as a Democratic Challenge: Citizenship and Inclusion in Germany and the United States* (Cambridge: Cambridge University Press, 2000), 81.

Related to participants' perceptions of insecurity was a widespread fear of detention and removal. Interviewees in France, Slovenia and the United Kingdom all discussed such fears quite openly, while Estonia was again an outlier in our study. The fear of removal was especially great in Slovenia since some Erased had been removed to Bosnia. The accounts of the Erased provided by Jelka Zorn in chapter 8 also record how people had been removed surreptitiously, and how some of the children of the Erased were placed by police on buses to Bosnia when they turned eighteen. In both France and the United Kingdom participants recorded their fears, which were in part based on knowing people in similar situations who had been removed, and also an awareness of the wider policy context – especially in France, where interviewees commented on the actions and declarations of President Sarkozy and his ministers. In the United Kingdom, participants expressed their fears of dawn raids and about being stopped in the street by police, often when they were simply going about their business. Again, such problems were not reported in Estonia where people were able to move quite freely across the state and between Estonia and Russia.

The provision of universal healthcare was not a theme taken up by Arendt, whose writings pre-date the establishment of welfare state systems. Nonetheless it is important to consider it in terms of her claims of total state domination. While one of the main points of distinction between EU nationals and those entitled to remain in the European Union and non-EU nationals is access to medical and health-related services, the above findings suggest greater differentiation than would be expected from Arendt's account: in France, Slovenia and Estonia stateless individuals enjoy considerable access to health services; in the United Kingdom, while this remains a highly contested subject, there is evidence to suggest that doctors will still often treat such people.

The topic of health was most relevant in the context of mental well-being: in several settings, the loss of status had generated profound psychological distress and contributed to depression and other mental illness. This was most acute in Slovenia, where the effects of the erasure were total, and in the United Kingdom where participants spoke of a situation of imposed idleness, in the absence of opportunities to work, which was often compounded by traumatic experiences of exile for several of the refused asylum seekers interviewed. In terms of physical well-being, participants in Slovenia were older, in generally worse health than in other regions sampled, and with fewer opportunities for treatment. Unlike the *sans papiers* in France, the Erased did not have access to the usual insurance system. Many had long-standing illnesses or mental health conditions that apparently remained largely untreated. In the United Kingdom and France interviewees were primarily young and healthy. Participants in the United Kingdom said that when they required medical assistance, doctors had treated them well, therefore one may surmise that attempts to restrict access to healthcare are not [yet] working. Again, Estonia stands out from the other countries sampled since universal health coverage is available to all legal residents, which the interviewees were. Something else noteworthy, although it was not universal, was the professionalism of doctors, who would often treat the sick regardless of their immigration status. Where the withdrawal of social provision forms part of a programme to encourage the unwanted to leave, such forms of professionalism can also represent a strong political statement.

Education as a basic right did not feature prominently in the interviews, except mostly in the case of Estonia where stateless ethnic Russians were restricted to separate schools and had little opportunity for higher education given the lack of Russian-language institutions. The parallel educational system is, however, shrinking and non-Estonians are therefore constrained by the lack of choice: the dilemma facing them is thus greater integration in Estonia, migration to Russia, or possibly seeking out educational opportunities elsewhere in the European Union. As reported by Raivo Vetik in chapter 9, the results of the Integration Monitoring Project currently suggest that there is less interest in integration by means of naturalisation and therefore one may infer that current educational infrastructure may be contributing to the divide between stateless ethnic Russians and the citizen ethnic Estonian majority. In the other countries, however, the theme of education did not feature extensively in the interviews; very few had school-age children. The issue of access to training and to higher education was discussed in greater detail with respect to the population in the United Kingdom. Some interviewees had started studies before the Asylum and Immigration (Treatment of Claimants, etc.) Act 2004 came into effect and were therefore able to continue their studies after the age of eighteen, in contrast to those on vocational training courses, including apprenticeships. In the field of education, the propensity of teachers – like the doctors mentioned above – to use their professional skills in aid of everyone, regardless of immigration status, could present a strong professional stance against government policies designed to withdraw all the advantages of civilisation from unwanted non-citizens. The situation with education is, however, more complex than with health; education is not as sporadic as health treatment, and the enrolment of a pupil or student despite their lack of status, as much as their non-enrolment for the same reason, is a strong and continuing statement that that status is not regarded as conclusive. It is more difficult for governments to resist the education of children; contravention of rights under the United Nations Declaration of the Rights of the Child is more controversial than withdrawing rights from adults, and can be politically problematic. Even those who advocate harsh treatment for unwanted adult non-citizens often baulk at withdrawing the means of everyday life from children, as with the resistance in the United Kingdom to the full implementation of the Asylum and Immigration (Treatment of Claimants, etc.) Act 2004, which could have meant some families with children being without shelter or food.

Although some participants expressed mistrust for state institutions and lumped the police, courts and Home Office or relevant ministries together, most still called upon the services of lawyers and other professionals to make their case before the courts. Access to courts and the justice system, however, varied from one state to another. The lack of access to justice was most profound in Slovenia where the state had been responsible for destroying documents and exerted its hegemony over every aspect of the lives of the Erased. For the Erased the burden of proof was especially high and it took more than a decade before some of them were able to assert their claims and demand that they recover their rights when the state had destroyed their documents. In Estonia, where participants enjoyed far fewer problems, there was no access to free legal aid. In the United Kingdom, where there is little free legal aid, participants spoke about how they were assisted by NGOs and support agencies, though they complained that the rate of response from governmental bodies, including the Home Office, was painfully slow. In France, however, participants claimed that there was fairly generous provision of legal assistance, certainly in the context of asylum claims. However, legal aid did not feature prominently in discussions with the *sans papiers* in France because their primary concern was regularisation of status – they had already managed to establish their presence in France, however unofficially, and had identified ways of working the system to survive.

With the exception of Estonia, where *de jure* stateless people were able to vote in both local and European elections, the participants were generally unable to vote. They did, however, express their political concerns and interest through activism and by drawing in NGOs as well as ordinary nationals into their struggles. As recorded in chapter 5, participants especially in France, but to a certain extent in both Slovenia and the United

Kingdom, were able to raise the problem of being stateless, undocumented and marginal as a rallying point.

Arendt's notion of the loss of a place in this world remains relevant to this study, not least because the populations treated in this research remain in Europe and many express hopes of vindicating their rights under European instruments or by means of political pressure and social action, as discussed in chapter 5. As stated above, one of the main points of distinction between the populations sampled in this study and the people of concern to Arendt is the degree to which they enjoy greater agency and access to courts and justice institutions. While some stateless groups have enjoyed voting rights, for example in European Parliament elections, the most relevant political rights addressed in this study relate to the right to organise, assemble and assert one's claims to basic or social rights, often through communal or other organisations. In the context of today's Europe, such rights may appear to be guaranteed and the case studies in this book record considerable activism and even appeals through the judicial process to assert rights. Stateless groups, whether the Erased in Slovenia or the *sans papiers* in France, have engaged NGOs and lawyers to seek clarification and enforcement of their rights under the ECHR, as well as through domestic legal routes. Indeed, the research teams in each of the four jurisdictions found that some stateless people had had access to legal advice and had been able to take cases to local courts. This finding suggests that the stateless people sampled for the purposes of this research project may indeed enjoy 'voice' and can assert a claim to a place in the world, unlike those in Arendt's account. It is important to note, however, that they still face considerable risks. A remaining dilemma is the degree to which stateless people are able to use the legal system to claim rights, while avoiding the 'rights trap' – namely, that in order to claim rights and state protections, unlawful migrants must raise their profile, bringing themselves to the attention of state authorities. So, while 'pariah groups' have in some cases become prominent political actors, as noted by Monika Krause and Jelka Zorn in chapters 2 and 8, they may have done so at great personal risk. The findings in this study raise a further question about what enhances minority groups' powers, including the ability to resist the withdrawal of basic human rights. It appears from the experiences in France and Slovenia that attitudes among the wider public are particularly important. One could ask, for example, how important a tradition of ready public protest in France, as against a lack of such a tradition in Slovenia, has played a part in the respective conditions of the *sans papiers* and the Erased.

Accounting for difference: key factors
and tentative explanations

There are many reasons why the experiences of stateless people differ from one country to the next. Structural explanations which take into consideration political histories still provide some of the most compelling reasons for the variation in experience and access to rights as described above. Both France and the United Kingdom are still coming to terms with post-colonial identities and being historically countries of immigration. The introduction of so much legislation over the past fifteen years, in an attempt to regulate the ways in which immigrants may access services, integrate according to accepted norms and apply for the rights to settle, remain, or be removed, suggests that the administrations of both France and the United Kingdom are struggling to assert their legitimacy over these policy areas. In France 'outsiders' such as North Africans and Muslim Arabs are perceived to challenge the republican model, which is both culturally specific and secular, while in the United Kingdom they are perceived as challenging the sense of fair entitlement and membership. Indeed, the increasingly vocal and xenophobic debates over the rights of new migrants, whether in the context of religious clothing or of language acquisition, further expose some of the fundamental problems at the heart of the French state and the United Kingdom.

In Slovenia and Estonia, the challenges of national unification, citizenship and the treatment of foreigners is more closely defined as a result of the introduction of new laws on citizenship, asylum and the creation of new constitutions over the past two decades. As mentioned above, the problems of statelessness do not relate to recent migrations but rather the political restructuring that took place after the fall of the Soviet Union and break-up of Yugoslavia. Yet, particular historical events still serve as markers which have determined the way in which nationality policies are organised. In the case of Estonia, the primary marker is the period before Estonia was occupied by the Soviet Union and drawn into that sphere. In the case of Slovenia, the defining point remains the date of secession from the SFRY and the initial opportunities for membership in the new state.

In addition to the structural explanations offered above, we have suggested four factors that may influence the degree to which stateless people may access rights in contemporary Europe.

Geo-politics

The relationship between the EU member state and the countries of origin, or generally rather countries where there is a perceived ethnic attachment for stateless individuals and groups, has a profound influence on the ways in which stateless people are treated. Power relations between EU states and their non-EU neighbours appear to have a particular bearing on the ways in which European states behave. For example, the power and proximity of Russia has influenced the ways in which the Estonian state has accommodated ethnic Russian non-citizens in its policy and society. By contrast, the relative weakness of Bosnia, Croatia, Serbia and Macedonia, as compared to Slovenia, a country which is seen as having victoriously escaped from the oppressive Yugoslavia, has negatively affected the lives of the Erased, deemed to be outsiders from the former Yugoslav republics. Similarly, in the case of France, its hegemonic relationship with the Southern Mediterranean has influenced the way in which it has both historically tolerated the presence of illegal migrant labour while increasingly publicising its use of removals to Algeria and elsewhere in North Africa.

Size and homogeneity of population

The large presence of ethnic Russian non-citizens in Estonia and the *sans papiers* of North African origin suggests that states are better able to accommodate the rights of non-nationals when there is a large and clear constituency. Indeed, such factors also appear to influence the ability of such stateless groups to organise and press for their rights. Having a clear sense of collective ethnic attachment has positively affected the ways in which Estonia and France have responded to claims made by stateless people within their jurisdictions, in contrast to the *de facto* stateless Erased in Slovenia. For the Erased, their heterogeneity (some ethnic Serbs, others Croat, Bosnian, Macedonian, or Roma) has enable the state and nationalist forces to label them as 'outsiders', 'southerners' and the like, all of which are defined in opposition to ethnic state of Slovenia.

Establishment and settlement on the territory

Related to the above, the degree to which stateless people are considered as migrants or established populations appears to affect the way in which they are treated by the state. In the case of the Erased, while they may have considered themselves established, for the Slovene state and much of the population they were perceived as foreigners who were not settled – or who could be uprooted. Ethnic Russians in Estonia are considered established but are identifiably 'foreign'. By contrast, in the French Republican model, the *sans papiers* may be closer culturally to the French and can be assimilated into the French community of North African origin. In the United Kingdom, despite the existence of diverse communities of settled populations, stateless people moving into those communities from outside the United Kingdom have not been accommodated into UK society in a way equating to the experiences of the *sans papiers* in France.

Support from citizen population, including third-sector organisations

As discussed in chapter 5, NGOs and the local population may play a critical role in improving the lives of stateless people by exercising voice and moral condemnation and by seeking ways in which the law may be clarified to protect stateless non-citizens. We note that while the Erased received little practical support, with legal assistance they were able to challenge their situation before the Constitutional Court and then have a case admitted before the ECtHR. The *sans papiers* have received considerable support from organisations such as *France Terre d'Asile* and have been able to establish their own 'collectifs'. At the other end of the spectrum, *de facto* stateless people in the United Kingdom have benefited from charity for both practical and legal support.

Across the four jurisdictions considered in this project, the experiences of *de facto* and *de jure* statelessness show interesting similarities and differences. Overall, however, they resemble each other in being disadvantaged by insecurity. Those who are not assured that there is a solid future for them cannot make plans or work towards a better life, for themselves or for their families. The longer people are left in a state of uncertainty, the more likely their disadvantage is to be replicated in the next generation and throughout a community.

A particularly unsettling aspect of that insecurity arises from the ability and occasional willingness of states to redefine their commitments to their various populations. Such redefinitions can be shattering to the individuals involved, and the effects are transmitted across decades and generations. The United Kingdom and France are both countries with former Empires and substantial populations with roots in their former overseas territories. The United Kingdom's influence ran even in countries that were not formally colonies, and where many of the current unwanted migrants originate, such as Iraq or Somalia. France has constant difficulties defining the status of Maghrebins, and in particular those from Algeria, whose country was once – not so very long ago – an internal part of France itself, even if the migrants in question often have personal ties in Africa rather than mainland France. The rejections of populations following the end of the Soviet Empire that are considered in this study are different in that they are also part of the self-definition of newly independent states. Slovenia's rejection of those of its permanent residents who did not become formal citizens on independence was perceived by those 'erased' from the register as being rendered stateless even if the formal position was that they had always belonged (albeit without practical consequence) to another constituent state of Yugoslavia. These three jurisdictions are similar, however, in that the population without protection is generally rooted in a community that had never been powerful or dominant – in the case of Slovenia, a disproportionate number of Roma were among the discarded. In Estonia, however, geo-politics worked in favour of the disenfranchised; rejection was not of weak or supplicant population who had migrated in search of economic advantage or a better life, or merely to avoid disaster, but of representatives of a former invading and dominant military power. Noticeably, the stateless of Estonia were the only population in the study that was largely truly *de jure* stateless. They were also the least disadvantaged in terms of everyday practical rights, and the most secure.

Paul Weis, an early scholar of statelessness, believed that remedies for statelessness needed to be available also to those who had a nationality that was not useful in offering them protection, as well as to those who had no nationality at all.[4] Hannah Arendt similarly counted among the meaningfully stateless those whose states did not offer them the basic protections. The framework of international law and of much of the activity of the United Nations even now focuses on those who are *de jure* stateless, so that it is difficult to assess the nature and especially the extent of the problem. There are relatively few statistics and it is often difficult to be certain to what types of population they refer. The lack of statistical and other information obscures the difficulties inherent in formal and legal international attempts to end statelessness. Many countries have ratified the Refugee Convention but few have ratified the Conventions relating to

---

[4] See n. 2 above.

statelessness; nevertheless many countries do grant citizenship to those who are *de jure* stateless. Such people are, in most parts of the world, relatively few, and there have been significant international efforts to avoid the creation of new *de jure* stateless populations when state organisation and boundaries change and there is a succession of states. Nevertheless, the growing tendency in Europe and elsewhere to institute a stronger *jus sanguinis* system in countries that have previously had a *jus soli* system will tend to produce more statelessness of both kinds in future generations.

Clearly the situation does not compare with that which inspired the work of Weis and Arendt. The expansion of human rights norms after the deprivations of the early and mid-twentieth century in Europe may not have achieved the sort of universal basic rights that many assume. Nevertheless, the concept that there is a bottom line of behaviour below which humanity should never fall is certainly embedded in Europe. Despite the hardening of many Europe-wide policies in relation to unwanted migrants – both as to the withdrawal of the means of life and as to the removal of the people themselves – there does remain a substantial underlying consciousness among much of the national and non-migrant population that there are fundamental issues of obligation and entitlement that state migration policies may not always fulfil. Especially where individuals and families have roots and are part of the social fabric, whether recently or in past generations, there is often not only a practical difficulty in removing them but a resistance to the very idea. Moreover, the practice of not removing children, often out of adherence to the letter and spirit of the United Nations Convention on the Rights of the Child 1959, means that people can be removed as they turn eighteen, but after years of settled life in the host state, to a country they have no memory of and no connections with. In effect, they are sent to countries where, even if the database of formal citizenship says they ought to be at home, they feel like foreigners, and may well be treated as such.

The ECHR has had something to offer the stateless of Europe. Article 3 – the right not to suffer inhuman and degrading treatment – was used in relation to the East African Asians' experience in the United Kingdom in 1973, and it is time for this fundamental aspect of states' treatment of their populations to be taken this seriously again. Article 8 – the right to respect for one's private and family life – is often the source of rights for migrants to remain with their families in host countries that otherwise seek to expel them. The right to live and develop one's life and personality in the place where one has one's home is, however, woefully under-developed, to the point that a Convention fundamentally rooted in a withdrawal of human rights linked to withdrawal of citizenship rights has its prohibition on the expulsion of a country's own citizens as a merely optional Protocol. More use could be made of Article 14, prohibiting discrimination, which was also adverted to in the East African Asians' case. Those affected by policies of exclusion are almost invariably minority communities, and the Strasbourg jurisprudence has been too ready to accept assertions that states' policies are to do with maintaining strong immigration and expulsion policies. The Strasbourg Court has been weak in resisting the characterisation of whatever form of immigration controls the governments and executives of the day see fit to implement as a manifestation of the maintenance of public order. It is to be hoped that the Court will move to analyse the substance of such arguments and countenance the idea that there are objective considerations and that real public order may sometimes be best maintained by adverting also to the founding principles of the ECHR itself.

12

Conclusions

CAROLINE SAWYER AND BRAD K. BLITZ

Fifty years ago, against the background of attempts to resettle the casualties of political disaster and to ensure that there could be no more war and dehumanisation in Europe, Hannah Arendt was pessimistic about the ideal of universal human rights. She asserted that in a world of nation-states there could always be statelessness, and that without a nationality through which to establish their claims, the stateless would lack the right to any rights. Despite the international and regional Conventions and their courts and committees that appear to guarantee rights to everyone in the European jurisdiction, the research set out in this book demonstrates that aspects of Arendt's pessimism are justified today. Many of her claims regarding the limitations of the human rights regime to guarantee protection remain true, and her assertion that since what matters to the stateless is the inability to assure state protection, so *de jure* and *de facto* statelessness are equivalent, is notably borne out in this study.

Arendt offered a grounded theory of statelessness, drawn from her own experience, explicitly critical of the human rights regime which was then being established. In drawing conclusions from fieldwork with today's irregular migrants and unwanted immigrants, we have confirmed the observation made when we began considering this project – namely, that although there have been considerable strides in the machinery of human rights, political theory with respect to statelessness has hardly moved on since Arendt's day. This may be in large part because of the dearth of empirical work on the daily lives of the stateless, looking at the common experiences of those without status, for reasons that may vary – they may be refused asylum seekers; economic migrants whose immigration status is irregular whether through knowing evasion of rules, or misunderstanding, or error; people who believed themselves to be nationals but found they were not, or who had been citizens but had had their citizenship withdrawn. What the stateless populations have in common is established lives without status, and no intention and often no realistic prospect of being able to live in an alternative country.

While the ideal of human rights has been entrenched and is acknowledged throughout Europe, there is still validity in Arendt's notion of the 'hollowness' of universal human rights or their implementation through systems of supra-national protection. We suggest that the term 'fragility' may be a more appropriate term for consideration, since basic and social and even political rights are often guaranteed in a variety of ways, as are claims to citizenship. Nevertheless the grounds for these claims may be withdrawn, or the rights they promise may turn out to be unattainable. The concept of 'fragility' is born out of our analysis of the interaction between the three bundles of rights – namely, basic, social and political rights. While very few non-citizens enjoy rights to vote, historically the denial of access to political rights has been followed by the retraction of social and other benefits such as rights to education, employment, or healthcare. Here we record individuals' experiences of how the loss of social rights led in its turn to the degradation of other basic rights and directly created situations of poverty, vulnerability and hopelessness, the contemporary face of the rightlessness Arendt described.

In spite of much recent writing on the rights of non-citizens, very few theorists have been prepared to tackle the practical faces of statelessness and offer a focused critique of the human rights regime that takes account of how it functions in implementation. Access to many of the necessary means to establish a decent life – the right to work, for example, or the right to education – are often increasingly dependent on proof of status which may itself be refused or withdrawn. Human rights are therefore made inaccessible to sections of the population, because of the lack of state adoption of practical human rights measures, the absence of enforcement mechanisms built into certain forms of formal rights, or the simple inability of those leading marginal lives to lead any challenge to their deprivations. Some people cannot negotiate the complexities of their position; some fear that challenge will lead to exposure and removal. Often, however, this is no accident, or failing of a larger state endeavour, but a result of the overwhelming of the human rights endeavour by competing policies which use the denial or withdrawal of rights essential to everyday life as a means of controlling migration or redrawing populations.

The fieldwork approach of the project focused on access to rights rather than on nationality itself, since that is how individuals experience statelessness. Our expectations at the outset were that issues of access to nationality and citizenship would also be important, but the extent of their unimportance was borne upon us especially by the comparative element of the project. Participants in the study could not be concerned with political rights such as the right to vote while they were concerned with the more basic and social rights. Those who are without the right to work, and especially those living in insecurity and fear of the authorities, cannot consider the future of the society in which they live but which does not allow them to make any certain plans for their own future or that of their families. The comparative element of the project showed that the extent of personal security was not only directly related to access to practical daily rights but also that the extent of practical rights was not directly related to formal citizenship. This is not merely a theoretical assertion. It was striking that the population most obviously deprived of formal citizenship rights – the Estonian ethnic Russians – were the most secure and advantaged in their practical day-to-day rights. The most disadvantaged were the Slovenian Erased, who had not lost their formal citizenship but some of whom had otherwise lost everything, including accrued property rights. But the experiences of the participants in the United Kingdom and France reflected common as well as different aspects to their lives.

The reported experiences of many of the participants in this study demonstrate how difficult it is for them to realise even basic human rights and needs such as even decent accommodation and a family life: the language of international human rights holds little real currency for the most vulnerable people sampled in this study. The complexity of the lives of the participants in this study reflects the complexity of the issues with which they struggle. The study, however, also reveals common factors as well as contrasts among their experiences. These offer material for analysis and consideration of ways in which the margins of life in Europe need to be re-set so that existing populations, whose departure or removal is unlikely, can be integrated appropriately, to the benefit of the communities and countries in which they live.

There is an importance to the language of universal human rights, especially when it is spoken by the entrenched populations of the countries where the marginalised populations live. There have been notable social action campaigns and cases have been supported and taken before the ECtHR at Strasbourg. Not only the ability of the Court to award damages to individuals for breach of rights, but also the opprobrium of a decision against a country, carries considerable weight. It can embarrass states and prompt reform of particular practices. Nevertheless, despite the existence of popular good will towards particular individuals, families, or communities, or interpretations of European and international laws, or public protest, there seems to be little that these can do to unsettle states' claims of sovereignty over issues of nationality and immigration, the equation of those policies with proper public order and the consequent destabilisation of ideas of integration and practical universal basic rights.

The liberal and theoretical discourse, which vaunts the idea of a universal human rights regime, might suggest that what the project fieldwork uncovered about the current position of the stateless of Europe was at most the result of some heavy foot-dragging by the state authorities across Europe, or a failure of various state systems, including legal systems, to implement those basic rights. There has certainly been resistance to the exclusion and expulsion of the stateless in Europe, in forms such as the organised *sans papiers* movement of France, with its wider public support, or in the applications to international tribunals made with the support of NGOs such as the Soros Foundation. There have been some striking successes, but otherwise resistance to the liberal idea of universal basic human rights may often appear almost unnecessary, because that universality is illusory at the level of legal rules, and increasingly at the level of daily domestic practice.

The philosophy behind the theoretical and liberal discourse has not translated into either legal rules or political discourses. International rules on universal positive rights are often more limited than is popularly (or even academically) understood, especially in their applicability to the real lives of the stateless. Concern for the stateless may be deflected by reference solely to the *de jure* stateless, with the relevance of *de facto* statelessness often misunderstood or ignored, notwithstanding that the borderline between the two is often fuzzy. Where there are directly applicable rules, even if states have signed up to them, they are usually unenforceable. The enforceability of rights under the ECHR is often illusory, too. The rights it guarantees are essentially negative, and notwithstanding its willingness to accept the principle that the Convention is a 'living instrument', in interpreting its terms the Strasbourg Court has shied away from imposing obligations on states that could amount to limiting their ability to regulate their own populations. With some departures, it has had a relatively weak approach to the rights of people to live in the place in which they have established their home and to exercise the basic rights of citizenship. The convergence of the European Union and the ECHR only lends weight to the argument of those who see Europe as fortified against foreigners. An ironic twist, contradicting the logic of the cosmopolitan theories of contemporary philosophers of rights, is the degree to which the European Union, while promoting an identity as a progressive and tolerant region, has made efforts to 'harmonise' the effective exclusion of potentially burdensome non-citizens, ensuring that none but the most desperate will be able to benefit from its promises of safety and security, and effectively ensuring that many of the only slightly less desperate, and many who believe they belong in Europe, are excluded as well.

The weakness of internal European systems in making any robust assertion of the universality of basic and social rights is particularly of concern where domestic policies spill into exclusion of those who are not immediately obvious as foreigners, or do not consider themselves to be so – those who have long-established homes in the European Union, especially if they have had or still have citizenship of a member state – and would expect to be protected by the European legal and constitutional system. The right to a personal identity as a citizen or settled resident is an area of jurisprudence ripe for further exploration and development by the Strasbourg Court as well as domestic jurisdictions. The forthcoming judgements of the Strasbourg Court on the United Kingdom's treatment of the Ilois, or Chagos Islanders, may be particularly interesting for the issue of the Court's treatment of the incidents of citizenship, as with the outcome of the application of the Erased in *Makuc* v. *Slovenia* (Application No. 26828/06). The domestically stateless have hitherto been ineffectively protected by the supra-national jurisdiction at Strasbourg, but that this is a contemporary and growing issue is surely indicated by the occasion of *Rottmann*, the first case on statelessness in the Luxembourg Court in early 2010. The development of its jurisprudence will no doubt depend, as will that of the Strasbourg Court, on perceived political realities as well as legal reasoning. A general trajectory towards the protection of individuals' basic rights is not a forgone conclusion, but it is to be hoped that there is a better future for the realisation of the universal human rights ideal in Europe.

In deciding what to do about making the human rights ideal real for all those who really are within the jurisdiction of the European states, and working out what rights, and mechanisms of access to those rights, are appropriate, the experiences of today's displaced, marginalised and excluded are a good place to start. The various spheres of argument may influence one another: moral protest against the inhumanity of excluding those perceived to be undesirable from basic rights such as the right to work may combine with differently motivated economic arguments by those who desire a pool of unskilled, undemanding workers. The realisation of universal human rights may be approached simultaneously in different ways. There should be an analysis of the costs and benefits of exclusion which sees beyond the headline desire to get rid of unwanted populations. If residents are not allowed to become members of society, and are not persuaded to go, they risk forming disadvantaged populations whose internal exclusion is damaging to the social fabric. This is not put forward here as a moral issue, but as a practical one. There may appear to be political or economic imperatives to restricting rights to the obviously economically desirable, but they may be outweighed by the practical consequences not only of hosting dispossessed residents but of destabilising the existing communities to whom those people may feel attached. The question of who should be admitted and accorded rights is not a purely or simply economic one; even the most desirable worker grows old or may fall ill and become a burden, and, as with the strong development of EU law on third-country nationals, the admission of family members is necessary for the ideal of free movement and a market in labour skills. The current discourse of admission and naturalisation appears to include not only economic desirability but also cultural loyalty to the host country, especially in Western countries. Those who are deprived of the means of everyday life are, however, then also deprived of the means of demonstrating their loyalty.

A warning flag, however, is that citizenship is again being asserted in an idealised form, with tests of loyalty and knowledge used as entry criteria. Such tests require acceptance or adherence to certain values and scripts. The requirement that non-citizens should have to demonstrate particular social behaviours may undermine other European liberal traditions of respect for cultural diversity and tolerance and, as a result, especially if those behaviours are equated with entitlement to formal citizenship and the lack of citizenship is equated with disloyalty and disentitlement from basic rights, may also call into question broader social stability. Attempts to re-define citizenship and the bases for membership in culturally narrow ways must not detract from the moral and political obligations to respect basic human rights irrespective of nationality and immigration status. The demonstration of loyalty to the new country can entail conflicts with memory and identity for newer citizens and so create tensions within the citizen population. This entails broader political questions, and raises constitutional issues in the deepest sense, for all the population.[1]

---

[1] The ECtHR gave judgment in the case of *Kirić* (formerly *Matuc*) *and others* v. *Slovenia* (App. No. 26828/06) on 13 July 2010, too late for discussion in this book. It held Slovenia in breach of Articles 8 (respect for family and private life) and 13 (effective remedy) and required the restoration of permanent resident status to the Erased.

BIBLIOGRAPHY

Abizadeh, A. (2008) 'Democratic Theory and Border Coercion: No Right to Unilaterally Control Your Own Borders', *Political Theory*, 36(1), 37

Ablayatifov, R. (2004) 'The Resettlement, Adaptation and Integration of Formerly Deported Crimean Tatars in Ukraine: Evaluation of Impact of Governmental Programmes of 2002', Paper presented at the 12th NISPAcee Annual Conference: 'Central and Eastern European Countries Inside and Outside the European Union: Avoiding a New Divide', Vilnius

Adler, M. (1995) 'The Habitual Residence Test: A Critical Analysis', *Journal of Social Security Law*, 2, 179

Agamben, G. (2004) *Means Without End* (Minneapolis, MN: University of Minnesota Press)

Agar, A. and A. Strang (2000) *Indicators of Integration: The Experience of Integration – Final Report* (London: Home Office)

Aleinikoff, T. (1986) 'Theories of Loss of Citizenship', *Michigan Law Review*, 84(9), 1471

Alt, J. (1999) *Illegal in Deutschland* (Karlsruhe: Von Loeper Literaturverlag), www.joerg-alt.de/publikationen/materialanlagen/materialanlagen.mtml, accessed December 2006

(2007) *Slovenia: Amnesty International Condemns Forcible Return of 'Erased' Person to Germany*, www.amnestyusa.org/document.php?lang=e&id= ENGEUR680022007, accessed 1 February 2008

Amnesty International (2005) *Slovenia: Briefing to the UN Committee on Economic, Social and Cultural Rights*, 35th Session

Anderson, A. (2005) 'Missing Boundaries: Refugees, Migrants, Stateless and Internally Displaced Persons in South Asia', *Pacific Affairs*, 78(2), 320

Andreev, S. (2003) 'Making Slovenian Citizens: The Problem of the Former Yugoslav Citizens and Asylum Seekers Living in Slovenia', *Southeast European Politics*, 4(1), 1

Andrijasevic, R. (2006) 'How to Balance Rights and Responsibilities on Asylum at the EU's Southern Border of Italy and Libya', COMPAS Working Paper, WP-06–27 (Oxford: COMPAS)

Anya, I. (2007) 'The Right to Healthcare for Vulnerable Migrants', *The Lancet*, 370 (8 September), 827

Arakan Project (2008) *Issues to Be Raised Concerning the Situation of Stateless Rohingya Women in Myanmar (Burma). Submission to the Committee on the Elimination of Discrimination Against Women (CEDAW) for the Examination of the Combined 2nd and 3rd Periodic State Party Reports (Cedaw/C/Mmr/3) – Myanmar* www.burmalibrary.org/docs6/CEDAW_Myanmar_AP_Submission-Final-Web.pdf

Hannah Arendt (1951) *The Origins of Totalitarianism* (New York: Schocken Books)

    (1958) *The Human Condition* (Chicago, IL: Chicago University Press)

    (1961) *Between Past and Future* (London: Faber & Faber)

    (1968) *The Origins of Totalitarianism* (New York: Harcourt Brace Jovanovich)

    (1970) *On Violence* (London: Allen Lane)

    (1982) *The Jew as Pariah* (New York: Grove Press)

    (1986) *The Origins of Totalitarianism* (London: André Deutsch)

Aspal, S., K. Kallas and K. Kasearu (2008), in M. Lauristin, K. Korts and K. Kallas (eds.), *Integration Strategy 2008–2013* (Tartu: University of Tartu Institute of Baltic Studies), 54

Audit Commission (2000) *Another Country*, www.audit-commission.gov.uk/SiteCollectionDocuments/AuditCommissionReports/NationalStudies/anothercountry.pdf

Aurescu, B. (2007) 'The 2006 Venice Commission Report on Non-Citizens and Minority Rights – Presentation and Assessment', *Helsinki Monitor*, 18(2), 150

Ba, O. (2009) *Je suis venu, j'ai vu, je n'y crois plus* (Paris: Max Milo Éditions)

Badiou, A. (2007) 'L'intellectuel de gauche va disparaître, tant mieux', *Le Monde* (14 July)

Balibar, E. (1999) 'Le droit de cité ou l'apartheid', in E. Balibar *et al.* (eds.), *Sans-Papiers: l'archaïsme fatal* (Paris: Éditions La Decouverte), 113.

Balton, D. A. (1990) 'The Convention on the Rights of the Child: Prospects for International Enforcement', *Human Rights Quarterly*, 12, 120

Barany, Z. (1998) 'The Socio-Economic Impact of Regime Change in Eastern Europe: Gypsy Marginality in the 1990s', *East European Politics and Societies*, 14(2), 64

Barrington, L. (1995) 'The Domestic and International Consequences of Citizenship in the Soviet Successor States', *Europe-Asia Studies*, 49, 731

Barry, B. 'The Quest for Consistency: A Skeptical View', in B. Barry and R. Goodin (eds.), *Free Movement: Ethical Issues in the Transnational Migration of People and Money* (Hemel Hempstead: Harvester Wheatsheaf)

Batchelor, C. A. (1995) 'Stateless Persons: Some Gaps in International Protection', *International Journal of Refugee Law*, 7(2), 232

    (1998) 'Statelessness and the Problem of Resolving Nationality Status', *International Journal of Refugee Law* 10(1–2), 172

(2006) 'Transforming International Legal Principles into National Law: The Right to a Nationality and the Avoidance of Statelessness', *Refugee Survey Quarterly*, 25(3), 8

Bates, E. (2008) 'Avoiding Legal Obligations Created by Human Rights Treaties', *International & Comparative Law Quarterly*, 57, 751

Bauböck, R. (1994) *Transnational Citizenship: Membership and Rights in International Migration* (Aldershot: Edward Elgar)

  (1997) 'Changing the Boundaries of Citizenship', in R. Bauböck (ed.), *From Aliens to Citizens* (Aldershot: Avebury)

  (2005) 'Changing Meanings and Practices of Citizenship', *PS: Political Science and Politics*, 28, 667

  (ed.) (2006) *Migration and Citizenship: Legal Status, Rights and Political Participation* (Amsterdam: Amsterdam University Press)

  (2007) 'The Rights of Others and the Boundaries of Democracy', *European Journal of Political Theory*, 6(4), 398

Beckman, L. (2006) 'Citizenship and Voting Rights: Should Resident Aliens Vote?', *Citizenship Studies*, 10(2), 153

Beirens, H., R. Hek, N. Hughes and N. Spicer (2007) 'Preventing Social Exclusion of Immigrant and Asylum Seeking Children: Building New Networks', *Social Policy and Society*, 6, 219

Benhabib, S. (1996) *The Reluctant Modernism of Hannah Arendt* (London: Sage)

  (2001) *Transformations of Citizenship* (Amsterdam: Van Gorcum)

  (2004) *The Rights of Others: Aliens, Residents, and Citizens* (Cambridge: Cambridge University Press)

Bentwich, N. (1935) 'The League of Nations and Refugees', *British Yearbook of International Law*, 16, 114

Bernstein, R. (1996) *Hannah Arendt and the Jewish Question* (Oxford, Polity and Cambridge, MA: MIT Press)

  (2005) 'Hannah Arendt on the Stateless', *Parallax*, 111, 46

  (2008) 'Are Arendt's Reflections on Evil Still Relevant?', *Review of Politics*, 70(1), 64

Beznec, B. (2008) 'The Impossible is Possible: An Interview with Aleksandar Todorović', J. Zorn and U. Lipovec Čebron (eds.), *Once upon an Erasure: From Citizens to Illegal Residents in Slovenia* (Ljubljana: Študentska založba), 19–31

Bhabha, J. (1998) 'Enforcing the Human Rights of Citizens and Non-Citizens in the Era of Maastricht: Some Reflections on the Importance of States', *Development & Change*, 29(4), 697

Black, J., QC, (n.d.) www.18redlioncourt.co.uk/index.php/barristers/black/125

Blake, M. (2002) 'Discretionary Immigration', *Philosophical Topics* 30(2), 273

  (2006) 'Universal and Qualified Rights to Immigration', *Ethics and Economics*, 4, ethique-economique.net/IMG/pdf/BLAKE.pdf

Blitz, B. K. (2006) 'Statelessness and the Social (De)Construction of Citizenship: Political Restructuring and Ethnic Discrimination in Slovenia', *Journal of Human Rights*, 5(4), 453

(2007) 'Democratic Development, Judicial Reform and the Serbian Question in Croatia', *Human Rights Review*, 9(1), 123

(2009) 'Libyan Nationals in the United Kingdom: Geo-Political Considerations and Trends in Asylum and Return', *International Journal on Multicultural Societies*, 10(2), 106

Blitz, B. K. and M. Lynch (eds.) (2011) *Statelessness and Citizenship: A Comparative Study on the Benefits of Nationality* (Cheltenham: Edward Elgar)

Blitz, B. K. and M. Otero-Iglesias (2011) 'Stateless by Any Other Name: Unsuccessful Asylum Seekers and Undocumented Migrants in The United Kingdom' (*Journal for Ethnic and Migration Studies*, forthcoming)

Bloch, A. (2000) 'Refugee Settlement in Britain: The Impact of Policy on Participation', *Journal of Ethnic and Migration Studies*, 26, 75

Booth, W. (1997) 'Foreigners: Insiders, Outsiders and the Ethics of Membership', *Review of Politics*, 59, 259

Bosniak, L. (2006) *The Citizen and the Alien: Dilemmas of Contemporary Membership* (Princeton, NJ: Princeton University Press)

Bowring, B. (2008) 'European Minority Protection: The Past and Future of a "Major Historical Achievement"', *International Journal on Minority and Group Rights*, 152(3), 413

Boyden, J. and J. Hart (2007) 'The Statelessness of the World's Children', *Children & Society*, 21(4), 237

Brilmayer, L. (2006) 'From "Contract" to "Pledge": The Structure of International Human Rights Agreements', *British Yearbook of International Law*, 77, 163

British Medical Association General Practitioners' Committee (2006) 'Guidance for GPs' www.bedshertslmcs.org.uk/Guidance/guidanceDocuments/Overseas%20visitors%20March%202006.doc

Brock, G. and H. Brighouse (2005) *The Political Philosophy of Cosmopolitanism* (Cambridge: Cambridge University Press)

Brownlie, I. (1963) 'The Relations of Nationality in Public International Law', *British Year Book of International Law*, 39, 284

(1998) *Principles of Public International Law* (Oxford: Clarendon Press)

Brubaker, R. (1992a) *Citizenship and Nationhood in France and Germany* (Cambridge, MA: Harvard University Press)

(1992b) 'Citizenship Struggles in Soviet Successor States', *International Migration Review*, 26(2), 269

Buck, T. (2005) *International Child Law* (London: Routledge/Cavendish)

Caloz-Tschopp, M. C. (2000a) 'La figure-sujet des sans-État dans l'œuvre de Hannah Arendt', in M. C. Caloz-Tschopp (ed.), *Les sans-État dans la philosophie de Hannah Arendt* (Lausanne: Éditions Paliot)

(2000b) *Les sans-État dans la philosophie de Hannah Arendt* (Lausanne: Éditions Paliot)

Camilleri, I. (2010) 'Malta's Migration Burden Biggest in EU – Study', *Times of Malta* (4 March), www.timesofmalta.com/articles/view/20100304/local/maltas-migration-burden-biggest-in-eu-study

Canovan, M. (1978) 'The Contradictions of Hannah Arendt's Political Thought', *Political Theory*, 6, 5

(1992) *Hannah Arendt: A Re-Interpretation of Her Political Thought* (Cambridge: Cambridge University Press)

Carens, J. H. (1987) 'The Case for Open Borders', *The Review of Politics*, 251

(1988) 'Immigration and the Welfare State', in A. Guttman (ed.), *Democracy and the Welfare State* (Princeton, NJ: Princeton University Press)

(1992) 'Migration and Morality: A Liberal Egalitarian Perspective', in B. Barry and R. Goodin (eds.), *Free Movement: Ethical Issues in the Transnational Migration of People and Money* (Hemel Hempstead: Harvester Wheatsheaf)

(2002) 'The Rights of Residents', in R. Hansen and P. Weil (eds.), *Reinventing Citizenship: Dual Citizenship, Social Rights and Federal Citizenship in Europe and the US* (Oxford: Berghahn)

(2005) 'On Belonging: What We Owe People Who Stay', *The Boston Review* (Summer), www.bostonreview.net/BR30.3/carens.html

Carty, H. (1983) 'Overseas Visitors and the NHS', *Journal of Social Welfare and Family Law*, 5, 258

Castles, S. and M. Miller (2003) *The Age of Migration*, 3rd edn. (Basingstoke: Palgrave)

Chakrabarti, S. (2005) 'Rights and Rhetoric: The Politics of Asylum and Human Rights Culture in the UK', *Journal of Law and Society*, 32, 131

Chan, J. M. M. (1991) 'The Right to a Nationality as a Human Right', *Human Rights Law Journal*, 12, 1

ChildRIGHT (2010) 'Court Report – Age Assessments of Asylum Seekers', *Children & Young People Now* (9 March)

Cholewinski, R. (1994a) 'The Protection of the Right of Economic Migrants to Family Reunion in Europe', *International & Comparative Law Quarterly*, 43, 568

(1994b) 'Strasbourg's "Hidden Agenda": The Protection of Second-Generation Migrants from Expulsion', *Netherlands Quarterly of Human Rights*, 12, 287

Cissé, M. (1997) 'Sans Papiers: Wir sind da! Die Bewegung der Illegalen in Frankreich', *Interim*, 433, 12

Clarke, L. (2010) 'Editorial: Immigrants or Foreign Residents?', (17 February), www.wantedinrome.com/articles/complete_articles.php?id_art=1000

Cohen, J. (1999) 'Changing Paradigms of Citizenship and the Exclusiveness of the Demos', *International Sociology*, 14, 245

Cohen, R. (1989) 'Citizens, Denizens and Helots: The Politics of International Migration Flows in the Post-War World', *Hitotsubashi Journal of Social Studies*, 21(1), 153

Colvin, M. (2001) 'The Schengen Information System: A Human Rights Audit', *European Human Rights Law Review*, 3, 271

Commissioner for Human Rights (2006) *Follow-Up Report on Slovenia (2003–2005): Assessment of the Progress made in Implementing the Recommendations of the Council of Europe Commissioner for Human Rights* (Strasbourg: Council of Europe), http://wcd.coe.int/ViewDoc.jsp?id=984025&Site=CommDH&BackColorInternet=FEC65B&BackColorIntranet=FE65B&BackColorLogged=FF679 P104_10139, accessed 21 December 2007

Coroller, C. (2007a) 'Paris: expulsions quotidiennes dans le Xxe, Série de reconduites à la frontière de *sans-papiers* aux enfants scolarisés', *Libération* (Paris) (12 May), www.liberation.fr/actualite/societe/253342.FR.php, accessed 25 May 2007

—— (2007b) 'Paris: sans-papiers arrêtés, enfants caches', *Libération* (Paris) (25 May), www.liberation.fr/actualite/societe/256008.FR.php, accessed 25 May 2007

—— (2009) 'SOS Racisme milite contre les expulsions de la "honte"', *Liberation.fr* (21 January), www.liberation.fr/societe/0101313547-sos-racisme-milite-contre-les-30–000-expulsions-de-la-honte

Council of Europe (2008) Commissioner for Human Rights, *'No One Should Have to be Stateless in Today's Europe'*, 9 June, www.unhcr.org/refworld/docid/48abd54e5.html, accessed 8 February 2009

Coventry Peace House (2008) *Statelessness: The Quiet Torture of Belonging Nowhere* (Coventry: Coventry Peace House), www.stateless.org.uk/stateless_book.pdf, accessed 28 January 2009

Cowan, D. and M. McDermont (2006) *Regulating Social Housing* (London: Routledge)

Craven, M. (2000) 'The International Law of State Succession', *International Law Forum du Droit International*, 23, 202

Crossette, B. (1998) 'Third of Births Aren't Registered, UNICEF Says', *New York Times* (July 8)

Dedić, J., V. Jalušić and J. Zorn (2003) *The Erased – Organized Innocence and the Politics of Exclusion* (Ljubljana: Peace Institute)

Dell'Olio, F. (2005) *The Europeanization of Citizenship: Between the Ideology of Nationality, Immigration and European Identity* (Aldershot: Ashgate)

Dembour, M.-B. (2003) 'Human Rights Law and National Sovereignty in Collusion: The Plight of Quasi-Nationals at Strasbourg', *Netherlands Quarterly of Human Rights,* 21, 63

Dennis, J. (2002) *A Case for Change: How Refugee Children in England are Missing Out* (London: The Children's Society, Refugee Council and Save the Children)

Department of Health (2009) *National Health Service: Implementing the Overseas Visitors Hospital Charging Regulations: Guidance for NHS Trust Hospitals in England*, www.dh.gov.uk/prod_consum_dh/groups/dh_digitalassets/@adh/@cn/documents/digitalnet/dh_081516.pdf

Detrick, S. (1999) *A Commentary on the United Nations Convention on the Rights of the Child* (The Hague: Martinus Nijhoff)

Dijk, P. van (1999) 'Protection of "Integrated" Aliens Against Expulsion under the European Convention on Human Rights', *European Journal of Migration and Law*, 1, 293

Doek, J. E. (2006) 'The CRC and the Right to Acquire and to Preserve a Nationality', *Refugee Survey Quarterly*, 25, 26

Donner, R. (1994) *The Regulation of Nationality in International Law* (Ardsley, NY: Transnational Publishers)

Dow, U. (ed.) (1995) *The Citizenship Case – The Attorney General of The Republic of Botswana vs. Unity Dow: Court Documents, Judgements' Cases and Materials* (ENTSWE LA LESEDI (PTY) LTD), www.law-lib.utoronto.ca/Diana/fulltext/dow1.htm

Dwyer, J. (2004) 'Illegal Immigrants, Health Care and Social Responsibility', *The Hastings Center Report*, www.thehastingscenter.org.Publications/HCR 3, 34

Eagle, A. *et al.* (2002) *Asylum Seekers' Experiences of the Voucher Scheme in the UK – Fieldwork Report*, www.homeoffice.gov.uk/rds/pdfs2/asylumexp.pdf

(2007) *Third Report on Slovenia*, adopted on 30 June 2006, made public on 13 February 2007 (Strasbourg: European Commission against Racism and Intolerance, www.coe.int/t/e/human_rights/ecri/1-ecri/2-country-by-country_approach/Slovenia_CBC_3.asp#TopOfPage, accessed 9 December 2007)

Eide, A. (1999a) 'The Non-Inclusion of Minority Rights: Resolution 217C(III)', in G. Alfredsson and A. Eide (eds.), *The Universal Declaration of Human Rights – A Common Standard of Achievement* (The Hague: Martinus Nijhoff), 701

(1999b) 'Citizenship and the Minority Rights of Non-Citizens', Working Paper, 5th Session, Working Group on Minorities, UN Doc. EICN.4/Sub2/AC.5/1999/WP.3

Einhard (1960) *The Life of Charlemagne* (Written c. 830) (Ann Arbor: University of Michigan Press, Ann Arbor Paperbacks)

Elman, R. A. (2001) 'Testing the Limits of European Citizenship: Ethnic Hatred and Male Violence', *NWSA Journal*, 13(3), 49

Engstrom, M. and N. Obi (2001) *Evaluation of the UNHCR's Role and Activities in Relation to Statelessness* (UNHCR Evaluation and Policy Unit) EPAU/2001/09, www.unhcr.org/research/RESEARCH/3b67d0fa7.pdf

Enzensberger, H.-M. (1994) *Die große Wanderung* (Frankfurt/Main: Suhrkamp)

Equal Rights Trust (ERT) (2009a) *Legal Working Paper: The Protection of Stateless Persons in Detention Under International Law* (4 February), www.equalrightstrust.org/view-subdocument/index.htm?id=398

(2009b) *Research Working Paper: The Protection of Stateless Persons in Detention* (4 February), www.equalrightstrust.org/view-subdocument/index.htm?id=399

Euro Mediterranean Human Rights Network (EMHRN) and Migreurop (2009) 'Illegal Refoulement of 500 Migrants to Libya: The EU Must Condemn Italian Authorities', Press release (11 May), www.migreurop.org/IMG/pdf/CP-Libye-english.pdf

European Commission (1997) *Agenda 2000 – Commission Opinion on Slovenia's Application for Membership of the European Union* (Brussels: European Commission), http://ec.europa.eu/enlargement/archives/pdf/dwn/opinions/slovenia/sn-op_en.pdf, accessed 6 December 2007

European Commission against Racism and Intolerance (ECRI) (2006) Estonian Country *Report* www.coe.int/t/e/human_rights/ecri/1-ECRI/2-Country-by country_approach/Estonia/Estonia%20third%20report%20-%20cri06–1% 20estonian.pdf

(2007) *Third Report on Slovenia*, adopted on 30 June 2006, made public on 13 February 2007 (Strasbourg: European Commission against Racism and Intolerance), www.coe.int/t/e/human_rights/ecri/1-ecri/2-country-by-country_approach/Slovenia_CBC_3.asp#TopOfPage, accessed 9 December 2007

Evans, A. C. (1979) 'Development of European Community Law Regarding the Trade Union and Related Rights of Migrant Workers', *International & Comparative Law Quarterly*, 28, 354

Evans, M. D. and R. Morgan (1998) *Preventing Torture* (Oxford: Oxford University Press)

Fehervary, A. (2003) 'Citizenship, Statelessness and Human Rights: Recent Developments in the Baltic States', *International Journal of Refugee Law*, 5(3), 392–423

Ferré, N. (1997) 'La production de l'irrégularité', in D. Fassin, A. Morice and C. Quimina (eds.), *Les lois de l'inhospitabilité* (Paris: Éditions la Découverte), 47

Fields, H. (1932) 'Closing Immigration throughout the World', *American Journal of International Law*, 26, 671

Fischer Williams, J. (1927) 'Denationalization', *British Yearbook of International Law*, 8, 45

Flanyak, C. M. (1992) 'Accessing Data: Procedures, Practices and Problems of Academic Researchers', in M. K. Dantzker (ed.), *Readings for Research Methodologies in Criminal Justice* (Oxford: Butterworth-Heinemann).

Frelick, B. (2009) 'Greece's Refugee Problem', *New York Times* (July 30)

Frelick, B. and M. Lynch (2005) 'Statelessness: A Forgotten Human Rights Crisis', *Forced Migration Review*, 24, 65

Gedalof, I. (2007) 'Unhomely Homes: Women, Family and Belonging in UK Discourses of Migration and Asylum', *Journal of Ethnic and Migration Studies*, 33, 77

Gelazis, N. M. (2004) 'The European Union and the Statelessness Problem in the Baltic States', *European Journal of Migration and Law*, 6(3), 225

Germain, C. M. (2003) 'Approaches to Statutory Interpretation and Legislative History in France', *Duke Journal of Comparative and International Law*, 13, 195

Gibney, M. J. (2004) *The Ethics and Politics of Asylum: Liberal Democracy and the Response to Refugees* (Cambridge: Cambridge University Press)

  (2008) 'Asylum and the Expansion of Deportation in the UK', *Government and Opposition*, 43, 146

Gibney, M. J. and R. Hansen (2003) 'Deportation and the Liberal State', UNHCR New Issues in Refugee Research Working Paper, 77 (February)

Gilbert, G. S. (1983) 'Right of Asylum: A Change of Direction', *International & Comparative Law Quarterly*, 31, 633

Ginsburgs, G. (1966) 'Soviet Citizenship Legislation and Statelessness as a Consequence of the Conflict of Nationality Laws', *International & Comparative Law Quarterly*, 15(1), 1

  (2000) 'The Right to a "Nationality" and the Regime of Loss of Russian Citizenship', *Review of Central and East European Law*, 26(1), 1

Goldstein, J. and R. Keohane (1993) 'Ideas and Foreign Policy: An Analytical Framework', in J. Goldstein and R. Keohane (eds.), *Ideas and Foreign Policy* (Ithaca, NY: Cornell University Press)

Goldston, J. A. (2006) 'Holes in the Rights Framework: Racial Discrimination, Citizenship, and the Rights of Noncitizens', *Ethics & International Affairs*, 20, 321

Goodman, R. and D. Jinks (1978) *International Law and the Movement of Persons Between States* (Oxford: Clarendon Press)

  (2004) 'How to Influence States: Socialization and International Human Rights Law', *Duke Law Journal*, 54, 621

Goodwin-Gill, G. (1974–5) 'The Limits of the Power of Expulsion in Public International Law', *British Yearbook of International Law*, 55, 55

Grant, S. (2007) 'International Migration and Human Rights: A Paper Prepared for the Policy Analysis and Research Programme of the Global Commission on International Migration (Geneva: Global Commission on Migration), www.gcim.org/attachements/TP7.pdf

Granville-Chapman, C. (2004) *Harm on Removal: Excessive Force Against Failed Asylum Seekers* (London: Medical Foundation for the Victims of Torture)

Green, S. (2000) 'Beyond Ethnoculturalism? German Citizenship in the New Millennium', *German Politics*, 9(3), 105

Groenendijk, C. A. and B. D. Hart (2007) *Multiple Nationality: The Practice of Germany and the Netherlands* (The Hague: T.M.C. Asser)

de Groot, G.-R. (1998) 'The Relationship between the Nationality Legislation of the Member States of the European Union and European Citizenship', in M. La Torre (ed.), *European Citizenship: An Institutional Challenge* (The Hague, London and Boston: Kluwer Law International), 115

(2000) 'The European Convention on Nationality: A Step Towards a *ius commune* in the Field of Nationality Law', *Maastricht Journal of European and Comparative Law*, 7(2), 117

Grossman, A. (2001) 'Nationality and the Unrecognised State', *International & Comparative Law Quarterly*, 50, 847

Grotius, H. (1925) *De Jure Belli Ac Pacis Libri Tres, Book II*, trans F.W. Kelsey (Washington, DC: Carnegie Institute)

Guild, E., K. Groenendijk and H. Dogan (1996) *Security of Residence for Aliens in Europe* (Strasbourg: Council of Europe)

Gyulai, G. (2007) *Forgotten Without Reason: Protection of Non-Refugee Stateless Persons in Central Europe* (Budapest: Hungarian Helsinki Committee)

Hammar, T. (1990) *Democracy and the Nation State: Aliens, Denizens and Citizens in a World of International Migration* (Aldershot: Ashgate)

Hammarberg, T. (2008) 'No one Should Have to be Stateless in Today's Europe', *Viewpoint* (9 June), www.coe.int/t/commissioner/Viewpoints/080609_en.asp/, accessed 10 June 2008

(2009) Document Comm DH(2009)9, Strasbourg (19 February), https://wcd.coe.int/ViewDoc.jsp?id=1409353&Site=CommDH&BackColorInternet=FEC65B&BackColorIntranet=FEC65B&BackColorLogged=FFC679

Hansen, R. (2000) *Citizenship and Immigration in Post-War Britain* (Oxford: Oxford University Press)

(2001) 'From Subjects to Citizens: Immigration and Nationality in the United Kingdom', in R. Hansen and P. Weil (eds.), *Towards a European Nationality* (Basingstoke: Palgrave Macmillan)

Hansen, R. and P. Weil (2000) *Dual Nationality, Social Rights and Federal Citizenship in the US and Europe: The Reinvention of Citizenship* (New York: Berghahn)

Hargreaves, S. and A. Burnett (2008) 'UK Court Decision: Healthcare and Immigration', *The Lancet*, 317 (31 May), 1823

Harvey, C. (2004) 'The Right to Seek Asylum', *European Human Rights Law Review*, 4, 17

Hasenclever, A., P. Mayer and V. Rittberger (2000) 'Integrating Theories of International Regimes', *Review of International Studies*, 26, 3

Hathaway, J. C. (1984) 'The Evolution of Refugee Status in International Law 1920–1950', *International & Comparative Law Quarterly*, 33, 348

Hathaway, O. A. (2002) 'Do Human Rights Treaties Make a Difference?', *Yale Law Journal*, 111, 1870

Helemäe, J. (2008) 'Self-Realisation at Work and Perceived Opportunities for it', in R. Vetik (ed.), *Integration Monitoring of Estonian Society*, (2008) (in Estonian), http://ec.europa.eu/ewsi/UDRW/images/items/docl_9870_693007823.pdf

Hobbes, T. (1968) *Leviathan*, ed. C.B. Macpherson (Harmondsworth: Penguin)

Hodgson, D. (1993) 'The International Legal Protection of the Child's Right to a Legal Identity and the Problem of Statelessness', *International Journal of Law, Policy and the Family*, 7(2), 255

Holborn, L. W. (1938) 'The Legal Status of Political Refugees', *American Journal of International Law*, 32, 680

Home Office (2007) *Asylum Statistics, United Kingdom 2007*, Home Office Statistical Bulletin, 11/08, www.homeoffice.gov.uk/rds/pdfs08/hosb1108.pdf

Honig, B. (ed.) (1995) *Feminist Interpretations of Hannah Arendt* (University Park, PA: Pennsylvania State University Press)

House of Commons Home Affairs Committee (2006) Immigration Control HC 775-III (*Fifth Report*, Session 2005–2006), Ev 149

Hudson, M. O. (1952) Document A/CN.4/50(1952-II), *Yearbook of the International Law Commission*, 7

Hughes, J. (2005) 'Exit in Deeply Divided Societies: Regimes of Discrimination in Estonia and Latria and the Potential for Russophone Migration', *Journal of Common Market Studies*, 43(4), 739

Human Rights Watch (2008) *Stuck in a Revolving Door: Iraqis and Other Asylum Seekers and Migrants at the Greece/Turkey Entrance to the European Union*, Human Rights Watch (Document 1–56432–411–7) (November), www.hrw.org/en/node/76211/section/10

Human Security Commission (2003) *Human Security Now: Protecting and Empowering People* (New York: Commission on Human Security), 133, www.humansecurity-chs.org/finalreport/English/FinalReport.pdf

Hurst, C. J. B. (1925) 'Wanted! An International Court of Piepowder', *British Yearbook of International Law*, 4, 61.

Immigration Asylum and Nationality Law and Practice (2003), 41 (statement by Barbara Roche, Minister for Immigration)

Integration Programme of Estonian Society 2008–2013 (2008) http://ec.europa.eu/ewsi/en/

Inter-American Program for a Universal Civil Registry and 'The Right to Identity' (2007) Adopted at the Fourth Plenary Session, held on June 5, www.iin.oea.org/2007/Res_37_AG/Res_2286-37_en.pdf

Internal Displacement Monitoring Centre (IDMC) (2007) 'India – Jammu and Kashmir: Displaced due to 1947 Partition of Indian Protest in Jammu to Demand Citizenship', www.internal-displacement.org/idmc/website/countries.nsf/(httpEnvelopes)/tbe66d867clf56b3c12572c30034b7b4!Open Documents&Click=

International Labor Organisation (ILO) (1998) *A Declaration on Fundamental Principles and Rights at Work* (Geneva: ILO)

(2004) *Towards a Fair Deal for Migrant Workers in the Global Economy* (Geneva: ILO)

(2006) *Follow-Up* referred to in the *Non-Binding Principles and Guidelines for a Rights-Based Approach to Labour Migration*

International Law Commission (1936) *Report of the Thirty-Ninth Conference* (Geneva: ILO)

(1999) 'Nationality in Relation to the Succession of States', *Yearbook of the International Law Commission 1999* A/CN.4/SER.A/1999/Add.1 (Part 2), 19

International Organization for Migration (IOM) (2000) *World Migration Report 2000* (Geneva: IOM)

(2007) 'Social Security: Proposal to Extend Future Regulations to Foreigners', *European Report* (30 July)

(2008) *World Migration 2008: Managing Labour Mobility in the Evolving Global Economy* (Geneva: IOM)

Inter-Parliamentary Union (2005) *Nationality and Statelessness: A Handbook for Parliamentarians* (Geneva: Inter-Parliamentary Union)

Isaac, J. (1992) *Arendt, Camus and Modern Rebellion* (New Haven, CT: Yale University Press)

Isin, E. (ed.) (2000) *Democracy, Citizenship and the Global City* (New York: Routledge)

Jalušić, V. and J. Dedić (2008) 'The Erasure – Mass Human Rights Violation and Denial of Responsibility: The Case of Independent Slovenia', *Human Rights Review*, 9, 93

Järve, P. and V. Poleschuk (2009) *Country Report: Estonia*, EUDO Citizenship Observatory, European University Institute in collaboration with Edinburgh University Law School, http://eudo-citizenship.eu/docs/CountryReports/Estonia.pdf

Jay, M. (1958) 'The Progress of International Law', *British Yearbook of International Law*, 34, 334

(1996) 'The Political Existentialism of Hannah Arendt', in M. Jay (ed.), *Permanent Exiles: Essays on the Intellectual Migration from Germany to America* (New York: Columbia University Press), 237

Jennings, R. Y. (1939) 'Some International Law Aspects of the Refugee Question', *British Yearbook of International Law*, 20, 98

Jones, J. M. (1956) 'The *Nottebohm* Case', *International & Comparative Law Quarterly*, 15, 230

Joppke, C. (1999) 'Asylum and State Sovereignty', in C. Joppke (ed.), *Challenge to the Nation State: Immigration in Western Europe and the United States* (Oxford: Oxford University Press)

Kallas, K. (2008) *Integration Strategy 2008–2013 – Final Report of the Feasibility Study* (Tartu: University of Tartu Institute of Baltic Studies), Part IV, Legal and Political Integration, 19

Kanstroom, D. (2007) *Deportation Nation: Outsiders in American History* (Cambridge, MA: Harvard University Press)

Kant, I. (1991) *Political Writings*, ed. H. Reiss (Cambridge: Cambridge University Press)

Kasearu, K. and A. Trumm, 'Material Well-Being and Satisfaction with Life among Estonians and Non-Estonians', in R. Vetik (ed.), *Integration Monitoring of Estonian Society* (2008) (in Estonian), http://ec.europa.eu/ewsi/UDRW/images/items/docl_9510_693007823.pdf

Kateb, G. (1984) *Hannah Arendt: Politics, Conscience, Evil* (Totowa, NJ: Rowman & Allanheld)

Kerber, L. (2009) 'The Stateless as the Citizen's Other: A View from the United States', in S. Benhabib and J. Resnik (eds.), *Migrations and Mobilities* (New York: New York University Press)

Kertzer, D. I. and D. Arel (eds.), *Census and Identity: The Politics of Race, Ethnicity, and Language in National Censuses* (Cambridge: Cambridge University Press)

Kionka, R. and R. Vetik (1996) 'Estonia and Estonians', in G. Smith (ed.), *The Nationalities Question in the Post-Soviet States* (London and New York: Longman), 129–46

Kogovšek, N. (2008) 'The Erasure: The Proposal of a Constitutional Law as the Negation of the Rule of Law', in J. Zorn and U. Lipovec Čebron (eds.), *Once upon an Erasure: From Citizens to Illegal Residents in the Republic of Slovenia* (Ljubljana: Študentska založba), 196

Kogovšek, N., J. Zorn, S. Pistotnik, U. Lipovec Čebron, V. Bajt, B. Petković and L. Zdravković (2010) *Brazgotine izbrisa: Prispevek h kritičnemu razumevanju izbrisa iz registra stalnega prebivalstva Republike Slovenije* (Ljubljana: Peace Institute)

Kohn, H. (1944) *The Idea of Nationalism* (New York: Macmillan)

Krasner, S. D. (1982) 'Structural Causes and Regime Consequences: Regimes as Intervening Variables', *International Organization*, 36, 185

Kristan, I. (1976) *Družbena ureditev SFRJ* (Ljubljana: Založba Obzorja Maribor)

Lambert, H. (2006) 'The EU Asylum Qualification Directive, its Impact on the Jurisprudence of the United Kingdom and International Law', *International & Comparative Law Quarterly*, 55, 161

Lane, M. (2006) 'A Philosophical View on States and Immigration', in K. Tamas and J. Palme (eds.), *Globalizing Migration Regimes: New Challenges to Transnational Cooperation* (Aldershot: Ashgate)

Larkin, P. (2007) 'Migrants, Social Security, and the "Right to Reside"', *Journal of Social Security Law*, 14, 61

Lauterpacht, H. (1948) 'The Universal Declaration of Human Rights', *British Yearbook of International Law*, 25, 354

(1948–9) 'The Nationality of Denationalized Persons', *Jewish Yearbook of International Law*, 164

Lavender, N. (1997) 'The Problem of the Margin of Appreciation', *European Human Rights Law Review*, 4, 380

Lederer, H. (1999) 'Typologie und Statistik illegaler Zuwanderung nach Deutschland', in E. Eichendorfer, *Migration und Illegalität* (Osnabrück: Universitätsverlag Rasch), 53

Le Figaro (2007) 'Immigration: Brice Hortefeux s'explique' (1 June)

Leibovici, M. (2006) 'Appartitre et visibilité: Le monde selon Hannah Arendt et Emmanuel Levinas', *Journal of Jewish Thought & Philosophy*, 14, 55

Leinsalu, M., D. Vågerö and A. E. Kunst (2003) 'Estonia 1989–2000: Enormous Increase in Mortality Differences by Education', *International Journal of Epidemiology*, 32, 1081

(2004) 'Increasing Ethnic Differences in Mortality in Estonia after the Collapse of the Soviet Union', *Journal of Epidemiology and Community Health*, 58, 583

Le Monde (2007) 'Des maires refusent d'obéir aux préfets sur les sans-papiers' (Paris) (13 September)

Linde, R. (2006) 'Statelessness and Roma Communities in the Czech Republic: Competing Theories of State Compliance', *International Journal on Minority & Group Rights*, 13(4), 341

Lipovec Čebron, U. (2008) 'The Metastasis of the Erasure', in J. Zorn and U. Lipovec Čebron (eds.), *Once upon an Erasure: From Citizens to Illegal Residents in the Republic of Slovenia* (Ljubljana: Študentska založba), 71

Lloyd, C. (2003) 'Anti-Racism, Racism and Asylum-Seekers in France', *Patterns of Prejudice*, 3(3), 323

Locke, J. (1964) *Two Treatises on Government*, Peter Laslett (ed.) (Cambridge: Cambridge University Press)

Loewenfeld, E. (1943) 'Status of Stateless Persons', *Transactions of the Grotius Society*, 27, 59

London Detainee Support Group (LDSG) (2007) *Difficulties in Removal of Undocumented Iranian Nationals* (London: LDSG), www.ldsg.org.uk/files/uploads/dossierssummaries0708.pdf

(2008) *Difficulties in Removal of Undocumented Algerian Nationals* (London: LDSG), www.ldsg.org.uk/files/uploads/dossierssummaries0708.pdf

(2009) *Detained Lives: The Real Costs of Indefinite Immigration Detention* (London: LDSG) (January), www.detainedlives.org/wp-content/uploads/detainedlives.pdf

Lynch, M. (2005) *Lives on Hold: The Human Cost of Statelessness* (Washington, DC: Refugees International)

McBride, J. (2009) *Access to Justice for Migrants and Asylum Seekers in Europe* (Strasbourg: Council of Europe), http://fra.europa.eu/fraWebsite/research/research_projects/proj_irregularimmigrants_en.htm

Macedo, S. (2008) 'Immigration', ms on file with author

Magocsi, P. R. (1997) 'Mapping Stateless Peoples: The East Slavs of the Carpathians', *Canadian Slavonic Papers*, 39(3–4), 301

Marston, G. (1993) 'The United Kingdom's Part in the Preparation of the European Convention on Human Rights, 1950', *International & Comparative Law Quarterly*, 42, 796

Mayhew, S. (2004) *A Dictionary of Geography* (Oxford: Oxford University Press)

Medved, F. (2007) 'From Civic to Ethnic Community? The Evolution of Slovenian Citizenship', in R. Bauböck, B. Perchinig and W. Sievers (eds.), *Citizenship Policies in the New Europe* (Amsterdam: IMISCOE, Amsterdam University Press), 213

Mekina, B. (2008) 'A Monument to the Erased', in J. Zorn and U. Lipovec Čebron (eds.), *Once upon an Erasure: From Citizens to Illegal Residents in the Republic of Slovenia* (Ljubljana: Študentska založba), 44–51

Miller, D. (1995) *On Nationality* (Oxford: Clarendon Press)

(2004) 'Immigrants, Nations and Citizenship', Paper delivered at CRASSH Conference, Cambridge University, www.crassh.cam.ac.uk/oldwww/events/2003–4/MillerPaper.pdf

(2005) 'Immigration: The Case for Limits', in A. Cohen and C. Wellman (eds.), *Contemporary Debates in Applied Ethics* (Oxford: Blackwell)

Minahan, J. (2002) *Encyclopaedia of the Stateless Nations: Ethnic and National Groups Around the World*, 4 vols. (Santa Barbara, CA: Greenwood Press)

Modinos, P. (1962) 'Effects and Repercussions of the European Convention on Human Rights', *International & Comparative Law Quarterly*, 11, 1097

Montagna, N. (2001) 'La primavera dei migranti', *Posse*, 2, 12

Morris, L. (2002) *Managing Migration: Civic Stratification and Migrants' Rights* (London: Routledge)

Muršič, M. (2008) 'The Erasure is Always and Everywhere', in J. Zorn and U. Lipovec Čebron (eds.), *Once upon an Erasure: From Citizens to Illegal Residents in the Republic of Slovenia* (Ljubljana: Študentska založba), 32

Mydans, S. (2009) 'Thailand Is Accused of Rejecting Migrants', *New York Times* (January 17)

National Audit Office (2007) *The Cancellation of the Bicester Accommodation Centre* HC 19 2007–2008, www.nao.org.uk/publications/0708/the_cancellation_of_bicester_a.aspx

9ème collectif de sans papiers (2005), Occupation de la Fédération 93 du PS' (14 February), http://pajol.eu.org/article719.html

Niessen, J., T. Huddleston and L. Citron (in cooperation with A. Geddes and D. Jacobs) (2007) *Migrant Integration Policy Index* (London: British Council and Migration Policy Group)

Office of the High Commissioner for Refugees (OHCHR) (2008) *Promotion and Protection of All Human Rights, Civil, Political, Economic, Social and Cultural Rights, Including the Right to Development: Report of the Independent Expert* on *Minority Issues, Gay McDougall*, A/HRC/7/23 (28 February) www.unhcr. org/refworld/docid/47d685ea2.html

(2008) 'Addressing Situations of Statelessness', *UNHCR Global Appeal 2009 Update*, 1 December, 45, www.unhcr.org/publ/PUBL/4922d4370.pdf

(2009), *Statistical Online Population Database*, http://apps.who.int/globalatlas/ dataQuery/reportData.asp?rptType=1, accessed 27 November 2009

Open Society Institute (OSI) Justice Initiative (2006a) *Human Rights and Legal Identity: Approaches to Combating Statelessness and Arbitrary Deprivation of Nationality*, Thematic Conference Paper (May), http://dev.justiceinitiative. org/db/resource2/fs/?file_id=17050

(2006b) 'Written Comments on the Case of Makuc and Others *v.* Slovenia, Application No. 26828/06', www.soros.org/initiatives/justice/litigation/ makuc/written-comments-20071015.pdf

Oxford Mail (2004a) 'Lesson Learned' (Friday 23 July), http://archive.oxfordmail. net/2004/7/23/10133.html

(2004b) 'Meeting to Discuss Grievances Over Coverage' (Thursday 12 August), http://archive.oxfordmail.net/2004/8/12/9616.html

Parekh, B. (1994) 'Three Theories of Immigration', in S. Spencer, *Strangers and Citizens* (London: River Orams Press)

Parekh, S. (2004) 'A Meaningful Place in the World: Hannah Arendt on the Nature of Human Rights', *Journal of Human Rights*, 31, 41

Passerin d'Entrèves, M. (1994) *The Political Philosophy of Hannah Arendt* (London: Routledge)

Pattie, C., P. Seyd and P. Whiteley (2004) *Citizenship in Britain: Values, Participation and Democracy* (Cambridge: Cambridge University Press)

Patton, M. (1990) *Qualitative Evaluation and Research Methods* (Newbury Park, CA: Sage)

Perić, T. (2003) 'Personal Documents and Threats to the Exercise of Fundamental Rights of Roma in Europe', *Roma Rights*, 3, 7, www.errc.org/cikk. php?cikk=28

Petersen, R. D. and A. Valdez (2005) 'Community Sample of Gang-Affiliated Adolescents', *Youth Violence and Juvenile Justice*, 3, 151

Pignoni, R. (2008a), 'The Story of Velimir Dabetič', in J. Zorn and U. Lipovec Čebron (eds.), *Once upon an Erasure: From Citizens to Illegal Residents in the Republic of Slovenia* (Ljubljana: Študentska založba), 39

(2008b) 'The Double Erasure of Ali Berisha', in J. Zorn and U. Lipovec Čebron (eds.), *Once upon an Erasure: From Citizens to Illegal Residents in the Republic of Slovenia* (Ljubljana: Študentska založba), 41

Pinkerton, C., G. McLaughlan and J. Salt (2004) *Sizing the Illegally Resident Population in the UK*, Home Office Online Report, 58/04

Pistotnik, S. (2008) 'Chronology of the Erasure 1990–2007', in J. Zorn and U. Lipovec Čebron (eds.), *Once upon an Erasure: From Citizens to Illegal Residents in the Republic of Slovenia* (Ljubljana: Študentska založba), 222

Plender, R. (1986) 'Immigration Law Trends', *International & Comparative Law Quarterly*, 35, 531

(1990) 'Competence, European Community Law and Nationals of Non-Member States', *International and Comparative Law Quarterly*, 39, 599

Rawlings, R. (2005) 'Review, Revenge and Retreat', *Modern Law Review*, 68, 378

Rawls J. (1971) *A Theory of Justice* (Cambridge, MA: Harvard University Press)

(1993) *Political Liberalism* (New York: Columbia University Press)

Richburg, K. B. (2003) 'Security Curtain Raised Along EU's New Eastern Front: Tightened Borders Draw Concerns About Impact on Neighboring Nations', *Washington Post* (July 31)

Ring, J. (1991) 'The Pariah as Hero: Hannah Arendt's Political Actor', *Political Theory*, 19, 433

Robertson, A. H. (1950) 'The European Convention for the Protection of Human Rights', *British Yearbook of International Law*, 27, 145

Rodier, C. (2000) 'Le mouvement de sans-papiers en France,' in M.-C. Caloz-Tschopp (ed.), *Les sans-État dans la philosophie de Hannah Arendt* (Lausanne: Éditions Paliot), 186

Rogers, N. (2003) 'Immigration and the European Convention on Human Rights', *European Human Rights Law Review*, 4, 53

Rubio-Marin, R. (2000) *Immigration as a Democratic Challenge: Citizenship and Inclusion in Germany and the United States* (Cambridge: Cambridge University Press)

Saar, E. (2008) 'Education', in R. Vetik (ed.), *Integration Monitoring of Estonian Society* (2008) (in Estonian)

Sales, R. (2002) 'The Deserving and Undeserving? Refugees, Asylum Seekers and Welfare in Britain', *Critical Social Policy*, 22(3), 456

Samore, W. (1951) 'Statelessness as a Consequence of the Conflict of Nationality Laws', *American Journal of International Law*, 45(3), 476

Sarkozy, N. (2007) 'Lettre de mission adressée à M. Hortefeux, Ministre de l'Immigration, de l'intégration, de l'identité nationale et du codéveloppe-ment' (9 July)

Sassen, S. (2006) *Territory, Authority, Rights* (Chicago, IL: Chicago University Press)

Sawyer, C. (2006) 'Not Every Child Matters: The UK's Expulsion of British Citizens', *International Journal of Children's Rights*, 14, 157

(2007) 'Elephants in the Room, or: A Can of Worms', *Journal of Social Security Law*, 17, 86

Sawyer, C. and P. Turpin (2005) 'Neither Here Nor There: Temporary Admission to the UK', *International Journal of Refugee Law*, 17, 688

Scelle, G. (1954) 'Le problème de l'apatridie devant la Commission due Droit International de l'ONU', *Die Friedenswarte*, 52, 142

Schwartz, E. P. (2009) Assistant Secretary, Bureau of Population, Refugees, and Migration, 'Protecting Stateless Persons: The Role of the US Government', Conference on Statelessness: Sponsored by Refugee Council

USA, Washington, DC (October 30), www.state.gov/g/prm/rls/rmks/
remarks/131183.htm

Seckler-Hudson, C. (1934) *Statelessness: With Special Reference to the United States*
(Washington, DC: Digest Press)

Sen, A. (2001) *Development as Freedom* (Oxford: Oxford University Press)

Shachar, A. (2003) 'Children of a Lesser State: Sustaining Global Inequality through
Citizenship Laws', Jean Monnet Working Papers, 2, http://jeanmonnet
program.org/papers/03/030201.html

   (2005) 'Birthright Citizenship as Inherited Property: A Critical Inquiry', in
S. Benhabib and I. Shapiro (eds.), *Identities, Affiliations, and Allegiances*
(Cambridge: Cambridge University Press)

Shah, P. (2000) *Refugees, Race and the Legal Concept of Asylum in Britain*
(London: Cavendish)

Shapiro, I. (2003) *The Moral Foundations of Politics* (New Haven, CT: Yale
University Press)

Shaw, J. (2007) *The Transformation of Citizenship in the European Union: Electoral
Rights and the Restructuring of Political Space* (Cambridge: Cambridge
University Press)

Shklar, J. (ed. with S. Hoffman) (1998) *Political Thought and Political Thinkers*
(Chicago, IL: Chicago University Press)

Sidgwick, H. (1987 [1891]) *The Elements of Politics*, 2nd edn. (Basingstoke:
Macmillan)

Sikkink, K. A. and M. E. Keck (1999) *Activists Beyond Borders* (Ithaca, NY: Cornell
University Press)

Sikkink, K. A., S. Khagram and J. Riker (eds.) (2002) *Restructuring World Politics:
Transnational Social Movements, Networks, and Norms* (Minneapolis, MN:
University of Minnesota Press)

Simeant, J. (1998) *La cause des sans-papiers* (Paris: Presse de Sciences Po)

Simon Wiesenthal Centre (2009) SWC to New European Parliament Head:
Quarantine New MEPs Elected on Platform of Hate (10 August) (Paris:
Simon Wiesenthal Centre), www.wiesenthal.com/site/apps/nlnet/content2.
aspx?c=lsKWLbPJLnF&b=5711841&ct=7298057

Smith, R. M. (2002) 'Modern Citizenship', in E. Isin and B. Turner (eds.), *Handbook of
Citizenship Studies* (New York: Sage)

Social Research (2002) Special issue, 69(2)

Sokoloff, C. and R. Lewis (2005) 'Denial of Citizenship: A Challenge to Human
Security', *European Policy Centre*, Paper 28 (1 April), www.epc.eu/TEWN/
pdf/724318296_EPC%20Issue%20Paper%2028%20Denial%20of%20
Citizenship.pdf

Southwick, K. and M. Lynch (2009) *Nationality Rights for All: A Progress
Report and Global Survey on Statelessness* (Washington, DC: Refugees
International, 2009), www.refintl.org/sites/default/files/RI%20Stateless
%20Report_FINAL_031109.pdf

Soysal, Y. (1994) *The Limits of Citizenship: Migrants and Postnational Membership in Europe* (Chicago, IL: University of Chicago Press)

Spaventa, E. (2007) *Free Movement of Persons in the European Union: Barriers to Movement in Their Constitutional Context* (The Hague: Kluwer)

Spicer, N. (2008) 'Places of Exclusion and Inclusion: Asylum Seekers and Refugees' Experiences of Neighbourhoods in the UK', *Journal of Ethnic and Migration Studies*, 34, 491

Statistical Office of the Republic of Slovenia (2003) *Population Census Results*, www. stat.sc/popis2002/en/rezultati/rezultati_red.asp?ter=slo&st=7, accessed 6 December 2007

Stewart, A. (1995) 'Two Conceptions of Citizenship', *British Journal of Sociology*, 46, 63

StillHumanHere (2008), www.stillhuman.org.uk/

Storey, H. (1990) 'The Right to Family Life and Immigration Case Law at Strasbourg', *International & Comparative Law Quarterly*, 39, 328

Strangers into Citizens (2008), www.strangersintocitizens.org.uk

Struharova, B. (1999) 'Disparate Impact: Removing Roma from the Czech Republic', *Roma Rights*, 1, 47, www.errc.org/cikk.php?cikk=54

Šturm, L. (1984) *Upravnopravne institucije: izbrana poglavja*, 3rd edn. (Ljubljana: Law Faculty)

Summers, D. (2009a) 'Gordon Brown's "British Jobs" Pledge has Caused Controversy Before', *The Guardian* (30 January), www.guardian.co.uk/politics/2009/jan/30/brown-british-jobs-workers

(2009b) 'Brown Stands by British Jobs for British Workers Remark', *The Guardian* (30 January), www.guardian.co.uk/politics/2009/jan/30/brown-british-jobs-workers

Thiele, C. (2005) 'Citizenship as a Requirement for Minorities', *European Human Rights Law Review*, 6, 276

Thym, D. (2008) 'Respect for Private and Family Life Under Article 8 ECHR in Immigration Cases: A Human Right to Regularize Illegal Stay?', *International & Comparative Law Quarterly*, 57, 87

Times of Malta (2010) 'EU Makes Proposals to Strengthen Frontex, but Avoids Rules of Engagement' (24 February)

Torpey, J. (2000) *The Invention of the Passport: Surveillance, Citizenship and the State* (Cambridge: Cambridge University Press)

Tubb, D. (2006) 'Statelessness and Colombia: Hannah Arendt and the Failure of Human Rights', *Undercurrent*, 3(2), 39

Uehling, G. (2004) 'Evaluation of UNHCR's Programme to Prevent and Reduce Statelessness in Crimea, Ukraine', EPAU/2004/03 (Geneva: United Nations High Commissioner for Refugees Evaluation and Policy Analysis Unit), (March), www.unhcr.org/research/RESEARCH/405ab4c74.pdf

(2008) 'Livelihoods of Former Deportees in Ukraine', *Forced Migration Review*, 20, 19, www.fmreview.org/FMRpdfs/FMR20/FMR2008.pdf

United Nations (1960) *United Nations Convention Relating to the Status of Stateless Persons*, 1954 Convention, UN Treaty Series, www.unhcr.org/protect/ PROTECTION/3bbb25729.pdf

(1975) *United Nations Convention on the Reduction of Statelessness*, 1961 Convention, UN Treaty Series, vol. 989, 175, www.unhcr.org/protect/ PROTECTION/3bbb28608.pdf

(2006) *UN Secretary General's Study on Violence Against Children* (New York: United Nations), 27, www.unviolencestudy.org/

United Nations Committee on the Elimination of Racial Discrimination (2004) '*United Nations Committee on the Elimination of Racial Discrimination 2004. General Recommendation No. 30: Discrimination against Non-Citizens* (Geneva: Office of the High Commissioner for Human Rights), CERD/C/64/ Misc.11/Rev.3

United Nations Development Programme (UNDP) (1994) *Human Development Report* (New York: Oxford University Press), 22, http://hdr.undp.org/en/ media/hdr_1994_en_chap2.pdf

(2009) *2008 Human Rights Report: France, Bureau of Democracy, Human Rights, and Labor – 2008 Country Reports on Human Rights Practices* (February 25), www.State.Gov/G/Drl/Rls/Hrrpt/2008/Eur/119079.Htm accessed 4 December 2009

United Nations General Assembly (1948) *Universal Declaration of Human Rights* (10 December), 217A (III), www.unhcr.org/refworld/docid/3ae6b37/2c. html

(2008) *The Right to Development: Report of the Secretary-General on the Right to Development*, Document A/63/340, Sixty Third Session (2 September), http:// daccess-dds-ny.un.org/doc/UNDOC/GEN/N08/493/97/PDF/N0849397. pdf?OpenElement

(2009) *Human Rights and Arbitrary Deprivation of Nationality, Report of the Secretary-General*, Document A/HRC/13/34, Thirteenth Session (December 14), www2.ohchr.org/English/bodies/hrcouncil/docs/ 13session/A-HRC-13-34.pdf

United Nations High Commissioner for Refugees (UNHCR) (1997) *The State of the World's Refugees – A Humanitarian Agenda* (Oxford: UNHCR and Oxford University Press)

(1998) DIP *Guidelines: Field Office Activities Concerning Statelessness* (September) (Inter-Office Memorandum No. 66/98 and Field Office Memorandum No. 70/98), http://www.unhcr.org/refworld/docid/49a28afb2.html

(2007) 'The Excluded: The Strange Hidden World of the Stateless', *Refugees Magazine*, 147 (Geneva: UNHCR) (September), www.unhcr.org/publ/PUBL/ 46d2e8dc2.pdf

(2009) *Addressing Statelessness* (Geneva: UNHCR), www.unhcr.org/4b025e39.pdf

(2010) *Action to Address Statelessness: A Strategy Note* (Geneva: UNHCR), www. unhcr.org/4b960ae99.html

United Nations Human Rights Council (UNHRC) (2009) 'Arbitrary Deprivation of Nationality: Report of the Secretary-General', A/HRC/10/34, (26 January) (Geneva: UN Human Rights Council), www.unhcr.org/refworld/docid/49958be22.html

United States Congress (2009) HR 72 – *To Increase Global Stability and Security for the United States and the International Community by Reducing the Number of Individuals who are de jure or de facto Stateless and at Risk of Being Trafficked* (January 6), www.opencongress.org/bill/111-h72/text

United States Department of State (2007) *Kuwait – Country Reports on Human Rights Practices*, Bureau of Democracy, Human Rights, and Labor 2006 (March 6), www.state.gov/g/drl/rls/hrrpt/2006/78856.htm

Vandenabeele, C. (2007) 'Establishing Legal Identity for Inclusive Development: Bangladesh, Cambodia, Nepal', Presentation at 'Children without a State: A Human Rights Challenge Birth Registration and Irregular Migration' (Kennedy School of Government, Carr Center for Human Rights Policy and Committee on Human Rights Studies, Cambridge, MA: Harvard University)

Vandenabeele, C. and C. V. Lao (eds.) (2007) *Legal Identity for Inclusive Development* (Manila: Asian Development Bank)

Vasović, S. (2008) 'Deported to Death', in J. Zorn and U. Lipovec Čebron (eds.), *Once upon an Erasure: From Citizens to Illegal Residents in the Republic of Slovenia* (Ljubljana: Študentska založba), 190

de Vattel, E. (1916) *The Law of Nations or the Principles of Natural Law*, vol. 3 trans. C. G. Fenwick (Washington, DC: Carnegie Institute)

Verhoeven, A. (1998) 'Europe Beyond Westphalia', *Maastricht Journal of European and Comparative Law*, 5, 369

Vetik, R. (1993) 'Ethnic Conflict and Accommodation in Post-Communist Estonia', *Journal of Peace Research*, 30(3), 271–80

　(2001) *Democratic Multiculturalism: A New Model of National Integration*, (Mariehamn, Finland: Åland Islands Peace Institute)

　(2002) 'The Cultural and Social Makeup of Estonia', in P. Kostø (ed.), *National Integration and Violent Conflict in Post-Soviet Societies: The Cases of Estonia and Moldova* (London: Rowman & Littlefield)

　(2007a) 'Why the Estonian Position along the Human Development Index is not Improving', *Estonian Human Development Report 2007, Studies of Transition States and Societies*, 1(1), 3 (in Estonian)

　(2007b) *On the Boundary of Two Liberties* (Tallinn: Huma) (in Estonian)

Vetik, R. et al. (2008) 'Introduction and Trends', in R. Vetik (ed.), *Integration Monitoring of Estonian Society*, www.meis.ee/raamatukogu?book_id=196 (in Estonian)

Villa, D. R. (1999) *Politics, Philosophy, Terror: Essays on the Thought of Hannah Arendt* (Princeton, NJ: Princeton University Press)

Van Waas, L. (2008) *Nationality Matters: Statelessness Under International Law* (Antwerp: Intersentia)

Walzer, M. (1983) *Spheres of Justice: A Defense of Pluralism and Equality* (Oxford: Martin Robertson)

Weil, P., A. Spire and C. Bertossi (2009) *Country Report: France*, www.foyer.be/ IMG/pdf/EUDO-2009-France-linked.pdf

(1961) 'The Convention Relating to the Status of Stateless Persons', *International & Comparative Law Quarterly*, 10, 255

(1962) 'The United Nations Convention on the Reduction of Statelessness, 1961', *International & Comparative Law Quarterly*, 11, 1073

Weis, P. (1953) 'Legal Aspects of the Convention of July 28, 1951, Relating to the Status of Refugees', *British Yearbook of International Law*, 30, 480

(1979) *Nationality and Statelessness in International Law* (Alphen aan den Rijn: Sijthoff & Noordhoff)

Weissbrodt, D. (2001) *Prevention of Discrimination and Protection of Indigenous Peoples and Minorities – The Rights of Non-Citizens: Preliminary Report of the Special Rapporteur, Mr David Weissbrodt, Submitted in Accordance with Sub-Commission Decision* 2000/103, UN Doc. E/CN.4/Sub.2/2001/20/Add.1 (Geneva: UNHCR)

(2003) *Final Report on the Rights of Non-Citizens*, UN Doc. E/CN.4/Sub.2/2003/23 (Geneva: UNHCR)

(2008) *The Human Rights of Non-Citizens* (Oxford: Oxford University Press)

Weissbrodt, D. and C. Collins (2006) 'The Human Rights of Stateless Persons', *Human Rights Quarterly*, 28(1), 245

Weitkamp, R. (1995) 'Spielball des deutschen Arbeitsmarktes: Zur rechtlichen Hierarchisierung von MigrantInnen', in BUKO (ed.), *Zwischen Flucht und Arbeit: Neue Migration und Legalisierungsdebatte* (Hamburg: Verlag Libertäre Assoziation), 93

Wiegandt, M. H. (1995) 'The Russian Minority in Estonia', *International Journal on Minority and Group Rights*, 3, 109

Withol de Wenden, C. (1994) 'Immigrants as Political Actors in France', *West European Politics*, 17, 91

Young, I. M. (2000) *Inclusion and Democracy* (Oxford: Oxford University Press)

Young-Bruehl, E. (2006) *Why Hannah Arendt Matters* (New Haven, CT: Yale University Press)

Yuval-Davis, N., F. Anthias and E. Kofman (2005) 'Secure Borders and Safe Haven and the Gendered Politics of Belonging: Beyond Social Cohesion', *Ethnic & Racial Studies*, 28, 13

Zetter, R., D. Griffiths, S. Ferretti and M. Pearl (2003) *An Evaluation of the Impact of Asylum Policies in Europe* (London: Home Office)

Zolberg, A. (1995) 'Review of Y. Soysal, Limits of Citizenship', *Contemporary Sociology*, 24(4), 326

Zorn, J. (2005) 'Ethnic Citizenship in the Slovenian State', *Citizenship Studies*, 9(2), 135

(2007) 'New Borders, New Exclusions', in D. Zaviršek, J. Zorn, L. Rihter and S. Žnidarec Demšar (eds.), *Ethnicity in Eastern Europe: A Challenge for Social Work Education* (Ljubljana: Faculty of Social Work), 159

(2008) ' "We, the Ethno-Citizens of Ethno-Democracy" – The Formation of Slovene Citizenship', in J. Zorn and U. Lipovec Čebron (eds.), *Once upon an Erasure: From Citizens to Illegal Residents in the Republic of Slovenia* (Ljubljana: Študentska založba), 52

(2009a) 'A Case for Slovene Nationalism: Initial Citizenship Rules and the Erasure', *Nations and Nationalism*, 15, 280

(2009b) 'The Right to Stay: Challenging the Policy of Detention and Deportation', *European Journal of Social Work*, 12(2), 247

Zorn, J. and U. Lipovec Čebron (eds.) (2008) *Once upon an Erasure: From Citizens to Illegal Residents in the Republic of Slovenia* (Ljubljana: Študentska založba)

INDEX

Case-law and International Conventions are listed on pp. xi–xv.